**RISK MANAGEMENT
WITH FUTURES
AND OPTIONS**

RISK MANAGEMENT WITH FUTURES AND OPTIONS

KEITH REDHEAD

PRENTICE HALL EUROPE
London New York Toronto Sydney Tokyo Singapore
Madrid Mexico City Munich Paris

First edition published 1999
by Prentice Hall Europe
Campus 400, Maylands Avenue
Hemel Hempstead
Hertfordshire, HP2 7EZ

A division of
Simon & Schuster International Group
© Prentice Hall Europe 1999

All rights reserved. No part of this publication may be reproduced, stored in
a retrieval system, or transmitted in any form, or by any means, electronic,
mechanical, photocopying, recording, or otherwise, without prior permission,
in writing, from the publisher.

Typeset in 10pt Caslon 224 by
Dorwyn Ltd, Rowlands Castle, Hants

Printed and bound in Great Britain by
Biddles Ltd, Guildford and King's Lynn

Library of Congress Cataloging-in-Publication Data
Available from the publisher

British Library Cataloguing-in-Publication Data
A catalogue record for this book is available from the British Library

ISBN 0-13-010981-9
1 2 3 4 5   03 02 01 00 99

CONTENTS

Preface xi
Acknowledgements xii

1 INTRODUCTION
Financial futures 4
Financial options 7
Types of trader 9
The margin system 10
Further reading 13

2 MANAGING STOCK MARKET RISK WITH FUTURES
Introduction 15
Hedging with stock index futures 16
Removing or enhancing exposures 19
Stock index futures prices 22
Basis change and convergence 30
Conclusions 33
Further reading 34
Appendix 2.1: Calculating numbers of stock index futures contracts required for hedging 34
Appendix 2.2: Value at risk 36

3 MANAGING INTEREST RATE RISK WITH FUTURES
Introduction 39
The underlying markets 40
Basic principles 42

Interest rate computations and quotations   47
The determination of futures prices   48
The forward yield curve   55
Forward rate agreements (FRAs)   56
Cross hedging   60
Conclusions   61
Further reading   62

4 ADVANCED STRATEGIES FOR INTEREST RATE RISK MANAGEMENT
Introduction   63
The forward yield curve and basis risk   64
Sources of basis risk and hedge ratios   66
Strips and rolls (stacks)   68
Variation margin leverage and tailing   72
Hedging yield curve risk with futures straddles   74
Butterfly spreads   85
Inter-contract spreads   86
Conclusions   88
Further reading   89

5 MANAGING FIXED INTEREST RISK
Introduction   91
The underlying instrument   92
Futures contracts   93
Hedging the value of a portfolio   95
Hedging cash flow   96
Delivery   97
The price (conversion) factor   98
Invoice amount   99
The cheapest-to-deliver bond   99
Determination of bond futures prices   99
The role of implicit options   102
Implied repos   104
Basis and convergence   109
Conclusions   112
Further reading   113
Appendix 5.1: Discounting cash flows   113

6 USING FUTURES IN FUND MANAGEMENT
Introduction   115
Hedge design – equity portfolios   116
Hedge design – bond portfolios   119
Duration   122

Hedged equity portfolios as synthetic treasury bills   130
Hedged bond portfolios as synthetic treasury bills   131
Bond portfolio immunisation   131
Bond futures arbitrage as a means of enhancing bond portfolio returns   135
Asset reallocation   140
Conclusions   140
Further reading   141

7 OPTIONS – THE BASIC PRINCIPLES
Introduction   143
Call options   144
Put options   150
Writing options   155
Market practices and terms   158
Stock leverage and stock options   158
Exotic options   160
Warrants   163
Convertible bonds   164
Conclusions   168
Further reading   169

8 RISK MANAGEMENT WITH OPTIONS
Introduction   171
Options as hedging instruments   172
Zero-cost options   181
Hedging anticipated purchases   184
Delta hedging with options   185
Delta hedging of options   191
Hedging option sensitivities (Greeks)   193
Covered writing   194
Conclusions   200
Further reading   202
Appendix 8.1: Determining the appropriate strike price when using stock index options   202

9 TRADING WITH OPTIONS
Introduction   205
Basic principles   206
Vertical spreads   208
Reading derivatives prices   214
The effects of gearing   217
Time value and options trading   218
Volatility trading   224

Conclusions 241
Further reading 242

10 ARBITRAGE WITH OPTIONS
Introduction 243
Synthetics 244
Reversals, conversions and options boxes 246
Constructing synthetic options 249
Put–call parity 253
Option price convexity 259
Boundary conditions 263
Conclusions 269
Further reading 270

11 BLACK–SCHOLES OPTION PRICING MODELS
Introduction 271
The determinants of option prices 272
Option prices as the costs of replication 277
The basic Black–Scholes option pricing model 278
Early exercise 282
Variations on the basic Black–Scholes model 283
Pricing puts and American-style options 289
Valuing options on bonds 289
Volatility 292
The smile effect 295
ARCH and GARCH models 297
Conclusions 298
Further reading 299

12 SWAPS
Introduction 301
Hedging interest rate risk 302
Using swaps to reduce interest costs 305
How banks make profits from swaps 308
Warehousing 308
Currency swaps 311
Equity swaps 315
Floating rate notes (FRNs) 316
Swap pricing 317
Conclusions 320
Further reading 320

13 FORWARDS AND FUTURES IN CURRENCY RISK MANAGEMENT

Introduction 323
Currency markets 324
Quotation of exchange rates 325
The forward foreign exchange market 326
Pricing currency forwards and futures 330
Currency futures 339
Hedging currency risk with futures 339
A comparison of futures and forwards 346
The role of the corporate treasurer 348
Conclusions 360
Further reading 362
Appendix 13.1: Calculating numbers of futures contracts required for hedging 363

14 FINANCIALLY ENGINEERED INVESTMENTS

Introduction 367
Futures funds 367
Switching between stocks without trading in stocks 375
Synthetic bond portfolios 378
Options funds 381
Constructing a portfolio of capital protected funds 387
Credit derivatives and their potential role in fund management 388
The implications of implicit options in constant ratio funds 391
Conclusions 396
Further reading 396

References 397
Glossary 401
Index 431

PREFACE

Books on futures and options have to address a trade-off between rigour and accessibility. Some books put the emphasis on rigour, with the result that many people find them difficult to read. At the other extreme, there are books that show so little regard for rigour that readers are presented with oversimplified and superficial accounts, which can leave their understanding seriously incomplete. This book aims to provide an exposition that is neither oversimplified nor inaccessible.

Following the introductory chapter, which previews the main classes of derivatives, the markets and types of trader, there are five chapters on futures and forwards. The author has chosen to begin with futures, rather than options, partly because futures are conceptually easier, and partly because the instruments underlying options include futures; it is necessary to understand futures before one can fully appreciate the nature of options on futures. Although some chapters have the word 'futures' rather than 'forwards' in their title, many of the principles involved are as applicable to forwards as to futures.

Next come five chapters on options. The first of these provides a basic introduction to options. This is followed by chapters that provide progressively more advanced analysis of options in the context of the three categories of user: hedgers, speculators and arbitragers.

Integrated throughout the book are numerous examples and activities which are designed to illustrate the main principles being explained. Each activity comprises a relatively short, generally numerical, question followed by a worked solution. These allow readers to self-check their level of understanding as they progress through the text.

ACKNOWLEDGEMENTS

The activities and exercises in this text include questions from the Securities Institute examination in Financial Futures and Options, to whom I am grateful for their permission to include them. It is to be emphasised that, where given, the suggested solutions are mine, and that some of the questions have been amended in order to accord more closely with the ideas elucidated in the text.

INTRODUCTION 1

Most organisations and individuals face financial risk. Changes in stock market prices, interest rates and exchange rates can have great significance. Adverse changes may even threaten the survival of otherwise successful businesses. It is therefore not surprising that financial instruments for the management of such risk have developed. These instruments are known as financial derivatives. By providing commitments to prices or rates for future dates, or by giving protection against adverse movements, financial derivatives can be used to reduce the extent of financial risk. Conversely they also provide profit opportunities for those prepared to accept risk. Indeed, at least to some extent, they involve the transfer of risk from those who wish to avoid it to those who are willing to accept it.

Financial derivatives are financial instruments whose prices are derived from the prices of other financial instruments. Financial derivatives include forwards, futures, options and swaps. The instruments to which they relate include stocks, bonds, interest rates and currencies.

Although financial derivatives have existed for a considerable period of time, they have become a major force in financial markets only since the early 1970s. The 1970s constituted a watershed in financial history, partly because the fixed exchange rate regime (the Bretton Woods system) that had operated since the 1940s broke down, and partly because monetarism took over from Keynesianism as the orthodoxy in monetary policy. These developments established the context in which financial derivatives could develop, flourish and become a major force in world financial markets.

When the Bretton Woods system collapsed in the early 1970s, a regime of fixed exchange rates gave way to a financial environment in which exchange rates were constantly changing in response to the pressures of demand and supply. The fact that currency prices moved constantly, and often substantially, in the new situation meant that businesses faced new risks. Currency derivatives developed in response to the need to manage those risks. They also provided a vehicle for those market operators whose motivation was to profit from currency price fluctuations. In other words, the new system of variable exchange rates generated a need to find techniques to reduce the risks arising, and simultaneously created opportunities for speculation. Financial derivatives developed as a vehicle for these 2 forms of economic activity.

The new-found instability was not limited to currency markets. Short-term interest rates also became prone to fluctuation. Two major factors underlay this increase in interest rate instability. First, many governments attempted to manage exchange rate fluctuations by manipulating short-term interest rates. This involved the acceptance of interest rate instability in the hope of reduced currency volatility. Second, the adoption of monetarism entailed the adoption of money supply targets. It is impossible to achieve both money supply and interest rate objectives; one needs to be manipulated if the other is to be achieved. Before the 1970s, monetary authorities tended to maintain interest rates at constant levels and accepted the consequences in terms of money supply growth. The switch towards attempts to control the growth rate of the money supply entailed the acceptance that interest rates had to change frequently to whatever level was consistent with the desired growth rate of money supply (for example, if the money supply started to increase too rapidly, interest rates had to rise in order to reduce the demand for bank loans, such loans being a major source of money supply growth). So, from the 1970s short-term interest rates became more volatile than they had previously been.

This increased instability of short-term interest rates had implications for long-term interest rates, and hence bond prices, which are largely determined by long-term interest rates. Long-term interest rates might be seen as determined by an average of current and expected future short-term interest rates. It is thus to be expected that increased volatility of short-term interest rates would be accompanied by a raised volatility of long-term interest rates. The result is increased instability of bond prices. This in turn involves greater risk for both the issuers of, and investors in, bonds.

Not only are bond prices dependent upon long-term interest rates, but so too are the prices of other long-term assets such as company shares. Stock prices may be seen as the present values of expected future dividend payments, and the discount rates used to ascertain those present values are based on long-term interest rates. So increased instability in long-term interest rates implies enhanced volatility in share prices. This share price volatility is reflected in the volatility of stock indices, which provide measures of average share price movements, particularly since long-term interest rates affect all share prices and hence constitute a source of systematic risk (systematic risk is risk that is common to all, or at least most, stocks).

So, since the early 1970s financial market instability has increased. Financial derivatives have emerged as means of managing the risks associated with that instability, and also of taking advantage of it.

Forwards, futures and swaps involve commitments to exchanges of cash flows in the future at prices or rates determined in the present. An option provides the right, but not the obligation, to a future exchange at a price or rate determined in the present. Each instrument has its advantages and disadvantages.

Forwards can relate to commitments in the short and medium term (perhaps up to 5 years), and are relatively simple to understand and use. They tend to have the disadvantage of inflexibility of timing. Futures do not constrain the timing of the cash flows, but tend to be short-term (less than a year) and more difficult to understand and use. Swaps can be seen as series of forward contracts. They tend to be longer term than either forwards or futures (their maturities may exceed 10 years). However, they tend to be inflexible as to the timing of the future cash flows. Also, like forwards but unlike futures, they can be difficult to cancel or reverse.

Options have the advantage that the holder can choose to ignore them. If the price or rate of the underlying instrument (stock, stock index, bond, deposit, borrowing or currency) moves so that the price or rate stipulated by the option becomes unattractive, then the holder of the option may simply choose to disregard it. This may be particularly advantageous for a hedger.

A hedger is someone with an existing risk of a price (or rate) movement who uses derivatives as a means of reducing that risk. Since forwards, futures and swaps involve commitments, they tend to preclude the possibility of benefiting from otherwise favourable price (or rate) movements. Options provide protection against adverse movements while preserving the ability to gain from beneficial price or rate movements. Speculators also enjoy a corresponding advantage in that the facility of ignoring an option avoids the realisation of potentially large losses, an outcome that cannot be avoided with the other derivatives. However, these benefits of options, relative to the other derivatives, have to be paid for in the form of an option premium. A corresponding payment is not required when using forwards, futures or swaps.

Any use of a derivative in conjunction with another financial instrument (derivative or otherwise) can be regarded as financial engineering. Financial engineering can produce risk management tools that would be otherwise unavailable. In addition, it can be used to construct investments with risk-reward profiles that could not otherwise be produced but which match the requirements of many investors more closely than any existing investment vehicles. The potential of financial engineering using derivatives should make it clear to risk managers, bankers and those involved in investments, corporate finance and treasury that an understanding of financial derivatives is now a vital component of their professional expertise.

FINANCIAL FUTURES

A financial future is a notional commitment to buy or sell, on a specified future date, a standard quantity of a financial instrument at a price determined in the present (the futures price). It is rare for a futures contract to be used for the exchange of financial instruments. Indeed, many contracts have no facility for the exchange of the financial instrument. Instead, financial futures markets are independent of the underlying cash market, albeit operating parallel to that market. For instance, currency futures are different instruments from the currencies themselves, but currency futures prices move in ways that are related to the movements in currency prices. However, since futures markets are independent of the markets in the underlying instruments, this relationship is less than perfect and it is possible for futures prices to exhibit changes that have no parallel in the underlying currency markets.

The main economic function of futures is to provide a means of hedging. A hedger seeks to reduce an already existing risk. This risk reduction could be achieved by taking a futures position that would tend to show a profit in the event of a loss on the underlying position (and a loss in the case of a profit on the underlying position).

Positions in futures markets can be taken much more quickly and much more cheaply (in terms of transaction costs) than positions in the underlying spot markets. For example, a position in stock index futures can be established within a few minutes (from the time of the decision) at little cost in terms of commissions and bid–ask spreads. The construction of a balanced portfolio of stocks would take much longer and be more costly in terms of commissions and spreads. For these reasons, futures markets tend to be more efficient than the underlying spot markets; futures prices respond to new information more quickly. So futures have a second economic function, which might be termed price discovery. Futures prices may be indicative of what prices should be in the markets for the underlying instruments. This price discovery function is particularly important where the underlying spot market is poorly developed or illiquid, as in countries with poorly developed financial systems or for instruments that are not frequently traded.

Examples of hedging with futures

Consider a corporate treasurer who intends to borrow money in the middle of March for a three-month period. The treasurer may fear that interest rates will have risen by the date of the borrowing. Since a rise in interest rates would add to the cost of borrowing, a futures position is taken so that there would be an offsetting profit in the event of a rise in interest rates. This involves selling three-month interest rate futures.

Three-month interest rate futures are quoted on an index basis. The index is 100 minus the futures interest rate. So a futures interest rate of 6·5% p.a. would entail a quote of 100 − 6·5 = 93·5. As a result, the futures 'price' falls as interest rates rise. In order to profit from a price fall, the futures must be sold, with a view to subsequently buying back at a lower price.

Suppose that it is the middle of February and both spot and futures three-month interest rates stand at 6·5% p.a. The treasurer intends to borrow £500,000 in the middle of March. To hedge against the risk of a rise in interest rates, a futures contract is sold (£500,000 is the size of a contract on LIFFE).

Example 1.1

14 February

The treasurer intends to borrow £500,000 on 15 March. The current interest rate is 6·5% p.a.	The treasurer sells a futures contract at a price of 93·5.

If by 15 March the three-month interest rate had risen to 8% p.a. the treasurer would have to pay an extra 1·5% p.a. for 3 months on £500,000. However, the futures price would have fallen to 92 so that the futures contract could be bought back (closed out) at a lower price than that at which it was sold. The futures profit offsets the higher borrowing cost.

15 March

There is an increased borrowing cost of 1·5% p.a. for 3 months on £500,000.	There is a profit of 1·5 on the futures contract. This profit amounts to 1·5% p.a. for 3 months on £500,000.
Loss of £1,875.	Profit of £1,875.

The treasurer has successfully hedged by taking a futures position opposite to the underlying position. The increase in interest rates that caused a loss on the underlying position produced an offsetting profit from the futures contract.

Consider another example, this time based on stock index futures. The FTSE 100 Index stands at 3600 on 14 February and a fund manager expects to receive £900,000 on 15 March. The intention is to invest that money immediately in a balanced portfolio of shares. The fund manager fears that share prices will rise by 15 March, meaning that less stock can be bought with the £900,000.

Since the risk is that share prices will rise, the requisite futures position is one that would profit from a rise in share prices. Stock index futures are bought. A FTSE 100 futures contract relates to a value of stock equal to the futures index multiplied by £10. So, if the futures index were 3600, each futures contract would relate to 3600 × £10 = £36,000 worth of shares. Hedging a purchase of £900,000 of stock (at 14 February prices) requires the purchase of 10 FTSE 100 futures contracts.

The futures profit, when added to the £900,000, provides the £950,000 required to buy the quantity of stock that £900,000 would have bought on 14 February.

Example 1.2

14 February
Fund manager expects to invest £900,000 on 15 March, but fears that the stock index will rise above the current 3600, thus reducing the number of shares that could be bought with £900,000.

Fund manager buys 25 FTSE 100 futures contracts at a futures index of 3600.

Suppose that the index rises by 200 points by 15 March. The quantity of stock that could have been bought for £900,000 on 14 February now costs £950,000. This could be regarded as a loss of £50,000. However, if the futures FTSE 100 Index also rises by 200 points, there will be a futures profit of £50,000.

15 March
The FTSE 100 has risen to 3800. The fund manager needs an extra £50,000 to be able to buy the stock.

There is a futures profit of 200 index points at £10 per point on each of 25 contracts: 200 × 25 × £10 = £50,000.

Futures exchanges and contracts

There are more than 25 futures exchanges worldwide. The biggest are the Chicago Board of Trade (CBOT) and the Chicago Mercantile Exchange (CME). These are followed by the London International Financial

Futures and Options Exchange (LIFFE – pronounced 'life') and the Marché à Terme des Instruments Financiers (MATIF – located in Paris).

At the time of writing, the most important contracts, in terms of numbers traded, are the Eurodollar (short-term interest rate) futures on the CME, US Treasury bond futures (CBOT), Euroyen (short-term interest rate) futures (TIFFE – Tokyo International Financial Futures Exchange), German government bond futures (LIFFE), and French notional bond futures (MATIF).

Although volumes tend to be highest for interest rate and bond futures, important stock index and currency contracts are also traded. Stock index futures include contracts on the S&P 500 (CME), DAX (DTB – Deutsche Terminbörse, located in Frankfurt), Hang Seng (HKFE – Hong Kong Futures Exchange), FTSE 100 (LIFFE), CAC 40 (MATIF), IBEX 35 (MEFF RV – Meff Renta Variable, Spain), Nikkei 225 (OSAKASE – Osaka Securities Exchange), Nikkei Stock Index (SIMEX – Singapore International Monetary Exchange), All – Ordinaries Share Price Index (SFE – Sydney Futures Exchange) and Topix (TSE – Tokyo Stock Exchange).

The dominant exchange for currency futures is the Chicago Mercantile Exchange. The largest volumes at the time of writing were in the Deutschmark, yen, Swiss franc and British pound futures.

FINANCIAL OPTIONS

A call option provides the right (but not the obligation) to buy at a specified price (the strike or exercise price) during a period of time (or at a point in time). It thus provides a maximum buying price and protects the user from price rises above this maximum. Financial options may relate to individual stocks, stock indices, bonds, interest rates, currencies or futures. So someone wanting to buy shares could buy call options in order to put a ceiling on the amount to be paid for the shares. This would be hedging the purchase. Example 1.3 illustrates the use of a call option.

Alternatively, call options may be bought as an investment rather than as a means of hedging. They provide a low cost, highly geared, exposure to the shares. For example, a share may cost 200p and a call option on that share 10p. If a 20p rise in the share price causes a 10p increase in the option price, the purchase of the option provides half the capital gain with just 5% of the investment. Another way of looking at this is that the option provides a 100% profit, whereas the shares yield just 10%. However, the opportunity for high percentage profits is accompanied by the risk of heavy losses (with a strong possibility of a 100% loss).

A put option provides the right (but not the obligation) to sell at a specified price (the strike or exercise price) during a period of time (or at a point in time). It provides a minimum selling price, and hence protects the user against the price of the shares (or other underlying instrument) falling below that minimum. Put options can be used by potential sellers of shares to hedge against share price falls. The fact that the option involves no obligation means that if the share price is above the strike price, the shares can be sold at the market price; the right to sell at the strike price would not be exercised. Example 1.4 illustrates the use of put options in the context of hedging exchange rate risk.

Example 1.3

An investor buys a 300p BR call option contract for 15p per share (£150 per contract)

Outcome 1
The share price rises to 375p. The investor could exercise the option and thereby buy 1,000 shares at 300p per share

Outcome 2
The share price falls to 225p. The investor would not exercise the option. Instead the investor buys shares at 225p.

Example 1.4

A UK importer invoiced in US dollars needs to obtain $1,500,000.
 He buys pound sterling puts at an exercise price of £1 = $1·50 and thereby acquires the right to sell £1,000,000 for $1,500,000.
 Spot exchange rate is £1 = $1·50 and premium is 2·5 cents/£1 = $25,000.

Outcome 1
The pound strengthens to £1 = $1·65. $1,500,000 is bought for £909,091. The option is not exercised.

Outcome 2
The pound weakens to £1 = $1·35. £1,000,000 would buy only $1,350,000. The option to sell £1,000,000 for $1,500,000 is exercised.

Options exchanges and contracts

Most of the exchanges that trade financial futures also trade financial options. There are also exchanges that trade options but not futures, such as the European Options Exchange (EOE – located in Amsterdam) and the Marché des Options Négociables de Paris (MONEP).

At the time of writing, the option contracts with the highest volume of trading were on the S&P 100 stock index (CBOE – Chicago Board Options Exchange), the S&P 500 stock index (CBOE), Eurodollar (short-term interest rate) futures (CME), US Treasury bond (CBOT) and the DAX stock index (DTB).

During October 1995, the most actively traded stock options were CS Holding N (SOFFEX – Swiss Options and Financial Futures Exchange), IBM (CBOE), Intel (AMEX – American Stock Exchange), Micron Technology Inc. (PACIFIC – Pacific Stock Exchange, located in California), Microsoft Corporation (PACIFIC), Philips (EOE), Union Bank of Switzerland (SOFFEX) and Motorola (AMEX).

The most important exchange for currency options has been the Philadelphia Stock Exchange (PHLX). The highest trading volumes have been in the Deutschmark, yen and British pound contracts.

In addition to the exchange traded contracts, there are important over-the-counter (OTC) options; indeed, for some underlying instruments the OTC market is greater than that provided by the exchanges. OTC options are negotiated on a one-to-one basis between the provider (frequently a bank) and its client. They are not normally tradable with third parties.

In some cases, exercise of an option contract does not lead to an exchange of the underlying instrument. For example, stock index options involve a cash payment corresponding to the difference between the option strike price (index) and the actual index at the time of exercise. In the case of futures options, a futures contract is delivered upon exercise and that contract is immediately marked to market so as to realise the cash value of the difference between the option strike price and the current futures price.

TYPES OF TRADER

The main economic function of derivatives is the provision of a means of hedging, of reducing an existing risk. However, hedgers are not the only traders active on futures and options exchanges.

Speculators buy and sell derivatives simply to make profit, not to reduce risk. They buy when they believe futures or options to be underpriced, and sell when they view them as overpriced. Frequently, speculative trades heavily outnumber hedging trades.

Speculators are vital to derivatives markets. They facilitate hedging, provide liquidity, tend to ensure accurate pricing and can help to maintain price stability. It is unlikely that hedgers wishing to buy futures, for example, will precisely match hedgers selling futures in terms of numbers of contracts. If hedgers are net sellers, there will be a tendency for futures prices to fall and that may generate profit opportunities for speculators. Speculators will buy the underpriced futures. The purchases by speculators will allow the net sales on the part of the hedgers. In effect, speculators fill the gap between sales and purchases by hedgers. In so doing, they tend to maintain price stability since they will buy into a falling market, and sell into a rising one (in the event of hedgers being net buyers).

A liquid market is one in which there is considerable buying and selling on a continuous basis. In a liquid market, hedgers can make their transactions with ease and with little effect on prices. Speculative transactions add to market liquidity. In the absence of speculators, hedgers may have difficulty in finding counterparties and they may need to move prices in order to entice counterparties.

Speculators also help to make a market informationally efficient. A market is informationally efficient when prices fully reflect all available relevant information. Speculators are likely to consider all relevant information when deciding upon the appropriate price of a futures (or options) contract. If actual prices differ from those judged appropriate, they will be brought into line with the estimated prices by speculative trades; underpriced futures will be bought (and so their prices will tend to rise), while overpriced futures will be sold until their prices have fallen to the level considered correct.

In addition to hedgers and speculators, there is a third category of traders known as arbitragers. Arbitragers also help to make markets liquid, ensure accurate pricing and enhance price stability. Arbitrage involves making profits from relative mispricing. For example, bond futures prices should bear a consistent relationship to actual bond prices. If this relationship is violated, an arbitrage opportunity may arise. If the bond futures price is too high relative to the actual bond price, a profit can be made by buying bonds and simultaneously selling futures. Such trades will tend to restore the appropriate relationship between bond prices and futures prices (by raising bond prices and reducing futures prices).

THE MARGIN SYSTEM

Before dealing with specific types of futures contract, it is necessary to examine some features that are common to all futures markets. The margin system is central to futures markets. There are 3 types of margin: initial margin, maintenance margin and variation margin. The initial margin is a sum of money to be provided by both the buyer and the seller of a futures contract when they make their transaction. This margin is a small percentage of the face value of the contract (perhaps 1%). The initial margin is subject to variation (by a clearing house) and will depend on the volatility of the price of the underlying instrument concerned (initial margins may be as little as 0·1% or as much as 10% of the value of the instrument to which the futures contract relates). One function of initial margin is the provision of market discipline. The payment of initial margin may deter poorly capitalised speculators from entering the market.

Whereas initial margin is the sum to be initially deposited (with a clearing house), the maintenance margin is the minimum sum that must remain deposited while the futures position is held. Initial and maintenance margins are frequently identical in value. The margin is returned to the contract holder when the futures contract is closed out or matures. Initial and maintenance margins could be in the form of money (which may earn interest) or other securities (which continue to provide a yield to the holder of the futures position). The margin will be drawn upon (by the clearing house) in the event of the holder of a futures position failing to make a variation margin payment.

Variation margin is payable and receivable on a daily basis. It reflects the profit or loss made from a futures contract during the course of a day. If the futures price moves to the holder's advantage, the holder will receive variation margin; if the futures price moves adversely, a payment must be made. This process of realising profits and losses on a daily basis is known as marking to market. If a contract holder fails to make a variation margin payment, the contract will be automatically closed out and the outstanding sum deducted from the maintenance margin (which is set at a level that is expected to exceed any likely variation margin call).

When a futures deal is agreed between a buyer and a seller, a clearing house takes over the role of counterparty to both buyer and seller. So, although buyer A bought from seller B, once the deal is registered the clearing house becomes the seller to buyer A and the buyer from seller B. An implication of this is that there is no need to investigate the creditworthiness of the person or entity with whom a deal is made (the need for such investigation could slow up futures dealing and undermine market efficiency). All default risk is taken by the clearing house. The clearing house protects itself from counterparty default risk by means of the variation and maintenance margins. Marking to market prevents the accumulation of counterparty debt and the maintenance margin is a source from which one day's outstanding variation margin payment can be drawn.

So one implication of the margin system is the removal (or substantial reduction) of counterparty risk. As a result, dealers can feel free to trade instantaneously with any other traders. Another implication of the margin system is that futures are highly geared investments. For example, an initial margin of 1% of the underlying means that the exposure acquired is 100 times the initial money outlay.

Closing out

The majority of futures contracts are closed out before they mature. Since there are typically only 4 maturity dates each year, it is unlikely that the needs of futures users will coincide with one of these 4 dates (for most futures contracts there are maturity dates in March, June, September and December). Closing out involves taking a futures position opposite to the original position. If the position was opened by buying a contract with a March maturity date, it would be closed out by selling a March futures contract; likewise, a short position (futures sold) would be closed out by buying futures with the same maturity date. When futures contracts are closed out, the transactor is left with no futures position; the purchases and sales are deemed to cancel each other.

The closing transaction will typically not be with the same counterparty as the opening transaction; but, none the less, the transactions will cancel out, leaving the trader with no remaining futures position. This is because of the counterparty role of the clearing house. As soon as a futures trade is agreed, the clearing house becomes the counterparty to both buyer and seller. It is as if the buyer has bought from the clearing house and the seller sold to the clearing house. So when a closing out transaction occurs, the transactor is left with identical long (bought) and short (sold) positions with the clearing house and the clearing house deems these to cancel each other out.

Ticks

A tick is the smallest futures price movement permitted by the exchange on which the futures are traded. In the case of the FTSE 100 futures, the tick size is half an index point. Since the size of a futures contract is specified by LIFFE to be £10 per index point, it follows that a tick has the monetary value of £5. So one way of computing the profit or loss from such futures contracts is to multiply £5 by the number of ticks by which the futures price has changed.

Although the chapters on stock index futures, short-term interest rate futures, long-term interest rate futures and currency futures can, to a large extent, be read independently of each other, all of them require an appreciation of the foregoing common features – the margin system, the role of the clearing house, closing out and ticks.

Further reading

Other useful introductions to derivatives are available in the following books:
Rob Dixon and Phil Holmes, *Financial Markets* (Chapman & Hall, London, 1992), Chapters 8 and 9.
Keith Redhead, *Introduction to the International Money Markets* (Woodhead-Faulkner, Hemel Hempstead, 1992), Chapters 5, 6 and 7.
Janette Rutterford, *Introduction to Stock Exchange Investment*, 2nd edn (Macmillan, Basingstoke, 1993), Chapters 6 and 7.

For an insider's view, see
Alex Carpenter, *Inside the International Financial Futures Markets* (Woodhead-Faulkner, Cambridge, 1991).

MANAGING STOCK MARKET RISK WITH FUTURES

2

INTRODUCTION

Stock indices are now widely familiar; frequently quoted examples include the Dow Jones Industrial Average in the USA, the Nikkei 225 in Japan, the FTSE 100 in the UK, the DAX in Germany and the CAC 40 in France.

The first section of this chapter deals with hedging with stock index futures, including the use of beta in calculating hedge ratios. Beta is important since it measures the systematic risk (risk of general market movements) of a portfolio, and it is this component of risk that can be managed with stock index futures. This is followed by the overlay techniques of removing general market exposure (the market overlay) to isolate stock selection, or the isolation of general market exposure.

The chapter then considers the factors that are involved in the determination of stock index futures prices. Since the stock index portfolio is carryable, cash-and-carry arbitrage is an important factor in the process. In particular, cash-and-carry arbitrage tends to determine a range of values, the no-arbitrage band, within which the futures price (index) can be expected to fall. It is, however, argued that expectations-based speculation and hedging have a role to play in futures pricing and that cash-and-carry arbitrage can transmit futures price movements to the cash market, as well as producing effects of cash market movements on futures prices.

HEDGING WITH STOCK INDEX FUTURES

Stock index futures provide no facility for delivery and receipt of stock via exercise of the contract. Stock price movements are matched by compensatory cash flows. Futures contracts are available on many stock indices (frequently the index was created for the purpose of futures trading). Stock indices on which futures are traded include the S&P 100, S&P 500, Nikkei 225, FTSE 100, DAX, CAC 40 and the Hang Seng. There are contracts relating to all the major stock markets. Contract sizes are based on sums of money per index point. So if an S&P 500 contract is based on $250 per index point and the index (in the futures market) stands at 400, then each futures contract relates to 400 × $250 = $100,000 of stock. Similarly, at £10 per index point, a FTSE 100 of 6000 (in the FTSE 100 futures market) indicates that each futures contract relates to 6000 × £10 = £60,000 worth of shares.

When using stock index futures to reduce stock market risk, the anticipation is that any losses arising from movements in stock prices are offset by gains from parallel movements in futures prices. An investor might be anxious about the possibility that the prices of his or her stock might fall. He or she could reduce the risk of a reduction in the value of the portfolio by taking a position in the futures market that would provide a gain in the event of a fall in stock prices. In such a case the investor would take a short position in stock index futures contracts. By taking a short position, he or she guarantees a notional selling price of a quantity of stock for a specific date in the future. Should stock prices fall and stock index futures behave in a corresponding fashion, the notional buying price on that date would be less than the predetermined notional selling price. The investor could close out his or her position in futures by taking a long position in the same number of contracts. The excess of the selling price over the buying price is paid to the investor in cash in the form of variation margin. This gain on the futures contracts is received on a daily basis as the futures price moves (marking to market). Had the prices of stocks risen, the investor would have gained from his or her portfolio of equities, but lost on futures dealings. In either case, the investor has succeeded in reducing the extent to which the value of the portfolio fluctuates.

The use of futures to hedge the risk of a fall in stock prices does not require any alteration of the original portfolio. It is thus preferable to any form of hedging that involves changing the composition of the portfolio, such as liquidating part of the portfolio.

Hypothetical examples

In Example 2.1, the portfolio holder fears a generalised fall in equity prices and wishes to avoid a fall in the value of his or her portfolio.

Example 2.1

Cash (spot) market	Futures market
5 April Holds a balanced portfolio of equities valued at £1,000,000, but fears a fall in its value. The current FTSE 100 Index is 5000.	Sells 20 June FTSE 100 contracts at a price of 5000 each. He has thus committed himself to the notional sale of £1,000,000 of stock on the June delivery date at the level of equity prices implied by the futures price on 5 April. (£1,000,000 = 20 × 5000 × £10, where each futures contract relates to stock worth £10 per index point, hence 5000 × £10.)
10 May The FTSE 100 Index has fallen to 4750. Correspondingly, the value of the portfolio has declined to £950,000.	Closes out the futures position by buying 20 June FTSE 100 contracts at a price of 4750. The notional buying price of each contract is thus 250 below the notional selling price.
Loss on the portfolio = £50,000	Gain from futures trading = £50,000 (20 × 250 × £10)

By 10 May the portfolio holder feels that the fall in equity prices is complete and chooses to close out his or her futures position. Of course, this strategy is one that reduces variations in the value of the portfolio holder's assets. If, in Example 2.1, the FTSE 100 Index had risen, there would have been a cash market gain offset by a futures market loss.

Example 2.2 shows how a long position in futures can be used as a hedge. In this case, a fund manager anticipates receipt of £1 million on 10 January and intends to use it to buy a balanced portfolio of UK equities. He fears, one month earlier, that stock prices will rise before the money is received.

In Example 2.2, futures prices did not move precisely in line with the FTSE 100 Index and, as a result, the hedge was imperfect. Basis is the difference between the spot and futures indices. A change in basis will render a hedge imperfect. The possibility of a change in basis is known as basis risk. Another source of hedge imperfection might be differences in the percentage price changes between the hedged portfolio and the FTSE 100 Index arising from the portfolio having a beta different from that of the index. This latter source of imperfection can be dealt with by the use of hedge ratios.

Example 2.2

Cash (spot) market	Futures market
10 December Anticipates receipt of £1 million on 10 January. Current FTSE 100 Index is 5500. Fears a rise in the index.	Buys 18 March FTSE futures contracts at a price of 5500. He thereby notionally commits himself to paying £990,000 (18 × 5500 × £10) for stock on a future date.
10 January The new FTSE 100 Index is 5750.	Closes out by selling 18 March FTSE futures contracts at a price of 5700. He notionally guarantees a receipt of £1,026,000 (18 × 5700 × £10) upon maturity of the contracts.
Requires an additional £45,455 in order to buy the quantity of stock that £1 million would have bought on 10 December.	Profit from futures of £36,000.

Hedge ratios

Hedge ratios become necessary when the price behaviour of the futures contract is likely to differ from that of the instrument to be hedged. If the instrument to be hedged shows relatively large variations, then it is appropriate to use more futures contracts than in the case of a more stable instrument. It is unlikely that a portfolio of stocks, for which hedging is required, precisely corresponds to the composition of a stock index. It is thus probable that it will show more or less volatility than the index.

The beta factor of a stock is a measure of the extent to which it moves in line with stock prices in general. A balanced portfolio is likely to have a beta factor of about 1. A stock with only half the movement of the market as a whole would have a beta of 0.5, while one with double the degree of change has a beta of 2. The beta factor of a portfolio of stocks is the weighted average of the beta factors of the stocks that constitute the portfolio.

If the calculation indicates a beta factor of 1.2, then the portfolio tends to change by 20% more than the stock index. Hedging the portfolio would require the value of the stock index futures contracts used to exceed the portfolio value by 20%. The relatively large losses (or profits) arising from the high volatility require correspondingly large offsetting profits (or losses) from futures contracts, and this necessitates a relatively large number of futures contracts.

REMOVING OR ENHANCING EXPOSURES

Isolating stock selection

A fund manager may want to isolate the firm- or sector-specific exposure (if the expertise or opportunity is in stock selection), or to isolate the market exposure (if the expertise or perceived opportunity is in market timing). In order to isolate the stock selection dimension, the investor might remove market exposure by the use of a short position in stock index futures. The calculation of the appropriate number of futures contracts to sell will involve ascertaining the market exposure of the stock portfolio. The market exposure of the stock portfolio is not the same as its market value. Market value needs to be adjusted by the stock betas. A high-beta stock will tend to display disproportionately high responsiveness to overall market movements. Conversely, stocks with betas of less than one will tend to be less volatile than the market as a whole. (The stock market taken as a whole would have a beta of one, and stock index portfolios such as the S&P 500 are often treated as having betas equal to one.) Table 2.1 shows hypothetical stock betas and the corresponding market exposures, which are calculated by multiplying the market values of the stocks by the betas.

Having ascertained that the market exposure of the portfolio is $2,097,875, it is necessary to find the market exposure of a stock index futures contract. If the S&P 500 futures are to be used and the S&P 500

Table 2.1 Hypothetical stock betas and the corresponding market exposures

Stock	Value of shares ($)	Stock beta	Market exposure ($)
Aetna Life	531,250	1.1	584,375
American Express	600,000	1.2	720,000
Bethlehem Steel	432,500	1.0	432,500
Boeing	451,250	0.8	361,000
			2,097,875

index stands at 900, then each futures contract would relate to 900 × $250 = $225,000 of stock. (The use of the spot index is more appropriate than the futures index if the stock is to be held to or beyond the futures maturity date; see Appendix 2.1.) The requisite number of futures contracts would be $2,097,875/$225,000 = 9.32 contracts. This rounds down to 9 contracts. (Given the uncertainties relating to the measurement and stability of stock betas, rounding down would normally be preferred to rounding up.) Although this technique of selling stock index futures in order to neutralise the general market exposure of a specific stock portfolio is not perfect (due to the imperfect reliability of betas and the inability to trade fractions of futures contracts), it can remove most of the market exposure of a portfolio and thereby allow an investor to take positions on the performance of individual stocks or sectors relative to the market as a whole.

ACTIVITY 2.1

An investor has the following portfolio:

	Number of shares	Share price (p)	Share beta
Bank of Coventry	20,000	300	0.9
Coventry Motors	30,000	100	1.5
Nuneaton Manufacturing	10,000	600	1.3
Cheylesmore Stores	25,000	300	0.8

It is 15 February and the March FTSE futures price is 6000.
(a) How can the investor hedge the portfolio with futures?
(b) What factors might reduce the effectiveness of the measures taken in (a)?

Answer

(a) Calculate the market exposure of the portfolio by summing the market exposures of individual stocks (market exposure = number of shares × share price × beta):

$20{,}000 \times 300p \times 0.9 = 5.4\ m$
$30{,}000 \times 100p \times 1.5 = 4.5\ m$
$10{,}000 \times 600p \times 1.3 = 7.8\ m$
$25{,}000 \times 300p \times 0.8 = \underline{6.0\ m}$
$\phantom{25{,}000 \times 300p \times 0.8 = }23.7\ m$

The total market exposure is 23,700,000p (i.e. £237,000). The market exposure provided by one futures contract is:

$6{,}000 \times £10 = £60{,}000$

Hedging the portfolio with futures would involve selling:

$£237{,}000 / £60{,}000 = 3.95$ contracts.

Since futures contracts are indivisible, this would indicate either three or four contracts.

(b) Factors that could reduce hedge effectiveness include basis risk, the indivisibility of contracts, instability of beta and the presence of firm- or sector-specific risk (i.e. non-systematic risk).

Isolating market exposure

The specialist in market timing may wish to avoid exposure to non-systematic risk (i.e. risk unique to an individual stock or sector). In other words, the intention may be to gain market exposure while avoiding the risk that the stocks bought may underperform the market. Such an investor could obtain market exposure by buying stock index futures while keeping the investment fund on deposit; if the exposure is to a foreign market the deposit may be in either the home or the foreign currency. If the inclination is to take no view (and no risks) on currency movements, or if a bearish view is taken on the foreign currency, then the deposit would be in the home currency.

In effect, the fund manager is creating a futures fund. The market value of the stocks underlying the stock index futures bought might be matched to the sum on deposit. If the S&P 500 stands at 900 so that each futures contract reflects $900 \times \$250 = \$225{,}000$ of stock, then one futures contract would be bought for every $225,000 held on deposit. Note that if the deposit is held in a currency other than US dollars, currency fluctuations will remove the one-to-one relationship between the value of the deposit and the value of the stocks underlying the futures. So constant monitoring and rebalancing (i.e. changing the number of futures contracts held) may be necessary. Stock market movements would entail no such need for rebalancing since variation margin cash flows would tend to keep the size of the deposits in line with the value of stock underlying the futures contracts. For example, a rise in the market and hence futures prices will generate variation margin receipts that can be added to the deposit, so the deposit grows as the market rises.

STOCK INDEX FUTURES PRICES

The pricing of futures or forward contracts can be looked upon as being based on arbitrage. The arbitrage is between the futures or forward contract on the one hand and a financially engineered equivalent on the other. When the underlying instrument can be held during the life of the futures or forward contract, the arbitrage may be referred to as a cash-and-carry arbitrage. Instruments that may be held in this way include stock index portfolios, bonds and currencies (in the latter case, the cash-and-carry arbitrage tends to be referred to as covered interest arbitrage).

In the case of stock index futures, the arbitrager might buy the portfolio of stocks on which the index is based (or a good approximation to it) and hold it until the maturity date of the futures contract. In true arbitrage this portfolio would be financed by borrowing money. This purchase of stock via borrowing money with a view to holding the stock until a time in the future constitutes a financially engineered (or synthetic) futures position. If the cost of this synthetic futures position differs from the price of traded futures, an arbitrage opportunity may be available. If the actual futures price exceeds that of the synthetic, then a profit might arise from long cash-and-carry arbitrage that involves borrowing money and using it to buy the stock index portfolio while simultaneously selling futures. (In other words, the relatively expensive traded futures are sold and the cheaper synthetic futures are bought.) The proceeds from selling the stock via the futures would exceed the sum of money to be repaid. The excess would be the arbitrage profit.

If stock index futures are trading at a price below that of the synthetic, they would be bought and a synthetic short position taken. So in this case the cash-and-carry arbitrage would involve buying futures while short selling stock (selling borrowed stock) and putting the proceeds on deposit (or into other short-term risk-free assets) – the stock acquired when the futures contract matures is used to repay the stock borrowing. In this case the proceeds from depositing money (net of dividend obligations) exceed the amount required to buy the stock at the price guaranteed by the futures contracts, and this excess constitutes the arbitrage profit. It is to be noted that the stock transactions, the futures trades and the borrowing/depositing are all carried out simultaneously.

Fair futures prices and no-arbitrage bands

The fair futures price is based upon arbitrage. In the case of stock index futures, this would be a cash-and-carry arbitrage. The futures price should be such that there is no arbitrage profit from buying stock (with borrowed money) and simultaneously selling futures. The excess of the financing cost of holding the stock over the dividend receipts constitutes the net cost of carry. The selling price guaranteed by the futures should match the initial cost of the stock plus the net cost of carry. In other words, the futures price should provide a guaranteed capital gain that exactly compensates for the excess of the interest payments over the (expected) dividend receipts.

The formula for fair value premium is:

$$FP = I \times \left[\frac{(r-y)}{100} \times \frac{d}{365} \right]$$

where FP is the fair value premium, I is the FTSE 100 Index, r is the interest rate over d days, y is the percentage yield on the index portfolio and d is the number of days in the funding period.

For example, let I = 2400, r = 10% p.a., y = 5% p.a. and d = 91 days. Then:

$$FP = 2400 \times \left[\frac{(10-5)}{100} \times \frac{91}{365} \right]$$

= 30 points (so the fair futures price is 2430)

Short cash and carry involves selling stock short and buying futures. In this case the excess of interest over dividends is a net inflow and this gain should be matched by having a guaranteed future purchase price that exceeds the spot sale price by the amount of this net inflow.

ACTIVITY 2.2

If the rate of interest on risk-free bank deposits was 7.5% p.a. and if money could be borrowed at the same rate of interest estimate the price of a FTSE 100 futures contract which matures in 4 months on the basis of a spot index of 4,000 and a zero expected rate of dividend yield on the FTSE 100 portfolio. How would the answer change if the expected rate of dividend yield was 4.5% p.a. (while the other values are as before)?

Answer

Using the formula

$$FP = I \left[\frac{i-y}{100} \times \frac{d}{365} \right]$$

and treating 4 months as exactly one-third of a year gives (with zero expected dividend yield):

$$FP = 4000 \left[\frac{7.5 - 0}{100} \times \frac{1}{3} \right]$$

$$= 4000 \times 0.025 = 100$$

If the fair value premium is 100 then the fair futures price is 4000 + 100 = 4100. With an expected rate of dividend yield of 4.5 p.a. the calculation becomes:

$$FP = 4000 \left[\frac{7.5 - 4.5}{100} \times \frac{1}{3} \right]$$

$$= 4000 \times 0.01 = 40$$

If the fair value premium is 40 then the fair futures price is 4000 + 40 = 4040.

Example 2.3

The current level of the FTSE 100 is 3100 and that of the DAX is 1650. The settlement date is 10 days from now in both cases. Interest rates in the UK and Germany are 5.6875% p.a. and 7.75% p.a. respectively. The estimated rate of dividend yield on the FTSE 100 portfolio over the next 10 days is 4% p.a.

On the basis of this information it is possible to calculate fair prices for futures on the FTSE 100 and the DAX. An important difference is that the FTSE 100 is based only on share prices and makes no allowance for dividend receipts, whereas the DAX is a total return index. The DAX index is constructed to include reinvestment of dividends, but the FTSE 100 is not.

In the case of the FTSE 100:

fair futures price = spot index × [1 + (r − d)(n/365)]
= 3100 × [1 + (0.056875 − 0.04)(10/365)]
= 3101.43

In the case of the DAX:

fair futures price = spot index × [1 + r(n/365)]
= 1650 × [1 + 0.0775 (10/365)]
= 1653.5

So it would appear that cash-and-carry arbitrage (long and short) determines the futures price. The futures price thus determined is known as the fair futures price. However, the actual futures price may differ from the fair futures price. This is due to transactions costs such as commissions and bid–offer spreads.

An arbitrager must make a gain that covers transactions costs before showing a net profit. The actual futures price can deviate from the fair futures price by as much as the transactions costs without arbitrage becoming profitable. So the arbitrage pressure that tends to prevent deviations of actual futures prices from fair futures prices merely serves to keep the actual futures prices within a range (the no-arbitrage band) rather than ensuring equality with the fair futures price. Arbitrage occurs only when the actual futures price moves outside the no-arbitrage band (i.e. away from the fair futures price by the sum of the transactions costs). This is illustrated by the following activity.

ACTIVITY 2.3

The FTSE 100 is 3000. The three-month interest rate is 8% p.a. and the expected rate of dividend yield over the next 3 months is 4% p.a. What is the fair futures price for a futures contract maturing in 3 months' time?

How might an arbitrage profit be made if the actual futures price were (a) 3050 and (b) 3000, and there were no transactions costs? If the total transactions costs (commissions, bid-offer spreads, stamp duty) amounted to £250 per £30,000 of stock, would arbitrage profits still be available?

Answer
The fair futures premium is:

$3000 \times (0.08 - 0.04)/4 = 30$

so the fair futures price is 3000 + 30 = 3030.

(a) *If the actual futures price were 3050, then the futures would be overvalued. In the absence of transactions costs, a profit is available from a long cash-and-carry arbitrage which entails buying stock and selling futures. There is a guaranteed profit from the stock and futures of 50 index points (amounting to 50 × £10 = £500 per £30,000 of stock and one futures contract). The corresponding cost of carry is 30 index points (£300). So there is a net profit of 20 index points (£200).*

(b) *If the actual futures price were 3000, the futures would be undervalued. So stock should be sold and futures bought (short cash and carry). There is neither profit nor loss from the stock and futures position. The net cost of carry accrues as profit and is 30 index points (30 × £10 = £300).*

If the total transactions costs were £250, there would be no net profit remaining in case (a) and only £300 – £250 = £50 in case (b). The futures price has to deviate by 25 index points from its fair value before any arbitrage profits become available.

In this case there is a no-arbitrage band of 25 index points either side of the fair futures price (3005 – 3055). Futures prices within this band do not induce arbitrage since they offer no arbitrage profit.

In the absence of transactions costs, cash-and-carry arbitrage would tend to keep the actual futures price equal to the fair price because undervalued futures would be bought by arbitragers (pushing up the futures price) and overvalued futures would be sold (pushing the futures price down towards its fair value). In the presence of transactions costs, the cash-and-carry arbitrage merely keeps the futures price within the no-arbitrage band. When the futures price is within the no-arbitrage band there will be no further buying or selling by arbitragers to move the futures price towards the fair futures price (i.e. towards the middle of the no-arbitrage band).

If the futures price falls below the bottom of the no-arbitrage band, arbitragers would buy futures until the futures price reaches the bottom of the band, at which point arbitrage would stop. A futures price above the top of the no-arbitrage band would induce long cash-and-carry arbitrage which involves selling futures. The sale of futures would move the futures price to the top of the no-arbitrage band, but no further. Once the futures price is within the band, arbitrage opportunities cease.

ACTIVITY 2.4

The FTSE 100 is currently 5000, the three-month interest rate is 7% p.a., and the expected dividend yield on the FTSE 100 portfolio is 3% p.a.
(a) What is the fair price of a FTSE 100 futures contract due to mature in 3 months?
(b) If each stock transaction incurs costs of 0.6% of the value of the stock, within what range of values should the actual futures price lie? (Ignore transactions costs on futures contracts.)
(c) If the actual futures price were 5200, how could an arbitrager make a profit? What might be the effects of arbitragers pursuing such a profit?

Answer
(a) The futures premium over spot, FP, is given by

$$FP = I\,[(r-y)/100]\,[d/365]$$

treating d/365 as 0.25 (a quarter of the year) gives

FP = 5000 [(7 − 3)/100] 0.25 = 50

So the fair futures price is 5000 + 50 = 5050

(b) Both long and short cash and carry arbitrage involve the purchase and sale of stock. So each arbitrage incurs transactions costs amounting to 1.2% of the value of the stock. Based on an index of 5000 this amounts to 60 index points. So the no-arbitrage band would be 5050 +/− 60, i.e. 4990 to 5110.

(c) A futures price of 5200 would be above the no-arbitrage band. Arbitragers could sell the over-priced futures and simultaneously buy stock (long cash and carry arbitrage). These transactions would tend to reduce the futures price and to raise the spot index (and hence the fair futures price and the no-arbitrage band). The futures price would fall, and the no-arbitrage band rise, until the futures price equalled the top of the no-arbitrage band. At that point arbitrage would cease since it would no longer be profitable.

Basis trading

The cash market and futures indices are different, albeit related, instruments. The movement of the futures index can be subdivided into a part that is related to the cash index and an independent component. The extent to which the futures index moves independently of the cash index provides scope for changes in basis, which is the difference between the cash market and futures indices (here, basis will be defined as the cash market index minus the futures index). Such changes in basis provide both risks and opportunities.

The first step is to ascertain the fair price of the futures contract. This might be looked upon as the middle of the range of possible values. The fair futures price is the price that renders an investor indifferent between buying stock now and holding it on the one hand, and depositing money while buying futures with a view to acquiring stock on the futures maturity date on the other hand. This requires the futures to trade at a premium to the cash index that compensates for the excess of the interest rate over the expected dividend yield. The investor depositing money and buying stock via futures would gain from the excess of the interest rate over the expected dividend yield on stocks, but would suffer an offsetting loss by having to buy stock at the higher price implied by the futures price.

This relationship between cash and futures indices is maintained by cash-and-carry arbitrage. If the futures price is above its fair value, the arbitrager can profit from buying stock spot and selling futures. An underpriced futures contract would be purchased and stock sold short. Although in principle such arbitrage operations would keep the futures index at its fair value, in reality the futures price needs to deviate significantly from its fair value if arbitrage profits are to become available. The futures price must deviate from its fair value to the extent that the arbitrage profits at least offset the transactions costs and, since this arbitrage would not normally be totally riskless, some further profit may be required to compensate for the risk involved. Transactions costs would include bid–ask spreads on both stocks and futures, commissions and (in the UK) stamp duty. Such costs could amount to as much as 2% of the underlying index value. The fact that the stocks used in the arbitrage are unlikely to mirror the stock index precisely provides an element of risk (the beta of the portfolio used may differ in an unpredictable way from the stock index beta). The extent of deviation from fair value may be even greater on the downside if there are regulatory restrictions on short selling of stock.

So, rather than a unique arbitrage determined futures price, there will be a range of futures prices consistent with an absence of arbitrage opportunities. Arbitrage would merely operate to keep prices within such a range; 2500 may be the fair price of the futures, but arbitrage may merely serve to keep the futures price within 2% of that value; i.e. between 2450 and 2550. If a trader has ascertained that the fair price of the futures contract is 2500 and the no-arbitrage range is 2450 to 2550, he or she could time a futures purchase so that the futures price is in the lower part of this range (i.e. between 2500 and 2450). This would correspond to high basis and a good chance of a fall in basis (achieved as the position of the price within its range moves up). Such basis trading would tend to enhance the profits of hedgers, speculators and investors in futures funds.

Since cash-and-carry arbitrage merely determines a band of possible futures prices around the fair futures price, there may be opportunities for enhancing profits by buying futures when the futures price is towards the bottom of the range of possible values (i.e. below the fair futures price). A rise in the actual futures price relative to the fair futures price would add to the profits arising from movements in the fair futures price. Buying when the actual futures price is below the fair futures price enhances the probability of a rise of the actual futures price relative to the (no-arbitrage) band of possible values. If the futures contracts are held to maturity, such an addition to profit is assured since the actual futures price converges on to the fair futures price at maturity (at that point in time the spot price, the fair futures price and the actual futures price are the same).

The role of hedgers and speculators

So cash-and-carry arbitrage determines a band of futures prices that is consistent with an absence of arbitrage opportunities and tends to keep futures prices within that band. The width of that band will vary with the particular circumstances of different stock markets and different times, but a width equivalent to 2% of the level of the index might not be unusual. So arbitrage determines that the futures price will fall within a range of values – which could be a wide range – but does not determine where within that range the futures price will lie.

This provides a role for hedgers and speculators to influence futures prices. Net buying by hedgers and speculators would move the futures price towards the top of the no-arbitrage band, while selling would induce a price movement towards the bottom of the band. Since net purchases would result from bullish views and net sales from bearish views, it follows that market expectations will play a part in determining the position of the futures price within the band.

Not only might such expectations affect the position of the futures price within the no-arbitrage band, but also they have the potential of moving stock prices, and hence the position of the band. To understand the processes involved, consider the situation in which hedgers and/or speculators buy futures to the extent that the futures price rises above the top of the no-arbitrage band. When the futures price rises above the top of the band, the opportunity for long cash-and-carry arbitrage arises. Arbitragers buy stock and sell the (overpriced) futures. This tends to put upward pressure on stock prices (and hence the no-arbitrage band). So the arbitrage pricing mechanism is not inconsistent with expectations influencing the level of futures prices. Furthermore, expectations of future stock prices influence fair futures prices via this mechanism of raising current stock prices and hence the fair futures price. The process of futures prices moving outside the no-arbitrage band and thereby inducing cash-and-carry arbitrage constitutes a mechanism whereby futures price movements can lead spot price movements.

The role of risk

Pure arbitrage is defined as making riskless profits from unequal prices of similar instruments without any capital outlay. In the examples given, the similar instruments were futures and synthetic futures, and capital outlay was avoided by borrowing money or stock. However, the process is not absolutely riskless. Stock prices might move against the arbitrager during the time taken to assemble the portfolio. Furthermore, future dividends cannot be known with certainty. In consequence, some risk remains and arbitragers may require compensation for such risk. How much compensation depends upon their market views, the confidence with which those views are held and the degree of risk aversion (some dislike risk more than others). Any such compensation for risk tends to widen the no-arbitrage band, but by amounts that vary between arbitragers and over time. So the boundaries of the no-arbitrage band should be seen not as definite values, but as imprecise borders.

An alternative view of stock index futures pricing

Two strategies for acquiring a portfolio of stocks on a future date at a price determined in the present are (a) buying the stocks now and holding them to the future date, and (b) buying stock index futures to guarantee the purchase price while depositing the cash required to finance the purchase. The futures price should be such that there is no benefit from pursuing one rather than the other. If the futures price were not such that the 2 approaches involved the same net cost of acquiring the stock, there would be an arbitrage profit to be made by buying via the strategy with the cheaper price and selling by means of the strategy offering the higher price.

Suppose that it is 1 April and stock index futures mature on 1 July. Strategy (a) involves a 1 April cost equal to the cost of the stock on that date, and 1 July assets amounting to the stock plus dividends (plus interest on dividends, but this latter sophistication will be ignored for the sake of clarity of exposition). Strategy (b) involves a 1 July effective stock price equal to the 1 April futures price, and 1 July assets amounting to the stock plus interest on the money deposited.

These 2 strategies differ in the cost of the stock (the differences between the spot and futures prices on 1 April) and the difference between the returns; i.e. the difference between the dividends and the interest. For the 2 strategies to be equivalent, these 2 differences should offset each other. Typically, the excess of the interest over dividends (the advantage of strategy (b)) would be offset by the excess of the 1 April futures price over the 1 April spot price (the disadvantage of strategy (b)), as in Example 2.4.

BASIS CHANGE AND CONVERGENCE

Basis is often defined as the difference between the spot and futures indices (usually spot minus futures). Prior to maturity, basis will rarely

Example 2.4

1 April strategy
(a) Buy stock.
 Expenditure: stock at 1 April spot price.
 Assets on 1 July: stock plus dividends.

(b) Buy futures and deposit money.
 Expenditure: stock at 1 April futures price.
 Assets on 1 July: stock plus interest

(a) = (b)

July stock + dividends − April spot price
= July stock + interest − April futures price.
April futures price − April spot price = interest − dividends.

---

equal zero and will do so only if the financing cost interest rate equals the expected rate of dividend yield. However, at the maturity of the futures contract the futures index will equal the spot index.

The futures and spot indices will tend to converge as the futures maturity date approaches (the difference between the 2 indices is based on the expected difference between financing costs and dividend yields, and the cash flow significance of this difference falls as the time to maturity shortens). As a result, a hedger will lock in the spot index only if intending to close out very soon after taking out futures contracts, otherwise the locked-in index will fall between the initial spot and futures indices. This is illustrated by Figure 2.1, which makes the simplifying assumption of a constant spot index (this simplifying assumption does not negate the generality of the conclusion).

Consider a hedger attempting to lock in the value of a portfolio. The objective is to make a futures profit (or loss) that matches the loss (or profit) on the portfolio. The hedger will sell futures to achieve this aim. In Figure 2.1, the futures price starts at a premium to spot and declines over time towards the spot index. If the futures were closed out at maturity, there would be a futures profit equal to the initial difference between the spot and futures indices. This means that the total portfolio value, inclusive of the futures profit, would correspond to the initial futures index. On the other hand, if the futures were closed out almost immediately there would be no profit and the value of the portfolio would correspond to the initial spot index. If the futures were closed out halfway to maturity, the portfolio value should fall midway between the values implied by the

FIGURE 2.1   Convergence of future and spot indices

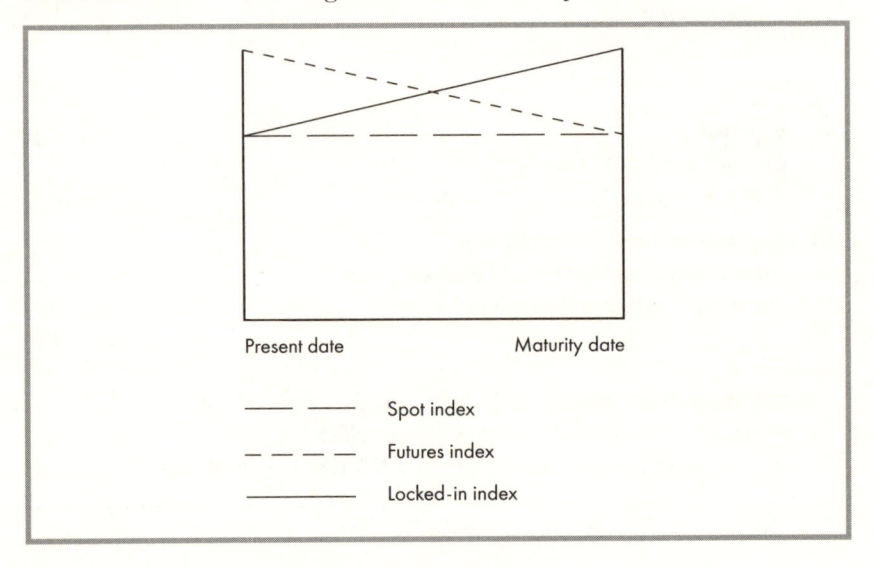

```
───── ─────   Spot index
─ ─ ─ ─ ─     Futures index
─────────     Locked-in index
```

initial spot and futures indices. The locked-in portfolio value is a function of the period to closing out the futures contracts.

This conclusion is not invalidated if the spot index fails to remain constant. Movements of the spot index would tend to be accompanied by equivalent movements in the futures index so that futures profits/losses tend to offset losses/profits on the portfolio being hedged. However, unless the futures contracts are held to maturity, there is no absolute certainty that the locked-in portfolio value will be achieved. This is because of basis risk, which is the possibility of unexpected changes in basis. The relationship between the spot and futures indices may not change precisely as expected (e.g. due to changes in interest rates or expectations of dividends). Unexpected changes in basis render hedges imperfect.

Table 2.2 Sources of basis risk when using stock index futures

1. The futures index relative to the spot index
    (a) Changes in the premium (or discount) of the fair futures index to the spot index caused by changes in short-term interest rates or expected dividend yields
    (a) Movements of the actual futures price relative to the fair futures price within the no-arbitrage band of futures prices
2. The stock index relative to the portfolio being hedged
    (a) The presence of non-systematic (diversifiable) risk
    (b) Changes in the portfolio beta

Unexpected changes in basis can have a number of causes, particularly if basis is defined in terms of a relationship between the futures index and the value of the portfolio being hedged. Changes in interest rates or expected dividends will cause unexpected alterations in the relationship between the fair futures index and the spot index. Any change in the relationship between the actual futures and fair futures price (such as might arise from a change in market sentiment about the stocks covered by the index) would further disturb basis in an unpredictable way. In addition, the relationship between the hedged portfolio and the spot index may unexpectedly change. This is particularly likely if the portfolio is not completely diversified and hence demonstrates non-systematic risk. Even if well diversified, a portfolio could experience an unpredictable change in its beta, with the result that the existing hedge ratio becomes inappropriate and hedge imperfection ensues. This is summarised in Table 2.2.

CONCLUSIONS

The asset underlying stock index futures is carryable. It is possible to buy the portfolio of stock on which the index is based and hold it to the futures maturity date. In consequence, cash-and-carry arbitrage is the basis for stock index futures pricing. However, the simultaneous purchase (or sale) of all the stocks used in the calculation of the index in amounts proportional to their weightings in the index is not usually practical. As a result, a surrogate portfolio is normally used, a portfolio that is easy to construct but whose value is expected to mirror the stock index. Since there are an infinite number of such surrogate portfolios, any delivery mechanism will involve substantial uncertainties. The uncertainties are avoided by having no possibility of physical delivery. The futures index and the spot index become equal on the futures maturity date and that maturity date convergence will entail a final marking to market cash flow. Transactions in stocks are undertaken in the spot market rather than by means of delivery against futures contracts.

Stock index futures provide a technique for employing overlay strategies. They can be used to reduce market exposure with a view to focusing the investment strategy on stock selection. Conversely, they can be used in futures funds to obtain general market exposure without any involvement in stock selection. These strategies could be interpreted in terms of hedging market exposure and enhancing such exposure: 2 opposite approaches to risk management.

Further reading

Sources with a strong focus on the use of derivatives (including stock index futures) in fund management include:
Keith Redhead, *Introduction to Financial Investment* (Prentice Hall, Hemel Hempstead, 1995).
Lewis Mandell and Thomas J. O'Brien, *Investments* (Maxwell Macmillan, Singapore, 1992).
Terry J. Watsham, *Options and Futures in International Portfolio Management* (Chapman & Hall, London, 1992).

A very readable account of the capital asset pricing model is available in:
Janette Rutterford, *Introduction to Stock Exchange Investment*, 2nd edn (Macmillan, Basingstoke, 1993), Chapter 9.

A rigorous account of the capital asset pricing model can be found in:
William F. Sharpe and Gordon J. Alexander, *Investments*, 5th edn (Prentice Hall, Englewood Cliffs, 1995), Chapter 8 (also see Chapter 9 on the arbitrage pricing theory, an alternative to the capital asset pricing model).

A useful source on stock index futures is:
C. M. S. Sutcliffe, *Stock Index Futures* (Chapman & Hall, London, 1992).

APPENDIX 2.1: CALCULATING NUMBERS OF STOCK INDEX FUTURES CONTRACTS REQUIRED FOR HEDGING

Basis is the difference between a spot (cash market) price and the corresponding futures price. Changes in basis reduce the efficiency of hedging with futures. One source of basis change arises directly from price movements. Futures prices tend to stand at premiums (or discounts) to cash market prices. This relationship between futures and cash prices, which is based on cost of carry, extends to the relationship between changes in futures prices and changes in cash prices. In the absence of a change in cost of carry, a futures premium would entail the extent of movement in the futures price exceeding that of the cash price. This means that basis changes as a result of price changes. The analysis that follows demonstrates that this source of basis change can be eliminated by an appropriate calculation of the number of futures contracts, a calculation that may seem to be counter-intuitive.

To determine the number of contracts when hedging with stock index futures, consider the hypothetical situation in which the FTSE 100 Index stands at 2000, the FTSE 100 futures index stands at 2200, and the portfolio to be hedged has a current market value of £550,000 and a beta of 1. Two alternatives for the calculation of the requisite number of contracts are (at £25 per index point):

$$\frac{\text{Value of hedged portfolio}}{£25 \times \text{spot index}} = \frac{£550,000}{£25 \times 2000} = 11 \text{ contracts}$$

and

$$\frac{\text{Value of hedged portfolio}}{£25 \times \text{futures index}} = \frac{£550,000}{£25 \times 2200} = 10 \text{ contracts}$$

The effectiveness of these alternatives can be judged in the context of two scenarios: 1. an immediate 10% fall in the market, and 2. the spot index being at 2000 on the futures maturity date. In both cases the portfolio is hedged by a short futures position.

1. The decrease in the value of the portfolio is £55,000. In the absence of any change in interest rates or expected dividend yield, the futures index would also exhibit a 10% fall to 1980. So the profit on each futures contract is 220 × £25 = £5,500. At £5,500 per futures contract, the £55,000 fall in the value of the portfolio is compensated for by 10 contracts. This suggests that the futures index should be used in the denominator when ascertaining the requisite number of futures contracts.
2. The value of the portfolio remains at £550,000. If futures are held to maturity they should provide an effective increase in the value of the portfolio based on the relationship between the initial spot and futures indices (2200/2000 = 1.1, i.e. a 10% increase in the value of the portfolio).

The achievement of this outcome requires a futures profit of £55,000. Convergence (to equality between the spot and futures indices on the futures maturity date) implies that the futures index falls by 200 so that the cash flow from each futures contract is 200 × £25 = £5,000. A total cash flow of £55,000 thus requires the use of 11 contracts. This implies that the index to be used in the denominator when calculating the number of futures contracts is the spot index.

The implication of this analysis is that the number of futures contracts to be used depends upon when they are likely to be closed out. If they are likely to be closed out immediately, then the futures index should be used in determining the number of contracts. If the futures contracts are to be held to their maturity date, the spot index should be used. A closing-out date between these extremes would suggest an index between the spot and futures indices based upon interpolation.

The need for leverage

When closing out takes place immediately after a futures position is established, the futures profit or loss includes a futures premium and hence is more than is required to offset cash market movements. The futures coverage thus needs to be **leveraged** downwards. This is achieved by dividing the exposure by the futures index, which will include the futures premium.

Consider the following data:

Cash exposure = £1,000,000
FTSE 100 futures price = 2500
Current FTSE 100 Index = 2451
Futures premium = 2%

A 100 point fall in the FTSE 100 Index would entail a 102 point fall in the futures price. As a result, the £40,800 cash market loss would be offset by a profit on:

$$\frac{£40,800}{102 \times £25} = 16 \text{ futures contracts}$$

Sixteen futures contracts relate to a current cash exposure of:

$$16 \times 2451 \times £25 = £980,400$$

The exposure covered is leveraged down in order to offset the distorting effect of the futures premium.

APPENDIX 2.2: VALUE AT RISK

Value at risk seeks to provide a measure of market risk in the form of a figure for the maximum possible loss over a particular time interval. The maximum possible loss is not treated in an absolute sense, but in a probabilistic sense. It is the loss consistent with a confidence limit, such as 99%, on a probability distribution (usually a normal distribution). In other words, the figure for the value at risk might be interpreted as the loss which has a chance of only 1% of being exceeded.

Looking at the case of measuring the market risk, or exposure, of an investment portfolio, 3 possible ways of producing the measurement would entail historical observations, variance/covariance models and Monte Carlo simulations. The simplest, and in some ways the most flexible, is the use of historical value change data.

The historical observation method might proceed by observing the last 200 value changes. If a 99% level of confidence were desired, then the second largest fall would be used, whereas a 97.5% level of confidence would use the fifth largest fall in value. These falls in value would be applied to the current portfolio value. The results of the computation would be the next day's portfolio value in the event of the second, or fifth, largest loss being experienced. The projected loss in the value of the portfolio is then regarded as the value at risk.

The value at risk thus calculated relates to daily value changes, whereas the concern may be with risk over a longer time horizon, for example a year. To convert a one-day value at risk into a value at risk for a longer period, the one-day figure is multiplied by the square root of the number of business days in the longer period. To obtain a one-year value at risk, the one-day figure would be multiplied by the square root of 250 (i.e. 15.8) on the basis of there being 250 business days in a year. The rationale for this procedure is based on the value at risk being a standard deviation measure; for example, at a 97.5% level of confidence, the value at risk corresponds to 2 standard deviations. Conversion of a standard deviation for one time period into that for another is based on the standard deviation being proportional to the square root of time (which in turn is based on variance being a linear function of time).

Variance/covariance models provide an alternative means of calculating the standard deviation. Unlike the historical observation approach, the variance/covariance models require that the probability distributions are normal. This requirement renders them more restrictive and less flexible.

The variance/covariance approach may use equations of the Markowitz type. This necessitates a substantial data input in the form of the standard deviations of the individual assets in the portfolio and the correlations between the returns on those assets. The Markowitz-type equation produces a value for the portfolio variance, the square root of which is the portfolio standard deviation. The value at risk is a multiple of the standard deviation depending on the desired level of confidence. At a 97.5% level of confidence, the value at risk equals 2 standard deviations.

It is to be noted that since the returns on options do not conform to a normal distribution, the variance/covariance models cannot be applied to options or portfolios incorporating options (unless the options are combined to produce synthetic futures).

Monte Carlo simulations involve using data on asset volatilities and covariances to execute a large number of computer runs that simulate alternative price behaviour patterns. The result is a distribution of prices. A cut-off point on that distribution is chosen to correspond with the desired confidence level. The amount by which that cut-off point falls short of the current value of the portfolio constitutes the value at risk.

All three approaches depend upon past volatility being a reliable guide to future volatility. They also depend upon the probability distribution being at least approximately normal. If it deviates substantially from a normal distribution, there is doubt as to whether a concept based on standard deviations is meaningful.

Using value at risk

As a measure of risk, or exposure, value at risk is more meaningful than the total value of the portfolio since it takes account of the probability of substantial price movements. It may be a particularly useful measure for futures funds, and other geared portfolios, since the gearing could cause the value at risk to exceed the size of the fund.

A fund manager may have a view as to the maximum acceptable loss. If the value at risk exceeds this maximum, the portfolio is clearly too risky. The fund manager is then faced with the decision of how to reduce the value at risk.

One approach would be to reallocate the portfolio so as to increase the proportion of low risk investments. Alternatively, derivatives may be employed. Put options could be purchased to prevent any loss in value exceeding the maximum acceptable loss while preserving upside potential. Futures could be used as a partial hedge to reduce portfolio volatility or as a means of portfolio reallocation. For example, selling stock index futures and simultaneously buying bond futures effectively rebalances the portfolio away from equities and towards bonds.

Using derivatives would be quicker and more flexible than changing the composition of the portfolio. This flexibility would be particularly valuable if value at risk proved to be unstable because the volatility of the assets in the portfolio was subject to change.

MANAGING INTEREST RATE RISK WITH FUTURES   3

INTRODUCTION

Both borrowers and lenders face interest rate risk. Borrowers lose from increasing interest rates, while lenders lose in the event of declines. If borrowers and lenders dislike risk and uncertainty, they will have an interest in finding techniques and instruments for reducing such risks. Short-term interest rate futures, which frequently take the form of three-month interest rate futures, are instruments suitable for the hedging of such risks. Three-month interest rate futures are notional commitments to borrow or deposit for a three-month period that commences on the futures maturity date. They provide means whereby borrowers or lenders can (at least approximately) predetermine interest rates for future periods.

This chapter begins with some description of the underlying short-term money markets and considers alternative money market instruments. It then looks at the use of three-month interest rate futures in their most basic hedging use (hedging against changes in the level of the yield curve). It will be seen that the basic hedge establishes a futures position opposite to the cash market position. For example, if the cash market position will lose from a rise in interest rates, the futures position taken is one that will profit from a rise in interest rates.

The next section considers the determination of the futures prices. Three-month interest rate futures prices are based on interest rate expectations, which may be deduced from the term structure of interest rates (the yield curve). It will be seen that arbitrage ensures that futures prices remain in line with the forward interest rates that can be generated by borrowing for one time period while simultaneously depositing the same sum of money for a different time period.

The chapter then provides an account of forward rate agreements (FRAs), which may be looked upon as over-the-counter futures (i.e. futures that are not traded on exchanges). The chapter ends with a brief consideration of the problems arising when cross hedging, i.e. hedging an interest rate with futures based on a different interest rate.

THE UNDERLYING MARKETS

There are a number of money markets that are sometimes collectively known as the parallel markets. The parallel markets comprise: (1) the inter-bank market, where banks borrow and lend among themselves (there is also corporate and local government participation); (2) the certificate of deposit (CD) market, where banks issue negotiable certificates as evidence that deposits have been made; (3) the commercial paper market in which the deposits are taken, and certificates issued, by companies rather than banks; and (4) the local government market, where deposits are taken by local (or regional) governments.

The first 3 of these have eurocurrency equivalents. The eurocurrency inter-bank market is particularly large. It involves borrowing and lending among banks (plus other entities of substantial worth such as large corporations, government bodies, central banks, and supranational agencies such as the International Monetary Fund). The distinguishing feature of the eurocurrency markets is that the lending and borrowing is in currencies other than the domestic currency; for example, a dollar deposit in London is a eurodollar deposit, and a yen deposit in Singapore is a euroyen deposit.

The inter-bank market, whether in the domestic currency or in eurocurrencies, is a wholesale market. Deposits and loans are in millions. Often money passes through several banks between the original lender and the ultimate borrower. Since deals are in large sums, individual banks cannot rely on inflows and outflows approximately matching on a daily basis. A bank making a loan or facing a withdrawal may need to borrow from other banks, while a bank receiving a deposit may lend it to other banks. Money brokers operate to bring borrowing and lending banks together.

The inter-bank markets are usually much larger, in terms of the aggregate value of transactions, than the discount market. The inter-bank interest rates have become the most common benchmarks for other interest rates. There are inter-bank offer rates which are the interest rates at which major banks can borrow from each other. Not only is there a different rate for each currency and each maturity of loan, but there may also be small variations between financial centres for the same currency and maturity. So, for example, LIBOR (London Inter-Bank Offered Rate) may differ from the corresponding rates in, say, Paris (PIBOR), Madrid (MIBOR) and Hong Kong (HIBOR). There are corresponding inter-bank bid rates at which major banks will take deposits from one another; these are known as LIBID, PIBID, MIBID, HIBID, etc. The offer rates always exceed the bid rates (a ⅛% bid–offer spread being typical). The average of the offer and bid rates is known as LIMEAN, PIMEAN, and so forth. The very small excess of offer rates over bid rates leads to banks, and other bodies, having deposits and outstanding debts simultaneously. The small excess of borrowing over deposit rates may be seen as a price worth paying for the convenience of having the high degree of liquidity provided by a short-term bank deposit.

Certificates of deposit (CDs) are bearer certificates denoting that a deposit has been made for a period, such as 3 or 6 months. As bearer certificates (not registered in a name), payment of principal plus interest at maturity is to whoever is in possession of the certificates on the maturity date. They are negotiable, i.e. they can be bought and sold between the issue and maturity dates. There are likely to be banks making markets in CDs, i.e. willing to buy and sell CDs (issued by other banks) on a continuous basis. This provides one illustration of the close relationship between the discount and parallel markets. In financial systems with discount houses, there is a tendency for those discount houses to operate as market makers in certificates of deposit as well as bills. In other financial systems, banks making markets in bills are likely to operate simultaneously as market makers in CDs.

Certificates of deposit offer advantages to both investors and the issuing banks (when compared with ordinary deposits). An investor can deposit for a period such as 3 months, and thereby receive an interest rate in excess of the rate attainable from a shorter-term deposit, while being able to turn the deposit into cash at any time by selling the CD. Simultaneously, the bank has money for 3 months and, because of the liquidity enjoyed by the investor, can pay an interest rate lower than that normally required to attract three-month deposits. So the investor has accessibility to cash, the bank has money for 3 months, the investor gets a higher interest rate than that on callable deposits (deposits that can immediately be used as cash), and the bank pays a lower interest rate than would normally be payable on three-month deposits.

Commercial paper is similar to certificates of deposit, but is issued by corporate borrowers rather than banks. It is a form of disintermediation whereby firms borrow directly rather than through the intermediation of banks. Large companies can often borrow at rates equal to, or even perhaps lower than, the interest rates that banks can borrow at. Since banks lend at higher interest rates than those at which they borrow, it

42 • **MANAGING INTEREST RATE RISK WITH FUTURES**

obviously pays large creditworthy firms to borrow directly from investors. For similar reasons, local government authorities may find it cheaper to take deposits directly rather than borrowing from deposit taking institutions such as banks.

Table 3.1 shows sterling interest rates on 13 December 1995. In each case the higher rate is the offer (borrowing) rate and the lower rate is the bid (deposit) rate.

Table 3.1 London money rates[a]

13 December	Overnight	7 days' notice	One month	Three months	Six months	One year
Inter-bank sterling	6⅞– 5½	6¾– 6⁷⁄₁₆	6¹¹⁄₁₆– 6⅜	6⁹⁄₁₆– 6⁷⁄₁₆	6⁷⁄₁₆– 6¼	6⁵⁄₁₆– 6³⁄₁₆
Sterling CDs	–	–	6¹⁵⁄₃₂– 6¹³⁄₃₂	6⁷⁄₁₆– 6⅜	6⁵⁄₁₆– 6¼	6¼– 6³⁄₁₆
Treasury bills	–	–	6⅜– 6¼	6⁵⁄₁₆– 6¼	–	–
Bank bills	–	–	6⅜– 6¹¹⁄₃₂	6⁵⁄₁₆– 6¼	6³⁄₁₆– 6⅛	–
Local authority deposits	6¹⁵⁄₁₆– 6¹³⁄₁₆	6¹³⁄₁₆– 6¹¹⁄₁₆	6²¹⁄₃₂– 6¹⁷⁄₃₂	6⁹⁄₁₆– 6⁷⁄₁₆	6⁷⁄₁₆– 6⁵⁄₁₆	6⁵⁄₁₆– 6³⁄₁₆
Discount market deposits	6½–6	6⅝– 6½	–	–	–	–

[a] UK clearing bank base lending rate 6½% from 13 December 1995.
Source: *Financial Times*, 14 December 1995.

BASIC PRINCIPLES

The basic principle of hedging with financial futures is that a futures position should be taken so that the feared interest rate change causes a profit on futures that compensates for the loss incurred on the assets or liabilities. Three-month sterling and three-month eurodollar futures contracts are notional commitments to borrow or lend for 3 months on specified future dates at interest rates agreed upon at the time of undertaking the contracts.

Both potential lenders and potential borrowers might find hedging desirable. Consider, for example, a company that anticipates receipts of £10,000,000 2 months hence and intends to lend this money. The company treasurer might expect interest rates to fall over the next 2 months and would like a means of reducing the impact of that fall. Alternatively, he may simply want to avoid the risk of interest rates falling. Either way he wants to hedge, i.e. insure himself against the possibility of a fall in interest rates. On the other hand, a potential borrower could be worried about the possibility of an increase in interest rates by the time that the loan is actually taken out. He will want to avoid such a rise in interest rates; in other words, he desires to hedge against the possibility that interest rates will increase.

Buying a June three-month sterling interest rate futures contract notionally commits the buyer to the deposit of £500,000, for 3 months from the June maturity date, at an interest rate determined in the present. The seller is simultaneously notionally committed to borrowing for that period and is also guaranteed that interest rate.

In Example 3.1, for the 3 months commencing 1 February, the interest cost on the loan would be £50,000 more than would have been the case had the interest rate remained at 10% p.a. However, there is an offsetting gain from the futures position. For a future three-month period, the hedger is committed to lending at 12% p.a. and borrowing at 10% p.a. This provides a gain equal to 2% p.a. on £10 million for 3 months, namely £50,000.

As with other futures contracts, the vast majority of short-term interest rate futures contracts are closed out prior to the maturity date. By the time of closing out, the hedger should have received, or paid, variation margin that offsets movements in the interest rate. A potential borrower, for example, having to pay more because of increased interest rates, should have received a sum of money to compensate for the higher interest

---

Example 3.1

Cash market
2 January
Treasurer intends to borrow £10 million on 1 February. Fears that interest rate will rise above the current 10% p.a.

Futures market

Sells 20 March futures contracts, thereby notionally guaranteeing that £10 million will be borrowed at 10% p.a. on the March maturity date.

1 February
Borrows £10 million at an interest rate of 12% p.a.

Buys 20 March futures contracts, thereby entering a notional commitment to lend £10 million at 12% p.a. on the March maturity date.

payments. If a contract is held to maturity, there will be a final cash settlement based on the exchange delivery settlement price (the futures price at maturity).

Price quotes

Short-term interest rate futures contracts are quoted on an index basis. The index is equal to 100 minus the annualised interest rate: for example, a three-month interest rate of 3% giving an annualised rate of 12% would mean that the contract would be priced at 88. It is to be emphasised that such prices are merely indices that are used in ascertaining profits and losses from futures trading and do not represent money payable for contracts.

Table 3.2 shows three-month interest rate futures prices on 13 December 1995. The figures show opening prices, settlement (closing) prices, changes in settlement prices since the previous day, the high and low prices during the day, the estimated volume traded during the day, and the open interest (number of contracts in existence).

A tick is the smallest price movement recognised and recorded by an exchange. In the case of most short-term interest rate contracts, it is 0.0025% of the face value of a contract. The eurodollar contracts each have a face value of $1 million and the value of a tick is $25, on both CME and LIFFE. In terms of the pricing system outlined above, each tick is depicted by 0.01. So a price change from 88 to 88.05 represents an increase of 5 ticks, amounting to $125. The difference between the 0.0025% and the 0.01 arises because the index used for pricing is based on annualised interest rates, whereas the interest actually payable is quarterly, so the annual interest rate must be divided by 4.

Suppose that a hedger buys, in December, a June three-month eurodollar interest rate contract at a price of 90 (annualised interest rate of 10%). The following day the price rises by one tick to 90.01 (annualised interest rate of 9.99%). Upon buying the contract, the hedger guaranteed the receipt of 2.5% over 3 months from the June maturity date on a eurodollar deposit of $1 million. A contract bought a day later would have guaranteed merely 2.4975% (9.99/4). Thus the hedger has guaranteed the receipt of $25,000, whereas one day later he would have guaranteed only $24,975. On the day following his purchase, he could close out his position by selling a contract and receive the value of one tick, $25, as his profit. By selling a contract the hedger acquires the notional right to borrow. The interest receivable from the long contract is $25,000, while the interest payable on the short contract would be $24,975. In the absence of closing out, the $25 would be paid to him as variation margin. Example 3.1 can now be rewritten as in Example 3.2, using the pricing convention outlined above.

Table 3.2 Three-month interest rate futures prices on 13 December 1995

	Open	Sett price	Change	High	Low	Est. vol.	Open int.
■ Three-month sterling futures (LIFFE) £500,000 points of 100%. Also traded on APT. All open interest figures are for previous day.							
Dec	93.51	93.51	–	93.52	93.50	6,454	72,020
Mar	93.80	93.80	–	93.82	93.78	9,083	93,158
Jun	93.92	93.92	–	93.93	93.90	5,553	65,503
Sep	93.91	93.91	–	93.92	93.89	3,143	44,805
Dec	93.77	93.78	–	93.79	93.77	1,269	31,627
■ Three-months PIBOR futures (MATIF) Paris Interbank offered rate (FFr 5 million)							
Dec	94.10	94.06	–0.17	94.13	93.87	37,962	33,968
Mar	94.62	94.51	–0.20	94.62	94.45	19,235	42,224
Jun	94.86	94.80	–0.12	94.86	94.77	6,653	36,125
■ Three-month euromark futures (LIFFE)[a] DM 1 million points of 100%							
Dec	96.10	96.08	–0.01	96.11	96.08	24,333	129,866
Mar	96.37	96.37	+0.01	96.39	96.36	19,484	169,252
Jun	96.42	96.44	+0.02	96.45	96.42	15,425	130,471
Sep	96.37	96.38	+0.02	96.40	96.37	11,508	104,530
■ Three-month eurolira futures (LIFFE)[a] L1000 million points of 100%							
Dec	89.51	89.51	–0.02	89.53	89.50	2,619	19,727
Mar	89.88	89.87	–0.02	89.90	89.92	3,518	33,866
Jun	90.18	90.18	–0.03	90.22	90.17	869	18,926
Sep	90.34	90.27	–0.02	90.34	90.27	372	11,321
■ Three-month euro Swiss franc futures (LIFFE) SFr 1 million points of 100%							
Dec	97.90	97.91	+0.03	97.91	97.88	3,113	14,628
Mar	98.11	98.12	+0.02	98.13	98.11	3,519	21,510
Jun	98.16	98.16	+0.02	98.17	98.14	1,091	11,725
Sep	98.08	98.07	+0.01	98.09	98.05	305	5,857
■ Three-month ecu futures (LIFFE) ecu 1 million points of 100%							
Dec	94.60	94.61	+0.03	94.63	94.60	865	5,245
Mar	94.84	94.83	+0.02	94.85	94.82	1,007	5,425
Jun	94.93	94.91	–	94.94	94.90	224	4,493
Sep	94.92	94.91	–	94.93	94.91	60	2,235
■ Three-months eurodollar (MM[b]) $1 million points of 100%							
	Open	Latest	Change	High	Low	Est. vol.	Open int.
Dec	94.23	94.21	–	94.23	94.19	40,611	284,140
Mar	94.60	94.56	–0.01	94.62	94.54	101,495	420,195
Jun	94.80	–	–	94.83	94.75	86,079	390,848

[a] LIFFE futures also traded on APT.
[b] IMM is the International Monetary Market, which is part of the CME.
Source: *Financial Times* 14 December 1995.

Example 3.2

Cash market
2 January
Treasurer intends to borrow £10 million on 1 February. Fears that interest rate will rise above the current 10% p.a.

1 February
Borrows £10 million at an interest rate of 12% p.a.

Loss is 2% p.a. on £10 million for 3 months, £50,000.

Futures market

Sells 20 March three-month sterling interest rate futures contracts at a price of 90.

Closes out by buying 20 March three-month sterling interest rate futures contracts at a price of 88.

Profit is 200 ticks at £12.50 per tick on each of 20 contracts, £50,000.

The transactions in the futures market have provided a perfect hedge to the cash market transaction. The possibility that futures interest rates might change by different amounts from cash market interest rates produces basis risk. Such incomplete matching of interest rate changes can render hedging imperfect. This is illustrated by Example 3.3, which

Example 3.3

Cash market
2 January
Treasurer intends to borrow £10 million on 1 February. Fears that interest rate will rise above the current 10% p.a.

1 February
Borrows £10 million at an interest rate of 12% p.a.

Loss is 2% p.a. on £10 million for 3 months, £50,000.

Futures market

Sells 20 March three-month sterling interest rate futures contracts at a price of 90.

Closes out by buying 20 March three-month sterling interest rate futures contracts at a price of 88.50.

Gain is 150 ticks at £12.50 per tick on each of 20 contracts, £37,500.

differs from Example 3.2 in that the futures interest rate rises by less than the cash market interest rate. Basis has changed from zero (90–90) to –0.5 (88.0–88.50) and, as a consequence, the gain on futures trading is insufficient to offset completely the loss from cash market transactions. The hedge is imperfect. Of course, if basis had changed so that futures interest rates were greater than cash market rates, the gain from futures trading would have been more than that required to offset the cash market loss.

ACTIVITY 3.1

(a) A corporate treasurer needs to borrow $10,000,000 for 3 months. It is 20 May and the money is to be borrowed on 1 August. How can the treasurer hedge against a rise in interest rates using futures?

(b) If eurodollar interest rates rise from 6% p.a. to 7% p.a. between 20 May and 1 August, what is the loss? If futures prices fell from 93.80 to 92.90 during the same period, how much futures profit would there be from the hedging strategy adopted in part (a)?

Answer
(a) Sell 10 September eurodollar interest rate futures contracts.
(b) (i) 1% on $10,000,000 over 3 months:
    0.01 × $10,000,000 × 0.25 = $25,000
    (ii) 90 ticks profit on each of 10 futures contracts at $25 per tick:
    90 × 10 × $25 = $22,500

INTEREST RATE COMPUTATIONS AND QUOTATIONS

Before addressing the issue of how short-term interest rate futures prices are determined, it is worth making some comments on the calculation and quotation of interest rates.

Simple returns are based on dividing the return over a period by the number of years in that period. However, such an approach ignores the fact that cash flows from investments can be reinvested. The compound rate of return is based on receipts being reinvested and hence producing their own returns. The formula is as follows:

The average compound rate of return (or geometric mean rate of return) = [(final value of investment)/(initial investment)]$^{1/N}$ – 1

where N = number of years.

48 • **MANAGING INTEREST RATE RISK WITH FUTURES**

For example, if an investment produces returns of 0, 10 and 20% in successive years, the average simple rate of return would be 10%, whereas the average compound rate of return would be $[(1.0)(1.1)(1.2)]^{1/3} - 1 = 0.097$, i.e. 9.7% p.a. When compounding (returns on returns) is allowed for, the underlying rate required for the realisation of a particular sum of money is lower (e.g. 9.7% p.a. as opposed to 10% p.a.). Examples of calculating the average compound rate of return are shown in Example 3.4. It is conventional to quote interest rates on a per annum basis irrespective of the maturity of the deposit or borrowing. For example, a three-month rate of 8% p.a. means 2% over 3 months and an actual return of $(1.02)^4 - 1 = 0.0824$ (i.e. 8.24%) over a year.

Example 3.4

1. 1st year 5% p.a.
   2nd year 6% p.a.

   Average compound rate of return over 2 years = $\sqrt{(1.05)(1.06)} - 1$
   = 0.055, i.e. 5.5% p.a.

2. 1st year 5% p.a.
   2nd year 6% p.a.
   3rd year 16% p.a.

   Average compound rate of return over 3 years = $[(1.05)(1.06)(1.16)]^{1/3} - 1$
   = 0.089, i.e. 8.9% p.a.

Note: The arithmetic average is reasonably accurate when rates vary little from year to year.

THE DETERMINATION OF FUTURES PRICES

The prices of short-term interest rate futures are influenced, for the nearer maturities at least, by arbitrage based on forward/forward calculations. Suppose that the three-month interest rate is 14% p.a., while the six-month rate is 15% p.a. A trader could borrow for 3 months and lend for 6, and thereby guarantee a profit from the 1% margin during the first 3 months. However, he is at risk from a rise in the three-month interest rate by the commencement of the second three-month period. There is a three-month rate for the second period, above which the loss on the second period will push the whole operation into a loss. That is the forward rate. Suppose that the trader lends £1 million for 6 months at 15% p.a. and borrows it for 3 months at 14% p.a. He will receive £1,075,000 at the end of the six-month period. Meanwhile, he must pay £1,035,000 at the end of the first 3 months and must borrow £1,035,000 in order to repay the debt. A £40,000 interest payment on this second loan would mean that the trader breaks even on the exercise, since the second debt could be repaid with the £1,075,000 from the £1 million originally lent. On a three-month loan of £1,035,000, £40,000 corresponds to a rate of interest of 15.46% p.a.

This is the forward rate and arbitrage tends to ensure that the futures rate approximates closely to it. If the futures rate were significantly below the forward rate, arbitragers would lend long and borrow short, using the futures market to guarantee future short-term interest rates. This would involve selling futures (commitments to future borrowing) and the increased sales would push down their prices. The fall in futures prices corresponds to a rise in futures interest rates. This increase in futures interest rates will tend to eliminate the scope for further arbitrage profits.

Forward interest rates

Forward interest rates are rates for periods commencing at points of time in the future and are implied by current rates for differing maturities. For example, the current three-month interest rate and the current six-month interest rate between them imply a rate for a three-month period which runs from a point in time 3 months from the present until a point in time 6 months hence.

Borrowing for 6 months and depositing for 3 months effectively creates a three-month borrowing deferred for 3 months (the three-month deposit offsets the first 3 months of the borrowing). Depositing for 6 months and borrowing for 3 creates a three-month deposit deferred for 3 months (during the first 3 months the asset and liability offset each other). The current three- and six-month interest rates imply rates for the deferred period; these implied rates are the forward interest rates. Consider the following data:

Spot three-month $8^{15}/_{16} - 9^{1}/_{16}$
Spot six-month $9^{15}/_{16} - 10^{1}/_{16}$

The forward three-month rate for a period commencing 3 months from the present is the rate that would yield the same return as the spot six-month rate, when compounded with the current three-month rate. Using mid-rates from the above figures:

$(1.0225)(1 + x) = 1.05$

0.0225 is the decimal rate for 3 months based on 9% p.a. and 0.05 is the decimal rate for 6 months based on 10% p.a. The rate x is the forward rate and is given by:

$x = (1.05/1.0225) - 1$
$ = 0.0269$

which is 2.69% over 3 months and hence 10.76% per annum (multiplying 2.69% by 4).

It may seem strange that the implied rate is not 11% p.a. since at first sight it might seem that the six-month rate would equal the average of the 2 three-month rates. Since the first three-month rate is 9% p.a., then to average 10% p.a. the second should be 11% p.a. The forward rate is less than 11% because there is compounding of the second three-month rate on the first, whereas the six-month rate involves no compounding. The effect of the compounding is that the second three-month rate is less than 11% p.a.

It is interesting to note that if the spot three- and six-month rates are the same, then the forward/forward rate will be lower than both of them. If both the three- and six-month rates were 10% p.a., then:

$(1.025)(1 + x) = (1.05)$
$x = (1.05/1.025) - 1$
$ = 0.0244$

i.e. 2.44% per quarter or 9.76% per annum. Again, this is because the 2 successive three-month rates benefit from compounding, whereas the six-month rate does not.

Thus far the analysis has been based on mid-rates. It is necessary to examine the effects of using the bid and offer rates. Different forward rates emerge according to whether the deferred rate is for a borrowing or a deposit. Returning to the first example and considering a deferred borrowing, the six-month rate would be 10 1/16% p.a., while the three-month rate would be 8 15/16% p.a. (the six-month borrowing would be at an offer rate, whereas the three-month deposit would be at a bid rate):

$(1.02234)(1 + x) = (1.05031)$
$x = (1.05031/1.02234) - 1$
$ = 0.0274$

(2.74% over 3 months, which is 10.96% per annum). The corresponding deferred deposit would involve depositing for 6 months at 9 15/16% p.a., while borrowing for 3 months at 9 1/16% p.a.:

$$(1.02266)(1 + x) = 1.04969$$
$$x = (1.04969/1.02266) - 1$$
$$= 0.0264$$

(2.64% over 3 months, which is 10.56% per annum). So the forward borrowing (i.e. offer) rate is 10.96% p.a., whereas the corresponding forward deposit (i.e. bid) rate is 10.56% p.a. The spread is 0.4% p.a. which approximates to ⅜% p.a. It is to be noted that the forward bid–offer spread is considerably larger than the spot market spread.

The forward rates are used as a basis for the calculation of fair prices for three-month interest rate futures and for forward rate agreements (FRAs).

ACTIVITY 3.2

The six-month interest rate is 10% p.a.
The three-month interest rate is 8% p.a.
Calculate the forward interest rate for the 3 months commencing 3 months from the present.

Answer
$$(1 + 0.08/4)(1 + x/4) = (1 + 0.1/2)$$
$$(1.02)(1 + x/4) = (1.05)$$
$$(1 + x/4) = (1.05)/(1.02)$$
$$x/4 = 1.0294 - 1$$
$$x = 0.1176$$

So the three-month rate available 3 months from the present is 11.76% p.a.

ACTIVITY 3.3

The following data is available:

Three-month interest rates are 6⅝–6½% p.a.
Six-month interest rates are 7⅜–7¼% p.a.

Within what range of prices would you expect the three-month interest rate futures price to fall if the futures contract is due to mature in 3 months?

Answer
Borrow short, deposit long.
$$1.03625/1.0165625 = 1.0193667$$
$$(1.0193667 - 1) \times 4 = 0.0774668$$
i.e. 7.74668% p.a. (7¾% p.a.)

Borrow long, deposit short.
1.036875/1.01625 = 1.0202952
(1.0202952 − 1) × 4 = 0.0811808
i.e. 8.11808% p.a. (8⅛% p.a.)
The no-arbitrage band of futures prices would be
100 − 7.74 = 92.26
to 100 − 8.12 = 91.88

Forward interest rates and arbitrage

The creation of a forward position in interest rates can be looked upon as a deferred deposit or borrowing. For example, a potential investor who anticipates the receipt of money 3 months hence and intends to deposit it for 3 months can, in the present, borrow money for 3 months and deposit it for 6 months. When the cash is received, it is used to repay the three-month borrowing, leaving the six-month deposit intact for the remaining 3 months. So there is no net cash inflow or outflow in the present, but a cash outflow after 3 months (debt repayment) and a cash inflow after 6 months (maturity of the six-month deposit). These cash outflows and inflows are equivalent to a three-month deposit made 3 months hence. The advantage of the creation of a forward position is that it guarantees the interest rate for the future three-month period, this interest rate being implied by the spot three-month and six-month rates.

If the rates that can be guaranteed by such forward transactions differ from the rates that can be guaranteed using futures contracts, an arbitrage opportunity may exist. Arbitragers could borrow via the cheaper method and deposit through the approach yielding the higher interest rate. This pursuit of arbitrage profits would tend to cause both spot and futures rates to move so as to eliminate arbitrage possibilities (by tending to bring the 2 deferred interest rates into equality). For example, if the futures interest rate is the lower one, arbitragers would sell futures (to guarantee being able to borrow at that lower rate), thereby causing the futures price to fall and hence the futures interest rate to rise until it has risen into line with the forward interest rate; see Figure 3.1.

A formula for calculating forward interest rates

A popular formula for ascertaining forward rates is as follows:

$$\left\{ \left[\frac{1 + (R_1 \times T_1/360)}{1 + (R_2 \times T_2/360)} \right] - 1 \right\} \times \frac{360}{T_1 - T_2}$$

FIGURE 3.1   Arbitrage between futures and synthetic forwards

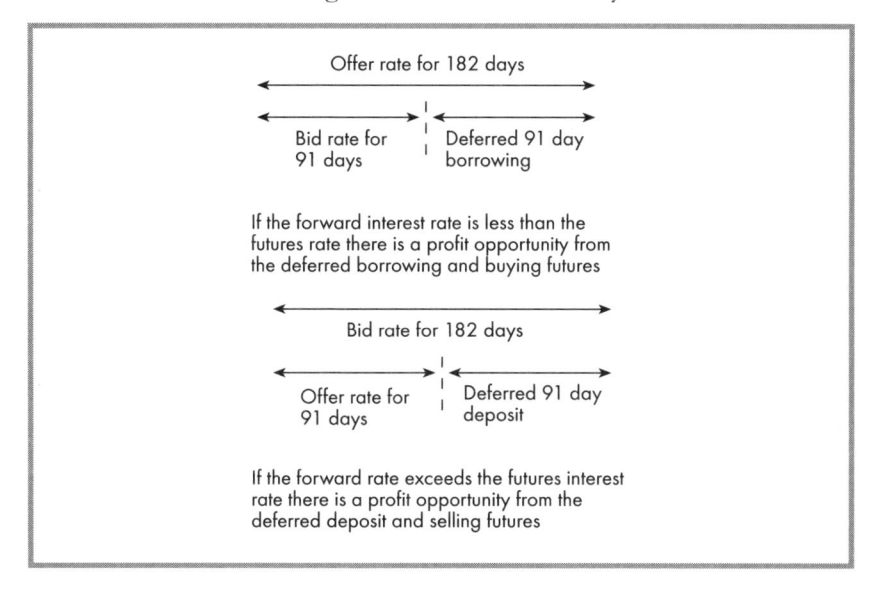

```
                    Offer rate for 182 days
         ←──────────────────────────────────→
         ←──────────────→ ←─────────────────→
          Bid rate for      Deferred 91 day
           91 days           borrowing
```

If the forward interest rate is less than the futures rate there is a profit opportunity from the deferred borrowing and buying futures

```
                    Bid rate for 182 days
         ←──────────────────────────────────→
         ←──────────────→ ←─────────────────→
          Offer rate for    Deferred 91 day
           91 days           deposit
```

If the forward rate exceeds the futures interest rate there is a profit opportunity from the deferred deposit and selling futures

where R_1 is the interest rate to the far end of the forward period, R_2 is the interest rate to the near end of the forward period, T_1 is the number of days to the far end of the forward period and T_2 is the number of days to the near end of the forward period. In the formula above, 360 has been used as the number of days in a year. This is the convention in the cases of most currencies other than sterling. In the case of sterling (and a few other currencies such as the Irish punt), 365 is used in the formula as the number of days in a year.

For the purposes of ascertaining arbitrage possibilities *vis-à-vis* futures prices, it is necessary to calculate both forward borrowing rates and forward lending rates, taking account of the bid–offer spreads. The difference between the forward borrowing and lending rates constitutes a price channel that is considerably wider than the usual ⅛ bid–offer spread. Arbitrage opportunities would require futures prices to fall outside the price channel.

Lending for 6 months at 15% p.a. and borrowing for 3 months at 14% p.a. gives:

$$\left\{ \left[\frac{1 + (0.15 \times 182/365)}{1 + (0.14 \times 91/365)} \right] - 1 \right\} \times \frac{365}{91} = 0.1546 \ (15.46\% \text{ p.a.})$$

Borrowing for 6 months at 15.125% p.a. and lending for 3 months at 13.875% p.a. gives:

$$\left\{ \left[\frac{1 + (0.15125 \times 182/365)}{1 + (0.13875 \times 91/365)} \right] - 1 \right\} \times \frac{365}{91} = 0.1583 \ (15.83\% \text{ p.a.})$$

54 • **MANAGING INTEREST RATE RISK WITH FUTURES**

The channel is between 15.46% p.a. and 15.83% p.a. Futures prices above 84.54 (100 − 15.46) would provide a possibility of arbitrage taking short futures positions, while prices below 84.17 (100 − 15.83) might provide arbitrage opportunities using long futures positions. In other words, if it is possible to lock in a borrowing rate, with futures, of less than 15.46% p.a. (the forward lending rate), there may be scope for arbitrage profit. Similarly, if it is possible to lock in a lending rate, with futures, of greater than 15.83% p.a. (the forward borrowing rate), there may also be scope for arbitrage profit. Transactions costs would widen the channel.

ACTIVITY 3.4

Interest rates are as follows:

six-month   12–11⅞% p.a.
three-month   11½–11⅜% p.a.

What would be the no-arbitrage band of futures prices? How could an arbitrage profit be made if the futures price were (a) 87 and (b) 89?

Answer

$$\text{Using} \left\{ \left[\frac{1 + (R_1 \times T_1/365)}{1 + (R_2 \times T_2/365)} \right] - 1 \right\} \times \frac{365}{T_1 - T_2}$$

and assuming that 3 months is 91 days and 6 months is 182 days,

(a) borrow for 3 months and deposit for 6 months:

$$\left\{ \left[\frac{1 + (0.11875 \times 182/365)}{1 + (0.1150 \times 91/365)} \right] - 1 \right\} \times \frac{365}{182 - 91}$$

(b) borrow for 6 months and lend for 3 months:

$$\left\{ \left[\frac{1 + (0.12 \times 182/365)}{1 + (0.11375 \times 91/365)} \right] - 1 \right\} \times \frac{365}{182 - 91}$$

$$= 0.1228, \text{ i.e. } 12.28\% \text{ p.a. } (12¼\% \text{ p.a.})$$

So the forward deposit rate is 11.91% p.a. and the forward borrowing rate is 12.28% p.a. There is no opportunity for arbitrage profits if the futures interest rate falls between these values (i.e. if the futures price is between 100 − 11.91 = 88.09 and 100 − 12.28 = 87.72).

(i) A rate of interest of 13% p.a. (100 − 87) can be guaranteed for the second three-month period. Depositing for the 3 months and locking in a 13% p.a. deposit rate for the second 3 months using futures will give a return that exceeds the cost of borrowing for 6 months. (In other words, the futures lending rate exceeds the forward/forward borrowing rate.)

(ii) *By selling futures a borrowing rate for the second three-month period of 11% p.a. can be guaranteed. So it is profitable to borrow for 3 months and sell futures to lock in a borrowing rate of 11% p.a. for the subsequent 3 months while simultaneously depositing for 6 months. The forward deposit rate would exceed the futures borrowing rate.*

THE FORWARD YIELD CURVE

A potentially very useful yield curve (from the point of view of ascertaining market expectations of interest rates) is the forward yield curve. Such a curve relates future short-term interest rates implied by long spot rates (forward rates) to the points of time to which those implied rates relate. For example, rates of return on five-year bonds and rates on four-year bonds imply rates on one-year instruments to be entered into 4 years from the present. The implied forward rate can be calculated by means of the formula:

$(1 + {}_4r_1) = (1 + r_5)^5/(1 + r_4)^4$

where r_5 is the five-year interest rate, r_4 is the four-year interest rate and ${}_4r_1$ is the one-year rate expected in 4 years' time.

This formula arises from the relation:

$(1 + r_5)^5 = (1 + r_4)^4 (1 + {}_4r_1)$

which states that a five-year investment at the five-year interest rate should yield the same final sum as a four-year investment at the four-year rate with the proceeds reinvested for 1 year at the one-year rate expected to be available 4 years hence.

Forward interest rates might be looked upon as being marginal interest rates. For example, the current four-year interest rate could be regarded as an average rate (average of the next four one-year rates), while the one-year rate for the period commencing 4 years from now is seen as the marginal rate. If the average rate is rising (the spot yield curve slopes upwards), then the marginal interest rate must exceed the average rate. For instance, if the five-year rate exceeds the four-year rate, then the one-year rate expected for 4 years hence must exceed the four-year rate. Conversely, a downward sloping spot yield curve would involve marginal (i.e. forward) rates being below the average (i.e. spot) interest rates. A five-year rate below the four-year rate requires the interest rate to be pulled down by a one-year rate, expected for 4 years from the present, i.e. lower than the current four-year spot rate. So the forward yield curve would be above an upward sloping spot yield curve and below a downward sloping one. This is illustrated by Figure 3.2.

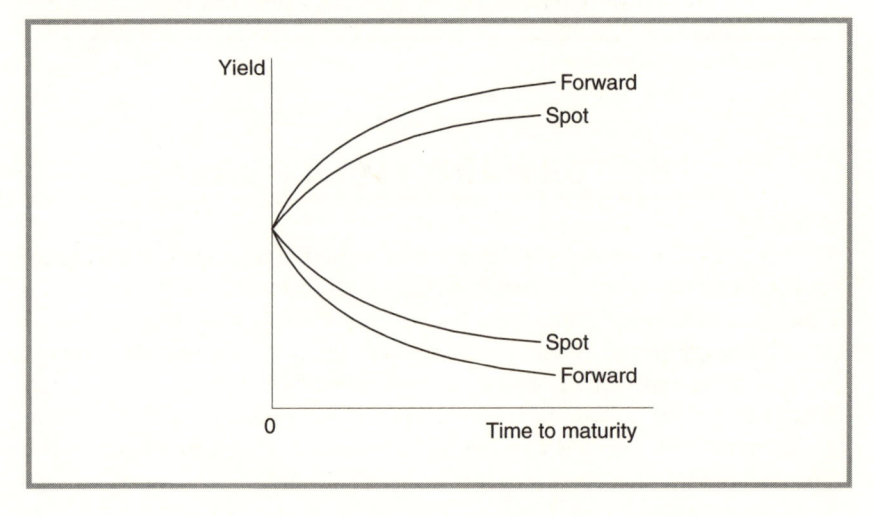

FIGURE 3.2 Spot and forward yield curves

FORWARD RATE AGREEMENTS (FRAS)

Forward rate agreements (FRAs), sometimes referred to as future rate agreements, provide a technique for locking in future short-term interest rates. They constitute a form of forward interest rate contract and are sometimes referred to as over-the-counter futures.

Hedging with FRAs

Risk is reduced by entering a notional agreement to lend or borrow in the future at a rate of interest determined in the present. A set of bid–offer spreads is published showing rates of interest for different future time periods; for example, the published spreads for sterling might indicate a bid–offer spread of 10.75–10.625 for sterling lent for a two-month period starting one month from the present, and 10.875–10.75 for a three-month period commencing nine months from the present. The customer and the bank agree that compensation will pass between them in respect of any deviation of interest rates, on the date that the loan was due to be made, from the rates published at the time of the agreement.

For example, a corporation has a floating rate loan of £1 million and would like to be certain what rate of interest it will be charged on the loan for the three-month period commencing 3 months from the present. It might ascertain from the published bid–offer spreads that for sterling three-month loans, taken out 3 months from the present, the spread is 10.625–10.5. The corporation could attempt to guarantee what its interest rate will be by entering an FRA, thereby notionally committing itself to borrow £1 million at 10.625% in 3 months' time. A settlement interest rate is used for calculation of the compensation payment to pass between the counterparties. Suppose that the spread for this rate stood at 11.625–11.5 when the contract period was reached. The 1% p.a. increase in rates would require the bank to pay the customer a sum equivalent to 1% p.a. for 3 months on a £1 million loan – totalling about £2,500. The money received would compensate the corporation for a rise in the rate of interest on its floating rate loan over the three-month period.

The change in the interest rate payable on a floating rate loan is likely to be equal to, or close to, the change in the settlement interest rate. Had interest rates fallen, the compensation payment would have been made in the opposite direction, so that the corporation would have lost on its FRA but gained from the lower rate on its floating rate loan. In either case an interest rate variation on the loan would have been offset by a gain or loss on the FRA. The corporation would have achieved its aim of removing uncertainty about the interest payable.

The actual compensation is slightly less than £2,500. This gross sum is discounted at the settlement interest rate since the compensation is paid at the beginning of the interest period, whereas the higher interest on the floating rate loan is paid at the end of the interest period. The compensation, plus interest obtainable on it during the interest period, would equal £2,500.

The interest rate that the parties attempt to lock in is not necessarily the current rate at the time of entering the FRA. The rate obtained by means of the FRA would reflect the forward interest rate. These points may be clarified by means of Example 3.5.

Example 3.5

A corporate borrower has a floating rate loan of £1 million, on which the interest rate is reassessed on a six-monthly basis. The latest reassessment has set the interest rate at 12% p.a., while the settlement interest rate is currently 11–10.875. The treasurer wishes to hedge the risk of a rise in interest rates by the date of the next interest rate reassessment. The FRA market is currently quoting 11.5–11.375 for 6 months against 12 months (interest rates for six-month loans made 6 months from the present). The company decides to hedge by buying FRAs, thereby notionally committing itself to borrow £1 million 6 months hence. By the beginning of the interest period, the spread stands at 12.5–12.375 and the interest on the floating rate loan is 13½% p.a.

Interest rate
1 February
Interest rate for February–July is set at 12% p.a. and LIBOR stands at 11–10.875. The company seeks to hedge against an interest rate increase occurring by 1 August.

FRA spread

Buys FRAs for six-month interest period commencing 1 August. The FRA interest spread is 11.5–11.375.

1 August
Interest rate for August–January is set at 13½% p.a. An extra 1½% must be paid, amounting to £7,500 (1½% on £1 million for 6 months).

The FRA spread stands at 12.5–12.375. Compensation is receivable in respect of 1% on £1 million for 6 months, amounting to £5,000.

The borrower suffers a loss of £7,500 which is offset by a £5,000 FRA gain. On 1 February the FRA spread was 11.5–11.375. The FRA gains and losses offset realised deviations from 12½% p.a. so that the effective interest payable, net of compensation, is 12½% p.a. The corporation has eliminated uncertainty about the future interest rate payable on its floating rate debt.

The removal of uncertainty would be incomplete if the interest rate charged on the loan could change by an extent different from the change in the settlement interest rate. For instance, if the interest on the loan in the example had risen to 13⅝% p.a., then the interest rate increase, net of compensation, would have been ⅝%. The borrower would have failed to guarantee a net increase of ½%. However, changes in borrowing rates are likely to be similar to settlement interest changes so that most of the uncertainty is removed.

Compensation formula

The payment made upon maturity of an FRA is given by the formula:

$$\frac{(R_s - R_f) \times (N/Y) \times A}{1 + R_s (N/Y)}$$

where R_s = settlement interest rate (when the FRA matures), R_f = FRA guaranteed interest rate (when the FRA is agreed), N = period (in days) of borrowing/lending to which the FRA relates, Y = number of days in a year

(365 for sterling, 360 for other currencies), and A = sum of money to which the FRA relates.

Example 3.6 illustrates the use of FRAs.

Example 3.6

A toy company has a seasonal borrowing requirement for the period July–October for the purpose of financing the stocks required to meet the pre-Christmas sales. On 15 January it uses an FRA to guarantee the interest payable on a £2 million three-month loan to be taken out on 15 July. On 15 January the rate for three-month LIBOR six-month forward is 10% p.a. Anticipating a borrowing at LIBOR + 1¼%, the toy company thus locks in an interest rate of 11¼% p.a.

On 15 July LIBOR stands at 12% p.a. The company could borrow £2 million at 13¼% p.a., which involves a repayment of £2,066,250 on 15 October. However, the bank providing the FRA compensates for the deviation of LIBOR on 15 July from 10% p.a. The compensation payment is 2% p.a. for 3 months on £2 million discounted at LIBOR to reflect the fact that the compensation is paid at the beginning of the period, whereas interest is payable at the end of the period. The sum paid by the bank to the toy company on 15 July is £9,786. The company thus borrows £1,990,214 instead of £2 million. At 13¼% p.a., the sum to be repaid on 15 October is £2,056,682. This is equivalent to paying 11.244% p.a. on £2 million for the three-month period. By using the FRA, the toy company has locked in an interest rate of about 11¼% p.a. and has thus avoided the 2% p.a. rise in interest rates:

$$\frac{(0.12 - 0.1) \times (92/365) \times £2,000,000}{1 + 0.12 (92/365)} = £9786$$

The bank providing the FRA need not be the bank providing the loan. Indeed, the FRA might be provided through a money broker rather than a bank. The cash flows under the FRA are limited to the money value of the deviation of LIBOR from the agreed future interest rate.

How banks make profits from FRAs

An FRA will have a bid–offer spread. The quote could be, for example, 6.14/6.10 for a '3 against 6' FRA. The bank would sell an FRA based on 6.14% but buy one at 6.10%. If the rate of interest at the three-month date is 7% the bank pays 0.86% on the FRA it sold, but receives 0.90% on the one that it bought. If the rate turns out to be 5% the bank receives 1.14%

FIGURE 3.3   FRA Cash Flows

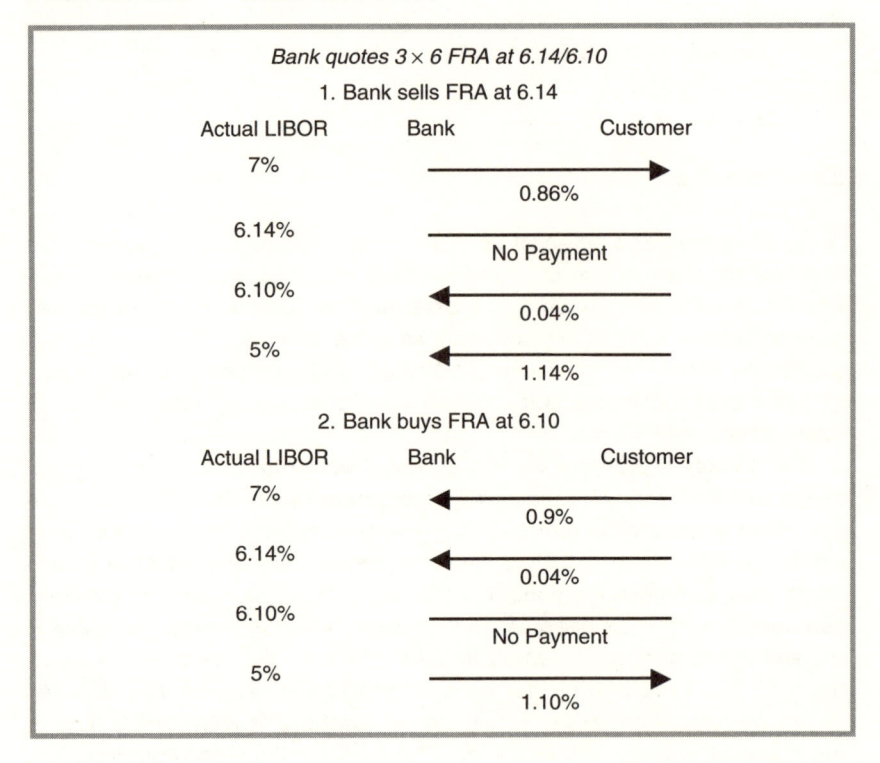

```
               Bank quotes 3 × 6 FRA at 6.14/6.10
                  1. Bank sells FRA at 6.14
         Actual LIBOR        Bank              Customer
             7%              ─────────────────────────►
                                        0.86%
             6.14%           ─────────────────────────
                                      No Payment
             6.10%           ◄─────────────────────────
                                        0.04%
             5%              ◄─────────────────────────
                                        1.14%

                  2. Bank buys FRA at 6.10
         Actual LIBOR        Bank              Customer
             7%              ◄─────────────────────────
                                         0.9%
             6.14%           ◄─────────────────────────
                                        0.04%
             6.10%           ─────────────────────────
                                      No Payment
             5%              ─────────────────────────►
                                        1.10%
```

on the FRA that it sold, and pays 1.10% on the one that it bought. Either way the bank makes a profit of 4 basis points (see Figure 3.3).

Finally, a difference in terminology between FRAs and futures may have been noticed. A potential borrower buys FRAs but sells futures: a potential depositor sells FRAs but buys futures.

CROSS HEDGING

Cross hedges involve hedging risk on one instrument with futures on another. For example, three-month certificates of deposit might be hedged with three-month interest rate futures, or movements of a single stock price might be hedged by using stock index futures. Cross hedging is subject to greater basis risk and there is a level beyond which basis risk becomes unacceptable. Basis risk can be measured by correlating the changes in the relevant cash market and futures prices. The nearer the correlation is to 1, the closer are the movements of the 2 instruments. A correlation coefficient of 1 indicates that the cash and futures instruments have moved precisely in line with each other, so that changes in the price of the cash market instrument could have been hedged perfectly by the futures instrument. The correlation coefficient of 1 indicates an absence of basis risk in the past and that bodes well for the future. A correlation coefficient of zero indicates that the 2 instruments have moved in completely unrelated ways in the past, and therefore basis risk is high. Low values of the correlation coefficient suggest that the futures instrument is unlikely to be suitable for hedging risk on the cash instrument. A rule of thumb might be that a correlation coefficient of at least 0.6 is required to suggest that the hedging would be reasonably successful: a correlation coefficient of 0.6 indicates that the proportion of the risk eliminated is 0.36, i.e. $(0.6)^2$.

The more dissimilar the cash market instrument and the instrument upon which the futures are based, the lower will be the correlation coefficient and the higher the basis risk. Three-month certificates of deposit (CDs) and three-month deposits are very similar, and hence futures on the latter (i.e. three-month interest rate futures) could safely be used to hedge risk on the former. There is less similarity between, say, a bond with 2 years to maturity and a three-month deposit, so it may be expected that the correlation coefficient is lower and basis risk higher. Reasonable effectiveness of the hedge would be less certain.

CONCLUSIONS

By their nature, interest rates are not instruments that can be held and carried. In consequence, short-term interest rate futures are not subject to the cash-and-carry pricing mechanism of other financial futures. Other financial futures are priced on the basis of the net cost of holding the instrument (e.g. a government bond) up to the futures maturity date. Since short-term interest rates are not carryable, a different pricing mechanism is involved. They are priced on the basis of interest rate expectations as embodied in the term structure of interest rates (the yield curve).

Although unlike other financial futures in this regard, they share the characteristic that arbitrage is the process that achieves and maintains the pricing relationship. Arbitrage tends to ensure a close relationship between futures interest rates and the forward interest rates implied by spot rates for differing maturities.

They also share with other financial futures the basic principle of hedging. The futures position should be opposite to the position that is being hedged. If the position to be hedged would lose from a rise in interest rates, the futures position should be one that profits in the event of a rise in interest rates: conversely for a risk of a fall in interest rates.

Hedging is rarely, if ever, perfect. One reason is that the instrument underlying the futures contract is rarely identical to the instrument being hedged. In the case of short-term interest rate futures, one source of difference is asset mismatch. This chapter has indicated a wide variety of short-term money market instruments; parallel money market instruments such as certificates of deposit and commercial paper exist alongside discount market instruments such as Treasury bills and bank bills, in addition to which there are deposits and loans.

At the end of this chapter, some difficulties arising from such mismatches between the futures instrument and the hedged instrument were indicated in the section on cross hedging. In addition to asset mismatch, there are date and maturity mismatches. Futures have a limited number of maturity dates available, and it is unlikely that a futures maturity date coincides with a deposit or borrowing date. In addition, short-term interest rate futures are usually for three-month deposits and borrowings, whereas the hedged position may be for a different period of time.

Date and maturity mismatches involve exposures to changes in the slope and curvature of the yield curve. The next chapter investigates the strategies available for reducing the risks arising from the possibility of changes in the slope and curvature of the yield curve.

Further reading

A useful account of short-term interest rate futures (including Treasury bill futures, which have not been covered here) is available in:
David A. Dubofsky, *Options and Financial Futures* (McGraw-Hill, Singapore, 1992), Chapter 16.

More information on forward rate agreements can be obtained from:
David Winstone, *Financial Derivatives* (Chapman & Hall, London, 1995), Chapter 9.

ADVANCED STRATEGIES FOR INTEREST RATE RISK MANAGEMENT

4

INTRODUCTION

Hedging is rarely perfect. The objective typically is one of minimising, rather than eliminating, risk. When hedging is undertaken in the ways described in Chapter 3, some risk remains. Probably the most significant remaining risk is basis risk. Basis risk arises from the tendency of futures prices to show movements that differ in unpredictable ways from the interest rate movements on the borrowing or investment being hedged. In other words, perfect hedging requires futures interest rates and cash market interest rates to move exactly in line with each other (or at least that any deviation should be predictable). There are other remaining sources of risk; for example, the marking to market of futures contracts that requires daily futures price movements to be reflected by daily cash flow movements (the immediate realisation of profits and losses) involves unpredictable cash flows that will attract unpredictable interest rates. Interest payments or receipts on the cumulative daily cash flows could distort the losses or profits on futures trading in unpredictable ways.

This chapter is concerned with the management of these remaining risks. One way of dealing with basis risk is to apply a hedge ratio based on a standard formula applicable to all futures contracts. Alternative techniques are based on the observation that basis risk largely arises from changes in the slope and curvature of the yield curve. One of these techniques is the strip, which involves the simultaneous use of contracts with different maturity dates (successive maturity dates). Another is the straddle, which involves purchases of contracts with one maturity date and simultaneous sales of contracts with another maturity date with a view to making profits from relative price movements. The straddle hedges against changes in the slope of the yield curve. This may be supported by the use of a futures butterfly, which hedges against changes in the curvature of the yield curve.

The distorting effects of interest on the cumulative daily cash flows (variation margin flows) arising from the marking to market of futures contracts can be dealt with by means of variation margin leverage or tailing. Variation margin leverage will be seen to be easy to operate but relatively inaccurate, whereas tailing is accurate but difficult to implement.

THE FORWARD YIELD CURVE AND BASIS RISK

Changes in the slope of the forward yield curve alter basis and are thus a source of basis risk. Example 4.1 illustrates a situation in which futures prices move from being at a premium to being at a discount with respect to cash prices (futures interest rates move from being lower to being higher than spot three-month rates). In this example, basis changes by one percentage point. From a cash market interest rate 0.5% above the futures rate, there is a change to a cash market rate 0.5% below the futures rate. As a result, the overall loss is $25,000 and the attempt to hedge fails completely. Indeed, a fall in the futures price would have rendered the effects of the hedging attempt perverse; for example, a fall in the futures price to 90 on 10 April would have added a $12,500 futures loss to the $25,000 cash market loss.

It is worth bearing in mind that basis always reaches zero at maturity. This observation can influence the choice of maturity date when buying or selling futures contracts. Maturity dates should fall after the date on which the risk to be hedged disappears (i.e. the date on which a deposit is made or loan taken out), otherwise there would be a period when hedging was absent. Using the earliest possible maturity date after the disappearance of the risk increases the probability that basis will be close to zero when the contract is closed out. In any event, the tendency for basis to converge towards zero as a contract approaches maturity implies that the closer a contract is to its maturity date, the less susceptible it is to changes in basis arising from yield curve movements. For this reason it is advisable to choose futures contracts that mature early after the risk of being hedged has passed.

Example 4.1

Cash market	Futures market
10 February	
Company plans to deposit $10 million on 10 April. Current rate of interest on three-month eurodollar deposits is 10% p.a.	Buys 10 June three-month eurodollar interest rate futures contracts at a price of 90.5.
10 April	
Company deposits $10 million at an interest rate of 9% p.a.	Sells 10 June three-month eurodollar interest rate futures contracts at a price of 90.5.
Loss equals 1% on $10 million for 3 months = $25,000 (0.01 × 10 million × 0.25).	There is no gain since the price is unchanged at 90.5.

It is to be emphasised that cash and futures prices typically do exhibit reasonably close correlation so that basis risk tends to be much less than the outright risk of unhedged positions (so long as the instrument being hedged is not very different from the futures instrument).

The fact that basis always reaches zero at maturity suggests that basis could be regarded as an element of loss (or profit) that cannot be hedged. If a contract is held to maturity, the basis can be seen as representing an interest rate change that cannot be avoided, but is at least known at the outset. If a contract is held to maturity, the futures interest rate when the contract was bought or sold is the locked-in rate and this differs from the spot rate on the date of buying or selling the contract by the value of the basis. In the absence of basis risk from other sources, the flow of variation margin would provide the hedger with an interest rate between the spot rate and the futures rate ruling at the time of entering the contract. Early closing out would provide a rate close to the original spot rate, whereas closing out near to the maturity of the futures contract would provide a rate close to the futures rate. The actual rate obtained could be treated as a linear function of time.

Figure 4.1 is based on the simplifying assumption that the spot three-month interest rate remains unchanged until the delivery date of the futures contract. It illustrates the convergence of the futures price towards the spot price. A hedger or trader who buys a futures contract today would receive variation margin payments as the futures price rises. The amount received would be approximately proportional to the time that elapses. The effective interest rate is the spot rate adjusted for the variation margin receipts. In Figure 4.1 the potential lender receives the spot rate of interest plus the variation margin receipts, which generates an effective interest rate in excess of the spot rate. The excess of the effective rate over the spot rate is dependent upon the time that elapses and is greatest if the futures contract is held to its delivery date. (It is to be noted that movements in the spot price that are paralleled by movements in the futures price would lead to mutually offsetting profits and losses, effectively leaving the situation as indicated by Figure 4.1; see also Figure 4.2.)

SOURCES OF BASIS RISK AND HEDGE RATIOS

When hedging with short-term interest rate futures, it is necessary to be aware of basis risk. Basis risk refers to the possibility that changes in the futures interest rate will not match changes in the interest rate on the position being hedged. Sources of basis risk include date mismatch, maturity mismatch and asset mismatch.

Date mismatch refers to a discrepancy between the date that a borrowing or deposit will be made and the maturity date of the futures contract.

FIGURE 4.1   Convergence of futures and spot prices

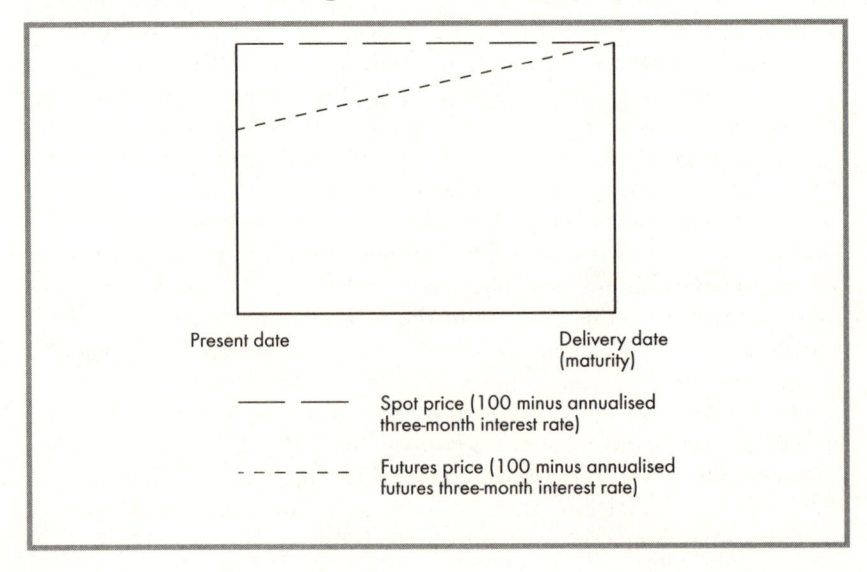

Present date   Delivery date (maturity)

——— Spot price (100 minus annualised three-month interest rate)

- - - - - Futures price (100 minus annualised futures three-month interest rate)

FIGURE 4.2 Effective interest rate equals the spot rate plus/minus the futures profit/loss

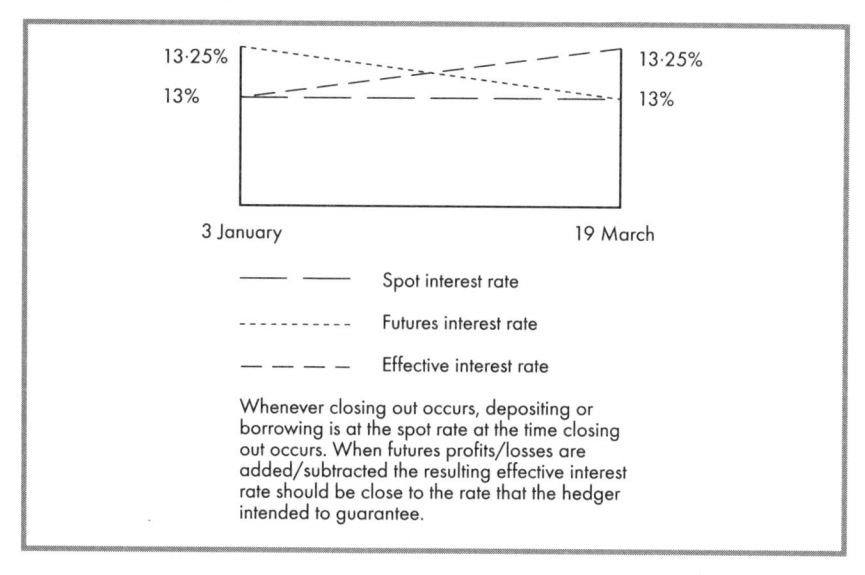

```
13.25%                                          13.25%
13%                                             13%


        3 January                    19 March

            ———  ———    Spot interest rate

            ----------  Futures interest rate

            ——  ——  —   Effective interest rate

        Whenever closing out occurs, depositing or
        borrowing is at the spot rate at the time closing
        out occurs. When futures profits/losses are
        added/subtracted the resulting effective interest
        rate should be close to the rate that the hedger
        intended to guarantee.
```

The three-month interest rate for the date of the borrowing or deposit may not move precisely in line with the three-month interest rate expected to be available on the futures maturity date.

Maturity mismatch arises because futures contracts normally relate to three-month borrowings or deposits, whereas the borrowing or deposit being hedged may not be for 3 months. Interest rates for different maturities are not likely to move exactly in line with each other. For example, three-month interest rates would not be perfectly correlated with six-month rates.

Asset mismatch arises when the instrument underlying the futures contract is not the same as the instrument being hedged. For example, three-month interest rate futures which are based on LIBOR would not provide a perfect hedge for three-month Treasury bills or three-month certificates of deposit. One reason for this is that different instruments exhibit different risk premiums, and the risk premium on one instrument may vary independently of the risk premiums on other instruments.

When basis risk is present, hedges are likely to be imperfect, futures interest rate movements failing to precisely offset cash market interest rate movements. Such imperfection can be minimised by the use of a hedge ratio. The standard hedge ratio is:

$$H = \rho \sigma_S / \sigma_F$$

where ρ is the correlation between cash market and futures interest rate changes, σ_S is the standard deviation of cash market interest rate changes, and σ_F is the standard deviation of changes in the futures interest rate. The requisite number of futures contracts is calculated by dividing the size of the exposure by the size of the futures contract and multiplying the result by the hedge ratio. So an exposure of £5 million, a contract size of £500,000 and a hedge ratio of 1.8 imply the use of 18 futures contracts; see Figure 4.3.

FIGURE 4.3 Dependence of variance of hedger's position on hedge ratio

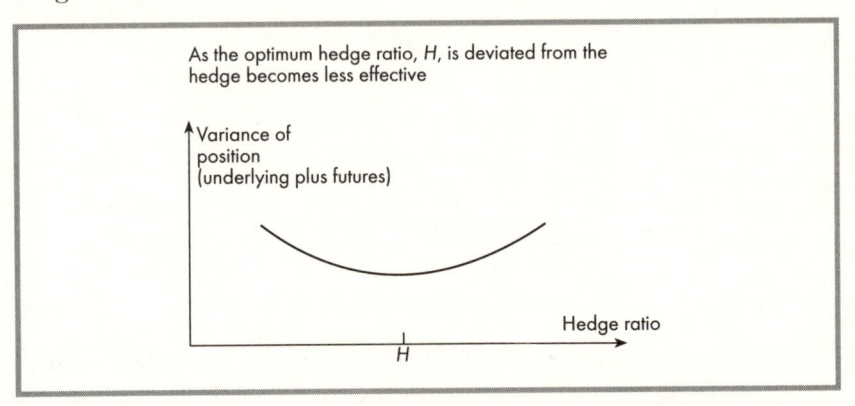

As the optimum hedge ratio, H, is deviated from the hedge becomes less effective

Variance of position (underlying plus futures) vs *Hedge ratio*, minimum at H.

It might be noted that the interest rate changes used in the calculation of the hedge ratio are based on actual borrowing or deposit periods and are not per annum rates. One result is that rates for longer periods will tend to have proportionately higher standard deviations. For example, changes in six-month rates might on average be expected to be double changes in three-month rates. If so, their standard deviations would tend to be twice as great. A result of this would be that hedging six-month borrowings or lendings with three-month futures would entail approximately twice the number of contracts required when hedging a three-month borrowing or deposit.

The hedge ratio equation shown above (p. 67) is applicable to any futures contract. For example, beta, which is used as the hedge ratio for stock index futures, is based on this equation.

STRIPS AND ROLLS (STACKS)

Consider a roll-over loan on which the interest is reassessed every three months. The borrower may face revisions of the interest rate on 1 May and 1 August. A strip hedge would involve taking out June and September futures contracts. This could prove difficult if there is inadequate liquidity in the more distant contract. Alternatively, a rolling hedge could be employed. Rolling hedges always use the nearest futures contract (subject to the maturity date of the contract falling after the earliest interest rate reassessment date). A simple rolling hedge involves hedging only the earliest interest rate change. The borrower sells June futures contracts sufficient to match the value of the loan in order to hedge the interest rate risk of 1 May. This leaves the 1 August risk, and any subsequent risks, unhedged. A piled-up roll involves hedging more than one future interest rate change by using the nearest contract. The face value of the contracts would be a multiple of the value of the loan; for instance, hedging for 2 interest rate reassessment dates would involve selling contracts with an aggregate face value of twice the value of the loan. On 1 May, at which date the contracts would have been closed out, September contracts are sold in order to hedge the 1 August risk (effectively replacing previously held contracts that hedged the 1 August risk). The advantage of piled-up rolls is that they avoid the liquidity problems that may arise from dealing in distant contracts while hedging risk on more than one future interest rate reassessment date. The disadvantages of piled-up rolls are that they involve a relatively large number of contracts and hence greater commission charges, and that they leave the hedger exposed to changes in the slope of the yield curve. Hedging distant interest rate changes with nearby futures contracts is effective if far and near rates move in line with each other, but if the near–far differential changes (i.e. the slope of the yield curve changes), then the effectiveness of the hedge may be reduced.

When hedging for periods that exceed three months, it may be desirable to use more than one maturity of futures contract. For example, when hedging an interest rate risk for the period 1 June to 1 December, equal numbers of June and September delivery date contracts would be appropriate. The six-month interest rate can be looked upon as being based on a three-month interest rate (June–September) compounded with a following three-month interest rate (September–December). A change in the six-month rate might be due to expectations of a higher rate for September–December which is not matched by a higher June–September rate. September three-month interest rate futures prices would respond to the expected change in the September–December rate, whereas the June futures prices would not.

Strip hedging makes use of futures contracts with successive maturity dates in order to hedge the interest rate risk on a deposit or borrowing which has an interest rate fixed for longer than the three-month period that is typical of short-term interest rate futures. So, for example, a one-year borrowing, at a rate fixed for one year, would be hedged with futures of 4 different maturities. By using futures with 4 successive maturity dates, a one-year futures contract is simulated.

This is based on the expectations explanation of the yield curve; in other words, the view that a long-period interest rate is an average of a series of short-term interest rates. So a six-month interest rate is seen as equal to the average of the spot three-month rate and the three-month rate expected for the following 3 months, whereas a one-year rate is equal to the average of the spot three-month rate and the rates expected for the following 3 three-month periods (so the one-year rate is the average of a succession of 4 three-month rates; see Example 4.2).

Example 4.2

$$(1.1)(1.12) = 1.232$$
$$(1 + x)(1 + x) = 1.232$$
$$1 + x = \sqrt{1.232}$$
$$x = \sqrt{1.232} - 1$$
$$= 0.11 \text{ (i.e. 11\% p.a.)}$$

The result of compounding a one-year rate of 10% p.a. followed by a one-year rate of 12% p.a. is the same as that of a two-year rate of 11% p.a.

The strip hedge can be seen as simulating a futures contract for deposit/borrowing periods greater than 3 months (e.g. 2 futures of successive maturities simulate a six-month futures contract). Equivalently, the strip hedge could be viewed as decomposing a longer period deposit or borrowing into a succession of three-month deposits/borrowings, each of which is hedged by a futures contract of corresponding maturity (this decomposition of the longer rate reflects the supposed equivalence of a long-term deposit to a succession of shorter-term deposits with reinvestment of proceeds at each maturity date).

An alternative to a strip hedge would be a stack hedge (piled-up roll), which would use only the futures with the nearest maturity. So, for example, a DM1 million 12-month borrowing to be taken out in September might be hedged with 4 September contracts (each relating to DM1 million for 3 months beginning in September) rather than the strip. It may be that liquidity is inadequate in the distant maturity contracts so that there are no counterparties to trade them with (at acceptable prices) and the hedger is forced to use the stack. If liquidity is adequate for the distant maturities, the strip is preferable.

The superiority of the strip can be seen by again referring to the expectations approach to the term structure of interest rates. A one-year interest rate may rise because the three-month rate expected 3 months hence increases. This would be reflected in the corresponding distant maturity futures. Consequently, a strip would provide compensation for the rate rise, whereas a stack would not.

The expectations approach to the term structure states that a depositor (borrower) would be indifferent between a one-year deposit (borrowing) and a succession of three-month deposits (borrowings) with compounding. Four three-month rates of 10% p.a. would be equivalent to a one-year rate of $(1.025)^4 - 1 = 0.1038$, i.e. 10.38% p.a. (note that Example 4.3 simplifies these calculations, sacrificing accuracy for the sake of clarity). If the expected interest rate for the third three-month period rises to 12% p.a., the one-year rate rises to $(1.025)^3(1.03) - 1 = 0.1092$, i.e. 10.92% p.a. The strip would provide a futures profit (or loss) to be set against the loss (or profit) from the interest rate change, whereas a stack would not.

It is to be noted that when using a strip (or stack) hedge, all contracts are entered into simultaneously and closed out simultaneously (when the deposit or borrowing is undertaken). The fact that futures contracts have different maturities does not imply that they should be transacted at different points in time.

Example 4.3

It is 25 June. A treasurer expects to borrow DM1 million for a year, at a fixed interest rate, on 20 September. The expectation is for a one-year rate of 10% p.a. based on:

Sep/Dec 10% p.a., Dec/Mar 10% p.a., Mar/Jun 10% p.a., Jun/Sep 10% p.a.

Correspondingly, the futures prices are:

Sep 90   Dec 90   Mar 90   Jun 90

The treasurer hedges using a strip, i.e. sells 1 Sep, 1 Dec, 1 Mar and 1 Jun contracts.

The expectation for Mar/Jun subsequently rises to 12% p.a. Hence the expected one-year rate rises to 10.5% p.a. and the March futures price falls to 88.

The additional borrowing cost is 0.5% on DM1 million for one year, i.e. DM5,000.

The futures profit is 2% on DM1 million for 3 months, i.e. 200 ticks on one contract: $200 \times DM25 = DM5,000$.

A hedge based on 4 September contracts instead of the strip would have failed.

> **ACTIVITY 4.1**
>
> (a) A corporate treasurer needs to borrow $10,000,000 for 3 months. It is 20 May and the money is to be borrowed on 1 August. How can the treasurer hedge against a rise in interest rates using futures?
>
> (b) If eurodollar interest rates rise from '% p.a. to 7% p.a. between 20 May and 1 August, what is the loss? If futures prices fell from 93.80 to 92.90 during the same period, how much futures profit would there be from the hedging strategy adopted in part (a)?
>
> (c) How would the answers to (a) and (b) change if the money was to be borrowed for a year?

Answer
(a) Sell 10 September eurodollar interest rate futures contracts.
(b) (i) 1% on $10,000,000 over 3 months
$0.01 \times \$10,000,000 \times 0.25 = \$25,000$
(ii) 90 ticks profit on each of 10 futures contracts at $25 per tick
$90 \times 10 \times \$25 = \$22,500$
(c) The best hedge would be a strip hedge involving 10 September, 10 December, 10 March and 10 June futures contracts. The loss due to the interest rate rise would be 4 times as much, i.e. $100,000. If all the futures prices fell by 90 ticks, then the total profit from the futures would be $22,500 × 4 = $90,000.

VARIATION MARGIN LEVERAGE AND TAILING

Variation margin receipts can earn interest, whereas payments incur interest charges (or involve interest forgone). When interest is added to variation margin, the effect is to increase profits or losses arising from futures positions. If no adjustment were made for this, it would mean that the total cash flows arising from futures would tend to produce overhedging, which would be particularly unfortunate when profits on the underlying position were more than offset by losses on futures.

To alleviate this overhedging, 2 techniques are available. The cruder but simpler is variation margin leverage. This technique has the advantage that it can be put into place at the beginning of the hedge period and left unadjusted. Its disadvantage is that it is only approximate. To take an example, suppose that money is to be borrowed for 3 months and the date on which the money is to be borrowed is 40 days hence. The hedger knows that variation margin will incur interest for the 91 days of the borrowing since interest on the borrowing is payable only at the end of the 91 days. So the variation margin would be enhanced, in the case of a 10% p.a. interest rate, by a factor of 1.025. In addition, since there will be variation margin flows prior to the date on which the futures are closed out (the date on which the money is borrowed), there would be interest payments or receipts prior to closing out and these interest payments/receipts might further exaggerate the cash flow effects of variation margin. However, there is no way of knowing beforehand what the pattern of such variation margin flows will be. A crude rule of thumb might be applied to the effect that all of the variation margin flows occur midway through the period of the hedge, which in this case would be 20 days before closing out. So the variation margin flows are treated as incurring interest for 20 + 91 = 111 days. At an interest rate of 10% p.a., the interest rate for 111 days would be $0.10 \times 111/365 = 0.0304$. So the cash flow effects of the variation margin are treated as being exaggerated by a factor of 1.0304. To offset this, the number of futures is factored down by dividing by 1.0304. This scaling down of the number of futures contracts that would otherwise be used is the variation margin leverage adjustment.

Tailing is more accurate but more cumbersome. The adjustment needs constant monitoring and frequent rebalancing. It involves scaling down the number of futures contracts by a discount factor based on interest rates for the period for which variation margin will be held. In this way, interest on variation margin is exactly offset by a reduced amount of variation margin (a reduction caused by reducing the number of futures contracts). In the example above, the discount factor might initially be 1.0359 (based on $0.10 \times (40 + 91)/365$). This discount factor would be adjusted daily to reflect interest rate changes and the passage of time.

ACTIVITY 4.2

It is 15 February and a company treasurer expects to borrow £20 million for 3 months on 15 April. The spot three-month interest rate is 12% p.a., the June three-month sterling futures price is 88, the coefficient of correlation between three-month interest rate changes and changes in the prices of futures maturing 2 months later is 0.95, the standard deviation of spot three-month interest rate changes is 2, whereas the standard deviation of three-month interest rate futures prices is 2.1 (for futures maturing in 2 months' time).

Design a hedge. What sources of possible hedge imperfection are present?

Answer
The basic hedge would involve dividing the exposure by the size of the futures contract and selling the resulting number of futures contracts:

20 million/£0.5 million = 40 contracts

This number needs to be adjusted for relative volatility.

$$40 \times \text{correlation coefficient} \times \frac{\text{Standard deviation of spot rate}}{\text{Standard deviation of futures price}}$$

40 × 0.95 × (2/2.1) = 36.19 contracts

This number should either be tailed or adjusted for variation margin leverage. If the latter approach is taken, then the previous number of contracts is reduced to

36.19 × (1/1.03) × (1/1.01) = 34.79

where 1/1.03 offsets interest on variation margin for the 3 months beginning 15 April and 1/1.01 offsets interest on variation margin prior to 15 April (making the simplifying assumption of a constant rate of receipt or payment of variation margin). The hedger would initially sell either 34 or 35 futures contracts.

Sources of hedge imperfection include basis risk, the possible unreliability of historical statistics as guides to future correlations and standard deviations, the inability to trade fractions of contracts, changes in interest rates and the uncertainty as to the timing of variation margin cash flows. Tailing is more accurate than using variation margin leverage.

HEDGING YIELD CURVE RISK WITH FUTURES STRADDLES

There are 3 dimensions of hedging yield curve risk. The first involves hedging against changes in the level of the yield curve. The second concerns hedging the risk that the slope of the curve may change; see Figure 4.4. The third hedging dimension relates to possible changes in the curvature of the yield curve.

There are 3 ascending levels of sophistication. Ideally, all 3 dimensions should be hedged. Hedging the level of the yield curve is the basic hedge, but the effectiveness of the hedge could be undermined if the slope of the yield curve changed (thereby causing basis to change). An

FIGURE 4.4   Shifts in the yield curve

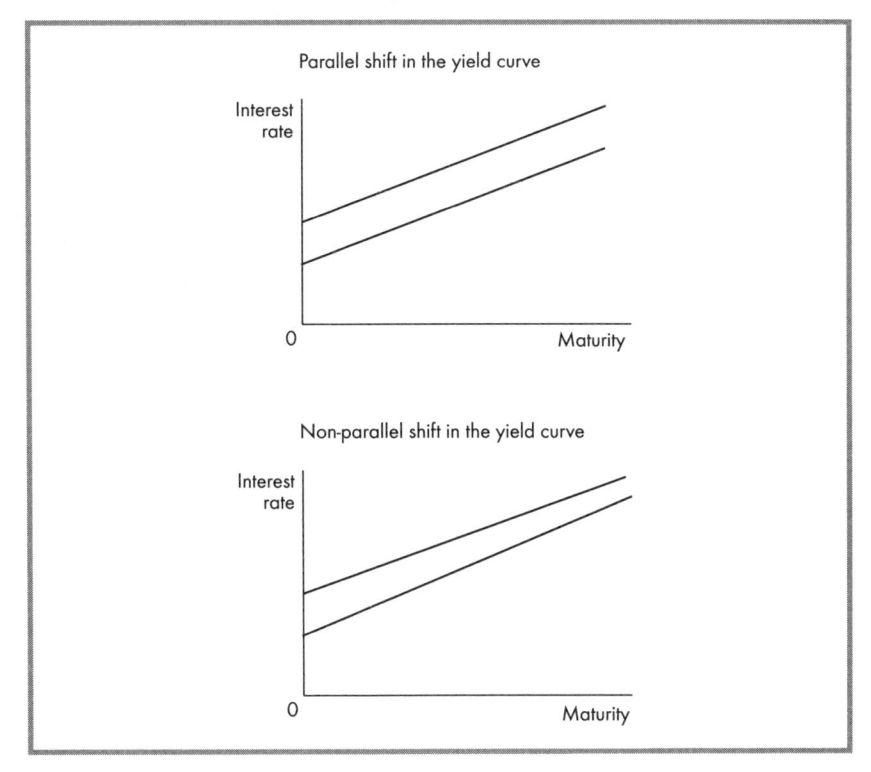

attempt to hedge against slope changes could be undermined by a change in curvature. So the most effective hedging strategy addresses all 3 dimensions.

As the hedging strategy is developed through these three levels of refinement, it becomes increasingly complex. To deal with the risk of slope changes, a futures straddle (inter-delivery or time spread) should be added to the basic hedge. Hedging curvature risk would involve adding a futures butterfly (a straddle of straddles) to the previous two hedges. So the most complete hedge would add together a basic hedge, a straddle and a butterfly. (Although the word 'most' has been used here, there is scope for even greater levels of refinement in hedging a yield curve.) If a borrower seeks protection from a rise in the slope of the yield curve, he can buy a futures straddle.

Suppose it is March and a corporate treasurer has a roll-over loan whose interest rate is reassessed six monthly on 1 June and 1 December. A strip hedge to protect him from rising (1 December) interest rates would involve selling December and March interest rate futures contracts. However, liquidity may be inadequate beyond the September contract. Protection against the 1 December risk can be obtained by selling

September contracts with a view to closing out the September contracts and replacing them with December contracts when liquidity in the latter becomes adequate.

While the 1 December risk is being protected by September contracts, the treasurer is vulnerable to an increase in the slope of the yield curve. September interest rates would rise by less than December interest rates, and hence September contracts would give incomplete protection. To offset this, the treasurer might take a futures position that would yield a profit in the event of the yield curve becoming more positively sloped. A more positively sloped yield curve involves September futures prices falling relative to June futures prices. So the hedger sells September contracts and buys June contracts. In other words, he buys a futures straddle. (Since September contracts are being sold in order to hedge the interest rate risk, the purchase of the straddle effectively involves raising the number of September contracts sold and buying some June contracts.)

Changes in the gradient of the (forward) yield curve reflect relative movements in forward interest rates. In particular, unequal movements in the forward rate relevant to the risk faced and the forward rate upon which a futures contract is based would tend to change basis and render a futures hedge imperfect. The following discussion will deal with this source of basis risk, which could be looked upon as arising from movements in the no-arbitrage band of futures prices. Movement of the futures price within the no-arbitrage band constitutes another source of basis risk, but needs to be handled by means of basis trading rather than hedging.

Futures straddles provide a technique for hedging changes in the slope of the yield curve. Before considering the construction of such a straddle, it would be useful to look at the effects of basis change on hedging with short-term interest rate futures. Example 4.4 illustrates a case with no change in basis (which remains at zero).

Example 4.5 differs from Example 4.4 in having a non-zero basis on the closing-out date. The change in basis renders the hedge imperfect.

Example 4.6 illustrates an extreme (but not implausible) situation in which the yield curve changes from being positive to being negative. This swivel of the yield curve renders the hedge perverse. A futures loss is added to the cash market loss.

Using straddles

Futures straddles involve buying and selling equal numbers of futures contracts for different delivery months (e.g. buying 5 June and selling 5 September would constitute a long straddle). The objective is to make a profit from an otherwise unfavourable change in the gradient of the yield curve. Consider the following case.

Example 4.4

Cash market
2 January
Treasurer intends to borrow £10,000,000 on 1 February. He fears that the interest rate will rise above the current 10% p.a.

1 February
Borrows £10,000,000 at an interest rate of 12% p.a.

Loss is 2% p.a. on £10,000,000 for three months, £50,000.

Futures market

Sells 20 March three-month sterling interest rate futures contracts at a price of 90.

Closes out by buying 20 March three-month sterling interest rate futures contracts at a price of 88.

Profit is 200 ticks at £12.50 per tick on each of 20 contracts, £50,000.

Example 4.5

Cash market
2 January
Treasurer intends to borrow £10,000,000 on 1 February. He fears that the interest rate will rise above the current 10% p.a.

1 February
Borrows £10,000,000 at an interest rate of 12% p.a.

Loss is 2% p.a. on £10,000,000 for 3 months, £50,000.

Futures market

Sells 20 March three-month sterling interest rate futures contracts at a price of 90.

Closes out by buying 20 March three-month sterling interest rate futures contracts at a price of 88.50.

Gain is 150 ticks at £12.50 per tick on each of 20 contracts, £37,500.

Example 4.6

Cash market	Futures market
2 January Treasurer intends to borrow £10,000,000 on 1 February. He fears that the interest rate will rise above the current 10% p.a.	Sells 20 March three-month sterling interest rate futures contracts at a price of 88.50.
1 February Borrows £10,000,000 at an interest rate of 12% p.a.	Closes out by buying 20 March three-month sterling interest rate futures contracts at a price of 89.00.
Loss is 2% p.a. on £10,000,000 for 3 months, £50,000.	Loss is 50 ticks at £12.50 per tick on each of 20 contracts, £12,500.

Suppose it is 26 March and that a corporate treasurer expects to borrow $5 million on 1 July for 12 months. The interest rate on the borrowing will be adjusted for changes in LIBOR on 1 January. The treasurer wants to hedge the interest rate, but finds that futures liquidity is poor beyond the September delivery month.

A $5 million borrowing for 12 months requires 20 short three-month eurodollar futures contracts. The simplest approach to hedging would be to sell 20 contracts for September delivery. Unfortunately, this involves time period mismatches. The futures contract relates to a notional borrowing covering the three-month period between the September and December futures maturity dates. The periods to be hedged are 1 July to 31 December and 1 January to 30 June. Although there would normally be a correlation between the September futures interest rate movements and the changes in the rates for the 2 six-month periods, the correlation would not be perfect.

It is useful to decompose each of the six-month periods into 2 successive three-month periods. So the 1 July to 31 December period becomes 1 July to 30 September followed by 1 October to 31 December. For the purposes of (simplicity of) exposition, it will be assumed that the futures maturities fall exactly in the middle of the delivery month. Again, for clarity of exposition, time will be described in terms of months (although in practice numbers of days would normally be counted).

The first three-month period has a timing mismatch of 2½ months relative to the September futures contract. The treasurer is vulnerable to the 1 July three-month rate rising relative to the mid-September three-month (futures) rate. In such a case, the futures profit would be inadequate to match the cash market loss. There is a need to hedge against a rise in nearby interest rates relative to distant ones. A futures straddle could be established in order to profit from a rise in nearby rates relative to distant ones (fall in nearby futures prices relative to distant ones).

In order to profit from a fall in nearby futures prices relative to distant ones, a futures straddle is sold, nearby futures are sold and distant ones bought. In the present example this would involve selling June contracts and simultaneously buying an equal number of September contracts. The question then arises as to the appropriate number.

The straddle relates to a three-month stretch of the yield curve (mid-June to mid-September), whereas the time mismatch is of 2½ months. If the mismatch were of 3 months, then to handle a $5 million exposure would require 5 straddles (selling 5 June and buying 5 September). However, since the mismatch is of just 2½ months, the appropriate number of straddles is factored down to (2½/3) × 5 = 4.17 (4 when rounded to the nearest whole number). So the first straddle involves the sale of 4 June and the purchase of 4 September contracts.

The second straddle would hedge the mismatch between the second three-month period (1 October to 31 December) and the September futures interest rate period (mid-September to mid-December). The risk here is of a rise in the 1 October three-month (forward) rate relative to the mid-September three-month (futures) rate. It is a risk of a rise in distant rates relative to nearby ones. A futures straddle aimed at making a profit from a relative rise in distant rates would be needed. In other words, the futures straddle should profit from a fall in distant futures prices relative to nearby ones (so as to compensate for futures profits being inadequate to meet higher interest costs for 1 October to 31 December). Nearby futures are bought and distant ones sold.

Again, the question arises as to the requisite number of straddles. Since the straddle relates to a three-month period (mid-June to mid-September) and the timing mismatch is just half a month, the number of straddles needed is (½/3) × 5 = 0.83 (1 to the nearest whole number). So the second straddle consists of buying 1 June and selling 1 September contract (i.e. one long straddle).

Next, the 1 January to 30 June interest period needs to be hedged against changes in the slope of the yield curve. Dividing the six-month period into 2 successive three-month periods produces a borrowing for 1 January to 30 March, which has a three-and-a-half month mismatch with the September futures. The later period, 1 April to 30 June, involves a six-and-a-half month mismatch.

The futures straddle hedging the basis risk relating to the first 3 months would need to hedge against a rise in distant interest rates relative to nearby ones (fall in distant futures prices relative to nearby ones); such an eventuality would mean that profits from September futures would not completely compensate for a rise in the 1 January three-month (forward) interest rate. So a long straddle, the purchase of nearby and sale of distant futures contracts, is appropriate. The number of straddles required is (3½/3) × 5 = 5.83 (6 to the nearest whole number).

Hedging the basis risk relating to the later period also requires a long straddle, for the same reasons as for the earlier period. The requisite number of straddles would be (6½/3) × 5 = 10.83 (11 to the nearest whole number).

The total futures position can now be ascertained as follows:

Basic hedge			Sell	20 September
1st straddle	Sell	4 June	Buy	4 September
2nd straddle	Buy	1 June	Sell	1 September
3rd straddle	Buy	6 June	Sell	6 September
4th straddle	Buy	11 June	Sell	11 September
Total	Buy	14 June	Sell	34 September

Buying 14 June futures contracts and selling 34 September futures provides the requisite net 20 short contracts. (Note that it would be more accurate to use the decimalised, rather than whole, numbers of contracts in the foregoing calculation. The result of doing so is buy 13.32 June and sell 33.32 September, which rounds to 13 June and 33 September.)

Subsequent adjustments

As time passes, liquidity will develop in the December and subsequent contracts. Consequently, it becomes possible to use more distant futures. This is particularly desirable in the case of hedging the 1 January to 30 June risk. It is informative to look at how the hedge might stand at a later date, e.g. 6 months later, on 26 September.

If, by 26 September, there is adequate liquidity in both the December and March contracts, then the basic hedge for the 1 January to 30 June risk might take the form of a short position in 10 March futures contracts. To ascertain the requisite number of straddles, it is again useful to split the six-month period into 2 successive three-month periods: 1 January to 31 March and 1 April to 30 June.

Hedging the risk relating to the first 3 months involves a time mismatch of 2½ months between the three-month interest period being hedged (1 January to 31 March) and the three-month interest period to which the March futures contract relates (mid-March to mid-June). There is a risk that the 1 January to 31 March interest rate will rise relative to the mid-March to mid-June futures interest rate. It is necessary to take a straddle position that will profit from a rise in nearby rates relative to distant ones (nearby futures price fall relative to distant futures price). In this way, any inadequacy of profits from the March futures would be compensated for. Futures straddles should be sold. The number of straddles would be (2½/3) × 5 = 4.17 (4 to the nearest whole number). So the ideal straddle (if contracts were divisible) would take the form of selling 4.17 December contracts and buying 4.17 March contracts. Together with the basic hedge of selling 5 March contracts to cover the 1 January to 31 March period, the net result is the sale of 4.17 December and 0.83 March contracts.

It can be seen that when the straddle involves futures contracts whose maturity dates fall either side of the risk date, the appropriate hedge consists of a combination of the 2 maturities. The numbers of the 2 maturities are proportional to the periods between the risk date and the maturity dates, the futures contract whose maturity falls closest to the risk date having the greatest weighting. In the case under consideration, the December futures have a weighting of 2½/3 and the March futures a weighting of ½/3. The result is 4.17 December contracts and 0.83 March contracts (of course, since contracts are not divisible, this becomes 4 December and 1 March).

The interest risk relating to 1 April to 30 June involves a time mismatch of half a month relative to the March futures contracts. The risk is of a rise in distant interest rates relative to nearby ones. A futures straddle that would profit from such an eventuality (fall in distant futures prices relative to nearby ones) involves buying nearby (December) contracts and selling distant (March) contracts. The number of straddles to be bought is (½/3) × 5 = 0.83. So, bearing in mind the need to deal in whole numbers of contracts, one December contract is bought and one March contract sold.

The total hedge position as of 26 September comprises the following:

Basic hedge			Sell	10 March
1st straddle	Sell	4.17 December	Buy	4.17 March
2nd straddle	Buy	0.83 December	Sell	0.83 March
Total	Sell	3.34 December	Sell	6.66 March

It is to be noted that the mid-point between the 2 risk dates of 1 January and 1 April is mid-February. This mid-point has a time mismatch of 2 months from the December futures maturity date and one month from the March futures maturity date. The total number of contracts arising from the calculation above involves March and December contracts in a 2 to 1 ratio, with the higher weighting being for the futures contract whose maturity is closest to the mid point between the risk dates.

Rolling straddles forward

When the December contracts mature, and if adequate liquidity has developed in the June contracts, the December–March straddles would need to be replaced by March–June straddles. If the basic hedge remains a short position in 10 March contracts, then substituting the new straddles for the old ones produces the following:

Basic hedge	Sell	10 March		
1st straddle	Sell	4.17 March	Buy	4.17 June
2nd straddle	Buy	0.83 March	Sell	0.83 June
Total	Sell	13.34 March	Buy	3.34 June

Of course, it must be borne in mind that it is not possible to trade fractions of contracts. So in practice the total would be short 13 March and long 3 June (giving a net short position of 10 contracts).

Non-linear yield curves

An implicit assumption thus far has been that the yield curve is a straight line (or nearly so) over the relevant portion. It must be borne in mind that perfect linearity is not likely to be encountered. The foregoing technique is therefore subject to some error, the size of which will rise with increasing discrepancies between the period of the timing mismatch and the period covered by the futures straddle.

Example 4.7

On 20 March there is a need to hedge a three-month borrowing due on 20 December. There is poor liquidity in the December contracts, but adequate liquidity in the June and September contracts.

September contracts are sold. Spot and futures three-month interest rates are:

Spot	June futures	September futures	December forward
10% p.a.	10.25% p.a.	10.5% p.a.	10.75% p.a.

By 20 June, liquidity is adequate in the December contracts, but interest rates are:

Spot	September futures	December futures
11.25% p.a.	11.75% p.a.	12.25% p.a.

The December forward rate that can be guaranteed with futures is 12.25% p.a., which is 1.5% p.a. higher than the previous forward rate for December.

However, the profit from the September futures relates to just 1.25% p.a. There is an incomplete hedge because the yield curve has become steeper (more positive). This hedge imperfection would have been avoided if, on 20 March, a June–September futures straddle had been bought. That would have provided a profit from the rise in September futures rates relative to June rates of 0.25% p.a.

Note: (1) If the borrowing were to be taken out midway between 20 September and 20 December, the number of straddles would be halved. (The straddle relates to a 13 week section of the yield curve, whereas the risk arises from a 6½ week section.) (2) If the borrowing were to be taken out midway between 20 September and 20 December, equal numbers of September and December contracts would be appropriate (up to the September futures maturity date). (3) Variation margin leverage should be applied.

ACTIVITY 4.3

Assume that it is now 2 April and that you wish to hedge a $50 million one-year loan commencing on 15 May with three-month roll-overs. The three-month interest rates are 9.500—9.625 and the only quoted futures are:

    Jun   90.18
    Sep   89.93
    Dec   89.63

How would you construct the appropriate hedge?
(Based on Securities Institute Financial Futures and Options examination, July 1993, Question 9.)

Answer
Hedging the position of the yield curve would require a strip using 50 June, 50 September, 50 December and 50 March contracts. The absence of March contracts suggests that this strategy should be amended to 50 June, 50 September and 100 December contracts.

*   Since the borrowing and roll-over dates do not coincide with futures maturity dates, there is a need to hedge against changes in the slope of the yield curve. As a result, the above strategy will require amendment.*

*   The 15 August roll-over can be hedged with a weighted combination of June and September contracts. If it is the case that 55 days have elapsed since the June futures maturity and 36 days remain to the September futures maturity, then the numbers of short contracts required to hedge the 15 August roll-over would be:*

$(36/91) \times 50 = 19.8$ June contracts

and $(55/91) \times 50 = 30.2$ September contracts

A parallel analysis indicates that the 15 November roll-over should be hedged by selling 19.8 September and 30.2 December contracts.

The number of short June contracts required to hedge the initial borrowing on 15 May would be 50 adjusted by a June–September straddle. The risk is that nearby rates rise relative to distant ones (so that the June futures fail to hedge the May exposure completely). A straddle is constructed that profits from a rise in nearby rates relative to distant ones; in other words, a fall in nearby futures prices relative to distant ones. June futures are sold and September contracts bought. If the time between 15 May and the June futures maturity date is 36 days, then the straddle involves:

$(36/91) \times 50 = 19.8$ June futures sold

and $(36/91) \times 50 = 19.8$ September futures bought

The short position in 50 December contracts to hedge the 15 February roll-over would need to be adjusted with a September–December futures straddle. The risk is that the distant interest rate (for February) could rise relative to the nearby one (for December); i.e. distant futures prices could fall relative to nearby ones. Such a change in the slope of the yield curve would reduce the hedging effectiveness of the December futures contracts. The appropriate straddle involves selling distant maturity contracts (December) and buying nearby ones (September), thereby generating a profit from a fall in distant futures prices relative to nearby ones. If the number of days between the December futures maturity date and 15 February were 56 days, then the numbers of futures contracts required are:

$(56/91) \times 50 = 30.8$ September contracts bought

and $(56/91) \times 50 = 30.8$ December contracts sold

Totalling numbers of contracts provides:

June	$-19.8 - 50 - 19.8 = -89.6$
September	$-30.2 - 19.8 + 19.8 + 30.8 = 0.6$
December	$-30.2 - 50 - 30.8 = -111$

These numbers need to be adjusted for variation margin leverage. For the time period between closing out the futures and paying the interest on the loan, an adjustment may be made by dividing the numbers of futures contracts by 1.024 (9½% divided by four gives approximately 2.4%). A further adjustment may be made for the period between contracting the futures and closing them out. This is problematical since the pattern of variation margin cash flows cannot be predicted.

Figure 4.5 provides an illustration of the analysis above.

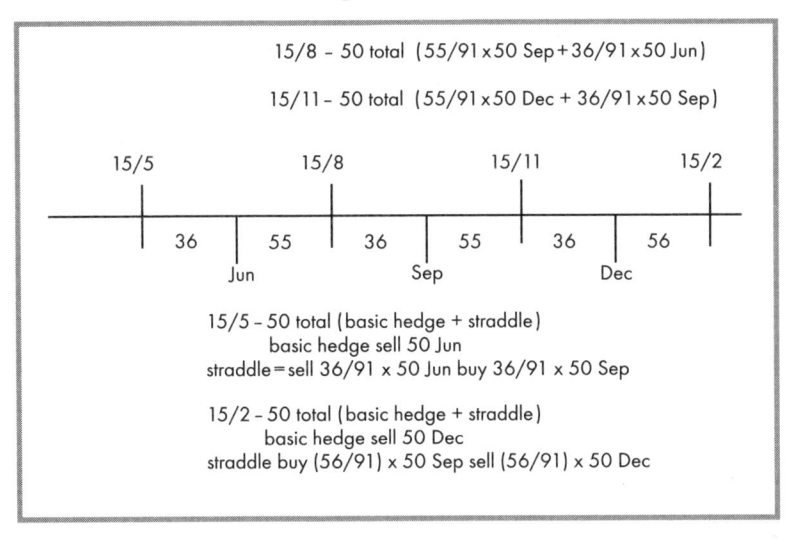

FIGURE 4.5 Calculating numbers of contracts

```
                    15/8 - 50 total (55/91 x 50 Sep + 36/91 x 50 Jun)
                    15/11 - 50 total (55/91 x 50 Dec + 36/91 x 50 Sep)

    15/5            15/8            15/11           15/2
     |               |                |              |
     |----36----|----55----|----36----|----55----|----36----|----56----|
                    Jun              Sep             Dec

    15/5 - 50 total (basic hedge + straddle)
           basic hedge sell 50 Jun
           straddle = sell 36/91 x 50 Jun buy 36/91 x 50 Sep

    15/2 - 50 total (basic hedge + straddle)
           basic hedge sell 50 Dec
           straddle buy (56/91) x 50 Sep sell (56/91) x 50 Dec
```

BUTTERFLY SPREADS

A complex type of spread is the butterfly. In the case of butterfly spreads, the view is on the relationship between 2 spreads. A butterfly is a spread of spreads.

Suppose that three-month eurodollar futures contracts have the prices shown in Table 4.1 for the next 3 maturity months. The value of a spread is obtained by subtracting the farther price from the nearer price. Within the butterfly the nearby spread is 150 ticks, while the deferred spread is 50 ticks. The value of the butterfly spread is 100 ticks (150 − 50).

Table 4.1 Eurodollar futures contracts prices

June	September	December
92.00	90.50	90.00

If the butterfly spread is expected to strengthen (more positive/less negative), the butterfly spread is bought; in the opposite case, the butterfly is sold. Example 4.8 illustrates a case in which the expectation of a strengthening of a butterfly spread leads a trader to buy that spread. It is based on three-month eurodollar futures.

86 • ADVANCED STRATEGIES

Example 4.8

On 5 July (see Table 4.2) the nearby spread is 50 ticks and the deferred spread is 100 ticks. So the value of the butterfly is –50 ticks. The trader expects that the nearby spread will increase relative to the deferred spread. In other words, the butterfly spread is expected to strengthen. On 5 July he buys a butterfly spread:

> Buy 1 September contract at   90.50
> Sell 2 December contracts at   90.00
> Buy 1 March contract at   89.00

On 25 July (see Table 4.3) he closes out by selling that butterfly spread. Selling a butterfly spread involves selling the nearby spread and buying the deferred spread.

> Sell 1 September contract at   90.50
> Buy 2 December contracts at   89.75
> Sell 1 March contract at   89.00

Table 4.2   Prices on 5 July

September	December	March
90.50	90.00	89.00

Table 4.3   Prices on 25 July

September	December	March
90.50	89.75	89.00

There is a profit of 25 ticks on each of the 2 December contracts, which at $25 per tick is a profit of $1,250. The trader was correct in expecting that the butterfly spread would strengthen. The nearby spread increased from 50 to 75 ticks and the deferred spread fell from 100 to 75. So the butterfly strengthened from –50 to zero.

INTER-CONTRACT SPREADS

Inter-contract spreads involve the simultaneous purchase and sale of futures contracts relating to differing underlying instruments. The underlying instruments need not even be on the same exchange: for example, the spread might involve the three-month eurodollar interest rate contract on LIFFE and the domestic certificate of deposit contract on the International Monetary Market (IMM) in Chicago. It is possible for the contracts being bought and sold to have the same maturity months in the case of inter-contract spreads.

Inter-contract spreads are subject to greater risk than straddle spreads. There is greater likelihood of divergent price movements, and the more unrelated are the 2 instruments, the larger is the risk. A LIFFE three-month eurodollar straddle is less risky than an inter-contract spread between LIFFE three-month eurodollar and IMM domestic certificate of deposit contracts. The risk on the latter would in turn be less than that between LIFFE three-month eurodollar and Chicago Board of Trade (CBOT) US Treasury bond contracts. Since inter-contract spreads are riskier than straddles, all the contracts involved in an inter-contract spread normally require payment of the full initial margin: there may be no reduced initial margin as might occur in the case of straddles.

ACTIVITY 4.4

A trader in Euromark futures on LIFFE is considering a butterfly trade using the LIFFE 'designated strategy' trade, whereby the butterfly can be traded in a single transaction. Euromark futures prices are as follows:

	Bid	Offer
15 Dec 94	94.70	94.71
16 Mar 95	94.28	94.29
15 Jun 95	93.83	93.84
14 Sep 95	93.48	93.50
14 Dec 95	93.15	93.20

(a) Indicate the prices which would be bid and offered in the market for the butterfly strategy for December/March/June as a single trade.

(b) Assuming that the trader purchased the butterfly at the offered price, what would be the outcome of the strategy under the following out-turns?

	A	B
Dec 94	95.23	93.35
Mar 95	93.70	95.60
Jun 95	95.85	93.95

(Based on the Securities Institute Financial Futures and Options examination, December 1994, Question 9.)

Answer

(a) Long butterfly
(94.71 − 94.28) + (93.84 − 94.28) = 0.43 + (−0.44) = −0.01
Short butterfly
(94.29 − 94.70) + (94.29 − 93.83) = −0.41 + 0.46 = 0.05

The figures of −0.01 and 0.05 are net payments and hence would correspond to strategy prices of 0.01 and −0.05.

(b) A: Long butterfly
(95.23 − 94.71) + 2 (94.28 − 93.70) + (95.85 − 93.84) = 0.52 + 1.16 + 2.01 = 3.69
B: Long butterfly
(93.35 − 94.71) + 2 (94.28 − 95.60) + (93.95 − 93.84) = −1.36 − 2.64 + 0.11 = −3.89

CONCLUSIONS

Hedging with short-term interest rate futures is likely to be imperfect. The imperfection arises from the unexpected changes in basis. A major cause of unexpected change in basis is unexpected change in the term structure of interest rates. Specifically, the slope and curvature of the forward yield curve can change.

This chapter has considered some approaches to dealing with basis risk. One approach is the use of a generic hedge ratio (generic because it is applicable to all futures contracts, not just short-term interest rate futures). Another approach is the use of a futures strip, which is useful when the maturity of the deposit or borrowing exceeds 3 months. Futures straddles provide another technique. It was pointed out that the sources of hedge imperfection could be divided into asset mismatch, maturity mismatch and date mismatch. The generic hedge ratio can deal with the asset mismatch, the futures strip can remove the maturity mismatch and futures straddles are suitable for reducing the hedge imperfection arising from date mismatches.

The chapter ended with a method for hedging against changes in the curvature of the yield curve. This involved the use of futures butterflies.

The hedging techniques considered in this chapter and the previous one are applicable to the hedging of interest rate risk on short-term money market instruments. In order to hedge the risks arising from changes in long-term interest rates, it is appropriate to employ government bond futures. This is the subject of the next chapter.

Further reading

An authoritative account of the use of short-term interest rate futures contracts in advanced strategies can be found in:

M. Desmond Fitzgerald, *Financial Futures* (Euromoney Publications, London, 1983), Chapter 8.

A focus on uses by financial institutions can be found in:

Robert T. Daigler, *Financial Futures Markets* (Harper Collins, New York, 1993), Chapter 15.

MANAGING FIXED INTEREST RISK 5

INTRODUCTION

Government bond futures are often the most heavily traded contracts on derivatives exchanges. This partly reflects the huge quantity, and trading turnover, of government bonds worldwide. It also reflects the price volatility of such bonds, a volatility that arises from fluctuations in long-term interest rates. Since bond price movements arise from and reflect changes in long-term interest rates, government bond futures can alternatively be regarded as long-term interest rate futures. Such futures are of use to those concerned with the management of interest rate risk, as well as those who aim to manage bond price risk. Bond price risk and long-term interest rate risk can be regarded as the same risk seen from two different perspectives.

This chapter begins with a brief overview of the nature, and purposes, of government bonds. It then describes the characteristics of government bond futures and illustrates some elementary hedging applications. As with other futures contracts, hedging involves a futures position opposite to the one being hedged. If the risk is that bond prices will rise (long-term interest rates fall), the futures position taken is one that would profit from a rise in bond prices, i.e. futures are bought. If bond price falls would cause losses on the existing position, this could be hedged by selling futures (a short futures position would profit from falling bond prices).

As a preliminary to an account of the principles of futures pricing, certain concepts specific to bond futures are described. These relate to the delivery process, price factors, invoice amounts and the cheapest-to-deliver bond. The account of the determination of futures prices focuses on cash-and-carry arbitrage.

Two features that distinguish bond futures from three-month interest rate futures are that bonds can actually be delivered (by the seller to the buyer of futures) if the futures are held to maturity, and that the underlying instrument (a government bond) is carryable. This latter feature renders cash-and-carry operations possible. A long cash and carry involves buying bonds and selling futures (with a view to a possible sale of those bonds through the futures). A short cash and carry consists of a sale of bonds and purchase of futures (which may be used for the repurchase of the bonds). It will be shown that futures prices should be such that there are no arbitrage opportunities from such cash-and-carry operations.

This leads on to a consideration of implied repos. Instead of seeing cash-and-carry operations as determinants of futures prices (given short-term interest rates), implied repos are based on cash and carry generating short-term interest rates (given futures prices). Used in this way, cash-and-carry operations provide short-term investment and borrowing opportunities.

THE UNDERLYING INSTRUMENT

Bonds are used for long-term borrowing by the issuer. Central governments are major issuers of bonds (and in some countries they are called gilt-edged securities, or gilts). Such government issues are usually for the purpose of long-term borrowing, although they may also be sold as a means of conducting monetary policy.

Bonds are issued in a wide variety of forms. However, most government bonds conform to a conventional format. The conventional government bond or gilt:

1. pays a fixed coupon per period (usually 6 months);
2. has a definite redemption date;
3. has a market price expressed as a sum per £100 nominal.

A conventional government bond pays a fixed sum of money, known as the coupon, every 6 months. It has a definite redemption date on which the government is obliged to pay the nominal value, or par, of the bond to its owner. Its market price is expressed in relation to its nominal or par value. For example, pounds per £100 nominal or dollars per $1000 par (so a market price of £96 means that £96 must be paid for every £100 to be repaid at redemption).

Dated bonds – those with a specified redemption date – may be classed as short, medium or long term. This classification is based on their term to maturity when they are first issued, i.e. their initial maturity. One possible classification is to treat those with initial maturities of 5 years or less as being short term (in some countries such short-term bonds are called notes). Medium-term bonds might be those with initial maturities of 5 to 15 years and long-term bonds might be those with initial maturities over 15 years.

Undated bonds have no stated redemption date. The government, or other issuer, is never obliged to repay the nominal value but may simply pay the coupon forever. Such bonds could be redeemed by the government buying them back in the market.

Index-linked bonds are a form of investment that protects the investor from inflation. Both the sum to be repaid by the issuer at redemption and the periodic coupon payment are adjusted in line with a price index. Conventional bonds suffer from a fall in their real values (in terms of purchasing power) as a result of inflation. Since the values of index-linked bonds are adjusted upwards in line with an index of prices of goods and services, the investor is protected against an erosion of the real value of the bonds.

FUTURES CONTRACTS

The contracts available include futures on ecu (European currency unit) bonds and on government bonds of various countries. These countries include the United States of America (Treasury bonds), Japan, Spain, the United Kingdom (gilts), Germany (Bunds), France, Italy (BTPs) and Australia.

Table 5.1 shows some bond futures prices at the close of business on 13 December 1995. The information indicates the country of the bond, the exchange on which it is traded (which is not necessarily in the country of the bond), the size of a contract and the tick size (the size of the minimum price movement). So, for example, US Treasury bond futures are traded on the Chicago Board of Trade, the contract size is $100,000 nominal and the minimum price movement allowed by the exchange is $1/32 ($0.03125) per $100 nominal (i.e. $31.25 per contract).

In each case either 2 or 3 delivery months are shown. This is not the total of the available delivery months, but tends to be those with significant trading volume. The table shows opening prices (e.g. US Treasury bond futures for December delivery opened at $120^{16}/_{32}$), settlement (closing) prices, the change in the settlement price since the previous trading day, the highest and lowest prices achieved during the day, the estimated volume (number of contracts traded) for the day, and the open interest

Table 5.1 Bond futures prices

	Open	Sett price	Change	High	Low	Estimated volume	Open interest
■ Ecu bond futures (MATIF) ecu 100,000							
Dec	90.54	90.62	−0.20	90.76	90.38	4,850	8,134
Mar	89.38	89.54	−0.20	89.64	89.38	1,967	2,854
■ US Treasury bond futures (CBT) $100,000 32nds of 100%							
Dec	120.16	120.06	−0.06	120.20	120.00	32,966	80,699
Mar	120.10	119.31	−0.06	120.14	119.25	252,596	338,336
Jun	119.26	119.18	−0.05	119.29	119.14	485	15,349
■ Notional Spanish bond futures (MEFF)							
Dec	93.52	93.82	+0.26	93.88	93.35	43,589	29,471
Mar	93.40	93.66	+0.29	93.75	93.38	8,629	19,655
■ Notional UK gilt futures (LIFFE)* £50,000 32nds of 100%							
Dec	110.19	111.02	+0.05	111.09	110.19	4,429	29.925
Mar	110.10	110.18	+0.05	110.28	110.01	48,592	121,522
■ Notional German Bund futures (LIFFE)* DM250,000 100ths of 100%							
Mar	98.70	98.80	+0.13	98.89	98.58	80,911	209,046
Jun	97.98	98.17	+0.13	98.10	97.98	8	191
■ Notional French bond futures (MATIF) FFr500,000							
Dec	120.00	119.86	−0.48	120.16	119.78	132,703	61,516
Mar	119.24	119.14	−0.42	119.38	119.08	46,073	71,522
Jun	119.52	119.38	−0.48	119.54	119.40	71	3,349
■ Notional Italian government bond (BTP) futures (LIFFE)* lira 200 million 100ths of 100%							
Mar	106.25	106.17	−0.12	106.38	106.00	22,193	48,261
Jun	105.90	105.77	−0.12	105.90	105.90	33	989

*LIFFE open interest figures are for the previous day.
Source: *Financial Times*, 14 December 1995

(the number of contracts in existence at the end of the trading day). It is to be noted that the figures relate to specific contracts on particular exchanges; similar futures may trade on other exchanges (e.g. German government bond futures are also traded on the Deutsche Terminbörse).

Government bond futures are commitments to buy or sell government bonds during specified future months. A limited number of bonds are eligible for delivery in fulfilment of a futures contract, and the seller has the choice as to the specific bond. Contracts are commonly not held until maturity but are closed out by means of the holder taking out an opposite contract; for example, a buyer can close out by selling bond futures in an amount and for a delivery month corresponding to those of the contracts previously bought. Cash flows by way of variation margin reflect the change in futures prices between the dates of buying and selling.

Those using these financial futures for hedging may wish to safeguard either the value of securities or the cash flow arising from them.

HEDGING THE VALUE OF A PORTFOLIO

A portfolio manager may fear an increase in long-term interest rates, an occurrence that would reduce the prices of bonds held in a portfolio. He could attempt to avoid this effect on the value of the portfolio by taking a position in futures that would provide an offsetting gain from a fall in bond prices. To achieve this he would sell futures contracts. A fall in bond prices should be accompanied by a fall in the prices of bond futures. If a loss were made from a decline in the value of bonds, the portfolio manager would be compensated by profits from the futures position. He would be able to buy bond futures at a price lower than that at which he sold.

This process is illustrated by Example 5.1, which needs to be preceded by details of the specification of a particular long-term interest rate

Example 5.1

Cash market

2 January
The long-term interest rate is 6% p.a. The DM1 million bond portfolio is vulnerable to an increase in long-term interest rates.

15 February
The long-term interest rate has risen to 7½% p.a. Correspondingly, the value of the bond portfolio has fallen to DM865,000 (this figure could be anywhere between DM800,000 and DM1 million depending upon the maturities of the bonds held).

There is a loss of DM135,000 in the value of the bond portfolio.

Futures market

Sells 4 March German government bond futures contracts. Futures price is 100, reflecting a 6% p.a. interest rate.

Closes out by buying 4 March German government bond futures contracts. The price of the contracts has fallen to 82.22, reflecting a 7½% p.a. futures interest rate.

There is a profit of DM177,800 from the futures position.

futures contract. This German government bond futures contract has a nominal value of DM250,000 and the prices of contracts are expressed as Deutschmarks per DM100 nominal value. The price of the notional bond (upon which the futures are based) would be 100 when the long-run interest rate is 6% p.a., but would rise above 100 when the interest rate is lower; the converse applies for higher rates. The tick, the minimum price movement, is DM0.01 for these bond futures.

In Example 5.1, a portfolio manager with bonds worth DM1 million on 2 January is anxious about the possibility that interest rates might rise and thereby reduce the value of his bonds. He hedges by selling 4 bond futures contracts and is more than successful in offsetting the fall in the value of his bonds. The reason for this overcompensation is the fact that the average maturity of the bonds in his portfolio is less than that of the bond on which the futures are based. The value of a portfolio responds less to interest rate changes as the average maturity declines. In the light of this, he could have chosen to hedge with fewer than 4 futures contracts; 3 might seem appropriate, particularly when it is borne in mind that with 4 contracts a fall in interest rates would have entailed a futures loss greater than the increase in the value of the bond portfolio.

HEDGING CASH FLOW

Example 5.2 is that of a corporate treasurer intending to raise money by the sale of securities with a fixed coupon yield. His anxiety is that interest rates might rise before the sale is made, with the result that the raising of a particular sum of money would then entail a greater future cash flow commitment to the security holders.

The treasurer could use the DM355,600 futures profit to reduce his borrowing requirement from DM2 million to DM1,644,400 and hence reduce the annual servicing cost to DM123,330. A perfect hedge would have provided a futures profit of DM400,000 so that the cash flow required to service the debt returned to DM120,000 p.a. The futures gain was less than DM400,000 because the bond on which the futures are based has a maturity date and only the price of an irredeemable bond responds proportionately to interest rate changes. A more effective hedge would have been obtained by using 9 contracts, which would have provided a futures profit of DM400,050.

In both of the examples, the hedger would be able to ascertain the appropriate number of futures contracts required – 3 and 9 respectively – before selling the contracts. The ratio of the nominal value of futures

Example 5.2

Cash market	Futures market
2 January	
The corporation intends to raise DM2 million on 15 February by the sale of irredeemable bonds. The interest rate on undated bonds is 6% p.a. The treasurer wants to ensure that the cost of servicing the debt will be limited to DM120,000 p.a.	Sells 8 March German government bond futures contracts. Futures price is 100, reflecting a 6% p.a. interest rate.
15 February	
The interest rate on undated stock has risen to 7½% p.a.	Closes out by buying 8 March German government bond futures contracts. Futures price is 82.22, reflecting a 7½% p.a. futures interest rate.
The cost of servicing a DM2 million debt would now be DM150,000 p.a.	There is a profit of DM355,600 from the futures position.

contracts required to the nominal value of assets or liabilities to be hedged is known as the hedge ratio. Even with the correct hedge ratio, hedging may not be perfect. Imperfections will arise if the cash market and futures interest rates do not change to the same extent. However, this basis risk tends to be much less than the outright risk of unhedged positions since the difference between cash and futures interest rates fluctuates less than cash market rates.

DELIVERY

In most cases the months in which government bonds may be delivered in settlement of futures contracts are March, June, September and December. The seller chooses which bond to deliver, subject to the bond meeting certain criteria concerning maturity. In some cases (including UK gilt and US Treasury bond futures) the seller also chooses the day of the month on which delivery takes place (in the other cases there is no choice as to delivery date).

If the rate of coupon yield on the bond exceeds the interest rate on funds borrowed to finance the purchase of the bond, the bond will be delivered at the end of the month so as to maximise the benefit from the relatively high coupon yield. If the coupon is less than the financing cost, the bond would be delivered at the beginning of the month so as to avoid the net cost of holding the bond during the month.

THE PRICE (CONVERSION) FACTOR

The price factor will be described in relation to the LIFFE gilt futures contract (gilts are British government bonds). The description can be readily extended to the other bond futures contracts.

The gilt futures contracts each have a nominal value of £50,000. Likewise, the gilts delivered when a contract matures must amount to £50,000 in nominal value. Gilts may, however, have differing market values despite identical nominal values. A £50,000 bond issued when the market rate was 12% p.a. would provide a coupon of £6,000 p.a., whereas a £50,000 bond issued at a rate of 10% p.a. would yield £5,000 p.a. The market value of bonds will vary according to the size of the coupon yield. A bond yielding £6,000 p.a. is worth more than one with a coupon of just £5,000 p.a. If the seller delivers high coupon gilts, he expects to receive more money than if he delivers lower coupon gilts. To ensure that this happens, price factors are used in the calculation of the sums for which buyers are invoiced, the relevant adjustment being made by means of multiplying the futures price by the price factor.

To obtain the price factor for a gilt, its price, if it were to have a gross redemption yield of 9% p.a., is ascertained (the coupons and redemption value are discounted at 9% p.a.). This price is then divided by the nominal value of the gilt and the result is the price factor. Higher coupon yields are reflected in higher price factors.

If the bonds were perpetuities, the price factor would equal the ratio of the coupons. The price factor for an 11¼% p.a. bond would be 1.25 since an 11¼% p.a. coupon into perpetuity would render the bond 25% more valuable than one yielding a perpetual 9% p.a. However, most gilts have maturity dates (as does the gilt upon which futures contracts are based). Since the bonds are not perpetuities, the price factor tends to differ from the ratio of the coupons, with the factor approaching 1 as the period to maturity declines towards zero.

INVOICE AMOUNT

The futures price upon which the invoice amount is based might be referred to as the settlement price, which is the market price of futures contracts at a specific point in time prior to delivery. The principal invoice amount is the settlement price multiplied by the price factor and by the nominal value of the futures contract divided by 100:

$$\text{Principal invoice amount} = \text{Settlement price} \times \text{Price factor} \times \frac{\text{Nominal amount of a contract}}{100}$$

The sum for which the buyer is invoiced is equal to the principal invoice amount plus accrued interest on the bonds. The resulting invoice amounts would normally differ from the market values of the corresponding bonds.

THE CHEAPEST-TO-DELIVER BOND

The seller chooses which bond to deliver in fulfilment of the contract. It is in the interests of the seller to deliver the bond whose invoice amount exceeds the market price by the largest margin (or whose invoice amount falls short of the market price by the smallest margin). This is the cheapest-to-deliver (CTD) bond. Alternatively, the CTD can be seen as the bond that provides the greatest profit from long cash-and-carry arbitrage.

DETERMINATION OF BOND FUTURES PRICES

As with other assets that can be carried during the life of a futures contract, bond futures prices tend to be determined by cash-and-carry arbitrage. Long cash and carry involves buying bonds while simultaneously selling bond futures. Short cash and carry (in its pure form) involves borrowing bonds and selling them while buying futures. The futures price should be such that no profit is available from cash-and-carry arbitrage.

For no arbitrage profits to be available from long cash and carry, the financing cost of holding bonds should be matched by the returns from holding the bonds in the form of coupon receipts, plus capital gain (or loss) guaranteed by the futures premium (or discount) relative to the spot price of the bonds. Note that if the financing cost (based on short-term interest rates) exceeds the coupon yield, there will be a futures premium over spot to yield a capital gain, whereas if the financing cost is less than the coupon receipts, a futures discount, providing a capital loss, should exist.

An absence of arbitrage profits in the case of short cash and carry requires that the interest receipts from short selling are precisely offset by losses in the form of coupon amounts payable to the entity from which the bonds were borrowed, plus capital losses (or minus capital gains). One difficulty with short cash and carry, since it involves buying futures, is that the arbitrager has no control over which bond is delivered when the futures mature – it may not be the bond that was sold short. For this reason, the influence of short cash and carry may be significantly weakened, but the following account will assume that short cash and carry occurs and is effective.

Pricing bond futures

For long cash and carry, when there are no coupons before the futures delivery date:

$$S(1 + rt) = F$$

The cost of buying the bonds, plus the financing cost, rt, should equal the sum receivable from selling against the futures, F. If the futures price is higher, there is an arbitrage profit from buying bonds and simultaneously selling futures.

For long cash and carry, when there are coupons before the futures delivery date:

$$S(1 + rt) - D = F$$

What will be paid by the delivery date, $S(1 + rt)$, minus what is received, D (the future value of the coupons), should match the sum receivable from selling against the futures.

Alternatively:

$$(S - I)(1 + rt) = F$$

where I is the present value of the coupons. The buyer of the bonds could partially finance the purchase by borrowing I against the anticipated coupon receipts. The net cost of buying bonds, $S - I$, plus the financing cost, should equal the futures price.

In equation form, the pricing relationship that tends to be established by cash-and-carry arbitrage can be expressed as:

either $F = (S - I)(1 + rt)$
or $\quad F = S(1 + rt) - D$

where F is the fair futures price, S is the spot price of the bond, I is the present value of coupons receivable before the futures maturity date, D is the future value of coupons receivable before the futures maturity date, r is the short-term risk-free interest rate and t is the period (in years) to the futures maturity date.

In both equations, by subtracting S from both sides it can be seen that the futures premium (or discount) relative to spot matches the difference between the financing cost and coupon yield. Thus:

$$F - S = S.rt - I(1 + rt)$$
$$\text{and} \quad F - S = S.rt - D$$

where both D and $I(1 + rt)$ represent the future value of the coupon receipts.

The equations for futures pricing shown above are somewhat abstract and need to be amended in 3 ways to take account of reality. First, it has been implicitly assumed that there is no difference between the coupon payment date and the ex-coupon date; if there is a difference, I and D refer to coupons relating to ex-coupon dates prior to the futures maturity, but discounting (or interest accrual) is from the date of receipt of the coupon.

Second, it has been implicitly assumed that the bond has a price factor of 1; if this is not the case (and it hardly ever will be), F in the equations needs to be divided by the price factor. More precisely, F net of accrued interest should be divided by the price factor of the bond in order to ascertain the futures price. Since S and F relate to sums actually paid and received, they must include accrued interest (the rights to coupon payment between the last coupon payment date and the date on which the bond is bought and sold). The price factor involved would be that of the bond used, which would normally be the cheapest to deliver. Note that since the bond normally used in cash-and-carry arbitrage would be the cheapest to deliver, the behaviour of the futures price would tend to relate closely to that of the cheapest to deliver.

ACTIVITY 5.1

It is 30 June 1997 and Treasury 10% 2007 has just paid a coupon. The price of this gilt is £130 and its price factor is 1.06. The six-month interest rate is 7% p.a. If the December futures contract is held to maturity what is the most likely date on which delivery into the futures contract would occur? What is the fair futures price on 30 June?

Answer
The current interest yield on the gilt is $(10/130) \times 100 = 7.69\%$ p.a. If there was a full 6 months accrued interest the interest yield would be $(10/135) \times 100 = 7.41\%$ p.a. So at current values the interest yield exceeds the interest

rate (financing cost) and so it seems likely that any delivery would be made at the end of December.

The cost of buying and holding the gilt until the end of December would be [£130 × (1.035)] − £5 = £129.55.

This corresponds to a futures price of £129.55/1.06 = £122.217 (£122–07), which is the fair futures price.

Third, transactions costs have been ignored. If bid–offer spreads are allowed for in both the bond market and the interest rates, the result is a no-arbitrage band of futures prices rather than the unique fair futures price (the fair futures price is the price that would prevail in the absence of transactions costs). The no-arbitrage band can be described by the expression:

$$S_B(1 + r_B t) - D \leq F \leq S_o(1 + r_o t) - D$$

where S_B is the spot bid price (dirty price, i.e. inclusive of accrued interest), S_o is the spot offer price (dirty price), r_B is the interest rate for period t (bid rate), r_o is the interest rate for period t (offer rate), t is the time to maturity of the futures contract (in years), D is the future value of coupons (relating to ex-coupon dates prior to the futures maturity date) and F is the futures price (multiplied by the price factor and inclusive of accrued interest).

Arbitrage should operate to keep the futures price within the no-arbitrage band. If the futures price rises above the band, long cash-and-carry arbitrage will tend to bring it back into the band. This will involve bonds being bought (the consequent upward pressure on bond prices will tend to raise the band) and futures being sold (thereby pushing futures prices down into the band). If the futures price falls below the band, the underpriced futures should be bought and the bonds sold; in other words, short cash-and-carry arbitrage should (at least in principle) take place. Short cash-and-carry arbitrage will tend to lower the no-arbitrage band (via reducing the spot bond price) and will raise the futures price until it is again within the band.

It can be seen that futures prices do not slavishly follow spot prices. Futures prices can lead spot prices via cash-and-carry transactions. Furthermore, within the no-arbitrage band futures prices can vary independently of spot prices.

THE ROLE OF IMPLICIT OPTIONS

The seller of bond futures contracts has choices relating to when to deliver during the delivery month and which bond to deliver. In effect, this gives the futures seller long option positions, and the futures buyer has

Example 5.3

Suppose that the date is 1 June 1995. The cheapest-to-deliver bond matures on 25 May 2006 and has a coupon of 9.5%. The clean price of the bond is 104^{14}/$_{32}$. The price factor of the bond is 1.03419. All interest rates are 5.125% p.a.

In order to ascertain the fair value of the September futures contract, it is necessary to decide on the delivery day within the delivery month. Since the rate of return from holding the bond is about 9% p.a., whereas the financing cost is 5.125% p.a., the seller will hold the bond as long as possible. So delivery will be at the end of the delivery month, 30 September.

Accrued interest is (^{7}/$_{365}$) × 9.5 = 0.1822. So the dirty price of the bond is 104.4375 + 0.1822 = 104.6197. The fair futures price is the price, in the absence of transactions costs, that offers no arbitrage profits. On the basis of 121 days between 1 June and 30 September, the no-arbitrage principal invoice amount for 30 September is given by:

104.6197 × [1 + (0.05125 × ^{121}/$_{365}$)] − accrued interest

where accrued interest equals 9.5 × ^{128}/$_{365}$ = 3.3315. So the principal invoice amount is 103.0657. The fair futures price is obtained by dividing this by the price factor:

103.^{0657}/$_{1.03419}$ = 99.6583

Consideration of transactions costs (such as bid–offer spreads) would establish a no-arbitrage band of futures prices around this fair futures price.

---

the corresponding short option positions. The seller of futures must, in some way, pay for the options and the buyer be paid. This is accomplished by a reduction in the bond futures price below the level that would otherwise pertain. In this way, at delivery the futures seller receives a sum which is reduced by the value of the option premiums, while the futures buyer receives payment for the options in the form of having to pay less for the bonds when they are delivered upon maturity of the futures contract.

ACTIVITY 5.2

On 1 January the cheapest-to-deliver Treasury bond for June has a 12% coupon and a price factor of 1.5. Coupons are paid at the end of February and August. The bond price is $110 and the rate of interest 8% per annum.

104 • **MANAGING FIXED INTEREST RISK**

> (a) Calculate the fair price for the June Treasury bond futures contract implied by this data.
> (b) Explain why your answer may differ from observed market prices.
>
> (Based on the Securities Institute examination in Financial Futures and Options, December 1991, Question 23.)

Answer

(a) It is necessary to ascertain the futures price that provides no cash-and-carry arbitrage profits. First, the cost of the Treasury bond, inclusive of net cost of carry, must be ascertained. The (clean) bond price is $110 and accrued interest would be $4. The bond would be delivered at the end of June since the coupon yield exceeds the financing cost (rate of interest). The total cost of buying and holding the Treasury bond until the end of June is its initial cost plus the financing cost:

$$\$114 + \$114(0.08/2) = \$118.56$$

The net cost of carry must take account of coupon receipts plus interest thereon, $6 + $0.16. So the net cost of the long Treasury bond position by the maturity date of the futures contract (end June) is $118.56 − $6.16 = $112.4.

The futures price should be such as to generate an invoice amount equal to $112.4. Letting F represent the futures price:

$$(F \times \text{price factor of CTD}) + \text{accrued interest} = \$112.4.$$

The price factor is 1.5 and the accrued interest would be $(4/6) \times \$6 = \$4$, so

$$(F \times 1.5) + \$4 = \$112.4$$

So F = $108.4/1.5 = $72.27.

(b) Since the seller of a bond futures contract has the choice of when and what to deliver, that seller has implicit (i.e. embedded) options which would be paid for by reduced receipts, which in turn implies a lower futures price. On CBOT there is also the wild card option arising from the facility to deliver, after the market has closed, at the market closing price. This valuable option is reflected in a reduced invoice amount (and hence reduced futures price).

IMPLIED REPOS

Given the spot price of a bond (normally the cheapest to deliver), its prospective coupon payments and the bond futures price, there will be a short-term rate of interest that precludes arbitrage profits. That interest rate is the implied repo.

It is possible to use transactions in bonds and bond futures to invest or borrow at the implied repo rate. The very low risk nature of such constructions has led to their being referred to as synthetic Treasury bills.

Buying bonds and simultaneously selling futures constitutes an investment whose maturity is the same as that of the futures contract. The implied repo is the rate of return on that investment. Selling bonds and buying futures constitutes borrowing for the period to the futures maturity date at the implied repo rate. (Repo is an abbreviation of sale and repurchase: selling bonds and buying futures is a form of sale and repurchase arrangement.) There is a source of risk in the use of the construction for borrowing in that there is no certainty as to which bond will be delivered at maturity, and no certainty as to the date on which delivery will take place (these being at the discretion of the seller of futures contracts).

In equation form, the implied repo can be expressed as:

$$IR = \frac{F - S + I}{S - I} \times \frac{365}{T}$$

where IR is the implied repo, F is the (futures price × price factor of bond) + accrued interest, S is the spot dirty (i.e. inclusive of accrued interest) price of the bond, I is the present value of coupons received prior to the futures maturity date and T is the number of days to the delivery (maturity) date.

The net initial investment (or borrowing) can be represented as $S - I$ since part of the cost of the bond can be met by borrowing against coupons receivable (those relating to ex-coupon dates prior to the futures maturity). F represents the invoice amount at delivery (futures maturity). So, $F - S + I$ represents the sum receivable (or payable) at delivery minus the initial investment. This return divided by the initial net investment is then annualised. For currencies other than sterling, the annualising term is likely to use 360 rather than 365 days (most notably, 360 days would be used for the US dollar and the Deutschmark).

Implied repos are not limited to bond futures. Any futures contract can be used for the investment or borrowing operation. An interesting implication is that any 2 futures contracts can be arbitraged against each other through the medium of their implied repos (so, for example, a stock index could be arbitraged against pork bellies). The futures contract offering the lower implied repo is used for borrowing, while the futures with the higher implied repo will provide the investment vehicle.

ACTIVITY 5.3

It is 31 March 1998. The cheapest-to-deliver bond is Treasury 2015 8%. Bond futures for June maturity are priced at 102–00. The price factor of Treasury 2015 8% is 0.89. Two- and three-month interest rates are 7.5% p.a. Treasury 2015 8% has just paid a coupon and is priced at £91.

(a) On what date is delivery into the futures contract likely to occur?
(b) What is the implied repo to that date?
(c) How could an arbitrage profit be made?

Answer

(a) The coupon yield on the bond is £8/£91 = 8.79% p.a. which exceeds the financing cost of 7.5% p.a. The bond will be delivered on the last business day in June since the seller can profit from holding the bond as long as possible.

(b) The implied repo is

$$[\{(102 \times 0.89) + 2\} - 91]/91 = 0.01956 = 1.956\%, \text{ i.e. } 7.824\% \text{ p.a.}$$

N.B. The £2 is the accrued interest at the end of June.

(c) Buy bonds and sell futures thereby investing at a risk free 7.824% p.a. The bonds are bought with money borrowed at 7.5% p.a. There is an arbitrage profit of 7.824 – 7.5 = 0.324% p.a. (This is a long cash-and-carry arbitrage.)

ACTIVITY 5.4

The following gilts prices were available at the close on 12 October:

| Treasury | 10% | 2003 | 98½ |
| Treasury | 12½% | 2003–05 | 116½ |

The price factors of these gilts in relation to the December and March long gilt futures contracts are:

		December	March
Treasury	10%	1.07818	1.07736
Treasury	12½%	1.27562	1.27286

The next coupon dates are 8 September and 21 November.
The offer rate was 15% p.a. for both two- and three-month money.

(a) Which of the 2 gilts is the cheapest to deliver against the December futures contract? What is the theoretical price of the December futures?

> (b) If the December and March gilt futures prices were 92.00 and 93.00 respectively, what December three-month interest rate futures price would have been implied?
> (c) What might be the effect of the seller's deliver option on prices of the gilt futures? How is this effect influenced by the current structure of interest rates and the length of time to delivery?
>
> (Based on the Securities Institute examination in Financial Futures and Options, December 1989, Question 23.)

Answer

(a) The current price of the Treasury 10% (inclusive of accrued interest) is:

$$98.5 + 0.932 = 99.432$$

and that of the Treasury $12\frac{1}{2}$% is:

$$116.5 + 4.863 = 121.363$$

Since the coupon yield is less than the financing cost, delivery would be on 1 December. On that date the cost of the gilts plus financing costs would be:

| Treasury | 10% | 101.475 |
| Treasury | $12\frac{1}{2}$% | 123.857 |

The invoicing amount for 1 December (per £100 nominal) would be:

(futures price (F) × price factor) + accrued interest

so the no-arbitrage conditions are:

Treasury   10% $(F \times 1.07818) + 2.301 = 101.475$

which implies a futures price (F) of 91.98:

Treasury $12\frac{1}{2}$% $(F \times 1.27562) + 0.342 = 123.857 - 6.276$

which implies a futures price (F) of 91.91 (6.276 is subtracted because 6.25 of accrued interest is received on 21 November and deposited for 10 days).

The Treasury $12\frac{1}{2}$% requires a lower futures price to provide a breakeven situation, and so the Treasury $12\frac{1}{2}$% is the cheapest to deliver and the futures price would be expected to be $91^{29}/_{32}$ (based on 91.91).

(b) The relationship between three-month sterling futures and the gilt futures straddle would be based upon an arbitrage involving buying/selling the cheapest to deliver via the futures and simultaneously borrowing/lending money at an interest rate locked in by three-month sterling futures. The invoice amounts for December and March respectively would be:

$$(92 \times 1.27562) + 0.342 = 117.7$$

and:

$$(93 \times 1.27286) + 3.467 = 121.843$$
$$121.843/117.7 = 1.0352$$

which implies an annualised interest rate of $3.52 \times 4 = 14.08\%$ and a three-month interest rate futures price of 85.92.

(c) The fact that the seller has the choice as to when and what to deliver renders selling more attractive and buying less attractive. This tends to depress futures prices below the levels implied by cash-and-carry arbitrage. This is particularly so when there is uncertainty as to which gilt will be cheapest to deliver – an uncertainty that is increased by longer periods to maturity of the futures contracts.

CASE STUDY – ORANGE COUNTY

An illustration of a repo strategy that went badly wrong is provided by Orange County, California. The county treasurer resigned in December 1994 with the announcement of losses of around $1.5 billion.

The treasurer had been involved in reverse repurchase agreements (repos) wherein securities owned by Orange County were sold to a dealer, while simultaneously an agreement was made to repurchase those securities at a specified price on a future date. Since both the sale and repurchase prices were agreed at the outset, this effectively provided Orange County with loans for the periods up to the predetermined repurchase dates at fixed interest rates.

Much of the money borrowed in this way was used to buy more securities, which themselves were sold under reverse repurchase agreements. As a result of this strategy for enhancing leverage, funds under management were raised from about $7.5 billion to more than $20 billion.

So long as such a strategy remains one of arbitrage, there should be yield enhancement from the arbitrage profits without a significantly raised interest rate exposure. If returns from the securities purchased exceed the borrowing costs under the reverse repurchase agreements, then there is a low risk enhancement to the returns on the net investment.

Problems arose when an element of speculation was allowed to enter the Orange County strategy. The arbitrage required the repos

> and the securities to match in terms of maturity dates. Such matching of maturities would have ensured similarity of the liabilities and assets, and would have avoided residual exposure on the maturity dates of the repos. Instead of such matching of maturities, the money borrowed was often used to buy bonds with distant maturity dates. Some of the borrowed money was even used for the purchase of inverse floating rate notes; such notes reduce their interest payments when market rates increase.
>
> The speculative dimension to the strategy provided an exposure to interest rate movements. A fall in interest rates would have raised the prices of the longer maturity securities (since there is an inverse relationship between interest rates and bond prices) and increased the returns on the inverse floating rate notes. However, interest rates rose, with the effect that the prices of the long maturity bonds fell and returns on the inverse floating rate notes declined.
>
> The crisis was brought to a head in December when banks refused to renew reverse repurchase agreements. Following the resignation of the treasurer, the portfolio was restructured and losses of $1.69 billion were realised.
>
> The Orange County case is sometimes cited as an example of the dangers of derivatives. However, it did not involve the use of derivative instruments. On the contrary, it demonstrated how highly leveraged exposure can be obtained without derivatives. Orange County was an example of speculation with money that was not risk capital, and provided a warning against overconfidence about the direction of market movements.

BASIS AND CONVERGENCE

The market price of a bond has 2 components: the clean price and the accrued interest. The latter refers to the right to interest receipts accumulated since the last coupon payment date. A purchaser of a bond realises the interest receipts that accumulated while the seller was holding the bond. The price paid for the bond will include compensation for the accrued interest unrealised by the seller. The remainder of the price is known as the clean price.

Division of the clean price, per £100 nominal, by the price factor renders the price comparable with the futures price. The difference between the price thus obtained and the futures price is known as the basis. In the case of the cheapest-to-deliver bond, basis is determined by the difference between the yield on the bond and the interest paid (or forgone) on the money required to finance the purchase of the bond. Basis converges to zero as the maturity date of the futures contract is approached. As maturity is approached, the period over which interest is paid and received shortens, and hence the monetary value of the interest differential declines towards zero.

Suppose that it is 2 October and a December futures contract has been sold as part of a cash-and-carry arbitrage operation. The cost of financing the holding of the bond exceeds the running yield obtained from the bond. This implies that the arbitrager will choose to deliver (the seller chooses the delivery date) at the earliest possible date (1 December) since there is a net loss to be expected from holding the bond after that date. It also implies that the futures price is at a premium to the spot price.

If the clean price of the cheapest-to-deliver bond is 121–00 and the price factor is 1.1 while the futures price is 112–00, then basis is obtained as follows:

$$\text{Basis} = \frac{121}{1.1} - 112 = -2$$

Figure 5.1 illustrates the expected erosion of the basis over time.

The fact that basis is expected to change over time means that the price that a hedger seeks to guarantee may differ from the spot price at the time of taking out the futures contracts. The greater the time lapse between agreeing the contracts and closing out, the higher will be the expected guaranteed price. Closing out soon after 2 October tends to provide an effective price close to the 2 October spot price, whereas closing out shortly before 1 December gives a price close to the futures price at which the contract was agreed.

If the risk being hedged occurs halfway between the present and the maturity date, the locked-in price will be the average of the present spot price and the price implied by the futures price. If it occurs after only a quarter of the time has elapsed, the price guaranteed would equal three-

FIGURE 5.1 Erosion of basis over time

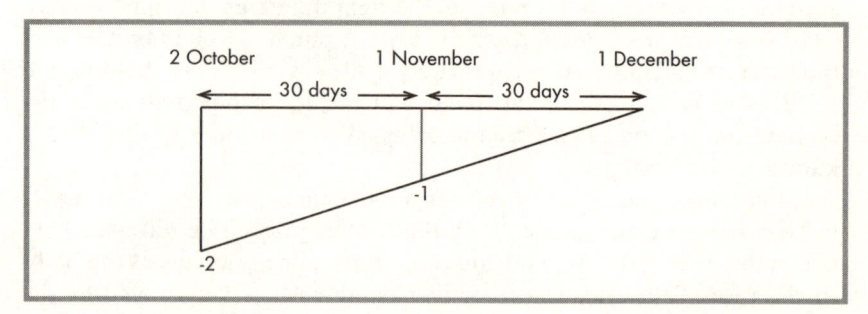

quarters of the initial spot price plus a quarter of the price implied by the futures price, and so on.

A holder of a futures contract may hold it to maturity. By so doing, he guarantees being able to buy or sell the cheapest-to-deliver bond at the price implied by the price of the futures contract bought or sold. In most cases, contracts are not held to maturity. This might be because the risk being hedged does not fall in a delivery month or because the bond (or other instrument) being hedged is not the cheapest-to-deliver bond.

Cash flows

It is useful to consider what types of cash flow might be involved in producing an effective price of the cheapest-to-deliver bond. Consider 2 extreme possibilities. First, suppose that the futures price corresponds to the expected price and that expectations prove to be correct. In such a case, the sum paid for the bond will change over time, while the futures price remains unchanged.

Second, suppose that the spot price remains constant. Whenever the contract is closed out, the same price is paid for the bonds. However, the futures price moves towards the spot price at a constant rate over time, becoming equal to it at maturity (the constancy of the rate depends upon financing costs remaining unchanged). This involves the payment (or receipt) of variation margin spread evenly over time. The spot price plus variation margin paid (or received) equals the price implied by the original spot and futures prices, i.e. the price that lies between the initial spot and futures prices, and which draws closer to the futures price as the maturity (delivery) date of the contract is approached. So if the contract were held to maturity, for example, the difference between the initial futures price and the unchanged spot price would have been paid (or received) in the form of variation margin.

Basis risk

As mentioned above, basis – the difference between the futures price and the adjusted spot price (clean spot price divided by the price factor) – reflects the financing cost relative to the coupon yield on the bond. A change in the interest rate on money borrowed to finance the purchase of a bond in cash-and-carry arbitrage would alter the basis. Such a change in basis introduces a degree of imperfection into the hedge, departing from the profile suggested by Figure 5.1. This possibility is known as basis risk. Fortunately, basis risk is likely to be low when the cheapest-to-deliver bond is being hedged. As the characteristics of the instrument being hedged diverge further and further from those of the cheapest deliverable bond, basis risk progressively increases. To the basis risk arising from the possibility of changes in financing costs must be added the basis risk from possible changes in the relative prices of the cheapest-to-deliver bond and the instrument being hedged. The greater the difference between the cheapest deliverable bond and the bond (or other instrument) being hedged, the greater the basis risk arising from this latter source. When basis risk is so large that there is not a close relationship between changes in the futures price and changes in the price of the instrument being hedged, the futures contract does not provide a suitable means of hedging.

CONCLUSIONS

Unlike the short-term interest rate futures contracts, long-term interest rate futures involve financial instruments that can be held and carried. These instruments are government bonds. The carryable nature of government bonds enables cash-and-carry arbitrage to operate as a pricing mechanism. The futures price should be such that there is no profit available from buying government bonds and simultaneously guaranteeing future selling prices by selling futures (or from selling bonds and buying futures).

There are many different government bonds, but it is necessary to have just one futures price (different futures for different bonds would entail liquidity problems). One solution to this apparent dilemma would be to have just one bond that could be delivered when a futures contract matured. This could entail the risk of cornering. Cornering occurs when a single entity buys futures and simultaneously acquires a substantial proportion of the deliverable asset. Sellers of futures are forced to buy the asset from the entity in order to deliver it to that same entity through futures contracts. That entity is able to profit from forcing up asset and futures prices.

The risk of cornering is reduced (probably eliminated) by allowing a number of different government bonds to be delivered against futures contracts. Since market prices will vary among bonds while there is just one futures price, there is a need to adjust the futures price so that the sum paid and received upon delivery reflects the market value of the bond that is delivered. This is achieved by multiplying the futures settlement price by a price factor that is based upon the specific characteristics of the delivered bond. Each bond will have its own price factor which is used for the calculation of invoice amounts for delivered bonds. Futures exchanges publish the price factors.

It will nevertheless be the case that one bond is more likely to be delivered than other bonds on the grounds of its invoice amount relative to its market price being the most favourable. This is known as the cheapest-to-deliver or cheapest deliverable bond. Market changes, such as a relative rise in the market price of a cheapest-to-deliver bond, can cause another bond to take over the role of cheapest-to-deliver.

Since the cheapest-to-deliver bond tends to be used in cash-and-carry arbitrage, the behaviour of the futures price often reflects that of the cheapest-to-deliver bond. The futures price tends to behave as if it relates to that specific bond. In consequence, the easiest bond to hedge using futures is the cheapest to deliver. When hedging other bonds, the hedge ratio needs to take account of the volatility of the hedged bond relative to the volatility of the cheapest-to-deliver bond. Volatility is measured by perturbation, a popular variant of which is the price value of a basis point. The calculation of volatility frequently involves duration.

These matters are developed in the next chapter.

Further reading

Material on bonds and bond futures can be found in:

David A. Dubofsky, *Options and Financial Futures* (McGraw-Hill, Singapore, 1992), Chapters 15 and 17.

Other sources on bond futures include:

Brian A. Eales, *Financial Risk Management* (McGraw-Hill, Maidenhead, 1995), Chapter 7.

Franklin R. Edwards and Cindy W. Ma, *Futures and Options* (McGraw-Hill, Maidenhead, 1992).

APPENDIX 5.1: DISCOUNTING CASH FLOWS

A sum of money received (or paid) in the present is worth more than the same sum received in the future. One explanation for this runs in terms of the fact that money can earn interest. A unit of money received now is worth more than the same unit received one year from now because it can earn interest over the year. If the interest rate is 10% p.a., then receipts in the present are worth 10% more than identical receipts one year hence.

To render a future cash flow comparable with a current one, the future sum is discounted. This involves dividing the future sum by 1 + the (decimalised) rate of interest. In the case of a receipt of S one year hence when the interest rate is 10%, the present value, PV, is given by:

$$PV = S/(1.1)$$

More generally:

$$PV = S/(1 + i)$$

where i is the decimalised rate of interest.

If the cash flow is to occur 2 years from now, then (assuming a rate of interest of 10% p.a.) because of compound interest, an identical sum in the present is worth 21% more. The present value would be:

$$PV = S/(1.1)^2 = S/(1.21)$$

More generally:

$$PV = S/(1 + i)^2$$

Correspondingly, the present value of a sum 3 years hence is $S/(1 + i)^3$, 4 years hence $S/(1 + i)^4$, and so on. It follows that the present value of a future stream of cash flows is:

$$PV = S/(1 + i) + S(1 + i)^2 + S/(1 + i)^3 + \ldots + S/(1 + i)^n$$

where the final receipt (or payment) occurs n years from the present. This can be more formally expressed as:

$$PV = \sum_{k=1}^{n} S/(1 + i)^k$$

which states that the present value equals the sum of the discounted cash flows (the cash flow amounting to S at the end of each year) relating to the next n years.

The time period may not necessarily be a year. If it is not, then an adjustment is required to the interest rate. For example, for six-monthly cash flows an interest rate of 10% p.a. would need to be expressed as a rate of 5%.

The cash flow may not be the same at the end of each time period, in which case the equation becomes:

$$PV = S_1/(1 + i) + S_2/(1 + i)^2 + S_3/(1 + i)^3 + \ldots + S_n/(1 + i)n$$

or:

$$PV = \sum_{k=1}^{n} S_k/(1 + i)^k$$

where $S_1, S_2, S_3, \ldots, S_n$ are the cash flows at the end of periods 1, 2, 3, . . . , n, respectively. There may also be a different interest rate (rate of discount) for each time period.

USING FUTURES IN FUND MANAGEMENT   6

INTRODUCTION

Previous chapters have considered how stock index and government bond futures can be used to hedge portfolios. Such hedging constitutes a major use for futures in fund management.

It has been seen that hedging involves taking a futures position that is opposite to the position at risk. To hedge against a fall in the value of a portfolio, futures are sold. In the event of a fall in asset prices, the short position in futures provides a profit that offsets the loss on the portfolio. The futures position can be closed out by buying futures at a lower price than that at which they were sold, thereby realising a profit.

Anticipatory hedging seeks compensation for a rise in share or bond prices. A fund manager intending to buy securities in the future, with cash expected to be received in the future, would be disadvantaged by a rise in asset prices. A prospective rise could be hedged by buying futures. In the event of share or bond prices rising, there should be a corresponding rise in futures prices. Futures could be closed out by selling at a price that is higher than the price at which they were bought. So there would be a futures profit to offset the increased cost of acquiring the securities.

The chapter begins by addressing the issue of hedge design, that is the determination of the appropriate number of futures contracts to use for a hedge. This involves deriving hedge ratios. The issue is considered for stock index futures and bond futures separately.

The chapter goes on to explain why fully hedged portfolios should exhibit the characteristics of a risk free instrument, such as a treasury bill. This outcome should be expected since a completely hedged portfolio is risk free, and arbitrage would tend to ensure that all assets of zero risk have the same expected rate of return. Again the analysis considers equity portfolios and bond portfolios separately.

Bond portfolio immunisation is considered next. This is a sophisticated form of hedging. It seeks to hedge against interest rate risk not from the perspective of the present, but from the perspective of one or more points of time in the future. It seeks to ensure that the cash flows from a bond portfolio match the cash flows required by the liabilities to be funded by the bond portfolio. For example, the desire may be to ensure that the cash flows received from the portfolio correspond to a series of future annuity payments. Immunisation pays attention not only to the effects of interest rate changes on the capital value of bonds, but also to the effects of interest rate changes on the returns obtainable from the reinvestment of coupons.

Bond futures arbitrage as a means of enhancing bond portfolio returns is considered next. The role of cash and carry arbitrage in the pricing of bond futures was described in Chapter 5. To the extent that the manager of a bond portfolio is able to take advantage of arbitrage opportunities, the profits from such arbitrage add to the returns of the portfolio. A bond portfolio manager has an advantage in relation to short cash and carry arbitrage. The fund manager may not need to take a short position in bonds, instead bonds already held in the portfolio might be sold (in this case the operation would be known as quasi-arbitrage).

The chapter ends with a consideration of how stock index and bond futures can be used to expedite asset reallocation. Sometimes the switch between asset classes, such as equities and bonds, needs to be undertaken very quickly. This may be because the switch is to be only temporary, or because market conditions are expected to change rapidly. A switch, for example from equities to bonds, can be expedited by means of a short position in stock index futures to eliminate the equity exposure and a long position in bond futures to create the exposure to bonds. If the switch is other than very temporary the fund manager may then take time to sell shares and buy bonds, unwinding the futures positions as the exposures are eliminated and created by transactions in shares and bonds. It is possible to transact in futures more quickly than in shares and bonds. Also this use of futures allows fund managers to take time over the decisions as to which shares to sell and which bonds to buy.

HEDGE DESIGN – EQUITY PORTFOLIOS

Hedge ratios become necessary when the volatility of the futures contract is likely to differ from that of the instrument to be hedged. If the instrument to be hedged shows relatively large variations, then it is appropriate to use more futures contracts than in the case of a more stable instrument. It is unlikely that a portfolio of stocks, for which hedging is required, precisely corresponds to the composition of a stock index. It is thus probable that it will show more or less volatility than the index.

The beta factor of a stock is a measure of the extent to which it moves in line with stock prices in general. A balanced portfolio is likely to have a beta factor of about 1. A stock with only half the movement of the market as a whole would have a factor of 0.5 while one with double the degree of change has a factor of 2. The beta factor of a portfolio of stocks is the weighted average of the beta factors of the stocks that constitute the portfolio.

If the calculation indicates a beta factor of 1.2, then the portfolio tends to change by 20 per cent more than the stock index. Hedging the portfolio would require the value of the stock index futures contracts used to exceed the portfolio value by 20 per cent. The relatively large losses (or profits) arising from the high volatility require correspondingly large offsetting profits (or losses) from futures contracts, and this necessitates a relatively large number of futures contracts.

ACTIVITY 6.1

On the basis of FTSE 100 futures contracts being priced at £25 per index point, how could a fund manager hedge the following portfolio against price falls when the index is 6000?

Stock	Stock price	Number of shares held	Stock beta
Cherwell Water	100p	200,000	0.6
Cave Construction	150p	100,000	1.4
St. Clements Inns	50p	500,000	0.8
EAP Services	200p	100,000	1.2

Answer
The market exposure of the portfolio is calculated as follows:

£200,000 × 0.6 = £120,000
£150,000 × 1.4 = £210,000
£250,000 × 0.8 = £200,000
£200,000 × 1.2 = £240,000
　　　　　　　　　£770,000

The market exposure of a futures contract is calculated as:

6,000 × £25 = £150,000

118 • USING FUTURES IN FUND MANAGEMENT

The fund manager should sell

£770,000/£150,000 = 5.13 *futures contracts.*

Since contracts are indivisible, the number to be sold would be 5.

ACTIVITY 6.2

Question
On 1 October a portfolio manager holds the following stocks. The number of shares, prices, and the betas are as follows:

Stock	Shares	Price	Beta
Honeywell	4,000	62⅝	1.20
Deere	8,310	24½	1.05
MCA	4,300	47⅞	0.95
K mart	7,500	32⅛	1.15

The portfolio will be liquidated on 30 November. The portfolio manager believes that the market will rally during October and November and would like to increase the beta to 1.3. The December S & P 500 futures price is 373. Construct a transaction that will increase the beta to 1.3. (The futures contract size is $250 per index point.)

Answer
Value of the portfolio

$\quad\quad$ 4,000 × 62.625
+ $\quad$ 8,310 × 24.5
+ $\quad$ 4,300 × 47.875
+ $\quad$ 7,500 × 32.125
$\quad\quad$ = $900,895

Market exposure of the portfolio

$\quad\quad$ (4,000 × 62.625 × 1.2)
+ $\quad$ (8,310 × 24.5 × 1.05)
+ $\quad$ (4,300 × 47.875 × 0.95)
+ $\quad$ (7,500 × 32.125 × 1.15)
$\quad\quad$ = $987,022.25

Portfolio beta = $987,022.25/$900,895 = 1.096
Additional beta required = 0.204

This amounts to additional market exposure of:

$900,895 × 0.204 = $183,782.58

Each futures contract provides an exposure of:

373 × $250 = $93,250.

So the number of futures contracts to be bought is:

$183,782.58/$93,250 = 1.97

which approximates to 2 contracts.

HEDGE DESIGN – BOND PORTFOLIOS

The hedger must decide upon the number of contracts required to accomplish the desired hedge. This calculation is simplest when hedging the cheapest-to-deliver bond:

$$\text{Number of contracts} = \frac{\text{Nominal value of position}}{\text{Nominal value of a contract}} \times \text{Price factor}$$

The multiplication by the price factor is necessary to adjust for the price difference between the cheapest-to-deliver bond and the notional bond on which the futures is based. A high coupon yield bond has a higher value to be hedged than a low coupon yield bond and will require a correspondingly larger number of contracts for the hedging (this difference will be greater the more distant are the maturity dates of the bonds).

Suppose that for the December 19XX contract month the cheapest-to-deliver gilt was the Exchequer 12½% 2010, whose price factor was 1.2. If the hedger wished to hedge £10 million nominal of this gilt, the requisite number of contracts would have been calculated thus:

$$\text{Number of contracts} = \frac{£10,000,000}{£50,000} \times 1.2 = 240$$

The hedger would have used 240 gilt futures contracts to hedge the position.

When hedging bonds other than the cheapest to deliver, account must be taken of the relative volatility of the bonds. Relative volatility can be measured in terms of the money value of a (say) 1% yield change per £100 nominal. If the bond being hedged is more volatile than the cheapest to

120 • USING FUTURES IN FUND MANAGEMENT

deliver, a correspondingly greater number of contracts will be required for the hedge (and vice versa for less volatile bonds). In this way, the larger price movements of relatively volatile bonds are handled. The formula becomes as follows:

$$\text{Number of contracts} = \frac{\text{Nominal value of position}}{\text{Nominal value of a contract}} \times \frac{\text{Price factor of}}{\text{cheapest to deliver}} \times \text{Relative volatility}$$

Thus, if the money value of a 1% yield change per £100 nominal were £5 for the gilt being hedged and £3.50 for the cheapest-to-deliver gilt, then the number of contracts necessary to hedge £10 million nominal of the gilts, in an example parallel to the previous one, would be as follows:

$$\text{Number of contracts} = \frac{£10,000,000}{£50,000} \times 1.2 \times \frac{5}{3.5} = 342.86$$

The appropriate number of gilt futures contracts is 342. A large number of futures contracts is necessary so that the profits/losses on futures succeed in offsetting the relatively large losses/profits on the gilt being hedged. Without adjusting for relative volatility, only £3.50 of every £5 price change would be offset.

Fixed interest securities other than government bonds can be hedged with government bond futures; however, it must be borne in mind that the more dissimilar are the cheapest-to-deliver bond and the instrument being hedged, the less effective is the hedge likely to be.

The definition of volatility used above is known as perturbation. This uses the impact of a specific interest rate change (e.g. 1%) on the price of the bond to be hedged and the cheapest deliverable. A frequently used interest rate change is the basis point (0.01%), in which case perturbation is alternatively referred to as the price value of a basis point (or PVBP).

The duration of a bond is a measure of the sensitivity of the price of the bond to changes in the rate of interest. To be more specific, duration is the relationship between the proportionate (or percentage) change in the value of the bond and the proportionate (percentage) change in $(1 + r)$ that caused it, where r is the redemption yield. Although the percentage change in $(1 + r)$ is closely related to the change in the percentage rate of interest, the two are not identical.

The following expression might be used to convert duration into a form approximating to perturbation (volatility).

$$\frac{1}{1 + \text{Redemption yield of bond}} \times \text{Price of bond}$$

The first term in this expression effectively changes the formulation:

$$\frac{\text{Proportionate change in price}}{\text{Proportionate change in } (1 + r)} \ (= \text{Duration})$$

into:

$$\frac{\text{Proportionate change in price}}{\text{Proportionate change in } (1+r)}$$

since it involves dividing duration by $(1 + r)$.

The second term in the expression converts proportionate changes in price into absolute changes in price. In these ways, duration is turned into the expression:

$$\frac{\text{Change in price}}{\text{Change in } (1+r)} \; (= \text{Perturbation})$$

This is expressed algebraically as:

$$\frac{\Delta P}{P} \times P = \Delta P \text{ (where } \Delta \text{ means 'change in')}$$

$$\frac{\Delta (1+r)}{(1+r)} \times (1+r) = \Delta(1+r) = \Delta r$$

Using duration to compute perturbation (or PVBP) is attractive since duration can be calculated easily and accurately, whereas direct estimates of perturbation (or PVBP) may be unreliable.

Relative perturbation (relative volatility) is expressed as:

$$\frac{1 + \text{Redemption yield of cheapest to deliver}}{1 + \text{Redemption yield of hedged bond}} \times \frac{\text{Price of hedged bond}}{\text{Price of cheapest to deliver}}$$

$$\times \frac{\text{Duration of hedged bond}}{\text{Duration of cheapest to deliver}}$$

ACTIVITY 6.3

An insurance company buys £5 million nominal of Treasury 11% 2007. This gilt has a price factor of 1.205, a duration of 6.1 years, a redemption yield of 12% p.a. and a price of £95. The cheapest to deliver gilt is Exchequer 10% 2005 which has a price factor of 1.11, a duration of 5.4 years, a redemption yield of 11⅞% p.a., and a price of £93. Suggest a hedging strategy.

Answer
Number of futures contracts to be sold

$$= \frac{£5,000,000}{£50,000} \times 1.11 \times \textit{relative volatility}$$

Relative volatility

$$= \frac{6.1}{5.4} \times \frac{95}{93} \times \frac{1.11875}{1.12} = 1.1526$$

So the number of futures contracts to be sold

$$= \frac{£5,000,000}{£50,000} \times 1.11 \times 1.1526$$

$$= 100 \times 1.11 \times 1.1526 = 127.94$$

Either 127 or 128 gilt futures contracts should be sold to hedge the holding of Treasury 11% 2007.

ACTIVITY 6.4

A fund manager has a portfolio of gilts with a nominal value of £5 million and a market value of £6 million. The duration of the portfolio is 10 years. The cheapest to deliver gilt has a price of £130, a price factor of 1.2 and a duration of 12 years. Ten- and twelve-year interest rates are both 8% p.a. How could the fund manager reduce the volatility of the portfolio of gilts as closely as possible to zero?

Answer

First calculate relative volatility:

$$\frac{10}{12} \times \frac{120}{130} \times \frac{1.08}{1.08} = 0.7692$$

(Note that £120 arises from £100 × £6m/£5m)

The number of gilt futures contracts to be sold is then given as:

$$\frac{£5,000,000}{£50,000} \times 1.2 \times .7692 = 92.3$$

Since it is not possible to trade in fractions of contracts the fund manager would sell 92 gilt futures contracts.

DURATION

Bonds and their valuation

The calculation of duration uses the principles of bond pricing. Bonds are fixed interest securities. The typical bond pays a constant sum to its holder at regular intervals (normally, annually or semi-annually). Bonds may be issued by governments (in some countries, government bonds are alternatively known as gilt-edged securities, or gilts), by private companies (in which case they may or may not be secured against assets of the company), or by financial institutions (which may be quasi-governmental, such as the World Bank).

A straight bond pays a fixed coupon at regular intervals over its life and then repays the initial issue price at the end of its life (alternatively known as its maturity date). Bonds come in many varieties. Some of the more important variations include irredeemable bonds, which have no maturity date but may simply continue to pay the coupon forever, index-linked bonds, which relate the coupon and principal to a measure of the price level, and floating rate notes, whose coupon payments vary in line with interest rates. The following exposition will concentrate on straight bonds.

As with other financial investments, bond prices are based on the present value of expected future cash flows. (Readers unfamiliar with the principles of discounting cash flows may find it useful to read Appendix 5.1 at this point.) The general formula for calculating a bond price is:

$$P = C/(1 + r) + C/(1 + r)^2 + \ldots + C/(1 + r)^n + B/(1 + r)^n$$

or

$$P = C \sum_{k=1}^{n} 1/(1 + r)^k + B/(1 + r)^n$$

where P is the fair price of the bond (strictly speaking, its dirty price, which includes accrued interest), C is the regular coupon payment per period, B is the nominal value to be paid to the bondholder at redemption, r is the rate of discount per period, and n is the number of periods remaining to redemption.

An important simplification that has been made in the above equation is the use of the same rate of discount for all the future cash flows. This assumes that interest rates are the same irrespective of the term of the investment (i.e. that the yield curve is flat). When valuing a bond, an investment analyst would use a different rate of discount for each cash flow in order to take account of the fact that different maturities have different interest rates.

Interest rates are not the only determinants of discount rates. Bonds with relatively high default risk need to yield a high expected rate of return to compensate for the risk. The rate of discount might be regarded as the required rate of return on a bond. High risk entails a high required rate of return and hence a high discount rate. It follows that for any particular stream of expected cash flows, high-risk bonds would have lower prices than low-risk bonds.

Although rates of discount vary according to the time to the receipt of a cash flow, it is possible to calculate a single rate of discount that would equate all future cash flows to the current price of the bond (this would be a form of average of the discount rates). This single discount rate is known as the redemption yield, or yield to maturity, of the bond. The redemption yield indicates the average annual return to be received by an investor holding the bond to maturity.

A bond will have a nominal or par value. This is the sum repayable at maturity and would normally be close to the initial sale price of the bond. Bond prices are often quoted in terms of units of currency per 100 nominal (e.g. dollars per $100 nominal). So, if a bond is priced at $96 per $100 par (nominal), $100,000 nominal of that bond would be valued at $96,000.

Bond prices, like the prices of other securities, are determined by supply and demand on the part of investors and borrowers. The primary market is the market in which issuers of bonds (i.e. borrowers) sell new bonds. The secondary market is the market in which existing bonds are bought and sold. The existence of the secondary market means that the buyers of bonds can get their money back (by selling their bonds) before the maturity dates of the bonds. This facility makes the purchase of bonds more attractive.

The market participants need to be able to ascertain the appropriate prices of bonds. This is done by means of the discounted cash flow model. A straight bond has a series of known future cash flows in the form of annual, or semi-annual, coupon payments plus the repayment of principal at maturity. These future cash flows are discounted in order to ascertain their present value, which is the fair price of the bond. The rate of discount will depend upon the perceived riskiness of the bond (risk of default by the issuer). Government bonds are frequently seen as being virtually riskless and hence their discount rates (required rates of return) are relatively low. So for a particular stream of cash flows, the prices of such low risk bonds would be relatively high. Corporate bonds vary in their levels of riskiness. Moody's and Standard and Poor's class bonds according to their riskiness, and those rated as relatively risky will have high required rates of return and hence high rates of discount. The riskiest bonds, known as junk bonds, have very high rates of discount and hence sell at relatively low prices.

Another factor affecting discount rates is the timing of the cash flow. If interest rates for distant maturities differ from interest rates for nearby maturities, then different rates of discount are applicable to cash flows anticipated at different points in time.

The most common type of bond is a straight bond with semi-annual coupon payments. Using the discounted cash flow model to value such a bond produces:

$$P = C/(1 + 0.5r_1) + C/(1 + 0.5r_2)^2 + C/(1 + 0.5r_3)^3 + \ldots + C/(1 + 0.5r_{2T})^{2T} + B/(1 + 0.5r_{2T})^{2T}$$

where P is the fair value of the bond, C is the half-yearly coupon payment, T is the number of years to maturity, r_1 is the interest rate applicable to six-month assets, r_2 the interest rate for one-year money, r_3 the interest rate on securities with an 18-month maturity, and so on. B is the principal sum (nominal value) that is repayable at maturity. The bond to which the equation relates pays out its next coupon in 6 months from the present.

The fair price of the bond is inversely related to interest rates. Higher interest rates (higher rates of discount) produce lower bond prices. If the bond has no maturity date (i.e. it is irredeemable) and if the yield curve is flat so that the discount rate is the same for all maturities, then:

$P = C/r$

The bond price is inversely proportional to the rate of discount (and rate of interest). For bonds with maturity dates, the inverse relationship is less than proportional. The inverse relationship weakens as the maturity becomes shorter. A bond whose maturity date is imminent will show no price sensitivity to interest rate changes.

Calculating bond duration

Beta is a measure of stock price volatility. The corresponding measure of volatility for fixed income investments such as bonds is modified duration. Modified duration is the percentage change in the bond price as a result of a particular change in the rate of interest (redemption yield). The computation of modified duration begins with the calculation of Macauley's duration (frequently referred to simply as duration).

Macauley's duration is the average period of time to the receipt of cash flows. Each time period (to the receipt of a cash flow) is weighted by the proportional contribution of that cash flow to the price of the bond. The calculation of Macauley's duration is illustrated by Example 6.1. Macauley's duration is transformed into modified duration by means of dividing it by $(1 + r/n)$, where r is the rate of interest (redemption yield) and n is the number of coupon payments per year:

Modified duration = duration/$(1 + r/n)$

$\%\Delta p$ = −modified duration × Δr

where $\%\Delta p$ is the percentage change in the bond price and Δr is the change in the redemption yield.

Duration (and hence modified duration) tends to rise with increasing maturity of the bond. This makes intuitive sense since distant cash flows are more affected by changes in the rate of discount, and hence rates of interest (low coupon bonds also exhibit relatively high sensitivity to discount rate changes since the repayment of principal at maturity provides a

Example 6.1

A bond with a final maturity of 2 years pays a coupon of £6 six monthly. The yield curve is flat at an interest rate of 10% p.a.
  The price of the bond is:

$$\frac{£6}{(1.05)} + \frac{£6}{(1.05)^2} + \frac{£6}{(1.05)^3} + \frac{£106}{(1.05)^4}$$

= £103.54 (= £5.71 + £5.44 + £5.18 + £87.21)

Duration equals:

$$\left(\frac{5.71}{103.54}\right) 0.5 + \left(\frac{5.44}{103.54}\right) + \left(\frac{5.18}{103.54}\right) 1.5 + \left(\frac{87.21}{103.54}\right) 2$$

= 0.028 + 0.053 + 0.075 + 1.685 = 1.841 years

---

high proportion of the present value of the future cash flows). So bond volatility, and hence bond risk, increases with lengthening bond maturity.

A coupon-paying bond does not have a single maturity date. Each coupon payment, as well as the final redemption of principal, provides a maturity date. A coupon-paying bond can be regarded as a cluster of pure discount bonds (bonds with no coupon but which simply pay a sum at maturity) with maturities corresponding to the coupon payment dates, in addition to the date on which redemption of principal is to take place. Duration is a measure of the average of these maturities; it is a weighted average, where the weighting is based on the contribution of each receipt of money to the current (dirty) price of the bond. So if a coupon, c, to be received in exactly 1 year from now has a present value of $V_1 = c/(1 + r)$, then its proportionate contribution to the fair price of the bond is V_1/P, where P represents the fair price of the bond. Its contribution to average maturity (duration) is correspondingly $(V_1/P) \times 1$ year. Likewise, a coupon receipt due 2 years hence has a present value of $V_2 = c/(1 + r)^2$ and contributes $(V_2/P) \times 2$ years to the duration of the bond. The principal repayment, B, contributes $[(B/(1 + r)^T)/P] \times T$ years, where T is the period to final maturity.

The equation for the duration of a bond can be written as:

$$D = (c/P) \sum_{t=1}^{T} t/(1 + r)^t + (B/P)T/(1 + r)^T$$

so each maturity, $t = 1, t = 2, t = 3, \ldots, t = T$, contributes to duration with the contribution being based on the present value of the money receipts of that maturity as a proportion of the total of such present values (i.e. the fair price of the bond). The discount rate, r, is the yield to maturity (redemption yield) of the bond.

Duration can be used as a measure of interest rate risk. The present value equation is:

$$P = \sum_{t=1}^{T} c/(1 + r)^t + B/(1 + r)^T$$

Differentiating with respect to $(1 + r)$ gives:

$$dP/d(1 + r) = -c \sum_{t=1}^{T} t/(1 + r)^{t+1} - BT(1 + r)^{T+1}$$

Multiplying both sides by $(1 + r)$ gives:

$$(dP/P)/[d(1 + r)/(1 + r)] = -D$$

This means that (minus) duration is equal to the proportionate change in the bond price divided by the proportionate change in 1 + redemption yield. It is thus a measure of the responsiveness of bond prices to changes in redemption yields. As such, it is a measure of interest rate risk. The negative of duration might alternatively be interpreted as the elasticity of bond prices with respect to (1 +) yield to maturity. It is necessary to use the negative of duration since there is an inverse relationship between bond prices and redemption yields.

It is as a measure of interest rate risk that duration is most useful.

ACTIVITY 6.5

It is 24 November 1992. Treasury 12% 1994 (which has just paid a coupon) has a final maturity date of 24 May 1994. The yield curve is flat at 8% p.a. Calculate (a) the duration, and (b) the modified duration, of the gilt.

What capital gain or loss would arise from a holding of £1 million nominal of this gilt in the event of a ¼% p.a. fall in interest rates (throughout the length of the yield curve)? Comment on the accuracy of this estimate of capital gain or loss.

Answer
The price of the bond would be:

$B = £6/(1.04) + £6/(1.04)^2 + £106/(1.04)^3$
$= £5.77 + £5.55 + £94.23$
$= £105.55$

The duration of the bond would be:

$$D = \left(\frac{£5.77}{£105.55}\right) 0.5 + \left(\frac{£5.55}{£105.55}\right) + \left(\frac{£94.23}{£105.55}\right) 1.5$$

$= 0.0273 + 0.0526 + 1.3391 = 1.419$

= 1.42 years (to 2 decimal places)

The modified duration would be:

M = 1.419/1.04 = 1.3644
 = 1.36 years (to 2 decimal places)

The value of £1 million nominal of the gilt would be:

£1,000,000 × £105.55/£100 = £1,055,500

The capital gain would be calculated from:

% change in bond price = − modified duration × change in redemption yield
= − 1.36 × −0.25 = 0.34%

So the capital gain would be 0.0034 × £1,055,500 = £3,588.7. Hence, the new value of the bonds would be £1,055,500 + £3,588.7 = £1,059,088.7. It is to be noted that £6/(1.03875) + £6/(1.03875)^2 + £106/(1.03875)^3 = £5.7762 + £5.5607 + £94.5742 = £105.9111. Hence, according to the discount model the new value of the bonds would be £1,059,111. So the modified duration approach predicts the new value of the bonds very closely – the error is less than £23.

Modified duration does not provide a precisely accurate answer since it assumes a linear price-yield relationship, whereas the relationship is actually convex.

ACTIVITY 6.6

A gilt portfolio consists of £10 million nominal of a two-year gilt with an annual coupon of 12% and £5 million nominal of a five-year zero coupon. The interest rate is 10% and the yield curve is flat.

(a) What is the price of each gilt and the value of the portfolio?
(b) What is the duration of each gilt and of the portfolio?
(c) If the price, price factor and duration of the cheapest-to-deliver gilt are £120, 1.15 and 8 years respectively, how many gilt futures contracts should be sold to hedge this portfolio?

(Based on the Securities Institute examination in Financial Futures and Options, December 1992, Question 9.)

Answer
(a) The price of the two-year gilt (per £100 nominal) is £12/1.1 + £112/(1.1)^2 = £103.47.

The price of the five-year zero coupon bond (per £100 nominal) is £100/(1.1)^5 = £62.09.
So the total value of the portfolio is:
(£10 million × 1.0347) + (£5 million × 0.6209) = £13.45m

(b) The duration of the two-year gilt is
[(10.91/103.47) × 1] + [(92.56/103.47) × 2] = 1.89 years
[10.91 = 12/1.1 and 92.56 = 112/(1.1)^2]
The duration of the five-year zero coupon bond is 5.
The duration of the portfolio is:
[(10.347/13.45) × 1.89] + [(3.105/13.45) × 5] = 2.61 years.

(c) The requisite number of futures contracts is given by:

$$\frac{\text{Nominal value of portfolio}}{\text{Nominal value of a futures contract}} \times \frac{\text{Price factor}}{\text{of CTD}} \times \frac{\text{Duration of portfolio}}{\text{Duration of CTD}}$$

$$\times \frac{\text{Price of portfolio}}{\text{Price of CTD}}$$

$$\frac{£15 \text{ million}}{£0.05 \text{ million}} \times 1.15 \times \frac{2.61}{8} \times \frac{13.45}{15} \times \frac{100}{120} = 84.1$$

To the nearest whole number, the number of contracts is 84.

ACTIVITY 6.7

A corporate treasurer intends to issue a 20-year fixed rate bond for £50 million. The legal formalities are expected to take another 2 weeks. The treasurer wants to hedge against the possibility of a rise in interest rates prior to issue. Using modified duration, it has been estimated that the bond to be issued has a price value of a basis point (the effect of a one basis point change in the interest rate on the price of the bond per £100 nominal) of 0.09982 and that the cheapest-to-deliver bond has a price value of a basis point (PVBP) of 0.08754. The cheapest-to-deliver bond has a price factor of 1.0224.

How might the risk be hedged? What factors could reduce the effectiveness of the hedge?

Answer
The number of futures contracts to be sold is given by:

$$\frac{\text{Nominal value of hedged bonds}}{\text{Nominal value of a futures contract}} \times \frac{\text{Price factor}}{\text{of CTD}} \times \frac{\text{PVBP of hedged bonds}}{\text{PVBP of CTD}}$$

$$\frac{£50 \text{ million}}{£50,000} \times 1.0224 \times \frac{0.09982}{0.08754} = 1,165.8 \text{ contracts}$$

The hedger should sell either 1,165 or 1,166 contracts. The effectiveness of the hedge would be reduced by a change in the slope of the yield curve which would cause the hedged bonds and the cheapest-to-deliver bonds (and hence

> the futures) to experience unexpected differences in the extent of price changes. There is also the risk of a change in the relationship between the price of the cheapest to deliver and the futures price, so that there is an unexpected difference in the extent to which their prices move. These two sources of hedge imperfection constitute basis risk.

HEDGED EQUITY PORTFOLIOS AS SYNTHETIC TREASURY BILLS

The principles of financial economics suggest that if an asset is riskless, and it trades in an efficient market, it should yield the risk-free rate of return (specifically, the rate of return on the ultimate risk-free asset, the Treasury bill, although short-term deposits in banks with good credit ratings constitute a reasonable approximation to risk-free assets). It follows that if a stock portfolio is fully hedged, its expected rate of return should equal that on risk-free investments.

That this is so can be seen by considering the cash-and-carry operation. Long cash and carry involves buying a portfolio of stocks and simultaneously selling futures. The fair futures price is one where the financing cost of holding the stock portfolio is matched by the sum of the expected dividend yield and the capital gain guaranteed by the futures premium over spot. A corollary of this is that the return from the cash-and-carry transactions, which takes the form of dividend yield plus capital gain, equals the rate of interest on short-term deposits. Short-term deposits in banks of high credit rating might be regarded as risk-free assets.

A further implication is that the cash-and-carry operation can be used as a means of making risk-free investments, of for borrowing money at the risk-free rate. Long cash and carry involves an initial cash outflow and a subsequent cash inflow such that the risk-free rate of interest is earned. So long cash and carry is equivalent to a risk-free investment and is often referred to as a synthetic Treasury bill (the cash and carry is risk free because the clearing house guarantees that the futures contract will be honoured). Conversely, short cash and carry involves an initial cash inflow (from the sale of stock) and a subsequent cash outflow (repurchase of stock) such that there is a net loss equal to the short-term risk-free interest rate. In other words, short cash and carry is equivalent to a short-term borrowing.

It is only strictly correct to regard an investment (or borrowing) as equivalent to a long (or short) position in Treasury bills if it is truly risk free. It is unlikely that cash and carry with stock index futures is absolutely risk free; hence, the description of such an operation as a synthetic Treasury bill should be treated with caution.

HEDGED BOND PORTFOLIOS AS SYNTHETIC TREASURY BILLS

If the coupon yield on a bond exceeds the short-term rate of interest, then arbitrage based on buying bonds and simultaneously selling futures (cash-and-carry arbitrage) must involve a futures discount in order to offset the excess of coupon yield over the financing cost. As maturity of the futures approaches, the convergence of the futures and bond prices would involve the futures price rising relative to the bond price.

A futures hedge of a bond holding would entail a short futures position. A rise in the futures price would cause a loss from a short futures position. This loss would be equal to the difference between the futures price and the bond price (i.e. equal to the futures discount), and is therefore equal to the excess of the coupon yield over the interest rate.

It follows that the excess of the coupon yield over interest rate is offset by a loss equal to that excess. The result is that a bond that is fully hedged with futures would yield a return equal to short-term interest rates. In other words, it would yield a return identical to that on risk-free assets, which would be consistent with the risk-free nature of a fully hedged bond. Analogous reasoning can be used for the case in which the coupon yield on a bond is less than the short-term rate of interest.

BOND PORTFOLIO IMMUNISATION

Interest rate risk on bond portfolios may be reduced by the following means:

1. *Dedicated portfolios* The prospective cash flows from the assets held correspond to the future cash flow requirements in both amount and timing. For example, the future payments to pensioners from an annuity fund might be synchronised with the coupon and the redemption receipts from the bonds that constitute the fund. Such a dedicated portfolio is difficult to construct.
2. *Maturity matching* The maturities of the bonds in the portfolio match the times at which cash flows will be required. This avoids the price

risk from interest rate changes but is subject to reinvestment risk (the rate of interest on invested coupon receipts is uncertain).
3. *Duration matching* The modified duration of the assets matches the time at which a cash flow will be required. Bond price changes tend to offset variations in returns from reinvested coupons. So both the bond price risk of interest rate changes and the reinvestment risk are substantially reduced. Immunisation by duration matching is less effective if the slope of the yield curve changes. Not only is duration matching a very effective means of immunising a bond portfolio, it may also be the easiest. The ease of the strategy arises from the facility of using bond futures to achieve the requisite adjustment. Any discrepancy between the duration of the liabilities (prospective cash outflows) and the duration of the assets can be removed by taking an offsetting position in bond futures.

Price factors and the cheapest to deliver

Before the examination of the application of bond futures to the manipulation of the duration of a portfolio, the reader will be reminded of the concepts of price factors and the cheapest-to-deliver bond.

Price factors bring bonds on to a common basis with bond futures contracts. For example, in the case of LIFFE Long Gilt contracts, the futures price is based on a notional gilt with a 9 per cent coupon. By assuming a 9 per cent p.a. redemption yield the notional gilt is priced at £100. Gilts with other coupons will have different prices when the 9 per cent p.a. redemption yield is assumed. For example, a 12 per cent coupon gilt might have a value of £125. In that case the 12 per cent coupon gilt might be said to have a price factor of £125/£100 = 1.25. The use of price factors makes it possible for bonds with different coupons and maturities to be rendered comparable to one another and to the notional gilt on which the futures contract is based. (Note that the method of calculating price factors varies between exchanges; this example was intended merely as a means of providing an intuitive feel for the principles involved.)

The seller of a futures contract has the choice as to which bond to deliver. The receipts for the bond (the invoice amount) are based on the futures settlement price and the price factor of the bond. This invoice amount normally differs from the market price of the bond. The seller would choose to deliver the bond whose market price is furthest below the invoice amount, or least far above it. This is the cheapest-to-deliver bond.

The futures price would tend to reflect the price behaviour of the cheapest-to-deliver bond. This is because the relationship between the futures price and the price of the underlying bond is determined by cash and carry arbitrage. Long cash and carry arbitrage involves buying bonds and simultaneously selling futures. The bonds that would be chosen would be the cheapest to deliver. Thus the cash and carry arbitrage links the futures price with the price of the cheapest-to-deliver bond.

Adjusting portfolio duration with futures

The volatility of a bond portfolio may be measured as the change in portfolio value arising from a basis point change in yield. This can be obtained by multiplying the modified duration by the value of the portfolio and by 0.0001 (the decimal of 1 basis point). Since multiplying the modified duration by the yield change gives the percentage change in the value of the portfolio, further multiplying by the value of the portfolio provides the change in money terms (see Figure 6.1).

Suppose that the portfolio has a duration of 15 years, a redemption yield of 8 per cent p.a., a value of £10 million, and that coupons are semiannual. Then portfolio volatility can be calculated as:

$$\frac{15}{1.04} \times £10 \text{ m} \times 0.0001 = £14{,}423$$

(1.04 is used since the redemption yield has to be divided by the number of coupon payments per year). So an interest rate change of 0.01 per cent p.a. (1 basis point) is expected to result in the portfolio value changing by £14,423.

FIGURE 6.1   Bond portfolio immunisation using futures

Bond portfolio immunisation

Interest rate risk on bond portfolios may be reduced by means of duration matching. The modified duration of the portfolio matches the time at which the cash flow will be required. Bond futures can be used to achieve duration matching.

Volatilities
1. Measure the volatility of the portfolio
   = modified duration × portfolio value × 0.0001
   i.e. volatility is the change in portfolio value from one basis point change in yield.
2. Calculate portfolio volatility when modified duration is at the desired level.
   = desired modified duration × portfolio value × 0.0001.
3. Measure the volatility of a futures contract. This requires calculation of the volatility of the cheapest-to-deliver bond per £50,000 nominal (the size of the gilt futures contract) and division of this volatility by the price factor of the cheapest-to-deliver bond.
4. Divide the difference between volatilities 1 and 2 by volatility 3. This gives the number of bond futures contracts to be bought or sold.

134 ● **USING FUTURES IN FUND MANAGEMENT**

Suppose that the portfolio manager seeks to reduce the portfolio duration to ten years, then the desired volatility is given by:

$$\frac{10}{1.04} \times £10 \text{ m} \times 0.0001 = £9,615.$$

So portfolio volatility needs to be reduced by £14,423 − £9,615 = £4,808. The desired one-third reduction in duration entails a one-third reduction in volatility.

The next step is to measure the volatility of a futures contract. This entails calculating the volatility of the cheapest-to-deliver bond and then dividing by its price factor. Suppose that the cheapest-to-deliver has a duration of 12 years, a redemption yield of 8 per cent p.a., a price of £110 (i.e. £55,000 per £50,000 nominal), and pays coupons twice a year. Then for £50,000 nominal (the size of the long gilt futures contract):

$$\frac{12}{1.04} \times £55,000 \times 0.0001 = £63.46.$$

If the cheapest-to-deliver has a price factor of 0.9875, then the volatility of a futures contract is calculated as £63.46/0.9875 = £64.26. So, in order to reduce the portfolio volatility by £4,808 it is necessary to sell £4,808/£64.26 = 74.8 contracts. Since futures contracts are indivisible, either 74 or 75 contracts would be sold in order to reduce the portfolio duration from 15 to 10 years.

Such a reduction in portfolio duration could be seen as a partial hedge, and a bond portfolio manager seeking to fully hedge the portfolio could be regarded as aiming to achieve a duration of zero. Activity 6.8 provides an example of complete hedging.

ACTIVITY 6.8

A bank buys £10 million nominal of Treasury 12½ per cent 2012. This gilt has a price factor of 1.302615, a duration of 8.6 years, and a price of £96¾. This purchase is financed by the issue of certificates of deposit. The cheapest-to-deliver gilt is Exchequer 12 per cent 2010 whose price factor is 1.238401 with a duration of 8.3 years and a price of £95⁵⁄₁₆. Both gilts have a redemption yield of 13 per cent p.a. How might the holding of gilts be hedged (assuming that the certificates of deposit have negligible duration)?

Answer

$$\frac{£10,000,000}{£50,000} \times 1.238401 \times \frac{8.6}{8.3} \times \frac{96.75}{95.3125} = 260.469$$

The risk of a fall in gilt prices can be hedged by the sale of 260 or 261 gilt futures contracts. The reader may note that the calculation is based on *dividing the volatility of the gilt portfolio by the volatility of a futures contract, and the terms based on redemption yields cancel out since the redemption yields are equal.*

Some caveats

A bond portfolio manager using duration-based immunisation needs to be aware of the need for frequent rebalancing for three reasons. First, modified duration declines more slowly than term to maturity. So the passage of a year will reduce modified duration by less than a year. Modified duration would then exceed the investment horizon. Second, the price-yield relationship for bonds is convex. So modified duration changes as interest rates rise or fall. Third, changes in the slope of the yield curve will affect duration. Finally, when using futures, attention needs to be paid to the significance of interest on variation margin cash flows. There may be a need to take account of this by factoring down the number of futures contracts, either by tailing or by use of variation margin leverage.

BOND FUTURES ARBITRAGE AS A MEANS OF ENHANCING BOND PORTFOLIO RETURNS

For a fund manager with a portfolio of gilts or money market investments bond futures arbitrage presents a means of enhancing returns without significantly changing the characteristics of the gilt portfolio. Although it is unlikely that such arbitrage operations would dramatically increase bond portfolio returns, even a half percentage point increase in annual returns would be worth striving for.

The arbitrage processes

As with other assets that can be carried during the life of a futures contract bond futures prices tend to be determined by cash-and-carry arbitrage. Long cash and carry involves buying bonds whilst simultaneously selling bond futures. Short cash and carry (in its pure form) involves borrowing bonds and selling them whilst buying futures. The futures price should be such that there is no profit available from cash-and-carry arbitrage.

For there to be no arbitrage profits available from long cash and carry, the financing cost of holding bonds should be matched by the returns from holding the bonds in the form of coupon receipts plus capital gain (or loss) guaranteed by the futures premium (or discount) relative to the spot price of the bonds. Note that if the financing cost (based on short-term interest rates) exceeds the coupon yield there will be a futures premium over spot to yield a capital gain whereas if the financing cost is less than the coupon receipts a futures discount, providing a capital loss, should exist.

An absence of arbitrage profits in the case of short cash and carry requires that the interest receipts from short selling are precisely offset by losses in the form of coupon amounts payable to the entity from which the bonds were borrowed plus capital losses (or minus capital gains). One difficulty with short cash and carry, since it involves buying futures, is that the arbitrager has no control over which bond is delivered when the futures mature – it may not be the bond that was sold short. For this reason the influence of short cash and carry may be significantly weakened, but the following account will assume that short cash and carry occurs and is effective.

Price factors bring bonds on to a common basis with bond futures contracts. For example, in the case of LIFFE Gilt contracts, the futures price is based on a notional gilt with a 9% coupon. By assuming a 9% p.a. redemption yield the notional gilt is priced at £100. Gilts with other coupons will have different prices when the 9% p.a. redemption yield is assumed. For example, a 12% coupon gilt might have a value of £125. In that case the 12% coupon gilt might be said to have a price factor of £125/£100 = 1.25. The use of price factors makes it possible for bonds with different coupons and maturities to be rendered comparable to one another and to the notional gilt on which the futures contract is based. (Note that the method of calculating price factors varies between exchanges, this example was intended merely as a means of providing an intuitive feel for the principles involved.)

The seller of a futures contract has the choice as to which bond to deliver. The receipts for the bond (the invoice amount) are based on the futures settlement price and the price factor of the bond. This invoice amount normally differs from the market price of the bond. The seller would choose to deliver the bond whose market price is furthest below the invoice amount, or least far above it. This is the cheapest-to-deliver bond.

The futures price would tend to reflect the price behaviour of the cheapest-to-deliver bond. This is because the relationship between the futures price and the price of the underlying bond is determined by cash-and-carry arbitrage. Long cash-and-carry arbitrage involves buying bonds and simultaneously selling futures. The bonds that would be chosen would be the cheapest to deliver. Thus the cash-and-carry arbitrage links the futures price with the price of the cheapest-to-deliver bond.

The equations

In equation form the pricing relationship that tends to be established by cash-and-carry arbitrage can be expressed as:

either $F = (S - I)(1 + rt)$

or $F = S(1 + rt) - D$

where F = fair futures price
S = spot price of bond
I = present value of coupons receivable before the futures maturity date
D = future value of coupons receivable before the futures maturity data
r = short-term risk-free interest rate
t = period (in years) to the futures maturity date

In both equations by subtracting S from both sides it can be seen that the futures premium (or discount) relative to spot matches the difference between the financing cost and coupon yield. Thus:

$F - S = S.rt - I(1 + rt)$

and $F - S = S.rt - D$

where both D and $I(1 + rt)$ represent the future value of the coupon receipts.

The equations for futures pricing shown above are somewhat abstract and need to be amended in three ways to take account of reality. First, it has been implicitly assumed that there is no difference between the coupon payment date and the ex-coupon date, if there is a difference I and D refer to coupons relating to ex-coupon dates prior to the futures maturity but discounting (or interest accrual) is from the date of receipt of the coupon.

Second, it has been implicitly assumed that the bond has a price factor of 1, if such is not the case (and such wouild hardly ever be the case) F in the equations needs to be divided by the price factor. More precisely F net of accrued interest should be divided by the price factor of the bond in order to ascertain the futures price. Since S and F relate to sums actually paid and received they must include accrued interest (the rights to coupon payment between the last coupon payment date and the date on which the bond is bought and sold). The price factor involved would be that of the bond used which would normally be the cheapest to deliver. Note that since the bond normally used in cash-and-carry arbitrage would be the cheapest to deliver the behaviour of the futures price would tend to relate closely to that of the cheapest to deliver.

Third, transactions costs have been ignored. If bid–offer spreads are allowed for in both the bond market and the interest rates the result is a no-arbitrage band of futures prices rather than the unique fair futures price (the fair futures price is the price that would prevail in the absence of transactions costs). The no-arbitrage band can be described by the expression:

$$S_B(1 + r_B t) - D \leq F \leq S_o(1 + r_o t) - D$$

where
- S_b = spot bid price (dirty price, i.e. inclusive of accrued interest)
- S_o = spot offer price (dirty price)
- r_B = interest rate for period t (bid rate)
- r_o = interest rate for period t (offer rate)
- t = time to maturity of futures contract (in years)
- D = future value of coupons (relating to ex-coupon dates prior to the futures maturity date)
- F = futures price (multiplied by the price factor and inclusive of accrued interest)

Note that this no-arbitrage expression can be used for futures on any asset that can be carried during the life of the futures contract.

Arbitrage should operate to keep the futures price within the no-arbitrage band. If the futures price rises above the band long cash-and-carry arbitrage would tend to bring it back into the band. This would involve bonds being bought (the consequent upward pressure on bond prices would tend to raise the band) and futures being sold (thereby pushing futures prices down into the band). If the futures price falls below the band the underpriced futures should be bought and the bonds sold, in other words short cash-and-carry arbitrage should (at least in principle) take place. Short cash-and-carry arbitrage would tend to lower the no-arbitrage band (via reducing the spot bond price) and raise the futures price until it is again within the band.

It can be seen that futures prices do not slavishly follow spot prices. Futures prices can lead spot prices via cash-and-carry transactions. Furthermore within the no-arbitrage band futures prices can vary independently of spot prices.

The role of implicit options

The seller of bond futures contracts has choices relating to when to deliver during the delivery month and which bond to deliver. In effect this gives the futures seller long option positions, and the futures buyer has the corresponding short option positions. The seller of futures must, in some way, pay for the options and the buyer be paid. This is accomplished by a reduction in the bond futures price below the level that would otherwise pertain. In this way at delivery the futures seller receives a sum which is reduced by the value of the option premiums whilst the futures buyer receives payment for the options in the form of having to pay less for the bonds when they are delivered upon maturity of the futures contract.

The implications

Long cash-and-carry arbitrage can enhance the returns on a money market fund without significantly changing its nature. Buying gilts and simultaneously selling gilt futures constitutes a hedged position, with no net exposure to gilts. Such a hedged position would be expected to provide a return equal to money market rates, such as that on low risk deposits, plus the arbitrage profit. The arbitrage profit constitutes an addition to what would otherwise be received.

Short cash-and-carry arbitrage can add arbitrage profits to the returns on a bond portfolio without any fundamental changes in the characteristics of that portfolio. Selling gilts and simultaneously buying gilt futures maintains the exposure to gilts. The strategy can be expected to provide the return otherwise expected from the gilts plus an additional element in the form of the arbitrage profit.

ACTIVITY 6.9

It is 17 July 1998. The FTSE 100 stands at 6000. The cheapest-to-deliver gilt has a price of £125, a price factor of 1.1, and a duration of 11 years. A fund manager wants immediately to reallocate the equity market exposure of a £1m portfolio to the bond market without initially choosing which bonds to buy. If the equity portfolio has a beta of 1.2, how can the reallocation be carried out using futures?

Answer

To eliminate the equity market exposure FTSE 100 futures are sold. The market exposure of the equity portfolio is £1,000,000 × 1.2 = £1,200,000. Each futures contract has a market exposure of 6000 × £10 = £60,000. The number of FTSE 100 futures contracts that should be sold is

£1,200,000/£60,000 = 20.

£1 million would buy £1,000,000/1.25 = £800,000 nominal of the cheapest-to-deliver gilt (1.25 is the gilt price divided by 100). The number of futures contracts that would match the volatility (interest rate sensitivity) of £800,000 nominal of the cheapest-to-deliver gilt is

(£800,000/£50,000) × 1.1 = 17.6.

So 17 or 18 gilt futures contracts would be bought. If the fund manager knew which bonds were to be subsequently purchased, the number of futures contracts would have been adjusted by the relative volatility of the desired bonds and the cheapest-to-deliver gilt.

ASSET REALLOCATION

Stock index and government bond futures can be used to expedite asset reallocation. A fund manager wanting to switch from stocks to bonds can change the fund's exposure very quickly and at low cost by selling stock index futures and buying government bond futures. This process is much quicker than selling stocks and buying bonds. Having switched the exposure using futures, the fund manager can take time and care over the decisions as to which stocks to sell and which bonds to buy. The futures positions would be lifted as new portfolios are established.

CONCLUSIONS

The ultimate economic purpose of derivatives is the provision of a means of risk management, in particular hedging. In the context of risk management, futures have uses in the spheres in fund management and corporate treasury. This chapter has examined the use of futures in fund management, whilst Chapter 13 focuses on the corporate treasury uses. Fund management makes particular use of stock index and bond futures, whereas corporate treasury primarily uses currency and interest rate derivatives. The use of options in both fund management and corporate treasury is examined in Chapters 7 to 11 and Chapter 14.

Further reading

Sources with a strong focus on the use of futures in fund management include:

Keith Redhead, *Introduction to Financial Investment* (Prentice Hall, Hemel Hempstead, 1995).

Lewis Mandell and Thomas J. O'Brien, *Investments* (Maxwell Macmillan, Singapore, 1992)

C.M.S. Sutcliffe, *Stock Index Futures* (Chapman & Hall, London, 1992).

OPTIONS – THE BASIC PRINCIPLES   7

INTRODUCTION

This chapter begins with a consideration of the nature of options, distinguishing between their intrinsic and time values. This distinction is then used as the basis for an elementary analysis of the determinants of option prices.

For every buyer of an option there must be a seller. The seller is often referred to as the writer. As with futures (but unlike stocks and bonds), options are brought into existence by being traded; if none is traded, none exists; conversely, there is no limit to the number of option contracts that can be in existence at any time. As with futures, the process of closing-out option positions (selling to close out long positions and buying to close out short positions) will cause contracts to cease to exist, diminishing the total number.

Another feature shared with futures is that traders are involved in a zero-sum game; the profits/losses of buyers of options will precisely match the losses/profits of writers. The profit of one is the loss of the other.

After a consideration of option writing the chapter looks at call options as alternatives, but in some ways equivalents, to leveraged purchases of stock (buying shares on margin). This is followed by a definition of option elasticity.

The chapter ends by looking at some variations on the option theme. A number of exotic options are described, as are warrants, warrants being a form of long-term option. Convertible bonds are described; convertibles are bonds with option characteristics in that they permit the holders to exchange the bonds for shares.

An option is the right to buy or sell a specified amount of a financial instrument at a pre-arranged price on, or before, a particular date. A right to buy is referred to as a call option, and the right to sell a put option. There are two other important distinctions; first, between European-style and American-style options. European-style options can be exercised (the right to buy or sell can be used) only on the maturity date of the option, which is known as the expiry date. An American-style option can be exercised at any time up to, and including, the expiry date. It is to be noted that the distinction has nothing to do with geography. Both types of option are traded throughout the world.

The other distinction is between over-the-counter (OTC) options and exchange-traded options. OTC options are the result of private negotiations between 2 parties (typically, a bank and a client). They may relate to any amount of any financial instrument at any agreed price and have any expiry date. In other words, they can be tailor-made to the specific requirements of the client buying the option. Exchange-traded options are bought and sold on an organised exchange. They are standardised as to the amount and price of the underlying instrument, the nature of the underlying and the available expiry dates. Contracts would relate to discrete blocks of the underlying and would provide a limited range of prices and expiry dates. Most exchange-traded options are American style.

CALL OPTIONS

Although options can relate to a wide variety of underlying instruments, this discussion will consider stock options (options on shares).

A call option gives the buyer of that option the right, but not the obligation, to buy shares at a particular price. That price is known as the exercise or strike price. At the time of buying the option there will be at least 2 exercise prices available to choose from. For example, when the price of BP shares was 533½p on 13 December 1995, the option exercise prices available were 500p and 550p. If the holder of a call option decides to exercise it, he or she will buy a specific number of shares at the strike price chosen when buying the option. The number of shares covered by one option contract varies from country to country; examples are USA 100, UK 1,000, Germany 50.

It could be profitable to exercise a call option if the market price of the stock turns out to be higher than the strike price. In the event of the market price being lower than the strike price, the option holder is not obliged to exercise, and presumably will not, since exercising would realise a loss. The buyer of an option thus has potential for profit without the risk of a loss. For this favourable situation, the buyer of an option pays a premium. Continuing the previous example, the premiums for BP call options, at the close of trading on 13 December 1995, were as shown in Table 7.1. January, April and July were expiry months. The expiry month of an option is the month in which it ceases to be exercisable. Option premiums (i.e. prices) are expressed in the same currency units as the shares, e.g. pence in the UK, dollars in the USA. Premiums are payable at the time the option is bought.

Table 7.1 Premiums for BP call options

Exercise (strike) price (p)	Premium (p)		
	January	April	July
500	38½	47	54
550	6½	17½	25½

Source: *Financial Times*, 14 December 1995.

Example 7.1

An investor buys a 500p call option on BP shares at a premium of 38½p per share when the share price is 533½p. Since each option contract on LIFFE relates to 1,000 shares, the cash outflow is £385.

Subsequently, the share price rises to 600p. The investor can then exercise the right to buy at 500p. There is a gross profit of 100p (£1,000 per option contract). This gross profit of 100p is the intrinsic value of the option. The net profit must take account of the 38½p premium paid for the option. The net profit is thus 100p − 38½p = 61½p (£615 per option contract). The investor has guaranteed that the effective price to be paid for the shares will not exceed 538½p, this consisting of the strike price plus the premium paid for the option.

The profit/loss profile at expiry

Since an option buyer is not obliged to exercise an option, he has the right simply to disregard it. In such an event the premium paid is lost, but there would be no further loss. The premium paid is the maximum loss that can be incurred. On the other hand, the profit potential is subject to no limits. In principle, there is no upper limit to the stock price and hence no upper limit to the potential profit. Figure 7.1 shows the profit/loss profile of a call option at expiry.

The option used for the illustration is the January 500p BP call whose premium is 38½p. If the buyer holds the option to the expiry date and the share price turns out to be 500p or less, there will be no point in exercising the option. There is no benefit from exercising an option to buy shares at 500p when those shares can be bought at the same, or a lower, price in the market. In such a situation, the option buyer makes a net loss because of the payment of the 38½p premium, which is non-returnable. This is shown in Figure 7.1 which depicts a loss of 38½p at all prices up to 500p.

If the price of the share turns out to be greater than 500p, it would be worthwhile to exercise the option. The option holder could choose to exercise the option to buy at 500p and then immediately sell the shares at the higher price, thereby realising a profit. At a share price of 538½XBp, this profit would exactly offset the premium paid. Hence, 538 1/2p is the breakeven price at which net profit is zero. At prices above 538½p, the gross profit exceeds the premium so that there is a net profit. (These figures would need some adjustment if bid–ask spreads and commission costs were to be taken into account.)

The gross profit referred to is alternatively known as the intrinsic value of the option. Intrinsic value can be defined as the profit to be obtained by immediately exercising the option (disregarding the premium) and is equal to the difference between the exercise price and the market price of the stock when the option is in-the-money.

An in-the-money call option is one whose exercise price is less than the market price of the stock, and which therefore offers an immediate gross profit. An at-the-money option is one whose exercise price is equal to the market price. An out-of-the-money call option is one whose exercise price is greater than the market price. Only in-the-money options have intrinsic value.

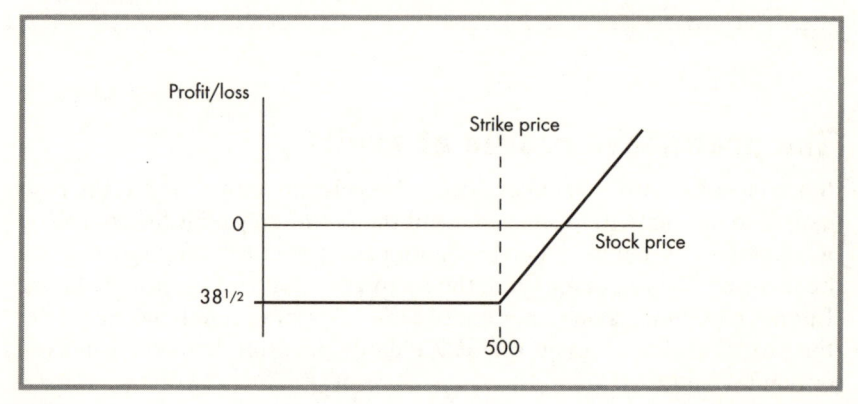

FIGURE 7.1   Profit/loss profile of a call option at expiry

ACTIVITY 7.1

The FTSE 100 is currently 3725. Call options with a strike price of 3700 are priced at 35 index points. The option contracts are based on £10 per index point and they are cash settled.

(a) What is the maximum loss to a buyer of the option?
(b) What is the breakeven stock index?
(c) Is there a maximum profit?
(d) If the option were exercised at an index level of 3750, what transactions would occur?

Answer

(a) The maximum loss to the buyer of an option is the premium paid. In this case it is 35 index points, which corresponds to a monetary sum of £350.

(b) If the option were exercised at an index level of 3735, there would be a gross profit (pay off) of 35 index points, amounting to £350. This matches the premium paid. So 3735 is the breakeven stock index.

(c) Since there is no upper limit to the stock index, there is no upper limit to the potential profits of a buyer of a call option.

(d) Since stock index options are cash settled, no shares change hands upon exercise. Instead there is a cash flow reflecting the intrinsic value of the option. In this case, the intrinsic value is 50 index points. Upon exercise the option holder will receive £500.

The profit/loss profile prior to expiry

At the time that a traded option expires, its price (premium) will be equal to its intrinsic value. Prior to expiry the premium would normally exceed the intrinsic value. This excess of the price of the option over the intrinsic value is known as the time value. When an option is exercised, only the intrinsic value is realised. The seller of an option would obtain a price that incorporates some time value as well as the intrinsic value; see Figure 7.2.

When account is taken of the time value, the profit/loss profile of an option differs from the at-expiry profile depicted in Figure 7.1. A prior-to-expiry profile is shown by the broken line in Figure 7.3. Time value is at its highest when the option is at the money. Time value declines as the option moves either into or out of the money and will approach zero as the market price of the stock diverges substantially from the exercise (strike) price.

The broken line indicates the market price of the option minus the initial premium paid (38½p in this case). When an option is purchased, the

FIGURE 7.2 The call option price (premium) as a function of the price of the underlying stock

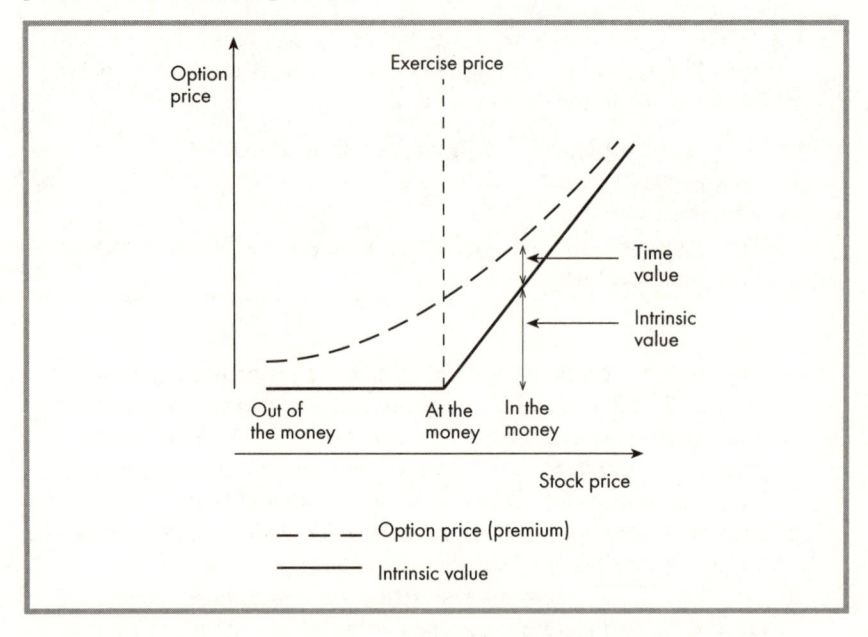

FIGURE 7.3 Profit/loss profile of a call option prior to expiry, showing its time value

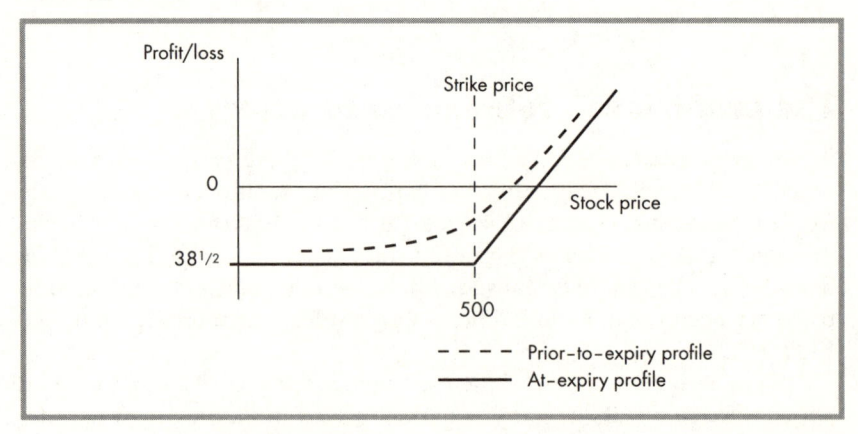

premium paid will be the market price and the profit/loss profile (broken line) will intersect the horizontal axis indicating zero net profit at the ruling stock price. (This is equivalent to saying that at the moment of purchase the value of the option is equal to the price paid for it.) As time passes and the stock price changes, the net profit will cease to be zero.

The net profit shown by the prior-to-expiry profile is the price that the trader could sell the option for minus the price (premium) that was paid for it.

Below the exercise price the price of the option consists of time value only, but above the exercise price the price consists of both time and intrinsic value. This ensures that the gradient of the prior-to-expiry profile increases as the share price rises. This gradient is known as the option delta and can alternatively be expressed as the change in the price of the option as a proportion of the change in the price of the stock. The delta approaches zero as the option becomes deeply out of the money and approaches one when it is deep in the money. The delta is approximately 0·5 when the option is at the money.

Determinants of the premium

The explanation of an option premium subdivides into ascertaining intrinsic value and assessing the influences on time value. The intrinsic value of a call option is equal to the stock price minus the exercise price of the option, with zero being the minimum intrinsic value. In principle, the option premium cannot fall below the intrinsic value. If the option premium were below the intrinsic value, there would be a guaranteed profit from buying the option and immediately exercising it (and selling the shares acquired). It would be irrational for anyone to sell an option for a price that is less than its intrinsic value, since more could be obtained from exercising it.

The determination of time value is more complex. Major influences on time value are the expected volatility of the stock price, the length of the period remaining to the expiry date, and the extent to which the option is in or out of the money.

The higher the expected volatility, the greater will be the premium. An option on a volatile stock has a strong chance of acquiring intrinsic value at some stage prior to expiry. Similarly, the probability of an option acquiring intrinsic value prior to expiry rises with the length of time remaining to its expiry date. It can be seen from Table 7.1 that the options with the more distant expiry dates have the higher premiums.

Time value is at its peak when the option is at the money and declines as the option moves either into or out of the money. Out-of-the-money options have less time value than at-the-money options because the stock price has further to move before intrinsic value is acquired. In-the-money options have less time value than at-the-money options since their prices contain intrinsic value which is vulnerable to a fall in the stock price, whereas at-the-money option premiums contain no intrinsic value. The risk that existing intrinsic value might be lost reduces the attractiveness of the option and lowers its price.

PUT OPTIONS

A put option gives its holder the right, but not the obligation, to sell shares at a specified price prior to, or on, the expiry date of the option.

The holder of an option can exercise it, sell it, or allow it to expire. It is worthwhile exercising an option – that is, exercising the right to sell shares at the strike price – only if the market price of the stock turns out to be lower than the strike price. If the strike price is greater than the stock price, the option is said to have intrinsic value. The intrinsic value would be equal to the excess of the strike price over the stock price. An option without intrinsic value might simply be allowed to expire since its holder is not obliged to exercise it, and presumably would not if the strike price were below the market price of the stock.

The buyer of an option pays a premium, which is the price of the option. The premium consists of the intrinsic value, if there is any, plus time value. It is likely that the holder of an option would choose to sell it in preference to exercising it or allowing it to expire. By selling the option he would receive the time value as well as any intrinsic value (whereas exercising the option realises the intrinsic value only).

Table 7.2 shows the premiums of BP put options at the close of trading on 13 December 1995. The price of BP shares was 533½p. The months referred to in Table 7.2 are expiry months. All the option contracts in the table belong to one class, namely BP puts. Within that class there are 6 series. Each series is characterised by a strike price and an expiry date (e.g. 500 January, 550 April). So at any one time the buyer of a BP put option would have 3 to choose from at each strike price. When the January expiry date is reached, options with an October expiry date would be introduced.

All prices in Table 7.2 are in pence. So, for example, it would cost 19½p (per share) to buy an option that provides the holder with the right to sell shares at 550p each at any time up to the January expiry date. (Since each option in the UK relates to 1,000 shares, the actual price of the option would be £195.) Substantial movements of the stock price would invoke

Table 7.2 Premiums for BP put options

Exercise (strike) price (p)	Premium (p)		
	January	April	July
500	1½	7	11½
550	19½	28½	33½

Source: *Financial Times*, 14 December 1995.

the introduction of new strike prices, so that there are strike prices either side of the stock price.

Example 7.2

An investor buys a 550p put option on BP shares at a premium of 19½p per share when the share price is 533½p. Since each option contract relates to 1,000 shares, the cash outflow is £195.

Subsequently, the share price falls to 400p. The investor can exercise the right to sell at 550p. There is a gross profit from the option of 150p (£1,500 per option contract). This gross profit of 150p is the intrinsic value of the option. The net profit from the option must take account of the 19½p premium paid for the option. The net profit is thus 150p − 19½p = 130½p (£1,305 per option contract). The investor has guaranteed that the effective selling price of the shares cannot fall below 530½p, this sum being the sale receipts of 550p minus the 19½p premium paid for the option.

The profit/loss profile at expiry

In the case of traded stock options, the premium is usually payable in full on the day following the purchase of the option. However, since the buyer is not obliged to exercise the option, and presumably will not do so if it involves selling at a loss relative to the market price of the share, the premium paid is the maximum loss the buyer of the option can incur. So, for example, a buyer of BP January 550p puts faces a maximum loss of 19 ½p per share, which amounts to £195 per contract, since each put option contract is for the sale of 1,000 shares.

The maximum profit is limited only by the fact that stock prices cannot fall below zero. Since it is conceivable that a stock price can fall to zero, the net gain from a put option can, in principle, be as much as the strike price minus the premium paid. The buyer of January 550p BP puts stands to gain as much as 550p − 19½p per share. This amounts to £5,305 per option contract. The option holder could buy shares at 0p and, by exercising the option, sell them at 550p.

Figure 7.4 shows the profit/loss profile of BP January 550p puts at expiry (i.e. on the day in January upon which the option ceases to be capable of being exercised). If the stock price is 550p or higher when the option expires, the holder of the option records a net loss of 19½p per share (£195 per option contract). If the stock price turns out to be less than 550p, there is a gross profit to be made by exercising the option.

Exercising the option will allow the option holder to sell shares at 550p, while buying them at a lower price. This gross profit from exercising the option minus the premium paid is the net profit. If the stock price lies between 530½p and 500p there is a net loss, whereas below the breakeven stock price of 530½p there is a net profit.

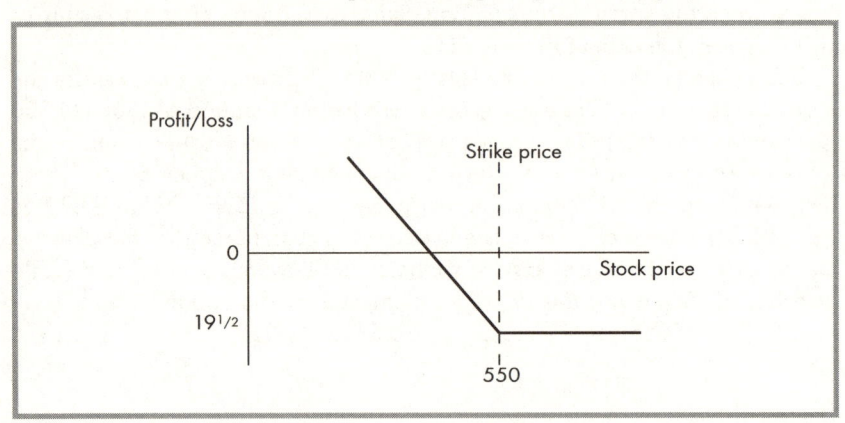

FIGURE 7.4 Profit/loss profile of a put option at expiry

The profit/loss profile prior to expiry

Intrinsic value is the gross profit to be made from exercising the option. At expiry an option would have only intrinsic value, which could be equal to zero. Prior to expiry the option would have time value as well as intrinsic value. The profit/loss profile of Figure 7.4 is based on intrinsic value only. Since intrinsic value is the gross profit to be made from exercising the option it will be zero at or above the strike price of 550p, whereas below 550p it will be equal to the difference between the stock price and the strike price. The net profit or loss at expiry is equal to the intrinsic value minus the premium paid.

Prior to expiry the price of an option will tend to differ from its intrinsic value. The difference is the time value and is shown by the vertical distance between the prior-to-expiry profile and the at-expiry profile in Figure 7.5. The prior-to-expiry profile indicates the current market price of the option minus the price that the present holder paid for it. As time passes, the prior-to-expiry profile will tend to converge on to the at-expiry profile, with the convergence becoming complete as expiry is reached.

This convergence reflects the tendency for the time value of an option to decline with the passage of time. This erosion of time value can be

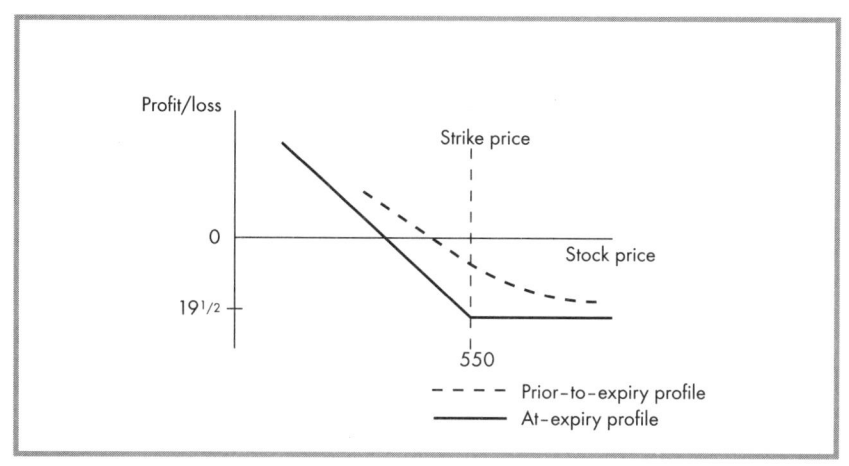

FIGURE 7.5   Profit/loss profile of a put option prior to expiry, showing its time value

explained in terms of the likelihood of a substantial increase in intrinsic value falling as the time available for the requisite stock price movement declines. A second factor affecting time value is the expected volatility of the stock price. With high volatility there is a relatively high chance of substantial gains in intrinsic value at some stage prior to expiry. So, the greater is the expected volatility of a stock price, the greater will the time value of an option on that stock tend to be.

A third factor affecting time value is the relationship between the stock price and the strike price of the option. Time value is at its highest when the stock price is equal to the strike price. When the stock price is equal to the strike price, the option is said to be at the money. As the stock price and strike price diverge, in either direction, time value declines.

When the stock price exceeds the strike price, the put option is said to be out of the money. A better price can be obtained by selling the shares in the market than by exercising the option. Time value declines as the option moves further out of the money (in other words, as the stock price rises), reflecting the decreasing likelihood of the stock price declining sufficiently to cause exercise of the option to become profitable.

When the stock price is lower than the strike price, the put option is said to be in the money. A better price can be obtained by exercising the option than by selling the shares in the market. It is possible to make a profit by buying shares at the market price and selling them at the price guaranteed by the option contract. Time value declines as the option becomes deeper in the money (i.e. as the stock price falls). This can be understood in terms of there being an increasing amount of intrinsic value that is at risk of being lost. The price of an in-the-money option contains the intrinsic value of that option. The buyer of an in-the-money option bears this risk, whereas the buyer of an at-the-money option does not. The risk borne rises as the option becomes deeper in the money. This risk is reflected in the time value. The buyer of an at-the-money option pays a higher price for time value than the buyer of an in-the-money option, with the price paid for time value declining as the option becomes deeper in the money.

The gradient of the prior-to-expiry profile is known as the delta and represents the ratio between the change in the price of the option and the change in the stock price. In the case of put options, deltas are negative. The delta increases in absolute value as the option moves deeper in the money (as the stock price falls). As the option becomes increasingly deep in the money, the prior-to-expiry profile approaches the 45° line of the at-expiry profile because of the decline in time value. This means that the delta approaches –1 when a put option becomes very deep in the money.

The delta decreases in absolute value as the option moves further out of the money. The prior-to-expiry profile approaches the horizontal line of the at-expiry profile since time value diminishes as the stock price moves away from the strike price of the option. The delta tends towards zero as the option becomes very deep out of the money.

ACTIVITY 7.2

Dixons shares are trading at 140p. The option prices are as follows:

Strike price	Calls			Puts		
	December	March	June	December	March	June
140	8	7	18	8	12	16
160	2	6½	10	19	25	27

Do any of the options appear to be mispriced? If so, what pricing principles are violated?

Answer
The March 140p call is underpriced because time value should rise with increasing time to expiry. The December 160p put is underpriced because the option price should not be below the intrinsic value.

WRITING OPTIONS

For every buyer of an option there must be a seller. The seller of an option is usually referred to as the writer. The buyer of an option is said to have a long option position, whereas the writer of the option is said to have a short position. The profit/loss profile of a short (written) option is the mirror image of that of the long (bought) option. Profits of the buyer must equal losses of the seller, and vice versa. Figures 7.6 and 7.7 compare long and short positions for call and put options respectively.

The premium paid by the buyer obviously equals the premium received by the writer. The profit (loss) of the buyer will always equal the loss (profit) of the writer. It should be noted that the buyer of a call option has loss potential limited to the premium paid, but unlimited profit potential. Conversely, the writer of a call has a maximum profit equal to the premium received, but unlimited loss potential. In the case of put options, the buyer has a maximum loss equal to the premium, which constitutes

FIGURE 7.6 Call option (at expiry) profiles

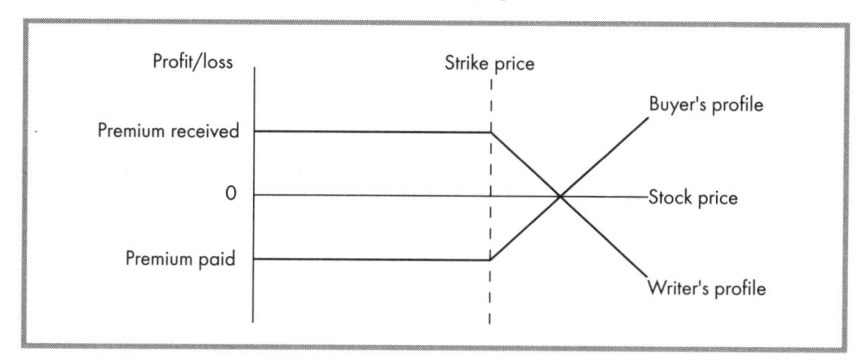

FIGURE 7.7 Put option (at expiry) profiles

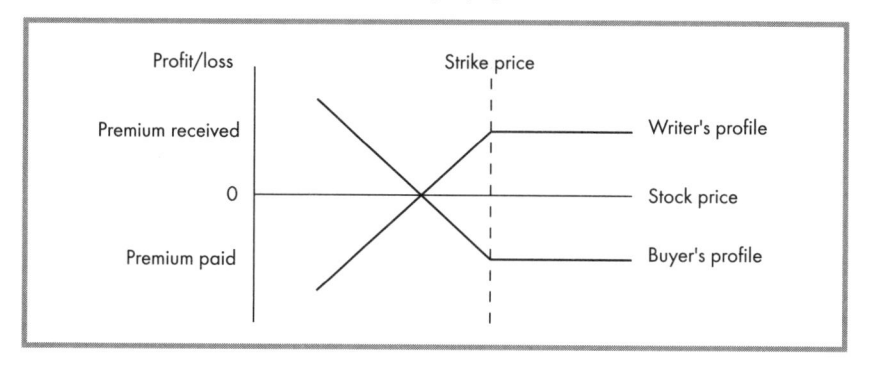

the maximum profit of the writer. With put options the maximum profit of the buyer (maximum loss of the writer) occurs at a stock price of zero.

In the case of traded options, a long option position can be closed out by writing an identical option, leaving no option position remaining. Likewise, a written option can be closed out by buying an identical option.

Example 7.3

An investor writes a 500p call option on BP shares at a premium of 38½p per share when the share price is 533½p. Since each option contract on LIFFE relates to 1,000 shares, the premium receipts amount to £385.

Subsequently, the share price rises to 600p. An option buyer might then exercise the right to buy shares at 500p. If the option writer is assigned to the option buyer (assignment of writers to meet the requirements of buyers who exercise is usually carried out on a random basis), the writer must sell shares for 500p to the option buyer. The option writer may need to buy shares at 600p in order to sell them at 500p. This entails a gross loss of 100p (the intrinsic value of the option). Taking account of the option premium received indicates a net loss of 61½p (£615 per option contract).

The loss of the option writer is equal to the profit of the option buyer.

ACTIVITY 7.3

The shares of Big Con plc stand at 110p. Put options with a strike price of 120p are priced at 14p.

(a) What is the intrinsic value of the options?
(b) What is the time value of the options?
(c) What might cause the time value to double with no change in intrinsic value?
(d) If the share price fell to 50p by the expiry date, what would be the profit/loss for the holder and writer of the options?
(e) What is the maximum loss for the writer of the options?

Answer

(a) *The intrinsic value is 120p – 110p = 10p.*
(b) *The time value is the premium minus the intrinsic value, 14p – 10p = 4p.*
(c) *The most likely cause of such an increase in time value is an increase in market expectations of volatility of the share price.*
(d) *The option holder could exercise to realise the intrinsic value of 70p. When the premium payment of 14p is considered, the net profit is 70p –*

14p = 56p. The option writer would pay 120p for shares worth 50p. This loss of 70p is partially offset by the premium receipt of 14p. The net loss to the writer is therefore 70p − 14p = 56p. It can be seen that the profit of the buyer is equal to the loss of the writer.

(e) The maximum loss for the writer would occur in the event of the share price falling to zero. It would equal the strike price minus the premium received, 120p − 14p = 106p. The writer would pay 120p for worthless shares, having previously received 14p per share for selling the options.

ACTIVITY 7.4

It is 10 June and shares in Covuni Plc are 98p. Option prices are:

	Calls		Puts	
Strike price	September	December	September	December
90p	9p	9½p	1p	1½p
100p	2p	3p	4p	5p
110p	1p	1½p	13p	13½p

(a) Why are the 100p put options more expensive than the 100p call options?
(b) Suggest two alternative strategies for hedging a holding of 1,000 shares (one strategy should use calls and the other puts). Under what circumstances would one be preferred over the other?
(c) How might a speculator make a profit from a 2p rise in the share price?
(d) If the September 90p options are held to expiry and the share price remains at 98p, what would you expect the option prices to be at expiry?
(e) If market expectations of share price volatility rose between 10 June and 11 June, while the share price remained at 98p, what should happen to the option prices?

Answer
(a) The put options have an intrinsic value of 100p − 98p = 2p. The call options have no intrinsic value, they are out of the money.
(b) i) Buy a 100p put option. Best when a large price fall is expected.
    ii) Write a 100p call option. Best when a small price fall is expected.
(c) Write a 100p put option.
(d) The 90p call would have an intrinsic value of 98p − 90p = 8p. At expiry time value is zero. So the option price should be 8p. The 90p put would have expired out of the money and hence would have zero value at expiry.
(e) Option prices should rise since time value is positively related to market expectations of volatility.

MARKET PRACTICES AND TERMS

All the call options on a particular underlying stock together constitute a class of options. Similarly, all the puts on the same underlying stock would together comprise another class. Within each class there will be a number of series. An option series is specific to a particular exercise price and a particular expiry month, as well as to a particular stock and call/put categorisation. So, for example, $50 December calls and $60 January calls on the stock of ABC are 2 different series within the same class (the class being ABC call options).

An opening purchase is a transaction whereby the buyer of an option becomes its holder; a closing purchase is a transaction in which a writer of an option buys an option identical to the one previously written, whereupon the 2 positions are deemed to cancel each other out. An opening sale is a transaction in which the seller of an option becomes its writer; a closing sale involves the cancellation of a previously purchased option.

Premiums in respect of traded options are normally payable via the broker to the clearing house on the morning following the day of the trade. Payment to the writer of the option would come from the clearing house, which usually acts as a registrar for all open contracts. If the holder of an option exercises it, the clearing house, using a random selection process, chooses a writer who is then assigned to sell (in the case of calls) or buy (in the case of puts) to or from the holder at the exercise price.

There are often position limits to the number of options in any one class that can be held or written by any one individual or organisation.

STOCK LEVERAGE AND STOCK OPTIONS

It is possible to buy stock in a leveraged way. This means that part of the cost of the stock is met with borrowed money. The shareholder's equity is the difference between the value of the stock and the outstanding debt. The proportionate changes in the value of the equity exceed the proportionate changes in the stock price.

Leverage = stock value/owner's equity

or:

= stock value/(stock value minus debt)

If, for example, the leverage were 2 and the stock price rose by 10%, then the owner's equity would have risen by 20%. If the leverage had been 1·5, the 10% stock price rise would have provided a 15% rise in the owner's equity. So:

Leverage = % change in owner's equity/% change in stock price

and:

% change in owner's equity = leverage × % change in stock price.

The beta of a leveraged holding of shares is equal to the stock beta multiplied by the leverage. So if the stock beta is 1·2 and the leverage is 1·5, the leveraged shareholding has a beta of 1·2 × 1·5 = 1·8.

An alternative way of obtaining a leveraged position in stock is to buy a call option. A call option gives the right to buy a particular quantity of stock at a particular price during a specified time period. The price of the call option is a fraction of the price of the stock, but provides a high level of exposure to changes in the stock price.

The change in the option price per unit rise in the stock price is known as the option delta. If the price at which the option holder has the right to buy shares (the option strike price) is equal to the share price, the option delta will be approximately 0·5. The option delta would rise and fall with the stock price (but not in proportion to changes in the stock price). The elasticity of the option price is the percentage change in the option price divided by the percentage change in the stock price.

Option delta = Change in option price/change in stock price

Option elasticity = % change in option price/% change in stock price

or

$$\text{Option elasticity} = \frac{\text{Change in option price}}{\text{Option price}} \bigg/ \frac{\text{Change in stock price}}{\text{Stock price}}$$

Option elasticity = Option delta × Stock price/Option price.

Option elasticity is similar to the leverage mentioned earlier. The leverage of a shareholding bought on margin (i.e. partially financed with borrowed money) can be expressed as:

% change in shareholder's equity/% change in stock price

which is the same as option elasticity if the value of the option is looked upon as the owner's equity.

The beta of a call option can be calculated in a way that is analogous to the derivation of the beta of a leveraged holding of shares. The beta of a call option equals the stock beta multiplied by the elasticity of the option.

EXOTIC OPTIONS

Exotic option is a generic name that refers to variations on the basic option theme. The following is an indicative, rather than an exhaustive, list of exotic options.

Lookback call options give the right to buy at the lowest price achieved during the life of the option. Lookback put options provide the right to sell at the highest price attained by the underlying instrument.

Asian options involve the average experienced price of the underlying taking the place of the spot price in ascertaining intrinsic value. So European options use the spot price on the expiry date, American options use any spot price observed during the life of the option, and Asian options use the average spot price during the life of the option.

Knock-in and knock-out options either come into being or cease to exist when particular prices of the underlying are reached. For example, down-and-out call options cease to exist if the price of the underlying instrument falls below a particular value. Such options tend to be cheaper than ordinary options.

Options on options may prove useful in certain circumstances. For example, a company tendering for a contract may take out an option to buy an option on the date on which the contract is due to be awarded. (An option would be preferable to a forward or futures position when the contract is awarded if the view is that currency movements are likely to be beneficial but some downside protection is desirable. In other words, the view is taken that the currency of the receivables will probably, but not certainly, rise against the base currency. Options, unlike forwards and futures, allow for profits from such a rise. If the beneficial currency movement is expected with certainty, hedging would seem inappropriate. An expectation of a detrimental currency movement would most likely lead to hedging with a forward or futures position – there would be little enthusiasm to pay a premium for the ability to profit from a currency movement that is not expected to occur.)

An option on an option is likely to be cheaper than the substantive option. First, the intrinsic value of an option on an option will be less than the intrinsic value of the substantive option because the delta of the substantive option would be less than one. Secondly, the volatility of an option price will be less than the volatility of the underlying instrument (again because the option delta will be less than one). Thirdly, if the option on an option has a shorter period to expiry than the substantive option – as is likely to be the case – the time value of the option on the option will be relatively low as a result.

Notational formulations

The minimum value of an American-style call option can be expressed as:

$$C = \max(0, S - K)$$

If the option is in the money the minimum value is S − K, the excess of the spot price over the exercise price. (Since an American call must be at least equal in value to a European call, this expression should, strictly speaking, use the discounted strike price in the place of the strike price. However, for the purposes of the following discussion, this refinement can be ignored.) If the option is at or out of the money, its minimum value is zero. So the minimum value of a call option is the greater of zero and the excess of the spot price of the underlying over the exercise price of the option.

The minimum value of an American-style put option can be stated as:

$$P = \max(0, K - S)$$

The minimum price of a put option is the greater of zero, and the exercise price minus the spot price. In other words, the minimum value is the intrinsic value and the intrinsic value cannot fall below zero.

The above notation can be used to describe exotic options. For example, lookback call options give the right to buy at the lowest price attained by the underlying instrument during the life of the option. In other words, the exercise price will be equal to the lowest price achieved by the underlying. In notation form:

$$C = \max[0, S_n - \min(S_0, S_1, \ldots, S_n)]$$

S_0, S_1, etc., are the observed prices of the underlying where the subscripts denote successive points in time. The minimum price of the call option is the highest of zero and the excess of the spot price over the exercise price. The spot price is the terminal price of the underlying, S_n, whereas the exercise price is the lowest spot price observed during the life of the option, i.e. $\min(S_0, S_1, \ldots, S_n)$.

A lookback put option gives the right to sell at the highest observed price. In other words, the highest observed price becomes the exercise price:

$$P = \max[0, \max(S_0, S_1, \ldots, S_n) - S_n]$$

The intrinsic value of an in-the-money put option is the exercise price, i.e. $\max(S_0, S_1, \ldots, S_n)$, minus the spot price at the time of exercise, S_n.

Average strike options have strike prices that are an average of the actual spot prices experienced during the life of the option. In notation form:

$$C = \max\{0, S_n - [\Sigma S_i/(n+1)]\}$$

$P = \max\{0, [\Sigma S_i/(n + 1)] - S_n\}$

The strike price is $\Sigma S_i/(n + 1)$, where ΣS_i is the sum of the observed spot prices (at points of time $i = 0, 1, 2, \ldots, n$) and $n + 1$ is the number of observed spot prices. S_n is the spot price of the underlying at time n, which is the moment at which the option is exercised or at which it expires.

Asian options (average price options) involve the average observed price taking the role of the spot price in determining the minimum value (intrinsic value) of the option:

$C = \max\{0, [\Sigma S_i/((n + 1)] - K\}$
$P = \max\{0, K - [\Sigma S_i/(n + 1)]\}$

Down-and-out call options can be looked upon as conditional options. They behave like normal American-style call options so long as the price of the underlying remains above a particular level. In notation form:

$C = \max(0, S_n - K)$ if $\min(S_0, S_1, \ldots, S_n) > H$ (where $H < K$)
$C = 0$ if $\min(S_0, S_1, \ldots, S_n) \le H$

So long as none of the observed spot prices ($S_0, S_1, \ldots, S_n$) falls to H (which is below the exercise price K), the option behaves in the same way as a normal call. If the price of the underlying declines to H or less, the option ceases to exist.

Correspondingly, there are down-and-in calls that come into existence only if the price of the underlying falls to, or beyond, a specific value. Down-and-out puts (otherwise known as up-and-out puts) cease to exist if the price of the underlying rises to a particular level which is greater than the exercise price. Up-and-in puts come into existence when the price of the underlying rises to a particular level.

Compound options, which are options on options, can also be described using notational form. For a call on a call:

$C = \max[0, \max(0, S_n - E) - K]$

The option on the option has an exercise price of K, whereas the option whose price (or minimum value) constitutes the price of the underlying for the option on it has an exercise price of E. In the case of a call on a put, the expression is:

$C = \max[0, \max(0, E - S_n) - K]$

A put on a call would be:

$P = \max[0, K - \max(0, S_n - E)]$

whereas a put on a put could be described by:

$P = \max[0, K - \max(0, E - S_n)]$

This is not an exhaustive list of exotic options; however, it is indicative of the range of such options. Furthermore, in order to avoid excessive complexity, time value has been ignored. The notation has been concerned solely with intrinsic values, i.e. minimum values.

The discussion has thus far largely ignored potential uses of the exotic options. It is difficult to be prescriptive about potential uses since it is impossible to foresee every possible circumstance. However, some suggestions can be provided.

Lookback options could be useful for a fund manager who expects a stock price to reach a particularly high or low level temporarily during the lifetime of the option. Average strike options might be attractive to an importer seeking to ensure that the purchase price of foreign currency is in line with the average purchase price faced by that importer's competitors. Asian options are useful for those who make frequent purchases or sales of the underlying, and hence experience a variety of spot prices. Hedgers would use Asian options to obtain compensation in the event of average purchase prices being too high or average sale prices being too low. The conditional options (down-and-outs, etc.) are a means of reducing the costs of options; such options would tend to be relatively cheap because they exclude some profit possibilities. Compound options might also be regarded as a means of reducing costs using options, particularly when a contingent risk is being hedged. An exporter tendering for a contract in foreign currency might want an option to buy another option with a view to exercising the option on an option in the event of the tender being successful. The option on an option could be much cheaper than the underlying option, particularly if it has a much shorter time to expiry (i.e. the time to the acceptance of the tender is much less than the subsequent period to the payment for the project). This reduction of initial financial outlay on the hedging instrument could be carried further by making the option on an option conditional upon success of the tender (i.e. it could have no intrinsic value in the event of the tender being rejected).

WARRANTS

Warrants are long-term options. They may have expiry dates that lie as much as 5 years or more in the future (in contrast to stock options which often have a maximum life of 9 months).

Most warrants are issued by the company upon whose shares they are based. If they are exercised, the company will issue new shares. So, unlike options, warrants are usually used as a means of raising corporate finance. The issuing company receives the money from the sale of the warrants and subsequently receives the money paid upon exercise. In contrast to options, warrants tend to entail the expansion of the number of shares in issue.

Warrants are often attached to company debt, such as loan stock, when they are issued. The presence of such warrants renders the debt more attractive to the investor, and hence the issuing company can raise money on more advantageous terms in that it needs to pay a lower rate of interest than would otherwise be the case. In most instances, the warrant is detachable from the host debt instrument and can be traded in its own right. Some warrants are issued naked, i.e. without the presence of corporate debt instruments. Since warrants normally pay no dividend or coupon, they provide an issuing company with a source of finance that involves no initial servicing costs.

Some warrants are not connected with the raising of corporate finance. Third party warrants (sometimes named 'covered' warrants) might be written by a bank without any involvement of the company on whose stock the warrants are based. One type of third party warrant is, however, used for the raising of corporate finance. This involves the company that is raising the finance issuing warrants on the stock of another company.

CONVERTIBLE BONDS

A convertible might be looked upon as a corporate bond with an attached warrant (call option). Convertibles are often referred to as convertible loan stock (or convertible unsecured loan stock, since most are unsecured) and involve the right to convert the loan stock into shares at specified rates and points of time. Convertible preference shares are preference shares with the right to convert to ordinary shares. Some convertibles provide the right to convert to other loan stock rather than shares.

The number of shares for which the bond can be exchanged is referred to as the conversion rate. So, for example, the convertible may allow the conversion of £100 par value of loan stock into 20 shares. Multiplication of the conversion rate by the share price provides the conversion value. A share price of £6 would imply a conversion value of £120. Convertible loan stock would also exhibit an investment, or straight bond, value. This is the value of the bond (or preference share) in the absence of the right to convert. The investment value is the price of a corresponding straight bond or preference share.

The market value of the convertible would normally be higher than the greater of the conversion and investment values. The excess of the market value over the greater of the conversion or investment value is often referred to as the premium. Figure 7.8 illustrates the relationship

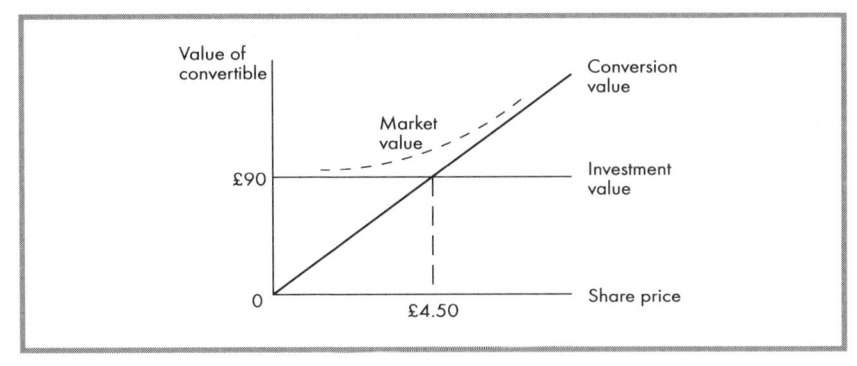

FIGURE 7.8 Relationship between the conversion, investment and market values of a convertible

between the conversion, investment and market values of a convertible. It is assumed that the conversion rate is 20 and that the investment value is £90 per £100 par value.

Figure 7.8 illustrates the convertible as a loan stock with an attached option (warrant). The investment value is that of the naked loan stock, while the excess of the market value over the investment value corresponds to the option premium. In this example, the option has a strike price of £4·50. The excess of the conversion value over the investment value corresponds to the intrinsic value of the option.

It must be realised that the investment value, and hence the strike price of the implicit option, is not immutable. A rise in interest rates would lower the investment value and strike price. Similar effects would arise from a decline in the credit standing of the company, such a decline requiring a higher rate of return which, given a constant coupon or dividend, implies a fall in the price of the loan stock (or preference share).

Convertibles are hybrids in that they constitute a compromise between bonds and shares. They provide more upside exposure to share price movements than bonds, but less than ordinary shares. They provide less downside protection than bonds, but more than shares. The percentage rate of dividend or coupon yield would be less than that of a straight bond (because the market value exceeds the investment value), but probably more than that of the ordinary share (a rate of dividend yield on the share that exceeds the rate of coupon yield on the convertible would probably induce conversion of the convertible into the share).

The fact that the convertible involves a lower rate of coupon yield than a straight bond renders it attractive to the issuer. The attached option causes the investor to require a lower coupon yield. Convertibles thus provide a cheaper source of finance than loan stock or preference shares. Their advantage over ordinary shares, from the point of view of the issuer, is that they constitute a form of deferred equity. In particular, the voting rights do not accrue to the holder until conversion takes place.

Holders of a convertible have the right to convert during a conversion period. If conversion does not take place during that period, the convertible might simply become a loan stock or preference share. So, for example, a convertible might offer the right to convert on 1 June of the sixth, seventh, eighth, ninth or tenth year of its life and, if conversion does not take place on any of those dates, it then becomes unsecured loan stock maturing at the end of a life of a further 10 years, at which point it would be redeemed at par. The conversion rate would normally imply a high purchase price of the share (if acquired through conversion) on the issue date of the convertible so that a significant share price advance would be necessary for conversion to become worthwhile. It is to be noted that this conversion price per share, based on the issue price of the convertible, is not the same as the strike price of the implicit option as illustrated in Figure 7.8 (which is based on the investment value). The conversion price is the market value of the convertible divided by the number of shares obtained upon conversion. At the time of issue the conversion price will be greater than the share price.

The price of the option component of the convertible is determined in the same way as the price of any other option. Its value is influenced by time to expiry, volatility, interest rates, and the share price, in the same way as other options. However, the strike price will be variable since it is dependent upon the investment (straight bond) value of the convertible. The investment value of the convertible is influenced by interest rates and the credit standing of the issuing corporation.

The question arises as to why the holder of a convertible would exercise the right to convert, since it might be expected that the market value would exceed the conversion value so that the sale of the convertible would appear to be preferable to conversion. The circumstances in which conversion would take place are (1) call by the issuing corporation, (2) the existence of a final conversion date, or (3) the dividend yield of the share rising above the coupon yield of the convertible.

Sometimes the issuer of the convertible has the right to call it. This means that the holder must either accept redemption of the convertible (probably at the par value of the loan stock) or convert it into shares. If the latter provides the greater value, conversion will take place. When the final conversion date passes, the implicit option disappears, leaving only the investment value of the convertible. If the conversion value exceeds the investment value on the final conversion date, it would be rational to exercise the right to convert.

The excess of the conversion price over the share price, when expressed as a percentage of the share price, is known as the conversion premium:

CONVERTIBLE BONDS • 167

$$\text{Conversion price} = \frac{\text{Market value of convertible}}{\text{Number of shares on conversion}}$$

$$\text{Conversion premium (\%)} = \frac{\text{Conversion price} - \text{Share price}}{\text{Share price}} \times 100$$

In most circumstances the conversion premium would be positive. However, a time may come when the dividend on the share exceeds the coupon on the convertible (the coupon is fixed, whereas the dividend is likely to rise over time). If conversion dates are at distant intervals (such as a year apart), the prospect of a lower rate of yield on the convertible than on the share could render it less valuable than the shares into which it might be converted. So a share dividend above the coupon of the convertible, together with a long time before the next conversion date, could entail a negative conversion premium. The prospect of a negative conversion premium subsequent to a conversion date could lead to conversion on that date.

ACTIVITY 7.5

A convertible has a maturity of 10 years and pays an annual coupon of £10. It has a conversion rate of 100 and the current share price is £1.10p. Conversion can take place on 1 June of the fifth, sixth, seventh and eighth years. The yield curve is flat at 12% p.a.
1. Calculate the investment and conversion values of the convertible. What would be the significance for the market value of the convertible if conversion could take place in year 5 only rather than in any of the 4 years?
2. If at the end of the eighth year one- and two-year interest rates were 5% p.a., what would you expect the price of the convertible to be at that time?

Answer
1. Investment value:

= £10/1·12 + £10/(1·12)² + £10/(1·12)³ + £10/(1·12)⁴ + £10/(1·12)⁵ + £10/(1·12)⁶ + £10/(1·12)⁷ + £10/(1·12)⁸ + £10/(1·12)⁹ + £10/(1·12)¹⁰ + £100/(1·12)¹⁰

= £56·5 + £32·2 = £88·70

Conversion value:

= 100 × £1·10 = £110

The ability to convert in year five only would reduce the time to expiry of the option and hence reduce its value. So the convertible would have a lower market value.

2. £10/(1·05) + £110/(1·05)² = £109·30

(Strictly speaking, it would not be a convertible at the end of the eighth year since the facility to convert would no longer exist.)

CONCLUSIONS

Call options give the right, but not the obligation, to buy at a specified price (the strike or exercise price) up to (or on) a future date (the expiry date). They thus allow a purchase to be delayed while guaranteeing a maximum buying price. Put options give the right, but not the obligation, to sell at a specified price up to (or on) a particular date in the future. A put option thus provides a means of delaying a sale while guaranteeing a minimum selling price. The absence of obligation means that if the price turns out to be more favourable than the strike price (lower for buying, higher for selling), the option need not be exercised; the transaction can then be carried out at the market price. The most that can be lost when buying an option is the premium (price) paid for it. This is another implication of the absence of obligation. On the other hand, a call option has unlimited profit potential, whereas the profit from buying a put option is limited only by the fact that the stock (or other underlying) price cannot fall below zero.

Most traded options are closed out before the expiry dates. For a long option position (option bought), closing out is accomplished by the sale of an identical option. Although exercise does not take place, profits (or losses) are experienced because option prices change over time. In particular, a rise in the stock price would cause an increase in the price of a call option (and fall in the price of a put option), whereas a fall in the stock price would tend to result in a higher put option price (and a lower call option price).

For every buyer of an option there must be a seller (the seller is frequently referred to as the writer). Indeed, it is the process of buying and selling options that creates them; if they are not bought and sold, they will not exist. The writer of a call option must deliver the stock for the strike price if the buyer chooses to exercise the option. The writer of a put option must buy at the strike price if the option buyer chooses to exercise the right to sell. The profits/losses of option writers equal the losses/profits of the buyers. The buyer's profit is the writer's loss, and vice versa. The maximum profit for the writer is the premium received. This profit accrues if the option expires unexercised. The writer of a call has unlimited loss potential, while the writer of a put has a loss potential limited only by the fact that stock prices cannot fall below zero.

Short option positions (written options) can be closed out by buying identical options. In the case of exchange traded options, the clearing house will deem long and short positions to cancel each other out. Since the clearing house takes the role of counterparty to every option trader as soon as options are traded, closing out need not be with the original counterparty. A trader can close out by entering a transaction with any other trader. The process of closing out option contracts will tend to reduce the number of contracts in existence (effectively, the process of closing out will destroy an options contract if both counterparties are involved in closing-out transactions).

Further reading

Introductions to options are available in:
Robert W. Kolb, *Financial Derivatives* (Kolb Publishing, Miami, 1993), Chapter 3.
Keith Redhead, *Introduction to the International Money Markets* (Woodhead-Faulkner, Hemel Hempstead, 1992), Chapter 6.
Janette Rutterford, *Introduction to Stock Exchange Investment*, 2nd edn (Macmillan, Basingstoke, 1993), Chapter 7.

RISK MANAGEMENT WITH OPTIONS   8

INTRODUCTION

This chapter begins with an account of the mechanics of fixed hedging with options. This includes an evaluation of the relative merits of using long and short option positions. It also indicates the pay off profiles that result from combining options with a position in the underlying instrument. It then goes on to describe 2 forms of zero-cost option: the participating forward and the cylinder. These constructions are zero cost when the receipts from writing options finance the costs of buying options.

The chapter then looks in more detail at the uses of options. These uses include fixed hedging (wherein the position being hedged matches the quantity to which the option relates, e.g. hedging 1,000 UK shares with one option contract), and delta hedging (which involves the number of option contracts bearing a frequently adjusted ratio to the size of the underlying position).

This leads on to a consideration of how written options may be hedged. An account of delta hedging a written option, using futures or the underlying instrument, is followed by a discussion of how other option series can be used to hedge option sensitivities such as gamma and vega.

The chapter then considers the subject of covered writing. Covered writing involves selling options against an existing position in the underlying, e.g. writing calls against a holding of stock. It is shown that this can be seen either as a technique of yield enhancement or as a hedging strategy.

OPTIONS AS HEDGING INSTRUMENTS

The ultimate economic function of financial derivatives (forwards, futures, swaps and options) is to provide means of risk reduction. Someone who is at risk from a price change can use options to offset that risk. A call option can be seen as a means of ensuring a maximum purchase price (if the market price exceeds the strike price, then the option may be exercised in order to buy at the strike price). A put option provides a minimum selling price (exercise of the right to sell might occur in the event of the market price being below the strike price). So options can be regarded as means of insurance against adverse price movements.

A hedger needs to compare the use of options with at least 2 alternatives. Those alternatives are leaving the exposure unhedged and covering it with futures or forwards. Consider a hedger with a long position (such as a holder of stock) who seeks protection from a fall in the stock price. The protection can be obtained by buying a put option. The result is illustrated by Figure 8.1.

The put option protects the hedger from a price fall. Profits from the option offset losses on the stock. However, profits from the rise in the stock price are not offset by losses from the option (apart from the premium paid for the option). So gains are made from a rise in the stock price. Thus, the net outcome of combining a stockholding with a put option is equivalent to a call option. The combination is known as a synthetic call option.

If the choice is between hedging with the option and not hedging at all, the choice is effectively between the long position and the synthetic call option. If the holder of stock is convinced that the stock price will not fall, then he or she will not be prepared to pay a premium for a put option to protect the position from a price fall. At the other extreme, if the hedger feels certain that the price will fall, he or she will either sell the stock or cover it completely by an offsetting short position (in markets where futures or forwards are available, the short position can be achieved by selling futures contracts or selling forward). The exposure to the price movement is thereby eliminated completely.

FIGURE 8.1 Using a put option for protection

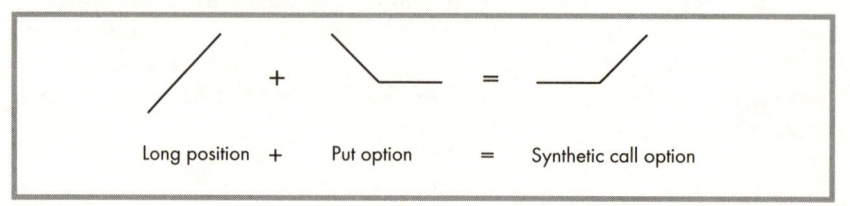

Long position + Put option = Synthetic call option

It follows that options will be used only when there is uncertainty as to the direction of price movement. Even then futures or forwards (or selling stock) are preferable if the hedger believes that the balance of probabilities is that the stock price will fall. The option becomes a possible choice if the hedger either has no view as to future price movements or believes a rise to be the more likely. As illustrated by Figure 8.1, hedging a stockholding with a put option effectively creates a call option. The hedger should construct such a position only if prepared to buy a naked call option (i.e. a call option that is not used for hedging an existing exposure). Option premiums tend to match the (statistical) expectations of profit from holding the options. The statistical expectation is based on possible profits weighted by their probabilities of occurrence. If the hedger believes that the stock price is more likely to rise than fall, then that hedger would value the option more highly (because of the high probability of profits) than the market (which bases option premiums on stock price rises and falls having equal probability).

So it would appear that a hedger will use options only in the event of believing that the stock price movement is uncertain, but more likely to be favourable than unfavourable. Other factors may impinge on the decision. There is attitude to risk. If a hedger is strongly risk averse, then the position would be either liquidated or covered with forwards or futures. Use of options involves some risk, even if it is only the risk of losing the premium paid for the option. An importer may use options to hedge against a rise in the currency of invoice rather than futures or forwards so as to profit from a beneficial currency movement. Hedging with futures or forwards will not provide gain from a beneficial exchange rate movement. Since any unhedged competitors would gain, the competitive position could thus be undermined.

Long versus short option positions

Hedging against a price fall can be carried out by buying a put option and protection against a price rise can be obtained from the purchase of a call option. Alternatively, a call option might be written (sold) as a means of protection from a price fall or a put option written as a means of hedging against a price rise. Writing options is the better approach if the price change is relatively modest, whereas buying options is the more effective strategy in the event of a substantial movement in the price of the stock (or other financial instrument being hedged). Figure 8.2 compares the purchase of a put option with the sale of a call option.

In the example illustrated by Figure 8.2, the 2 options have the same exercise price of 100. The put is priced at 5 and the call at 6. The long (i.e. purchased) put provides protection against a fall in the stock price below

FIGURE 8.2 Comparison of long put and short call options

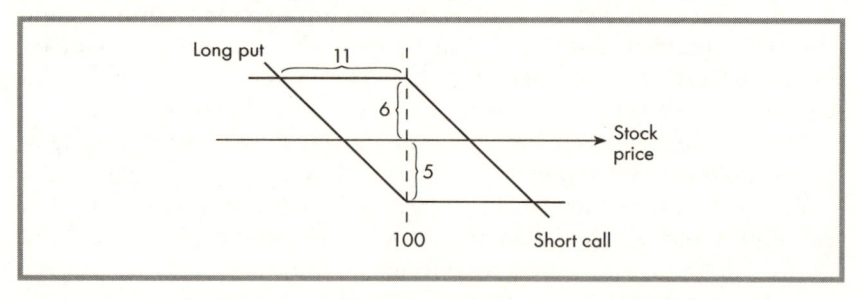

[Figure: graph showing long put and short call payoff lines crossing at stock price 100, with markers 11, 6, and 5 indicating premium differences]

100 but, considering the premium of 5, the put option does not confer a net advantage over an unhedged position until the stock price has fallen below 95. So the long put is beneficial in the event of a substantial price fall.

By writing the call for 6, a premium receipt is obtained and that receipt can be seen as providing downside protection. A stock price fall from 100 to 94 would leave the hedger no worse off since the loss of 6 on the stock would be offset by the premium receipt. However, the downside protection is constant in money terms and stock prices below 94 would entail a net loss. Of course, stock prices above 94 would entail a net profit. So the short call is advantageous in the case of a modest stock price fall.

The short call is superior to the long put down to a stock price of 89. This is demonstrated by Figure 8.2. The net profit from the put option does not exceed that of the call option until the stock price has fallen sufficiently to generate an intrinsic value for the put option of 5 (to offset the put premium) plus 6 (to match the call premium). So the short option position is superior to the long option position until the stock price has moved by the sum of the 2 option premiums. In this case, a hedger seeking protection from a price fall but anticipating a fall of less than 11 would prefer the short call, whereas a hedger fearing a greater fall would buy a put option.

Combining options with positions in the underlying instrument

In order to ascertain the effects, in terms of a profit/loss profile, of combining an option with a position in the underlying instrument, it is necessary to sum the profits and losses of the 2 positions at each possible price of the underlying instrument. Taking a holding of sterling currency as an example, and supposing that the spot price of sterling is $1.61/£, the profit/loss profile of the currency holding would be a diagonal line, as shown in Figure 8.3.

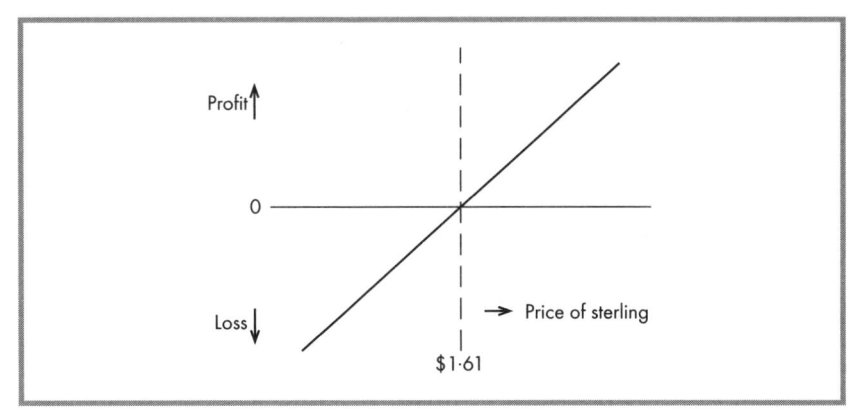

FIGURE 8.3   Profit/loss profile of a currency holding

[Graph showing profit/loss line crossing zero at $1.61 price of sterling, sloping upward from lower-left to upper-right]

If the price of the pound remains at $1.61, there is neither a profit nor a loss. A rise in the pound above $1.61 entails profits (equal to the excess of the new price over $1.61). If the price of sterling falls below $1.61, there will be losses; every cent that the pound falls below $1.61 will be an extra cent of loss.

Suppose that a put option on sterling has a strike price of $1.60 and a premium of 3 cents/£. The profit/loss profile of such a put option is depicted by Figure 8.4. At the currency price of $1.60 and above, the put option would not be exercised. In consequence, the 3 cent premium that has been paid would constitute a net loss. As sterling falls below $1.60, the option acquires intrinsic value; in other words, there is a pay-off from exercising the option. At $1.57 the intrinsic value (the pay-off from exercising the right to sell at $1.60 currency worth $1.57) is 3 cents/£. So when the price of sterling is $1.57, the intrinsic value of the option equals the premium paid. The currency price of $1.57 is the breakeven price and if the pound falls below $1.57 there is a net profit: the intrinsic value exceeds the premium paid.

Figure 8.5 shows the combination of the holding of sterling (referred to as a long position in sterling, a long position being one that benefits from a price rise) and the put option (referred to as a long put because it has been bought).

The combined position is ascertained by summing the profits and losses on the 2 constituent positions. It is useful to begin by considering the profit/loss in the event of the price of sterling being equal to the option strike price, i.e. $1.60. At $1.60 there is a loss of 3 cents/£ from the option (since it has no intrinsic value) and a loss of 1 cent/£ from the currency (which would have fallen from $1.61 to $1.60). So when the price of the pound is $1.60, there is a total loss of 4 cents/£; the combined position shows a loss of 4 cents at $1.60. A fall in sterling below $1.60

FIGURE 8.4   Profit/loss profile of a put option

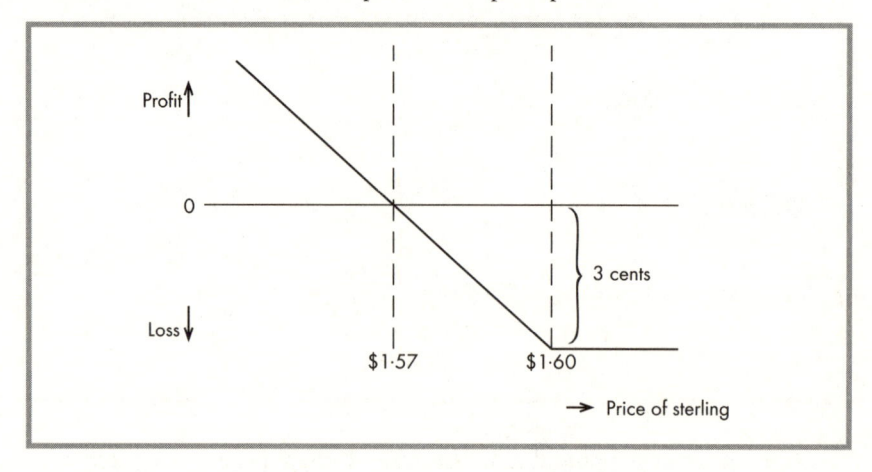

FIGURE 8.5   Combination of holding sterling and the put option

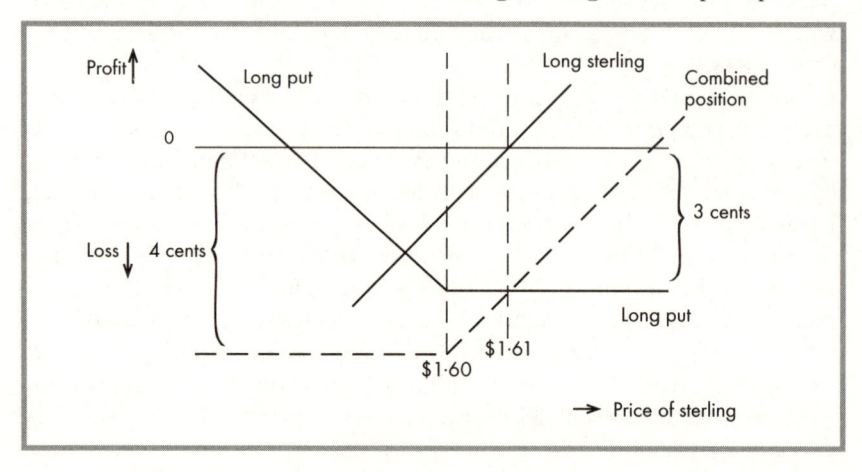

entails further losses on sterling being offset by profits on the option (the option acquires 1 cent in intrinsic value for every cent fall in the pound below $1.60); the net effect is that the overall loss remains constant at 4 cents/£ irrespective of how low sterling falls.

If the price of sterling ends up above $1.60 the option will have no intrinsic value and will therefore show a loss equal to the premium paid, i.e. 3 cents/£. However, the long position in sterling will benefit from a rise in the price of the pound: the higher the price, the greater the benefit. These benefits from a rising pound are not offset by increased losses on the option: the loss on the option cannot exceed the premium paid and hence remains constant at 3 cents/£. So the combined position shows a 1 cent improvement for every 1 cent increase in the price of sterling above $1.60. It is to be noted that above $1.60 the combined position will always be worth 3 cents less than a simple position in sterling, this 3 cents being the loss on the put option.

Example 8.1

It is 6 April. The $/£ spot rate is $1.6085/£. Philadelphia Stock Exchange sterling currency May expiry option prices (in cents per pound) are as follows:

Strike price	Calls	Puts
1.55	6.28	0.65
1.60	2.99	2.22
1.65	1.03	5.23

A UK exporter is due to receive US dollars in early May and intends to convert them to sterling. The exporter would lose from a rise in the price of sterling and thus has a short position in sterling. This could be hedged by buying (Figure 8.6) a call option or writing (Figure 8.7) a put option. Buying a call will be suitable if a large rise is feared, and a put might be written if it was thought that any rise would be modest.

FIGURE 8.6 Hedging a short sterling position by buying a $1.60 call option

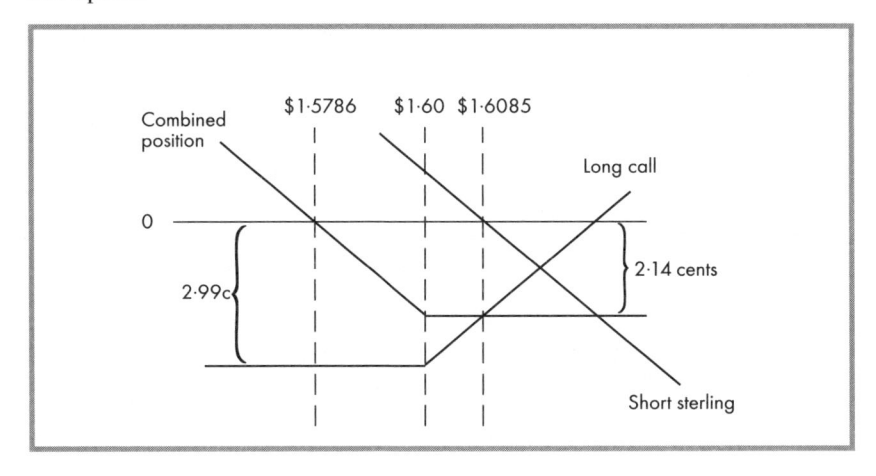

178 • RISK MANAGEMENT WITH OPTIONS

FIGURE 8.7 Hedging a short sterling position by writing a $1.60 put option

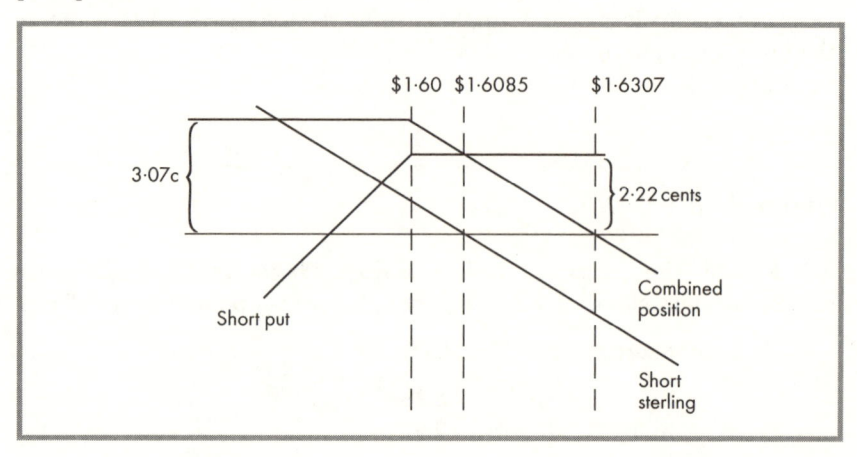

ACTIVITY 8.1

The GEC option prices are as follows, whilst the share price is 236p.

Strike price	Calls			Puts		
	Oct	Jan	Apr	Oct	Jan	Apr
220	19	30	39	1½	7	12
240	5	17	27	9	14	22
260	1	11	18	25	28	32

1. Draw the profit/loss profile for the buyer of a January 220p call option. What is the breakeven price at expiry? Indicate the maximum profit and maximum loss.
2. Draw the profit/loss profile for the writer of an April 260p call option. What is the breakeven price at expiry? Indicate the maximum profit and maximum loss.
3. Draw the profit/loss profile for the buyer of an April 240p put option. What is the breakeven price at expiry? Indicate the maximum profit and maximum loss.
4. Buy 1,000 shares and buy one January 240p put option. Draw the profit/loss profile of the combined position. Identify the breakeven share price at expiry and the maximum profit and loss.
5. Buy 1,000 shares and write one January 240p call option. Draw the profit/loss profile of the combined position. Identify the breakeven share price at expiry and the maximum profit and loss.

OPTIONS AS HEDGING INSTRUMENTS • 179

Answer
Figures 8.8 to 8.12 illustrate the profit/loss profiles for each question.

1. (a) 250p, (b) no maximum profit, (c) 30p.
2. (a) 278p, (b) 18p, (c) no maximum loss.
3. (a) 218p, (b) 218p, (c) 22p.
4. (a) 250p, (b) unlimited profit potential, (c) 10p.
5. (a) 219p, (b) 21p, (c) 219p.

FIGURE 8.8   Answer 1

FIGURE 8.9   Answer 2

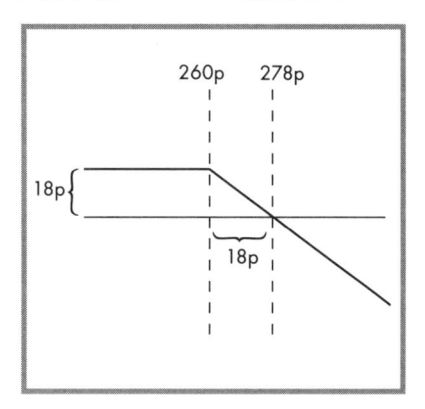

FIGURE 8.10   Answer 3

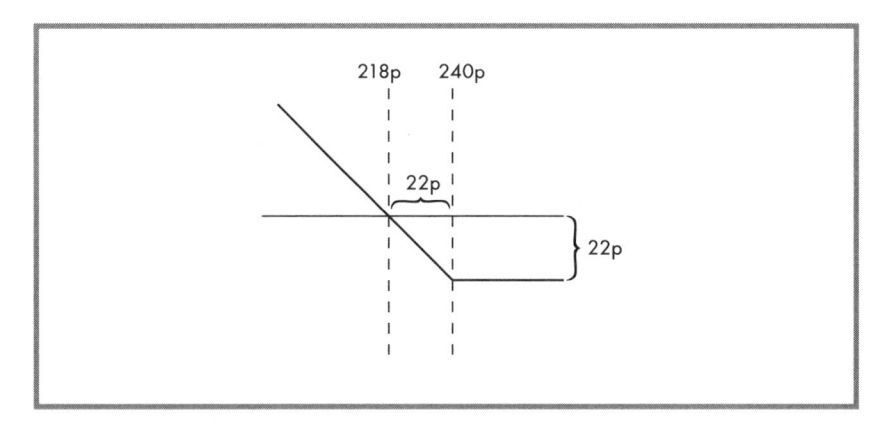

180 • **RISK MANAGEMENT WITH OPTIONS**

FIGURE 8.11   Answer 4

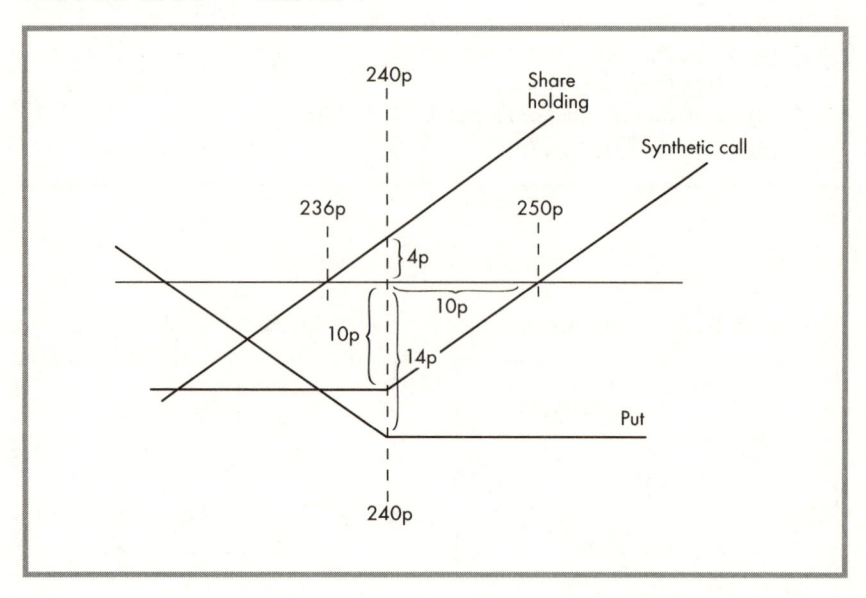

FIGURE 8.12   Answer 5

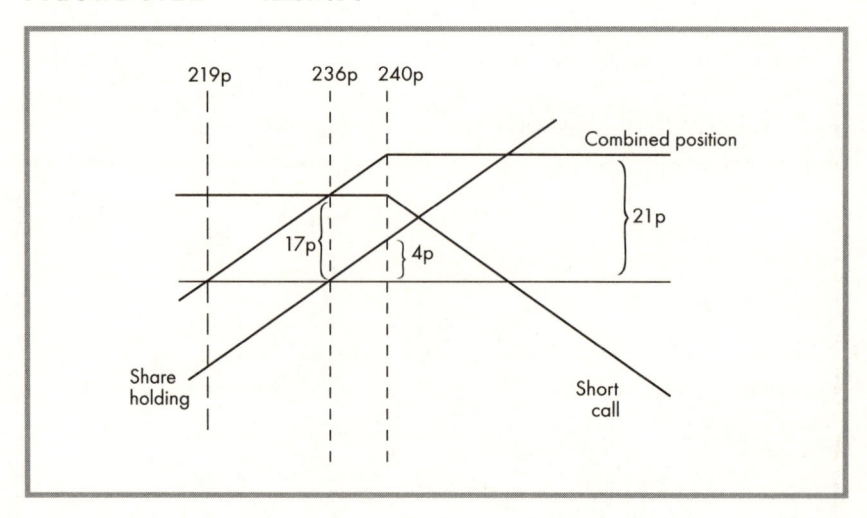

ZERO-COST OPTIONS

Buying an option involves paying a premium, whereas selling an option gives rise to the receipt of a premium. Zero-cost options are instruments that can be broken down into constituent options. They consist of long option positions financed by the sale of other options. They can be subdivided into participating forwards and range forwards.

All the constituent options in a participating forward have the same strike price. For the purpose of hedging against a price fall, a purchase of out-of-the-money puts could be financed by the sale of a smaller number of in-the-money calls (in other words, the stock price is greater than the strike price). The resulting configuration could be as illustrated by Figure 8.13.

The put options would completely cover the hedger against a price fall, whereas the call options would not fully negate the benefits of a price rise. So the net effect is that of a forward contract that allows some participation in the benefits of a price rise. (At first sight this strategy may seem to offer benefits without costs. Alas, benefits must be paid for, in this case by way of the strike price being below the stock price – so the guaranteed selling price is unfavourable.)

The other form of zero-cost option has a number of names, including range forward, cylinder and split-synthetic. The constituent options have different strike prices. A price fall could be hedged against by buying a put option with a strike price below the stock price and financing its purchase by writing a call option with a strike price above the stock price. This has the advantage of allowing some profit from a rise in the stock price (up to the strike price of the call option), but at the cost of having no protection against a price fall until the stock price reaches the strike price of the put option. A short range forward (cylinder) is illustrated by Figure 8.14. A long range forward (long cylinder) is illustrated by Figure 8.15.

FIGURE 8.13 Participating forward

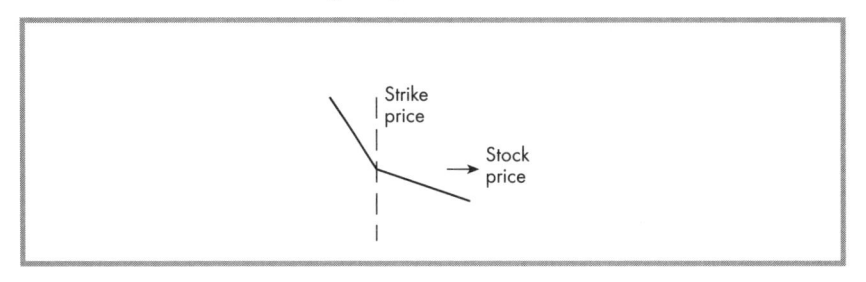

182 ● **RISK MANAGEMENT WITH OPTIONS**

FIGURE 8.14 Range forward zero-cost option (cylinder)

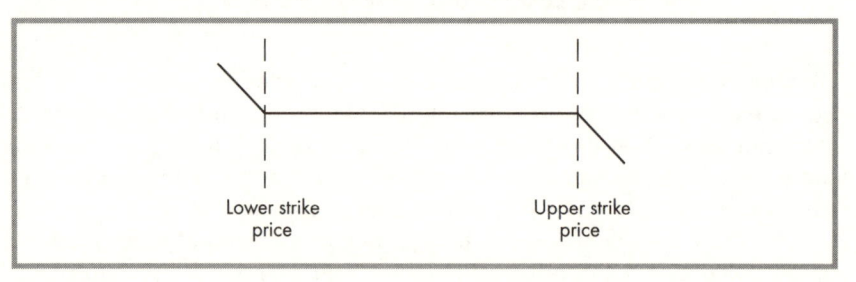

FIGURE 8.15 Option cylinder (range forward)

A long cylinder is used to hedge a short position (i.e. used to hedge against price rises). A high strike price call is bought and a low strike price put is written.

The spot price usually lies between the two exercise prices.

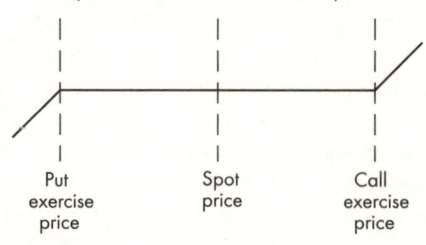

The cylinder allows price movements within a range (between the strike prices) but prevents extreme values. The call provides a maximum price and the put a minimum price.

If the receipts from selling the put match the cost of buying the call the cylinder is referred to as a zero cost option.

ACTIVITY 8.2

It is 20 May. A British company needs to sell sterling in order to pay a US dollar invoice 3 months from the present.
(a) How can options be used to provide protection against a fall in the pound whilst retaining the ability to profit from a rise in the pound?
(b) How can options be used to hedge against a fall in the pound whilst avoiding a net premium payment?
Illustrate your answers using the following information, indicating maximum profits, maximum losses, and breakeven points for the combined positions (options plus currency).

ZERO-COST OPTIONS • 183

Spot exchange rate $1.6244 per £1.
Options due to expire in three months have the following prices:

Strike price ($ per £)	Option prices (cents per £)	
	Calls	Puts
1.62	2.66	2.17
1.63	2.21	2.63

Answer
(a) Buy a $1.62 put option.

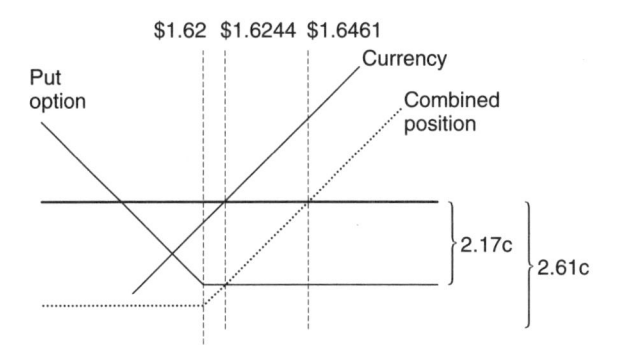

Maximum loss is 2.17 + (162.44 − 162) = 2.61 cents
Breakeven currency price $1.6461
There is no upper limit to the profit

(b) *Construct a short cylinder by buying a $1.62 put and writing a $1.63 call. This entails a net premium receipt of 2.21 − 2.17 = 0.04 cents per £1.*

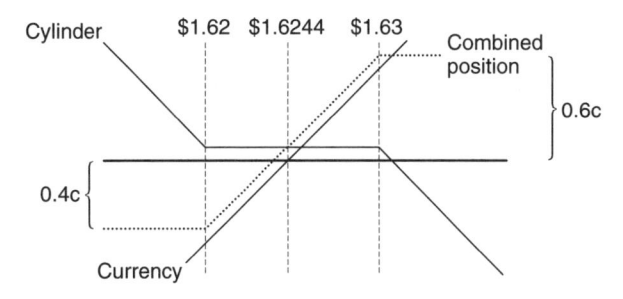

Maximum profit is 0.6 cents
Maximum loss is 0.4 cents
Breakeven currency price is $1.6240

Caps, floors, and collars

Caps, floors, and collars are successions of interest rate options. The buyer of a cap establishes a maximum level to the interest rate payable over a number of future periods. For example, a borrower may have a five-year debt on which the interest rate is reassessed every 6 months based on sterling LIBOR. A cap might provide compensation in the event of sterling LIBOR exceeding 7% p.a., thereby providing an upper limit to the interest rate payable. If sterling LIBOR remains below 7% p.a. the seller of the cap makes no payments to the buyer of the cap. An interest rate in excess of 7% p.a. leads to the seller of the cap paying a sum equal to the additional interest cost.

The notional principal may be £10 million. If sterling LIBOR rises to 8% p.a., the seller of the cap pays the buyer a sum equal to 1% p.a. on £10 million for 6 months (10,000,000 × 0.01 × 0.5 = £50,000). If, 6 months later, the rate has fallen to 7.5% p.a. the compensation to be paid will be £25,000.

A floor fixes a minimum level to an interest rate. A depositor might buy a floor in order to ensure that interest receipts do not fall below a particular level. If the interest rate falls below the strike level, the seller of the floor pays the buyer a sum of money to compensate for the difference between the actual and strike interest rates.

A cap could be looked upon as a succession of future call options, and a floor as a succession of put options. A collar could be regarded as a succession of cylinders (a cylinder involves either buying a call at a high strike price and selling a put at a low strike price, or buying a put at a low strike price and selling a call at a high strike price). A borrower could limit the potential interest payments by buying a cap whilst simultaneously selling a floor. The sale of the floor prevents the borrower benefiting from a fall in the interest rate below the floor level. A zero cost collar entails the receipts from the sale of the floor being sufficient to finance the purchase of the cap.

Conversely a depositor might buy a floor and finance the purchase by selling a cap. The depositor thus guarantees that the interest receipts will not fall below the floor level, but at the cost of foregoing any potential interest receipts above the cap level. The collar ensures that the interest flows cannot fall outside a range of values, the effective interest rate is subject to an upper and lower limit.

HEDGING ANTICIPATED PURCHASES

Options can be used to hedge intended purchases of stocks. Suppose it is 12 November 19XX and that a portfolio manager intends to buy XYZ stock with funds expected to become available at the end of November. The current price of XYZ stock is $236 and the portfolio manager wishes to avoid the risks of having to pay a much higher price in December. The prices of XYZ call options are found to be as shown in Table 8.1.

The portfolio manager could buy December 240 call options at 17. Each option contract provides the right, but not the obligation, to buy 100 XYZ shares at a price of 240 per share. The price of the option is 17 per share, which amounts to $1,700 ($17 × 100) per option contract.

If when the stock was purchased in December the price were 260, the portfolio manager could exercise the options and thereby buy stock at 240. This represents a saving of 20 per share at a premium cost of 17 per share: a net profit of 3 per share.

By exercising an option the hedger obtains its intrinsic value. If instead he sold the option, he would receive the time value as well as the intrinsic value. The time value might be 10 and hence the sale price of the option would be 30. The portfolio manager would have bought options for 17 and sold them for 30. There would have been a net profit of 13 per share rather than the 3 obtained from exercising the options. The 13 per share profit from the options partially offsets the increased price of the stock, whose effective price becomes 247 (260 – 13).

If the stock price were 240 or less at the time the stock was purchased, the options held would have no intrinsic value and therefore could not be profitably exercised. However, they would still have time value. For example, if the share price were still 236, the December 240 call options might be selling at 13. The options would have been bought for 17 and sold for 11 (assuming a bid–offer spread of 2). The net cost of 6 (i.e. $600 per contract covering 100 shares) compares favourably with the net cost of 17 ($1,700) incurred if the option is allowed to expire unexercised.

Table 8.1   XYZ call options

Exercise price	Premium		
	November	December	January
220	19	30	39
240	5	17	27
260	1	11	18

DELTA HEDGING WITH OPTIONS

In the previous example the hedger did not obtain full cover for the proposed stock purchase. The stock price rose by 24, while the net profit per share obtained from the options was only 13. Delta hedging provides a means of obtaining full compensation for the adverse stock price movement.

The delta of an option is the ratio of the change in the price of that option to the change in the price of the underlying stock. Delta hedging involves buying more than one option for each block of 100 shares covered. If, for example, the delta were 0.5, the hedger would buy 2 options for each block of 100 shares covered. When the option price changes by half as much as the stock price, twice as many options are bought (since each call option represents the right to purchase 100 shares, this implies 2 options per block of 100 shares covered). By using the appropriate ratio of options to shares, the extra cost of the stock to be purchased can be exactly offset by a profit from a rise in the price of the options.

In the previous example the stock price rose by 24, whereas the option price rose by 13. This implies that the average delta of the option was 0.54 (13/24) over the share price range 236–260. Approximately 1.85 (i.e. 1/0.54) options per 100 shares would have provided full cover against the stock price movement. The requisite number of options per 100 shares is the reciprocal of the delta.

A difficulty that arises with delta hedging is the tendency for the delta to change as the stock price moves. In the example, the delta would have been less than 0.5 at the stock price of 236 and greater than 0.5 at the stock price of 260. The requisite number of option contracts per 100 shares would have moved from above 2 to below 2. This suggests the need to adjust constantly the number of options held as the stock price moves. This is problematical not only because of the time and expense involved in constantly monitoring and adjusting option holdings, but also because option contracts are indivisible. Since fractions of contracts cannot be bought, precise cover cannot be achieved.

The lack of divisibility is not a significant drawback when large blocks of shares are to be purchased, but it can be very inconvenient when small blocks, such as 100 shares, are to be bought. Nevertheless, a hedger covering an anticipated purchase of 100 shares would have achieved a much better hedge with two option contracts (the number that would have been approximately the quantity indicated by the delta when the share price was 236p) than with the simple one option per 100 shares strategy.

Hedging the value of a stockholding

A put option guarantees a minimum selling price for a block of 100 shares (1,000 shares in the United Kingdom). Table 8.2 shows the premiums of XYZ put options at the close of trading on 12 November 19XX, at which time the price of XYZ stock was $236.

Table 8.2 XYZ put options

Strike price	Premium		
	November	December	January
220	1½	7	12
240	9	14	22
260	25	28	32

A holder of 500 XYZ shares would be able to ensure that the value of the stockholding could not fall below $110,000 (500 × $220) by buying five 220 put options. These options would provide the right to sell 500 XYZ shares at 220. The option prices are expressed in dollars per share, so the cost of providing such protection until the December expiry date would be $3,500 (500 × $7). Of course, should the stock price remain in excess of 220, the shareholder would not exercise the right to sell at 220.

Although the stockholder has the right to exercise the option and thereby sell stock at 220, he is more likely to sell, rather than exercise, the option. This can be understood by considering the elements that make up an option premium. The premium (i.e. the price) of an option can be subdivided into its intrinsic value and its time value. The intrinsic value represents the profit that could be obtained by immediately exercising the option. For example, a November 240 put option has an intrinsic value of 4 when the stock price is 236 since, by exercising the option, shares can be sold at 4 more than the price at which they are bought. The difference between the option premium and the intrinsic value is termed time value, which is 5 in the case of the November 240 put options. Time value can be regarded as a payment for the possibility that intrinsic value will increase prior to the date on which the option expires, i.e. the date beyond which it cannot be exercised. If a stockholder exercises an option, only the intrinsic value is received, whereas if the option is sold, both the intrinsic and time values are obtained. It thus makes sense to sell an option in preference to exercising it.

In Table 8.2 the 220 puts have exercise prices below the market value of the stock. Therefore, they cannot be exercised at a profit and have zero intrinsic value. Their price consists entirely of time value. Put options with exercise prices below the market price of the stock are said to be out of the money. When the stock price is equal to the exercise price, the option is said to be at the money. Put options with exercise prices above the stock price (the only ones with intrinsic value) are termed in the money.

Time value is at its highest when the option is at the money and declines as the stock price moves away from the exercise price (in either direction). If the stockholder bought December 220 put options at 7 on 12 November and saw the stock price fall by 20 the following day, he would simultaneously have seen the price of his options rise. A new option price of 14 would seem plausible (an intrinsic value of 4 plus time value raised from 7 to 10).

Faced with the choice between exercising the options and thereby selling stock at the exercise price of 220, and following the alternative route of selling stock at the new market price of 216 and simultaneously selling the options at 14, the investor will clearly favour the latter procedure. The $14 premium would include time value of 10, the receipt of which via selling the options gives an effective share price of 230 (223 after taking account of the original cost of the options) instead of the 220 from exercising the option ($213 after deducting the $7 original cost).

Had the stock price fallen to a more modest extent, say to 224, there would have been no benefit from exercising the options. However, there would have been some time value; 10 is plausible. Selling the stock at 224 and simultaneously selling the options at 10 gives an effective selling price of 234 ($227 allowing for the initial $7 premium paid).

In neither of the foregoing 2 cases did the stockholder succeed in maintaining the value of his stockholding. The effective stock prices were 223 and 227, after deducting the original premium, even when the options were sold rather than exercised.

Delta hedging provides a technique for maintaining the original value of the stockholding. In other words, it can ensure that the stock price plus profit on the options equals 236 per share. This is achieved by factoring up the number of options contracts purchased.

The delta of an option is a measure of the responsiveness of the option price to movements in the underlying stock price. It is the change in the option price divided by the change in the stock price. Put options have negative deltas because they become more valuable as the stock price falls. Deep out-of-the-money options have deltas close to zero, at-the-money options have deltas close to −0.5 and deep in-the-money options have deltas that approach −1.

An option buyer can be regarded as having acquired an asset. Delta hedging involves ensuring that increases in the value of one asset – the options – offset declines in the value of another asset – the stockholding.

Referring again to Table 8.2, it can be seen that the 240 put options are slightly in the money. December 240 put option deltas might plausibly be −0.625. Delta hedging involves factoring up the number of option contracts by the reciprocal of the delta, in this case 1.6 (i.e.

1/0.625). The hedger wishing to protect the value of 500 XYZ shares at $118,000 (500 × $236) can do so by purchasing eight (5 × 1.6) December 240 put options at 14. The initial cost of the options would be $11,200 (800 × $14). A $1 fall in the stock price would be accompanied by a $0.625 rise in the option price. So the $500 (500 × $1) loss on the value of the shares would be accompanied by a $500 (800 × $0.625) profit on the options.

Unfortunately, the movement of the stock price would tend to change the value of the delta; see Figure 8.16. So a delta hedge would need to be constantly monitored and the number of options increased or decreased in the light of changed circumstances. These circumstances include not only the underlying stock price, but also the time remaining to the expiry date of the option and the expected volatility of the stock price.

This need for monitoring and rebalancing the number of options contracts is a significant drawback of delta hedging, as is the possibility that the requisite number of options might not be a whole number. Options are indivisible and so perfect hedging is impossible when something other than a whole number of contracts is required. For a holder of a diversified portfolio, stock index options might be an attractive alternative to hedging individual stocks with their corresponding option contracts, because the problem of indivisibility becomes proportionately smaller when larger numbers of shares are being hedged.

FIGURE 8.16 The call option delta as a function of the stock price

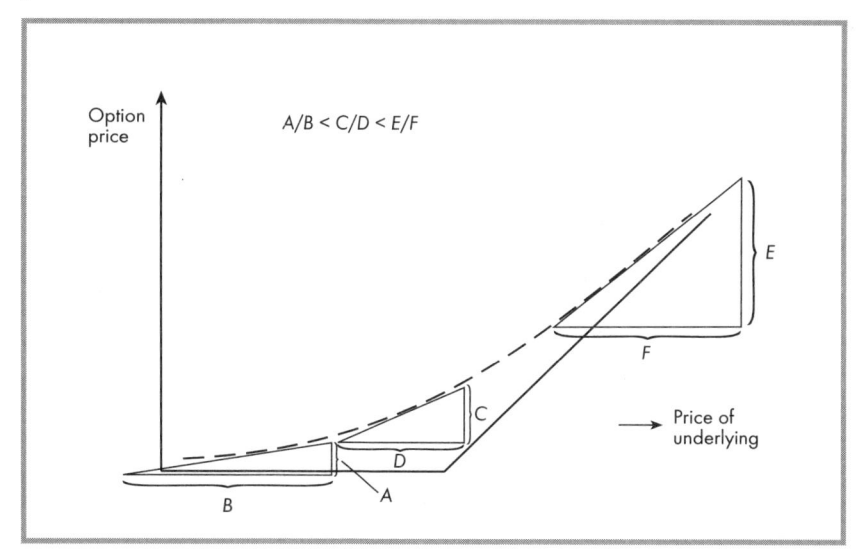

Example 8.2

$$\text{Delta} = \frac{\text{change in option price}}{\text{change in share price}}$$

Share price falls 1p
↓

Put option price rises 0.625p

$$\text{Delta} = \frac{0.625}{1.000} = 0.625$$

$$\text{Hedge ratio} = \frac{1}{0.625} = 1.6$$

1p share price fall on 5,000 shares
→ loss of £50

0.625p option price rise on 8 contracts (at 1,000 shares per contract)
→ profit of £50

Example 8.3

It is 12 November. Central Bank shares stand at 190p and the option prices are as follows (deltas in brackets):

Strike price	Calls			Puts		
	Dec	Mar	Jun	Dec	Mar	Jun
180	18(0.8)	28(0.7)	32(0.6)	7(–0.2)	16(–0.3)	22(–0.4)
200	10(0.2)	20(0.3)	23(0.4)	17(–0.8)	26(–0.7)	32(–0.6)

A fund manager wants to delta hedge a holding of 10,000 Central Bank shares.

Hedging a long position in stock requires the establishment of a negative delta with options. One approach would be to buy 14 March 200p puts. This fails to provide a perfect hedge since that would require about 14.3 contracts (1/0.7 = 1.429). Buying 25 June 180p would avoid such an initial imperfection, but the hedge may subsequently become imperfect as the delta changes and the hedge is rebalanced. Buying 50 December 180p puts reduces the extent of any hedge imperfection, but such a large number of contracts would involve substantial commission costs. Furthermore, options so close to expiry would be subject to rapid time value decay.

A negative delta can alternatively be produced by writing calls. This has the attraction of involving premium receipts and benefiting from time value decay, but involves the risk of early exercise which would destroy the position (the likelihood of such a possibility could be reduced by writing out-of-the-money calls with distant expiry). So writing 25 June 200p calls might be considered.

It may be the case that liquidity constraints dictate the use of near expiry contracts or the use of a combination of option series. A combination of option series may also be attractive for the purpose of balancing the various considerations referred to above.

DELTA HEDGING OF OPTIONS

Not only is it possible to use options to delta hedge a position in stocks (or other underlying instrument), it is also possible to use the underlying instrument to hedge an option position. If futures are available on an instrument, then futures, rather than the instrument itself, may be used for the delta hedging.

Consider the case in which a bank has written a call option on the FTSE 100 stock index and that the option relates to an amount of stock equal to £1,000 times the stock index. This gives a negative exposure to the stock index that can be offset by a long position in FTSE 100 futures contracts.

Since the futures contract is based on £25 per index point, the option coverage would correspond to 40 (£1,000/£25) futures contracts (assuming that the futures index moves on a one-to-one basis with the spot index). However, hedging the short option position would not normally require the purchase of 40 futures contracts since the option provides an exposure to the index equal to the index times £1,000 times the option delta. Consequently, the requisite number of futures contracts would be 40 times the option delta; see Figure 8.17.

This approach to hedging the written option (known alternatively as delta or dynamic hedging) involves constantly monitoring the hedge and changing the number of futures contracts whenever the option delta changes – a process known as rebalancing. Since it aims to ensure that the exposure provided by the futures (or the underlying instrument) always matches that of the option, it may be seen as the simulation of an option position. It might be noted that this dynamic hedging process involves buying futures in a rising market and selling in a falling market, so it can have a destabilising effect on the market.

192 • **RISK MANAGEMENT WITH OPTIONS**

FIGURE 8.17 Delta hedging a written call option

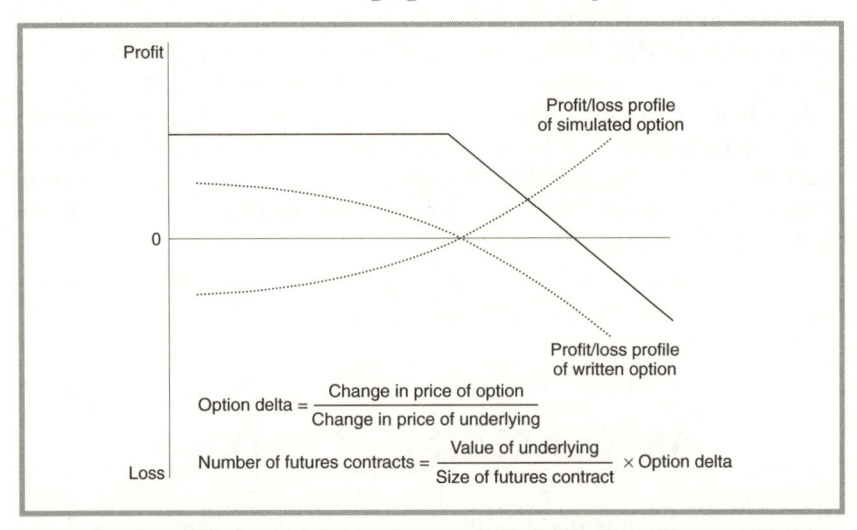

Profit/loss profile of simulated option

Profit/loss profile of written option

$$\text{Option delta} = \frac{\text{Change in price of option}}{\text{Change in price of underlying}}$$

$$\text{Number of futures contracts} = \frac{\text{Value of underlying}}{\text{Size of futures contract}} \times \text{Option delta}$$

ACTIVITY 8.3

(a) An equity options trader sells an at-the-money call option on 1,000 shares of the equity of XYZ plc for a 28-day period. The trade is hedged in the equity market using delta-weighted hedging until 7 days before expiry, when the position is closed by buying back a similar call in the market. Assuming that the trader always deals at the market's price, and neglecting the funding of interim cash flows, calculate the net profit or loss on the transaction, given the following information about the underlying share price and the option's delta:

Week	Share price (p) Bid	Offer	Option price (p) Bid	Offer	Option delta	Days remaining
1	98.5	101.5	2.5	4.0	0.54	28
2	103.5	106.5	5.5	7.0	0.78	21
3	105.5	108.5	6.5	8.0	0.89	14
4	108.5	111.5	9.5	11.0	1	7

(b) To what risks does the trader remain exposed during the period that the hedge is in place?

(Based on the Securities Institute examination in Financial Futures and Options, December 1993, Question 9.)

Answer
(a) Week 1: Sell call option for £25. Buy 540 shares at £101.5 = £548.10.
Week 2: Buy 240 shares at £1.065 = £255.60.

Week 3: Buy 110 shares at £1.085 = £119.35.
At close: Buy call option for £110. Sell 890 shares at £1.085 = £965.65.
Net loss: £25 − £548.10 − £255.60 − £119.35 − £110 + £965.65 = £42.40.

(b) The risk of a jump up or down in the stock before the hedge can be rebalanced. The risk of a rise in volatility. The risk of a rise in transactions costs/loss of liquidity in the underlying cash market.

HEDGING OPTION SENSITIVITIES (GREEKS)

It is often desirable to hedge option positions. For example, a bank that has written an option has resultant exposures that it may wish to hedge. Hedging often focuses solely on delta. However, there is also gamma (change in delta per unit change in the price of the underlying instrument, e.g. stock), vega (sensitivity of the option price to changes in volatility), theta (sensitivity of the option price to the passage of time) and rho (change in the option price per basis point change in short-term interest rates). The writer of the option may wish to hedge more dimensions than the delta.

Suppose that the option writer wanted to hedge the option delta, gamma (to render the delta neutrality more robust) and vega. The delta can be hedged by means of a position in the underlying or futures on the underlying. Gamma and vega can only be hedged by other option positions. Each sensitivity (or 'Greek') that is hedged requires at least one additional hedging instrument. So simultaneously hedging delta, gamma and vega necessitates at least three instruments. The hedging instruments for gamma and vega must be 2 option positions different from the one being hedged (unless it is possible to take a long position in an option that is identical to the written one, in which case all dimensions would be automatically hedged).

Each additional option position disturbs the other hedges since every option position introduces its own delta, gamma and vega. The underlying (or its futures) has zero gamma and zero vega, and hence does not disturb any hedge in these characteristics. It is thus possible to use option positions to hedge gamma and vega, and then a position in the underlying (or futures) to hedge the remaining delta.

Since each option contract has its own gamma and vega, the numbers of both of the options used for hedging must be solved for simultaneously.

Otherwise, a hedge in one dimension with one option would be disturbed when the other dimension is hedged with a different option position. So simultaneous equations must be used.

Consider the case in which option Z has been written and that option Z has a gamma of 0.7 and a vega of 1.3 (so that the written position exhibits a gamma of -0.7 and a vega of -1.3). The 2 option series chosen to hedge option Z are option X with a gamma of 0.8 and a vega of 1.2, and option Y with a gamma of 0.5 and a vega of 1.5.

The solution involves solving the following simultaneous equations:

$0.8X + 0.5Y = 0.7$ (1)
$1.2X + 1.5Y = 1.3$ (2)

The numbers on the right-hand side are the values of gamma and vega required to neutralise the gamma and vega of option Z. In the equations, X and Y represent the requisite numbers of option X and option Y. The solution can be obtained by multiplying equation (1) by 3 and then subtracting equation (2):

$$\begin{array}{ll} 2.4X + 1.5Y = 2.1 & (1) \times 3 \\ -(1.2X + 1.5Y = 1.3) & -(2) \\ \hline 1.2X \quad\quad\quad = 0.8 & \end{array}$$

So $X = 0.8/1.2 = 2/3$. Putting this value into equation (2) gives:

$1.2 (2/3) + 1.5Y = 1.3$
i.e. $1.5Y = 0.5$
$Y = 0.5/1.5 = 1/3$

So 2/3 of option X and 1/3 of option Y would establish gamma and vega neutrality (obviously, the size of the position to be hedged would entail whole numbers of option contracts, the 2/3 and 1/3 would be multiplied up in line with the number of contracts being hedged). The delta of the total option position (which is the net delta of the three options) could be hedged with the underlying (or futures on it).

Figure 8.18 illustrates the relationships between the price, delta and gamma of a call option.

COVERED WRITING

Covered writing refers to selling call options corresponding to assets held or selling put options when the liquidity for the purchase of the underlying is held. So covered writing involves the portfolio manager being prepared for the eventuality of being exercised against.

FIGURE 8.18 Price, delta and gamma of an option in relation to the price of the underlying instrument

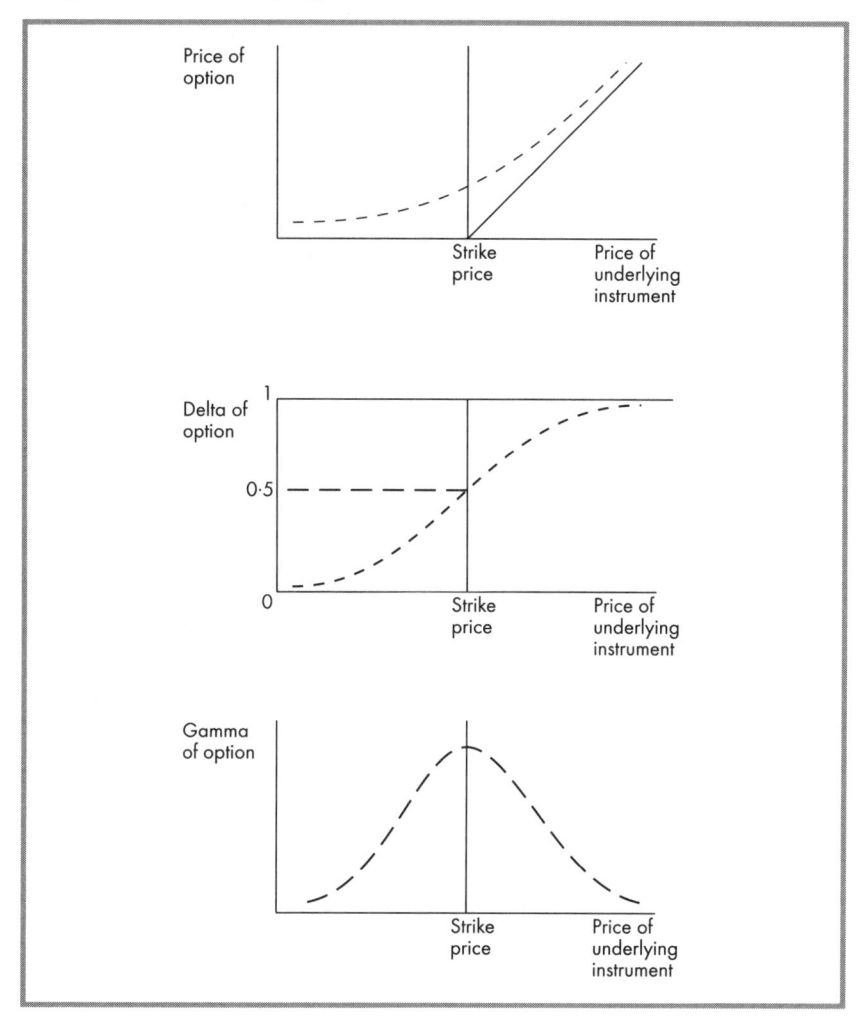

It may be the case that a portfolio manager has in mind a share price at which he would be prepared to buy and another at which he would be prepared to sell; see Figure 8.19. For example, he might be prepared to buy more shares in XYZ plc if the stock price falls to 180p and sell some of his existing holding if the price reaches 220p. In such a situation it might make sense for the fund manager to write 180p puts and write 220p calls. Writing these options would provide premium receipts whilst bringing about the desired transactions in the event of the stock price passing 180p or 220p.

ACTIVITY 8.4

A delta-neutral portfolio has a gamma of −40 and a vega of −60. Two additional options are available in the market. One has a delta of 0.6, gamma of 0.5 and vega of 1.5, while the other has a delta of 0.5, gamma of 0.8 and vega of 1.2.

(a) What positions in these new options should be taken to make the resulting portfolio gamma and vega netural?
(b) What would be the delta of the new portfolio incorporating these options?
(c) Suggest reasons for constructing a portfolio with these characteristics.

(Based on the Securities Institute examination in Financial Futures and Options, December 1991, Question 24.)

Answer

(a) If x and y are the holdings of the 2 options, then x and y must satisfy the equations:

$0.5x + 0.8y = 40$
$1.5x + 1.2y = 60$

These equations are satisfied by no x plus $50y$.

So gamma and vega neutrality are established by buying 50 of the second option.

(b) The delta of the new position would equal the delta of the original portfolio plus the delta of the new option holding:

$0 + 0.5 \times 50 = 25$

(c) The original portfolio was a position based on a bearish view of volatility. In other words, it was a short volatility trade. It was neutral with respect to the price of the underlying. The new portfolio is bullish on the price of the underlying and neutral with respect to volatility.

The transactions are consistent with an alteration of market view by a trader who does not wish to unwind the existing option positions.

Covered writing would also be a strategy that arises from a view that the market will be stable for a period of time.

If a fund manager expects the market to be stable, writing (i.e. selling) call options that are covered by his or her portfolio is a rational strategy. The premiums received from such covered writing (selling) augment the returns on the portfolio.

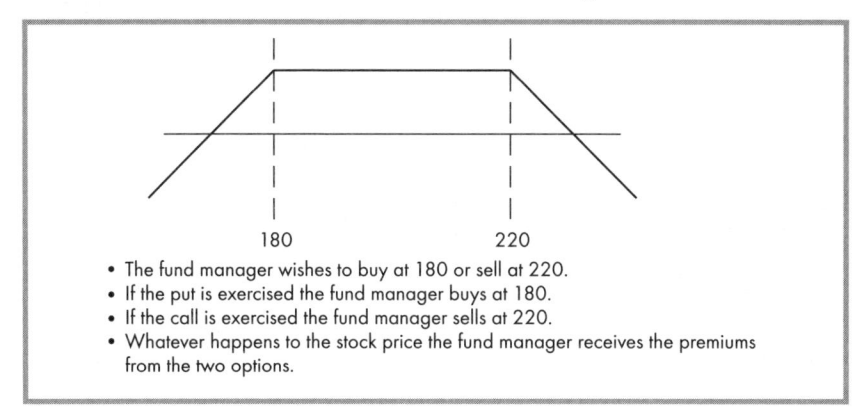

FIGURE 8.19 Illustration of covered writing

- The fund manager wishes to buy at 180 or sell at 220.
- If the put is exercised the fund manager buys at 180.
- If the call is exercised the fund manager sells at 220.
- Whatever happens to the stock price the fund manager receives the premiums from the two options.

The analysis can be expressed in terms of options on individual stocks covered by holdings of those stocks (for delivery if the option seller (writer) is assigned), or in terms of stock index options covered by a portfolio of shares.

Suppose it is 19 August and a fund manager has a balanced portfolio of UK equities with a value of £1 million and a beta of approximately 1. Suppose further that the FTSE 100 Index stands at 3067 and the FTSE 100 call options for September expiry with a strike price of 3100 are priced at 32. Since each contract relates to stock worth £10 per index point (3067 × £10), the fund manager can write up to 32 option contracts whilst being fully covered, £1,000,000/£30,670 = 32.6. (Note that the denominator is £10 multiplied by the current index and not £10 multiplied by the strike price.)

Selling 32 contracts would yield 32 × £320 = £10,240 (ignoring the bid–offer spread and other transactions costs). This yield is in addition to the dividend yield from the shares held. The drawback is that if the market rises by more than 33 points over the remaining life of the option, the fund manager will forgo any market rise beyond those 33 points; so this strategy would be attractive only if no strong market rise in the short term is expected.

Rates of return

The yield can be expressed as a rate of return on the net investment. The net investment is the expenditure on shares minus the receipts from selling options. For example:

Initial value of portfolio	£1,000,000
Less option premiums received	–£10,240
Net cash investment	£989,760

198 • RISK MANAGEMENT WITH OPTIONS

The potential rate of return can be expressed as 'return if unchanged' or as 'return if exercised'. The 'return if unchanged' is the rate of return in the event of the FTSE 100 Index remaining at 3067, in which event the 3,100 calls would not be exercised.

Unchanged value of portfolio	£1,000,000
Less net cash investment	−£989,760
Profit	£10,240

Rate of return = £10,240/£989,760 or 1.03%. It is to be emphasised that the appropriate denominator is the net cash investment and not the value of the portfolio.

When ascertaining the 'return if exercised' (which is the maximum return), it is necessary to take into account the profit on the portfolio arising from the market movement. (For clarity of exposition, dividends and transactions costs will continue to be ignored.)

Portfolio value upon exercise	£1,010,760	(£1,000,000 × 3100/3067)
Less net cash investment	−£989,760	
Profit	£21,000	

Rate of return = £21,000/£989,760 or 2.12%. It is to be noted that in the case of stock index options, 'portfolio value upon exercise' refers to the new value of the original portfolio minus the cash settlement made upon assignment. (Stock index options are cash settled, i.e. there is no delivery of stock if the option is exercised; instead, there is a cash settlement equal to the intrinsic value of the option.)

ACTIVITY 8.5

It is 15 March. FTSE option prices on LIFFE are:

Strike price	Calls			Puts		
	March	April	May	March	April	May
1800	64	88	110	23	47	65
1850	35	60	83	45	73	88
1900	16	38	60	77	103	115

The FTSE 100 Index is 1839. A portfolio manager has a balanced fund worth £1 million, with a beta equal to the beta of the FTSE 100 Index. Describe a strategy that could be pursued in order to increase returns in a stable market environment. Ignoring transactions costs and dividend receipts, calculate the rate of return achieved if on the option expiry date the FTSE 100 Index is (a) 1750, (b) 1839, and (c) 1950.

Answer
Write April 1850 call options. The number of contracts required for near complete cover is 54 (£1,000,000/£18,390 = 54.38).

Value of stock	£1,000,000
Less option premiums received	−£32,400
Net cash investment	£967,600

In cases (a) and (b) the option would be unexercised:

(a)
Value of stock	£951,604	[(1750/1839) × £1 million]
Less net cash investment	−£967,600	
Net profit/loss	−£15,996	
Rate of return	−£15,996 / £967,600 × 100 = −1.65%	

(b)
Value of stock	£1,000,000
Less net cash investment	−£967,600
Net profit/loss	£32,400
Rate of return	£32,400 / £967,600 × 100 = 3.35%

In case (c) the option would be exercised:

(c)
Value of stock	£1,005,982	[(1850/1839) × £1 million]
Less net cash investment	−£967,600	
Net profit/loss	£38,382	
Rate of return	£38,382 / £967,600 × 100 = 3.97%	

(In case (c) the rate of return would be a little higher than indicated since 0.38/54.38 = 0.7% of the portfolio would not be matched by options and would therefore benefit from the full rise in the index to 1950.)

Downside protection

The option premiums received can be looked upon as providing some protection against a fall in the value of the portfolio. In the previous case a decline in the value of the original portfolio to £989,760 after selling the options would leave the fund manager in his or her original position of holding assets to the value of £1,000,000 (£989,760 plus the option premiums received of £10,240). The written options might thus be regarded as providing 1.024% downside protection.

Thus, covered call writes provide additional yield, which can be interpreted as downside protection, at the cost of forgoing some (or all) of the upside potential; see Figure 8.20.

FIGURE 8.20 Covered call writing (buy–write)

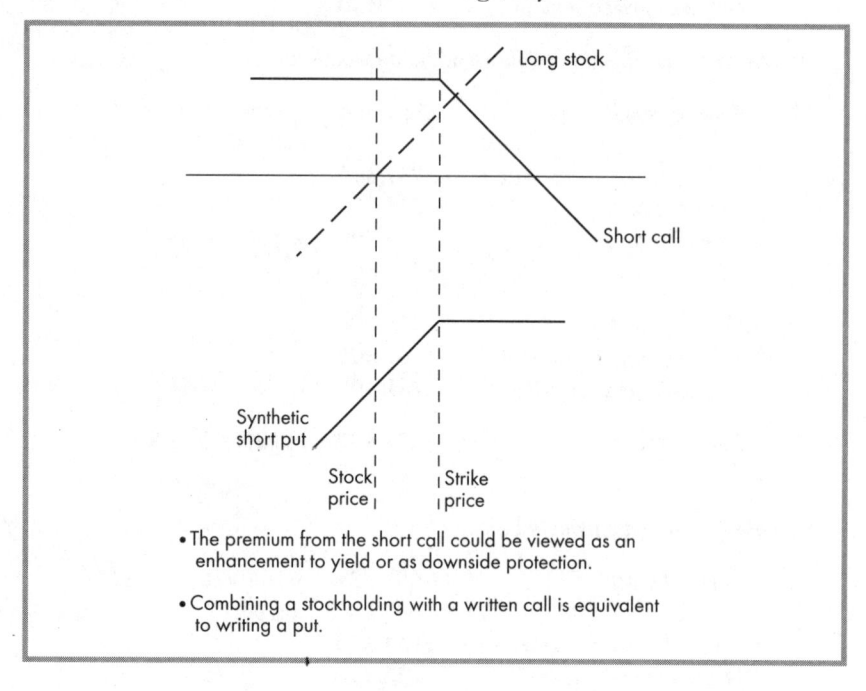

- The premium from the short call could be viewed as an enhancement to yield or as downside protection.
- Combining a stockholding with a written call is equivalent to writing a put.

CONCLUSIONS

Call options can be used to hedge future purchases by guaranteeing a maximum buying price (the option strike price). Put options can be used to hedge against a fall in price by guaranteeing a minimum selling price (the strike price). Alternatively, options may be written with a view to using the premium receipts to compensate for an adverse movement in the price of the stock (or other underlying instrument such as a currency or stock index). When the size of the position being hedged matches the amount of the underlying covered by the options (e.g. hedging 10,000 shares with 10 option contracts, each contract relating to 1,000 shares), the hedge is referred to as a fixed hedge.

Fixed hedges do not provide full protection against movements in the price of the underlying instrument because of the loss of time value. Delta hedging factors up the number of option contracts in order to provide a more complete hedge. Alternative strategies allow for hedging with no premium outlay, or the construction of positions with no downside exposure (as in the case of options funds).

Before hedging with options it is necessary to assess whether a hedge is desirable and, if so, whether options constitute the appropriate hedging instrument. For example, if there is no intention of ever selling a shareholding, there is no need to hedge its value. Also other risk reduction techniques, such as diversification, might be employed. There is also a choice to be made between options and other derivatives, such as futures. Table 8.3 outlines the relative merits of options and futures as hedging instruments.

A fixed hedge with options retains an exposure and entails a cost. While protection is obtained from a stock price movement in one direction, exposure is retained to a movement in the other direction. This profit potential is paid for in the form of the option premium. Futures and forwards tend to remove all exposure, but do not involve a premium (in the sense of a price to be paid). When comparing options with futures, it is necessary to assess whether the likelihood of the favourable stock price movement is sufficient to justify the cost of the option premium. If the alternative to hedging with options is not hedging at all, the potential hedger should consider whether or not the likelihood of an adverse stock price movement, and the damage it would do, is sufficient to justify the cost of the option premium.

Table 8.3 Options versus futures for hedging

Buying options	Allows profits from favourable stock price movements
	Involves no obligations
	Is suitable when expected stock price movements are large
	Entails exposure to volatility
	Requires the payment of premiums
Writing options	Loss of profits from favourable stock price movements
	Is suitable when expected stock price movements are small
	Entails exposure to volatility
	Involves the receipt of premiums
Futures	Outright risk replaced by basis risk
	Reduces expected portfolio returns towards short-term money market rates

Note: Buying a put option and writing a call option with the same strike price and expiry date is equivalent to selling a futures contract.

If a hedger wishes to reduce risk without taking a view as to future stock price movements, futures might seem to be most appropriate. If the hedger believes that the stock price movement is more likely to be beneficial than adverse, then the maintenance of upside exposure might justify the cost of the option. So the use of options rather than futures often implies an element of trading (speculation). However, there may be other circumstances that would render options preferable to futures; for example, an importer may wish to retain exposure to favourable exchange rate movements if competitors may be unhedged.

Further reading

For discussions of hedging with options, with particular focus on interest rates and currencies, see:

David Winstone, *Financial Derivatives* (Chapman & Hall, London, 1995), Chapters 14, 15 and 16.

Tim S. Campbell and William A. Kracaw, *Financial Risk Management* (Harper Collins, New York, 1993), Chapters 6, 8 and 10.

For treatments of hedging with options within the context of portfolio management, see:

Keith Redhead, *Introduction to Financial Investment* (Prentice Hall, Hemel Hempstead, 1995), Chapters 4 and 8.

Terry J. Watsham, *Options and Futures in International Portfolio Management* (Chapman & Hall, London, 1992), Chapter 5.

On the subjects of delta hedging and option price sensitivities, it is worth consulting:

Brian A. Eales, *Financial Risk Management* (McGraw-Hill, Maidenhead, 1995), Chapter 5.

APPENDIX 8.1: DETERMINING THE APPROPRIATE STRIKE PRICE WHEN USING STOCK INDEX OPTIONS

A fund manager may wish to guarantee a minimum portfolio value by hedging with put options. That minimum value could be a percentage of the present portfolio value and relate to a future point in time.

It is tempting to take the view that there is a proportionality between the value being guaranteed and the strike price used. For example, it might be supposed that protection against a fall in the value of the portfolio of more than 10% would be obtained from a put option with a strike price 10% below the current stock index. However, such an approach is appropriate only when the hedged portfolio and the index portfolio have identical betas and expected dividend yields.

One approach to the determination of the strike price would be to apply the capital asset pricing model and, in particular, the securities market line. The securities market line determines the required, or expected, return on a portfolio. It can be expressed as:

$$E(R_p) = R_f + B[E(R_m) - R_f]$$

where $E(R_p)$ is the expected rate of return on the portfolio being held, R_f is the risk-free rate of return (e.g. the Treasury bill rate or LIBOR), B is the beta of the portfolio being held, and $E(R_m)$ is the expected rate of return on the market portfolio (which might be treated as synonymous with the portfolio on which the stock index is based). The term $B[E(R_m) - R_f]$ can be seen as the reward for accepting risk. Risk and the reward for risk bearing (specifically, it is the general market risk, known as systematic risk, that is being referred to) are both directly related to the beta of the portfolio.

When ascertaining the appropriate strike price (where the strike price is a stock index value) it is necessary to see the maximum portfolio decline in terms of an excess rate of return. The excess rate of return is the difference between the portfolio rate of return and the risk-free rate (specifically, the portfolio rate minus the risk-free rate, $R_p - R_f$). The portfolio return embodies dividends as well as capital gain or loss. In the event of a fall in the stock index, the rate of dividend yield has to be subtracted from the portfolio value decline when calculating the negative excess return.

The beta of the portfolio being held gives the relationship between the excess return of that portfolio and the excess return of the stock index portfolio (whose beta is usually assumed to equal 1). The stock index portfolio has an expected excess rate of return of $E(R_m) - R_f$, whereas other portfolios have expected excess rates of return of $B[E(R_m) - R_f]$. So when the excess rate of return corresponding to the maximum fall in the protected portfolio is found, the corresponding excess rate of return on the stock index portfolio can be found by dividing by beta.

Since the excess return on the stock index portfolio is one that corresponds to a price fall in the hedged portfolio, it too can be expected to be negative. The actual return on the stock index portfolio will equal the risk-free interest rate minus the calculated excess return. This actual return includes the expected dividend yield. Subtraction of the dividend yield provides the capital gain or loss component of the rate of return.

204 • RISK MANAGEMENT WITH OPTIONS

When this rate of capital gain or loss is added to, or subtracted from, the current stock index value, the result is the stock index value that corresponds to the minimum portfolio value. In other words, it is the stock index to be used as the put option strike price when designing the portfolio hedge.

ACTIVITY 8.6

The FTSE is at 2000, its yield is 4% p.a. and the rate of interest is 10% p.a. You hold a portfolio with a value of £10 million, a beta of 2 and a yield of 2% p.a. and wish to insure against the value of this falling below £9 million after a year (with dividends distributed). At what exercise price should the puts be bought?

Answer
It is necessary to ascertain the FTSE Index that would correspond to a portfolio of £9 million after a year.

A 10% fall in the portfolio value to £9 million implies a total return on the portfolio of −8% (10% capital loss with a 2% yield). This in turn implies an excess return over the risk-free rate of −18% (treating the interest rate as the risk-free rate). Since the portfolio has a beta of 2, the corresponding excess return on the FTSE portfolio would be −18/2% = −9%. With an interest rate of 10%, an excess return of −9% implies an actual return of 1%. Since the FTSE has a yield of 4%, a return of 1% implies a decline in the FTSE by 3% to $2000 \times 0.97 = 1940$.

So the FTSE 100 Index that would correspond to a portfolio value of £9 million is 1940. A minimum portfolio value of £9 million thus corresponds to a minimum index value of 1940. The puts therefore should have a strike price of 1940. In equation form:

$$-0.08 = 0.1 + 2[E(R_m) - 0.1]$$
$$-0.18/2 = E(R_m) - 0.1$$
$$0.01 = E(R_m)$$
$$0.01 - 0.04 = -0.03$$
$$(1 - 0.03) \times 2000 = 1940$$

TRADING WITH OPTIONS 9

INTRODUCTION

Options may be used for the purpose of making trading (speculative) profits as well as for hedging. In other words, risk management with options may involve intentional increases in risk as well as reductions in risk. Speculators take on risk in the hope of making profits, and in so doing may allow hedgers to transfer their unwanted risk. Derivatives trading may be seen as a means whereby those wanting less risk (hedgers) transfer their unwanted risk to those wishing to accept more risk (speculators).

Futures also provide a means of transferring risk from hedgers to speculators. A major difference between futures and options in their trading uses is that futures give speculators exposure to just one dimension: the direction of movement in the price of the underlying instrument. Options can provide that exposure, but can also provide exposure to other dimensions such as volatility and time value decay. Since options prices are influenced by market expectations of volatility and by time to expiry, as well as by the price of the underlying instrument, they provide exposure to a number of dimensions. Strategies are available that allow speculators to gain exposure to any of these dimensions, or any combination of them.

This chapter begins with the use of options as a means of taking a position on a direction of movement of the price of the underlying. The techniques covered will encompass short and long positions in single option series, and vertical spreads. It should be borne in mind that these strategies usually involve simultaneous exposure to volatility and time value decay.

After a brief consideration of the relationship of the gearing effects of options to risk, the chapter goes on to look at trading based on time value. This includes a consideration of the strategies known as calendar, or horizontal, spreads. Such trading strategies seek to profit from the different rates at which time value declines with the passage of time. Theta is the measure of the decline in time value with the passage of time, so calendar spreads can be regarded as seeking to make profits from differences in theta between options with different expiry dates.

The chapter then turns to volatility trading. It will show the construction of straddles, strangles and butterflies. These are strategies that can be constructed to be delta neutral; they provide exposure to volatility without any initial exposure to changes in the price of the underlying instrument. These are followed by a consideration of ratio spreads, which are strategies that involve simultaneous exposure to volatility and the direction of price movement in the underlying instrument.

It will be seen that volatility has 2 dimensions: actual volatility and market expectations of volatility. Changes in market expectations of volatility cause changes in time value and hence the profit/loss profile of the strategy. Actual volatility will determine the position on that profit/loss profile.

The sensitivity of time value to changes in market expectations of volatility is usually referred to as vega (although Greek letters, particularly kappa, are often used instead). Volatility trades such as straddles and strangles may be constructed so as to provide an exposure to changes in market expectations of volatility while avoiding exposure to the direction of change in the price of the underlying; that is, they may have a non-zero vega together with a zero delta. Although delta neutrality may be achieved, theta neutrality would not be possible, nor would gamma neutrality (gamma is the change in delta per unit change in the price of the underlying instrument). Non-zero gamma benefits long positions, but is disadvantageous to short positions. Non-zero theta is adverse for long positions, but benefits short positions.

BASIC PRINCIPLES

Trading with options is based on views as to whether or not the existing price of an option series is likely to change. A trader believing that the price of an option series will rise might buy, while an option that is seen as prone to a price fall may be written.

As an option series moves into the money and becomes deeper in the money, its intrinsic value will rise and with it the value of the option. So trading strategies might be based on option series moving into the money, or becoming deeper in the money. These strategies parallel hedging strategies.

Trading strategies based on increases in intrinsic value are concerned with the direction and extent of movements in the price of the underlying instrument. The simplest trading strategies are those involving the purchase or sale of a single option series. A trader expecting a rise in the price of the underlying instrument might buy a call or write a put; see Figure 9.1. The choice between the long call and short put, along with choices relating to strike prices and expiry dates, would be influenced by factors such as the extent of the expected movement, the confidence with which the expectation is held and the level of risk that the trader is prepared to tolerate.

If the extent of the expected movement in the price of the underlying instrument is considerable, out-of-the-money long calls would be appropriate since the relatively low premiums would allow large percentage profits. If the expected rise in the price of the underlying instrument is considerable, a long call would be more appropriate than a short put with the same strike price. A more modest expectation might suggest the use of a short put. A long call would be more appropriate if the trader lacked strong confidence in his expectation or was particularly risk averse, since the short put entails the potential for very large losses in the event of a fall in the price of the underlying instrument.

The degree of confidence and the level of risk aversion would also influence the strike price chosen. A trader with little tolerance of risk might opt for the payment of a small premium in order to limit the sum of money risked, and would therefore choose an out-of-the-money call option. If a trader with limited confidence in his forecast, or who is very risk averse, were to write a put option, then an out-of-the-money option would be appropriate. The price of the underlying instrument would have further to move before it provided the writer with losses.

A trader anticipating a fall in the price of the underlying instrument might buy a put or write a call; see Figure 9.2. The considerations bearing upon the relevant choices parallel those mentioned in relation to the bullish trader.

FIGURE 9.1   (a) Long call; (b) short put

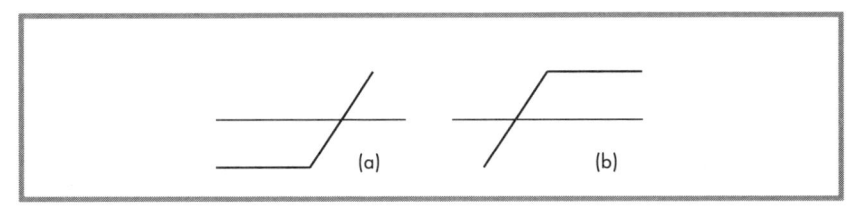

FIGURE 9.2   (a) Long put; (b) short call

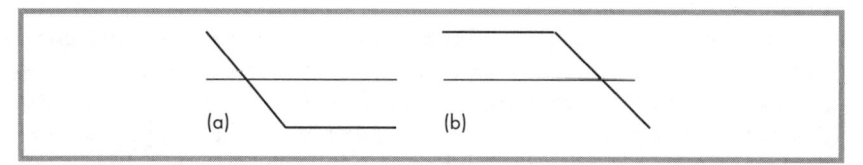

VERTICAL SPREADS

Vertical spreads involve the simultaneous buying and selling of options on the same underlying instrument for the same expiry month but with different exercise prices. Figure 9.3 illustrates a bull call spread.

FIGURE 9.3   Bull call spread

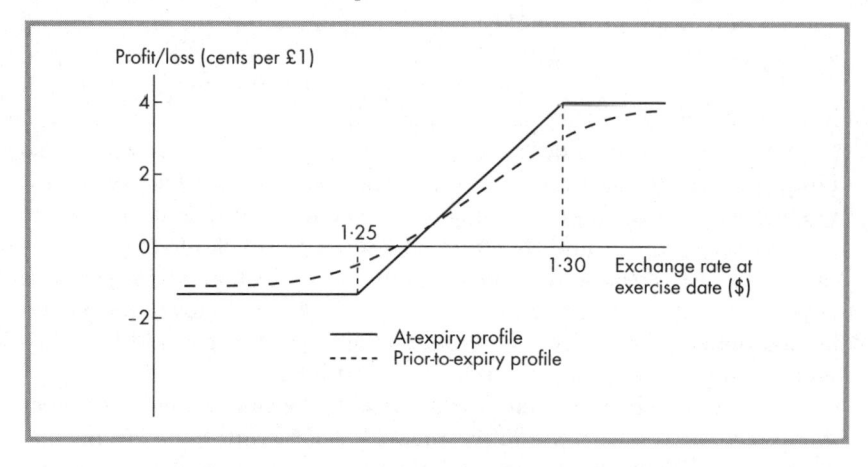

Spot exchange rate £1 = $1·22.
A $1·25 call is bought at a premium of 2 cents/£.
A $1·30 call is sold at a premium of 0·5 cents/£.

The vertical distance between the at-expiry and prior-to-expiry profiles represents the net time value. The net time value is the time value of the purchased option minus the time value of the written option. The net time value is positive when the purchased (i.e. long) option is at the money, but negative when the written (i.e. short) option is at the money (since the time value of an option is at its maximum when the option is at the money).

Example 9.1

Figure 9.4 illustrates a bull spread.
A $1·75 call is bought for 4 cents/£.
A $1·85 call is sold for 1 cent/£.
The net premium = 3 cents/£.
Below $1·75 neither option is exercised: the loss is the net premium of 3 cents/£.
Maximum profit occurs above $1·85:

   Profit from exercising $1·75 option
   Minus loss from exercise of $1·85 option
   Minus initial net premium
   Equals 7 cents/£

(Above $1·85 the additional profits from the long $1·75 call are offset by losses from the short $1·85 call.)

FIGURE 9.4 Bull spread

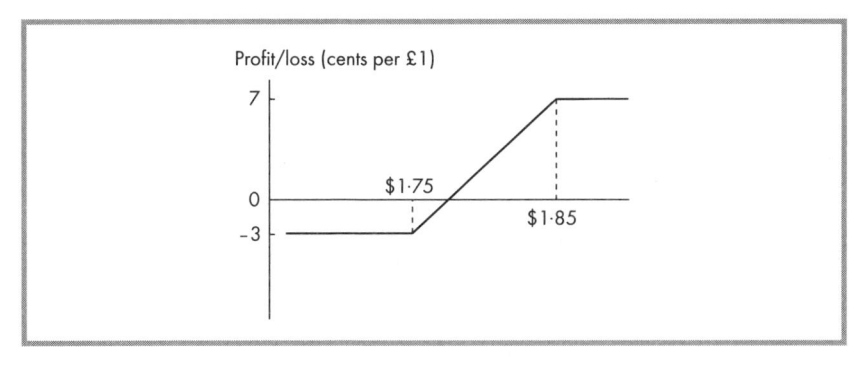

Figure 9.5 illustrates a bear put spread.

Spot exchange rate £1 = $1·22.
A $1·20 put is bought at a premium of 2·5 cents/£.
A $1·15 put is sold at a premium of 0·6 cents/£.

Considering the intrinsic value (at-expiry) profile, at spot prices above $1·20 neither option would be exercised and the transactor makes a net loss equal to the balance of the premiums: 2·5 − 0·6 = 1·9 cents. As the value of sterling falls below $1·20, there is a potential gain from selling sterling at the exercise price of $1·20 and buying it more cheaply. This

FIGURE 9.5   Bear put spread

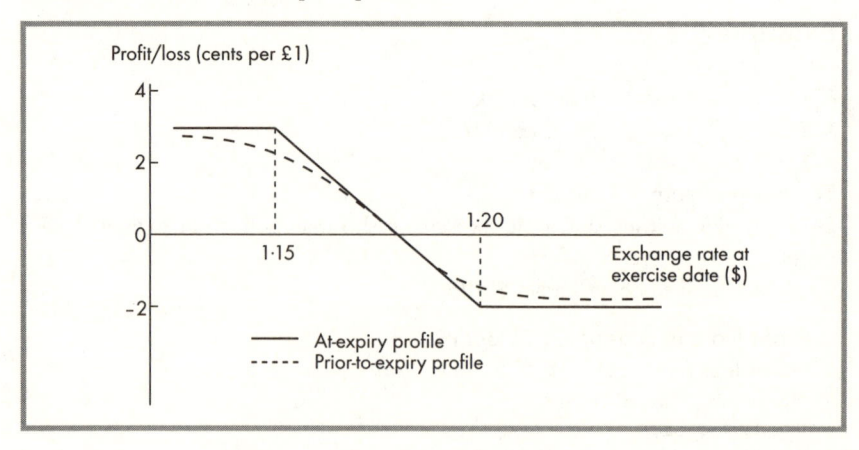

Figure: Profit/loss (cents per £1) vs Exchange rate at exercise date ($), showing at-expiry and prior-to-expiry profiles with strike prices at 1·15 and 1·20.

potential gain increases until it reaches 5 cents per £1 when the exchange rate is £1 = $1·15. The net gain at $1·15, taking account of the net premium, is 5·0 − 1·9 = 3·1 cents. If the price of sterling falls below $1·15, the $1·15 put will be exercised, obliging the transactor to buy at $1·15 while selling at a lower price. Thus, as the price of sterling falls below $1·15, the additional gains from exercising the $1·20 put are cancelled by the losses on the $1·15 put, leaving the net profit at a constant 3·1 cents per £1.

Example 9.2

Figure 9.6 illustrates a bear spread.
A $1·75 put is bought for 5 cents/£.
A $1·65 put is sold for 1 cent/£.
The net premium is 4 cents/£.
Above $1·75 neither option is exercised: the loss is the net premium of 4 cents/£.
Below $1·65 both options are exercised:

   Profit from $1·75 option
   Minus loss from $1·65 option
   Minus net premium paid
   Equals net profit of 6 cents/£

(Below $1·65 the additional profits from the long $1·75 put are offset by losses from the short $1·65 put.)

FIGURE 9.6 Bear spread

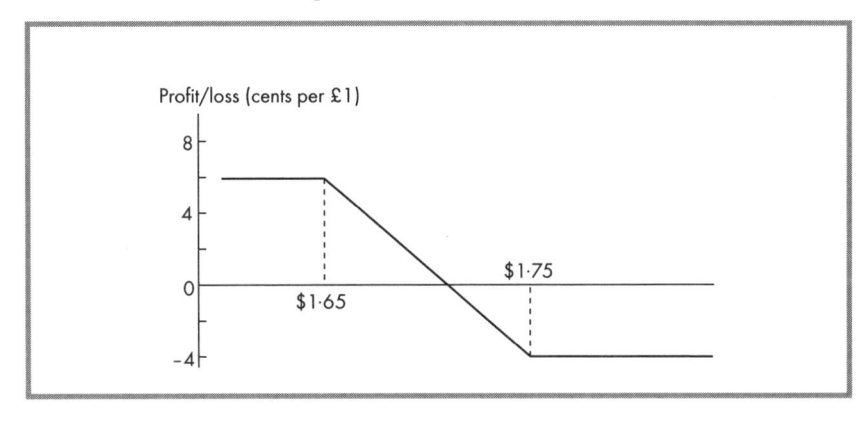

Profit/loss (cents per £1); levels marked at $1.65 and $1.75; profit around 5 below $1.65, loss around -4 above $1.75.

In addition to the bull call spreads and bear put spreads, there are bull put spreads and bear call spreads. Writing a put option with a high exercise price (and high premium) and buying a put option with a low exercise price (and consequent low premium) creates a bull put spread. A bear call spread involves selling a call option with a low exercise price (and high premium) and buying a call option with a high exercise price (and low premium).

ACTIVITY 9.1

It is 22 September. Options on Prudential trade as follows:

		Calls		Puts	
		Oct	Jan	Oct	Jan
Prudential	180	21	30	3	7
(*199)	200	10	17	12	14

Prudential is about to go xd with a net dividend of 3.5p. You believe that its price will continue to hold up close to 200p after the dividend.

(a) Suggest 2 distinct strategies you could conduct to take advantage of your view.
(b) What dangers are inherent to these strategies and how might you counter them?
(c) The following day Prudential is xd and prices have changed to the following levels:

		Calls		Puts	
		Oct	Jan	Oct	Jan
Prudential	180	23	31	3	4½
(*198)	200	10	18	10	12½

Calculate the profit or loss from your 2 strategies and comment on the way the option prices have moved.
(Based on the Securities Institute examination in Financial Futures and Options, December 1990, Question 25.)

Answer
(a) The strategy should reflect a mildly bullish view in the short term. Normally the stock would fall to 195·5p (199p − 3·5p) when it goes ex dividend. The view that the price will be close to 200p after the dividend (presumably immediately after the dividend) thus suggests a strategy that would profit from a small upward movement. Possible strategies would include short 200p October puts and a 180p/200p bull spread. A put bull spread would seem better than a call bull spread since the latter may be prone to early exercise of the 180p calls. The short-term nature of the view suggests the use of October expiry options. The short option positions would also benefit from any expectation of low volatility contained in the view taken.
(b) The greatest dangers are present in the simple short put strategy. This gives considerable downside risk in the event of a fall in the stock price. It also gives substantial risk from an increase in expectations of volatility. The use of the bull spread would ameliorate both of these risks.
(c) If October 200p puts had been written, a 2p fall in the option price, and hence a 2p profit, would have been realised. The 180p/200p put bull spread would have shown a profit of 2p also (2p profit on the 200p put and no change on the 180p put). Expectations have largely been borne out and profits made as a result. If the share price had moved to 200p, the 200p put price would have been lower and hence the profits higher.

ACTIVITY 9.2

It is 23 January and Ladbroke shares are 276p. Options with April expiry have the following prices.

Strike price	Calls	Puts
260	20	3
280	8	11

VERTICAL SPREADS

(a) Construct a vertical bear spread (i) with put options and (ii) with call options. In each case indicate the maximum profit, maximum loss, and breakeven share price.
(b) Construct a short cylinder. What is its cost?
(c) Diagrammatically show the combined position arising from a shareholding and (i) the vertical bear spread, and (ii) the short cylinder. What are the resulting maximum profits and losses?

Answer

(a) (i) Buy a 280p put and write a 260p put.
   The net premium cost is 11 − 3 = 8p. This is the maximum loss.
   The maximum profit is (280 − 260) − 8 = 12p.
   The breakeven share price is 272p.
   (ii) Write a 260p call and buy a 280p call.
   The net premium receipt is 12p. This is the maximum profit.
   The maximum loss is 20 − 12 = 8p.
   The breakeven share price is 272p.
(b) Buy a 260p put and write a 280p call. There is a net receipt of 5p.
(c) (i)

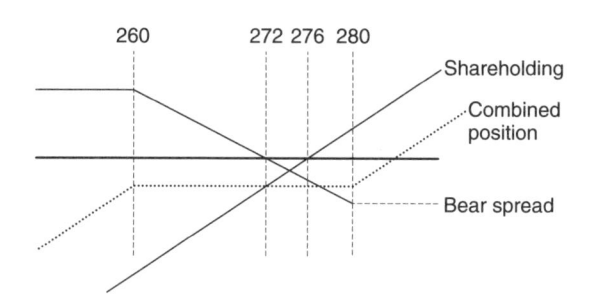

There is maximum profit.
The maximum loss is 260 + 4 = 264p.

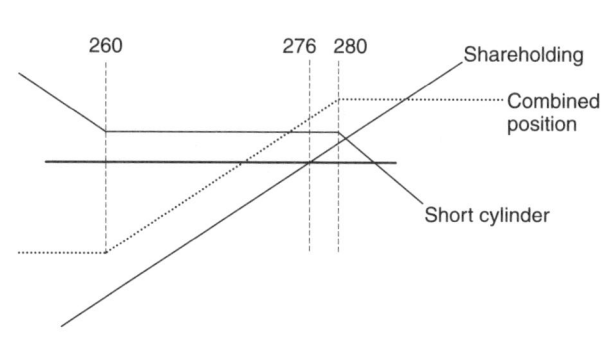

(ii)

There is a maximum profit of 9p and a maximum loss of 11p.

READING DERIVATIVES PRICES

Not only can derivatives prices be used for ascertaining market expectations of financial values, they can also be interpreted for the purpose of finding the probability distributions around the expected values. In other words derivatives prices contain information regarding market views as to the likelihood of particular price movements. One way in which this information can be obtained involves using option pricing models to deduce implied volatility, and hence the standard deviation of the probability distribution of prices. Unfortunately this procedure assumes that upward and downward deviations from the expected value have equal probability, and that potential values form a normal distribution. An alternative approach uses vertical option spreads, and this allows the distribution of potential values to take any form.

Vertical bear put spreads

The construction and interpretation of vertical bear put spreads will be based on the closing prices, on 12 February 1998, of the European style FTSE 100 index options traded on LIFFE (European style options were chosen since they had greater liquidity than American style options). The prices for the February expiry options (due to expire on 20 February, were as follows:

Strike	5375		5425		5475		5525		5575		5625		5675		5725	
Type	Call	Put	Call	Put	Call	Put	Call	Put	Call	Put	Call	Put	Call	Put	Call	Put
Price	188	15	143	23	105	35	73	53	47.5	77.5	28.5	108	15	145	7.5	187

A vertical bear put spread is constructed by buying a put option and simultaneously selling one with a lower strike price. For example a 5575 put is bought for 77.5p and a 5525 put sold for 53p. The net cost is 24.5p. In the event of the index being above 5575 on the expiry date, neither option would be exercised (it is not rational to exercise the right to sell at 5525 or 5575 if the actual market value is higher than both) and there would be a net loss equal to the net cost. If the index turns out to be less than 5525 there would be a net intrinsic value of 50 (the pay off from the long put minus the pay off from the short put). So an index below 5525 involves a net profit of 50p minus 24.5p, i.e. 25.5p. Investors are prepared to pay 24.5p for the possibility of a 50p net intrinsic value. This suggests an implied probability of 24.5/50, i.e. 49%, of an index value below 5525. The underlying index value was 5545.

Assume that the index will end up either below 5525 or above 5575, and not between 5525 and 5575. If there were an evens probability of a fall, the price of such an evens bet should be 25p. The actual price of 24.5p implies a view that the probability of a fall is 49% rather than 50%.

Looking at lower strike prices it can be seen that the 5375/5425 spread costs 23 − 15 = 8p. This suggests that market expectations are that an index below 5375 has an 8/50, i.e. 16% probability of occurrence. Conducting the same procedure for other spreads suggests the following probabilities:

<5375	<5425	<5475	<5525	<5575	<5625	<5675
16%	24%	36%	49%	61%	74%	84%

These figures imply probabilities for ranges of values as follows:

5375 to 5425	5425 to 5475	5475 to 5525	5525 to 5575	5575 to 5625	5625 to 5675
24 − 16 = 8%	36 − 24 = 12%	49 − 36 = 13%	61 − 49 = 12%	74 − 61 = 13%	84 − 74 = 10%

Vertical bull call spreads

A vertical bull call spread is constructed by buying a call option and selling another at a higher strike price (but with the same expiry date). Consider the 5525/5575 strike price options. Buying the 5525 and selling the 5575 entails a net outlay of 73 minus 47.5 equals 25.5p. The investor is prepared to pay 25.5p for the possibility of a net intrinsic value of 50p. This maximum net intrinsic value (the pay off from the long option net of exercise losses on the short option) is realised in the event of the index exceeding 5575 on the expiry date of the options. The willingness to pay 25.5p for the possibility of a 50p pay off in the event of an index value greater than 5575 suggests an expectation of a probability of 25.5/50, i.e. 51%, that the index will exceed 5575.

Using the operational assumption that the index will either exceed 5575 or be less than 5525 on the option expiry date, equal probability of a rise and a fall would imply that 25p would be paid for the chance of the 50p pay off in the event of an index above 5575. The payment of 25.5p implies a slight inclination to expect a rise. The prospect of a rise is given a 51% probability. It might be noted that this is consistent with the 49% probability of a fall deduced from the put option prices.

Carrying out the same procedure for other spreads suggests the following probabilities:

>5425	>5475	>5525	>5575	>5625	>5675	>5725
84%	76%	64%	51%	38%	27%	15%

These figures imply probabilities for ranges of values as follows:

5425 to 5475	5475 to 5525	5525 to 5575	5575 to 5625	5625 to 5675	5675 to 5725
8%	12%	13%	13%	11%	12%

The put and call option prices thus imply the following probabilities:

	5375 to 5425	5425 to 5475	5475 to 5525	5525 to 5575	5575 to 5625	5625 to 5675	5675 to 5725
Puts	8%	12%	13%	12%	13%	10%	
Calls		8%	12%	13%	13%	11%	12%
Av.	8%	10%	12.5%	12.5%	13%	11%	

It might be noted that 79% of the probability distribution lies between 5375 and 5725. This suggests a standard deviation of approximately 140 around a mean of 5545 (the underlying index value).

It is possible to manipulate these figures to ascertain an implied annualised volatility. The standard deviation as a decimal is 140/5545 = 0.02525. To convert this from a 6 trading day to a 250 trading day (i.e. annual) volatility it is necessary to multiply by $(250/6)^{0.5}$, i.e. 6.455. The result is 0.1630. The implied annualised volatility is 16.30%. This is nearly double the average annual volatility over the previous three years.

Interest rate derivatives

At close of trading on 12 February 1998 the base lending rate was 7.25% p.a., three-month LIBOR was 7.53125% p.a., and March three-month sterling futures implied an interest rate of 7.48% p.a. Three month sterling futures option prices (March expiry) were as follows:

Strike	92.50		92.75		93.00	
Type	Call	Put	Call	Put	Call	Put
Price	0.07	0.05	0.01	0.24	0.00	0.48

Vertical bear put spread costs imply the following probabilities:

        < 92.50   < 92.75

         76%   96%

which implies:

         92.50 <   < 92.75

             20%

Vertical bull call spread costs imply the following probabilities:

>92.75		>93.00
24%		4%
	92.75< <93.00	
	20%	

Summarising and converting futures prices into interest rates (interest rate = 100 − futures price) gives the following distribution:

<7%	7%< <7.25%	7.25%< <7.5%	>7.5%
4%	20%	20%	76%

Unfortunately these probabilities add to 120%, whereas they should add to 100%. This possibly arises because actual, and potential, interest rates fall at 0.25% intervals (7.00%, 7.25%, 7.50%, etc). As a result particular interest rates are likely to fall into two adjacent bands (for example 7.50% falls into both of the last two bands). Since the inequalities shown above should be interpreted as less (more) than *or equal to* it is likely that the probability of a particular value appears twice.

As a crude correction for this, each of the above percentages could be multiplied by 100/120. This procedure results in the following distribution:

<7%	7%< <7.25%	7.25%< <7.5%	>7.5%
3.33%	16.67%	16.67%	63.33%

The mean of this distribution (statistical expectation) as reflected in the futures price was 7.48%. It is clear that the distribution was skewed towards the expectation of an increase in interest rates. This was consistent with the Bank of England's recent announcement to the effect that base lending rate was more likely than not to rise in the near future.

THE EFFECTS OF GEARING

Options can be looked upon as either low-risk or high-risk instruments. In both cases the interpretation of risk is based upon the gearing effect offered by options. An option can be bought for a fraction of the price of the stock (or currency or bond or stock portfolio) to which the option relates. The maximum loss from buying stock is the price of that stock, whereas the maximum loss from buying a call option on that stock is the option premium. So buying a call option on 100 shares of stock can be seen as less risky than buying 100 shares of stock. (The number of shares to which an option contract relates varies from country to country; at the time of writing, one option contract related to 1,000 shares in the United Kingdom, 100 in the United States and 50 in Germany.)

However, if the choice is between investing $1,000 in stock and spending $1,000 on stock options, then the options appear to be the more risky. Again, this arises from the gearing offered by the options. Since the price of the option is a fraction of the price of the stock, percentage changes in the option price are prone to be much greater than percentage changes in the stock price. Suppose that XYZ stock is priced at 100 and a call option to buy at 100 is priced at 5. A rise in the stock price to 110 might plausibly cause a rise in the option price to 13. The stock price rises by 10%, whereas the option price rises by 160%. This arises from the gearing offered by the option. However, the possibility of high percentage profits is accompanied by potential large percentage losses. A fall in the stock price to 90 might cause a fall in the option price to 3. The 10% fall in the stock price is accompanied by a 40% drop in the option premium (and hence a 40% loss on the option). It may be that a more substantial fall in the stock price, say to 75, virtually eliminates the value of the option so that a 25% fall in the stock price brings about a 100% fall in the option price. So if the choice is between $1,000 invested in stock and $1,000 in options, the latter is the more risky (as usual, higher potential profits are accompanied by greater risk).

The foregoing example involved an at-the-money option gaining just 8 in value as a result of the stock price rising by 10. One might think that the right to buy at 100 should rise in price by 10 as a result of a rise in the stock price from 100 to 110. However, although there is an additional 10 in intrinsic value, the other component of the option premium, known as time value, falls as the stock price moves away from the option strike price (the initial option price of 5 was entirely time value; at the stock price of 110, the time value of the option is 3). The change in the option price as a proportion of the change in the stock price is known as the delta of the option (in the present example the delta is $(13 - 5)/10 = 0.8$).

TIME VALUE AND OPTIONS TRADING

Time value is not only something that might be the basis of trading in itself; it is also something that should be borne in mind when a trade is primarily concerned with movements in intrinsic value. Consider a trade that involves the purchase of a single call option series. An at-the-money call could provide the holder with a loss even in the event of a rise in the price of the underlying instrument. If the rise in the price of the underlying instrument is modest and takes a long time to come about, the profit from the increase in intrinsic value could be more than offset by a fall in time value. This is more likely in the case of an option that is close to expiry, since such an option would be subject to the rapid time value decay that occurs close to the expiry date. This case illustrates the point that it is not only the direction and extent of the movement in the price of the underlying instrument, but also the speed of the movement that a trader must consider when contemplating a trade.

The point is even more apparent in the case of an out-of-the-money call. Such a call might fail to become in the money as a result of a rise in the price of the underlying instrument. In such a case, any chance of a profit depends upon the price rise of the underlying instrument occurring quickly, and well before expiry. The profit would depend upon the increase in time value resulting from the price rise of the underlying instrument outweighing the loss of time value caused by the passage of time.

Some trading strategies are based entirely on anticipated movements in time value. These strategies include calendar spreads, alternatively known as horizontal spreads. (The various expiry months are depicted horizontally in the financial press and so strategies using the same strike price but differing expiry dates are referred to as horizontal spreads. Strategies using the same expiry date but differing strike prices are referred to as vertical spreads, the various strike prices appearing vertically in the financial press. If the options used differ with respect to both expiry date and strike price, the strategy is called a diagonal spread.)

A calendar spread seeks to profit from the acceleration in time value decay as the expiry date approaches; see Figure 9.7. A trader using a calendar spread would take a short position in an option series with a nearby expiry month and a long position in a series with a distant expiry (the 2 series would be identical in every respect other than the expiry month). The short option position can be seen as a liability, whereas the long option is an asset. The time value of the option with the nearby maturity date would decay more rapidly than that of the option with the distant maturity date. The value of the liability declines more quickly than the value of the asset. If the other determinants of time value remain unchanged, the passage of time will yield a profit for the trader.

The rate of decline of an option premium per unit of time elapsing is known as the theta of the option. The (absolute value of the) theta of an option increases as expiry is approached. Thetas are greatest for at-the-money options.

In order to benefit most from the rapid time value decay of the near-dated option, the option should be allowed to run to the expiry date (it

FIGURE 9.7 Time value decay accelerates as the expiry date is approached

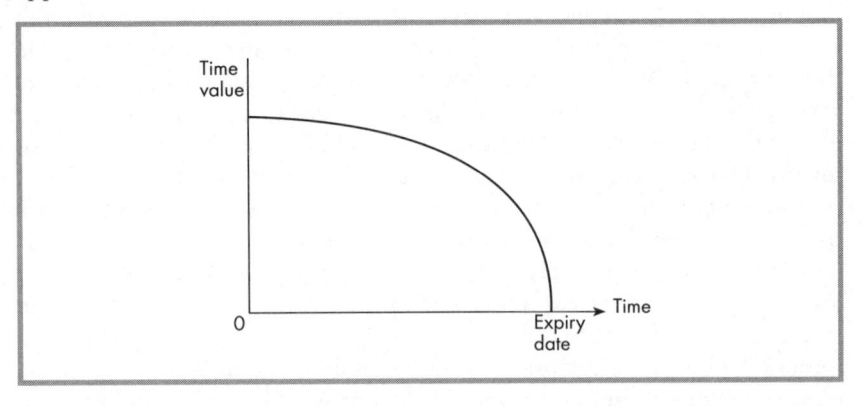

would be advisable to use out-of-the-money options for the near date so as to reduce the risk of early exercise; in other words, the risk that the option holder will exercise the option before the expiry date). The profit from the calendar spread is then equal to the time value of the far-dated option (on the expiry date of the near-dated option) minus the net premium cost of initially establishing the calendar spread. The time value of the far-dated option will be at its maximum when that option is at the money, and will decline as the price of the underlying instrument deviates from the exercise price. The profit/loss profile of the calendar spread thus takes the form indicated in Figure 9.8 (note that the intrinsic values cancel each other out); see also Figures 9.9 and 9.10.

FIGURE 9.8 Profit/loss profile of a calendar spread

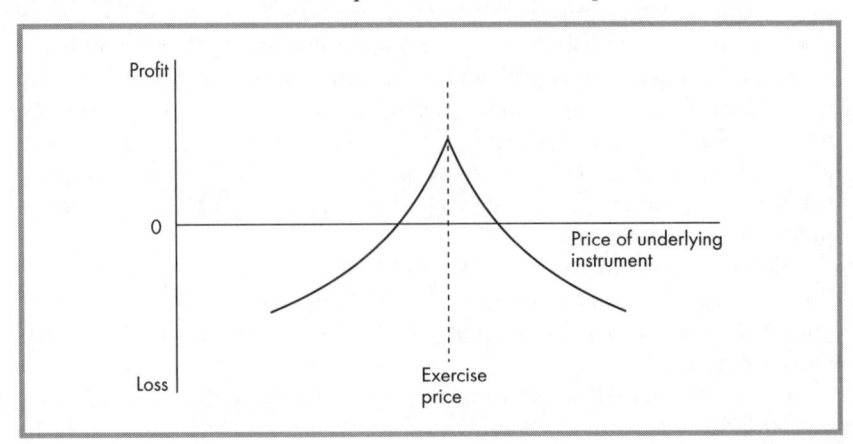

FIGURE 9.9 Calender spread created using two calls

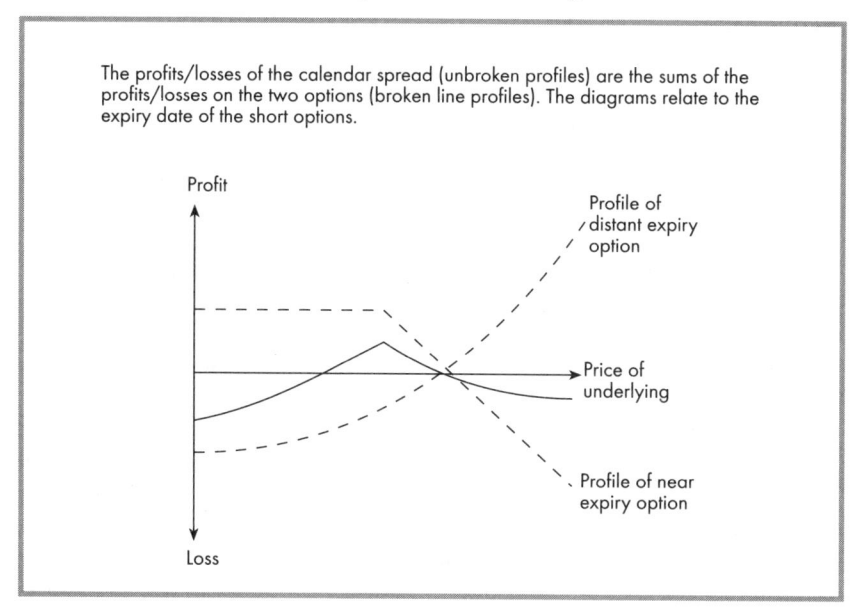

The profits/losses of the calendar spread (unbroken profiles) are the sums of the profits/losses on the two options (broken line profiles). The diagrams relate to the expiry date of the short options.

FIGURE 9.10 Calender spread created using two puts

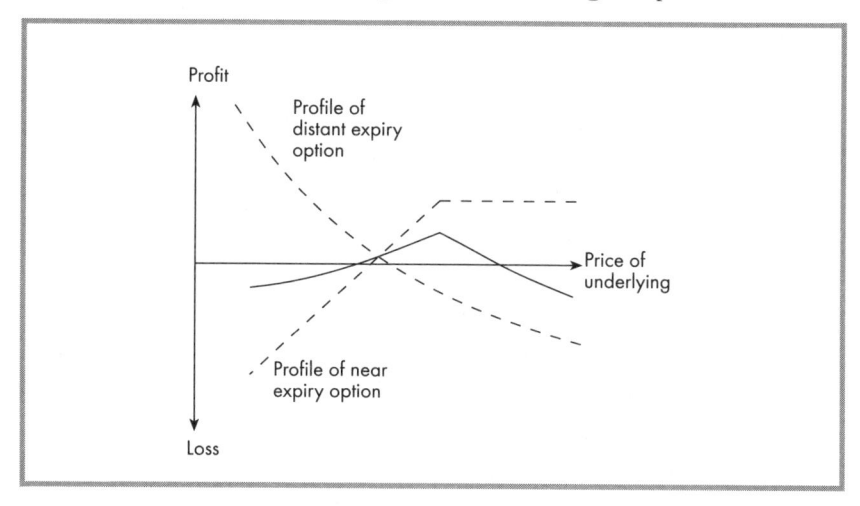

An increase in expected volatility would also raise the time value of the far-dated option. So increases in market expectations of volatility increase profits, whereas actual volatility reduces them.

Example 9.3

It is 12 November. Central Bank shares stand at 190p and the option prices are as follows:

Strike price	Calls			Puts		
	Dec	Mar	Jun	Dec	Mar	Jun
180	18	28	32	7	16	22
200	10	20	23	17	26	32

A calendar spread can be constructed by writing a December 200p call and simultaneously buying a June 200p call. The six-month difference between expiries will maximise the difference between the thetas. Use of out-of-the-money options reduces the likelihood of early exercise. A profit would be made in the event of the options being not far from at the money on the December expiry date. Profitability would be enhanced by an increase in market expectations of volatility (which would raise the time value of the long call).

Another trading strategy based on time value is often referred to as valuation trading. This involves identifying relatively over- and under-priced options and trading them in delta neutral combinations.

Coming to a view as to whether an option is over-, under- or correctly priced requires attention to the volatility implied by the option premium. Just as the theoretical option premium (alternatively known as the fair price) can be ascertained from knowledge of the determinants of option prices, including volatility, so too can the value of one determinant be ascertained from knowledge of the option premium and the other determinants. So it is possible to calculate, using models such as Black–Scholes, the volatility implied by an option premium. This is a major way of ascertaining market expectations of volatility, which is the only determinant of option prices that is not directly observable.

An overpriced option series is one whose premium implies a higher than average level of volatility; the converse applies for an underpriced option. If the underlying instrument and the expiry date are the same, the implied volatility should be the same. If implied volatilities differ, there may be an opportunity for valuation trading.

Suppose that a trader encounters the premiums for call options on the shares of Shoddigoods plc shown in Table 9.1, and using an option pricing model derives the implied volatilities and deltas indicated. (The options share a common expiry month.) The 330p calls are relatively underpriced, while the 390p calls are relatively overpriced. The valuation trader might write 390p calls while buying 330p calls. In order to achieve delta neutrality, and hence immunity from movements in the price of the underlying instrument, the numbers of options contracts should be in the ratio of the deltas. Writing seven 390p calls for every three 330p calls bought would achieve this delta neutrality.

This oversimplifies the decision facing the trader. The trader really seeks to trade the option series whose over- or underpricing is greatest in percentage terms. These may not coincide with those with the most extreme implied volatilities. The series with the most extreme implied volatilities would exhibit the greatest percentage deviations of time value, but if intrinsic value is present then this may not be reflected in the relative percentage deviations of premiums. If an option series has considerable intrinsic value, a high percentage deviation of time value may correspond to a relatively low percentage deviation of the premium.

Table 9.1 therefore needs to be adjusted. First, a column of theoretical (fair) prices needs to be added (see Table 9.2). In order to ascertain these fair prices, the trader needs a single measure of volatility to apply to each of the option series. This measure of volatility could be derived from the implied volatilities depicted in Table 9.1. Secondly, a column showing percentage deviations of actual premiums from fair prices is needed. It is this column that would guide the trader's actions. He would buy those with the greatest percentage undervaluation and sell those showing the highest percentage overvaluation. Although the 330p calls have the lowest implied volatility, the percentage undervaluation is greatest in the case of the 360p calls. The valuation trader would buy 360p calls and sell 390p calls. The ratio of five 390p calls to every three 360p calls would achieve delta neutrality.

Another class of trading strategies based on time value arises from the relationship between time value and market expectations of volatility.

Table 9.1 Premiums for call options

Strike price	Premium	Implied volatility	Delta
330	44	6.800	0.7
360	28	7.000	0.5
390	18	8.900	0.3

Table 9.2 Theoretical fair prices

Strike price	Premium	Fair price	% deviation of premium from fair price	Delta
330	44	46	−4.3	0.7
360	28	30	−6.7	0.5
390	18	15	+20.0	0.3

VOLATILITY TRADING

Volatility trading can be looked upon as taking positions on changes in market expectations of price volatility. The main strategies for trading volatility are straddles, strangles and butterflies.

Straddles

A long straddle is the simultaneous purchase of a call and a put on the same stock, at the same exercise (strike) price and for the same expiry month (see Figure 9.11). A short straddle is the simultaneous sale of 2 such options (see Figure 9.12). A trader buying a straddle is taking the view that volatility will be high in the future, whereas the seller of a straddle takes the view that volatility will be low.

Suppose that shares in Shoddigoods plc are 99p and that, on 1 December, January 100p call options are 2p, while January 100p put options are 3p. A long straddle could be constructed by simultaneously buying a January 100p call and a January 100p put so as to produce the profit/loss profile illustrated by Figure 9.13. The holder of the long straddle depicted in the figure would make net profits if the stock price moved outside the range 95p–105p. The maximum loss would be the sum of the premiums paid, 5p. This loss would be incurred if the stock price moved to, and stayed at, 100p.

FIGURE 9.11 Long straddle

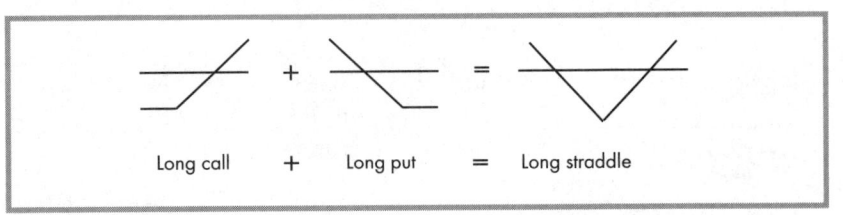

Long call + Long put = Long straddle

FIGURE 9.12 Short straddle

Long call + Long put = Long straddle

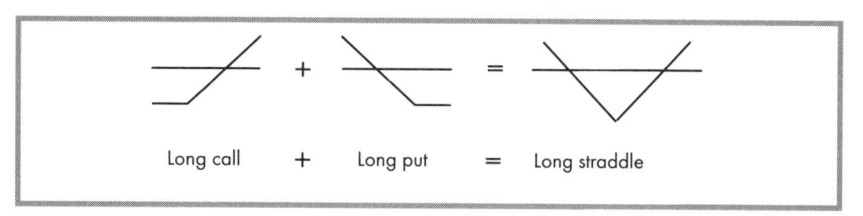

FIGURE 9.13 Long straddle

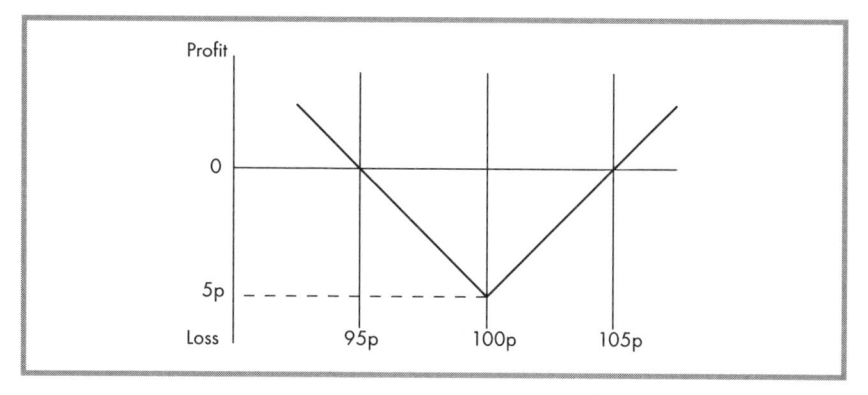

A short straddle could be produced by means of writing a January 100p call and simultaneously writing a January 100p put. The resulting profit/loss profile is illustrated by Figure 9.14. The seller of the short straddle shown in the figure will make a profit if the stock price remains within the range 95p–105p. The maximum profit of 5p, equal to the sum of the premiums received, would be made in the event of the stock price moving to and stabilising at 100p.

Thus the holder of a long straddle hopes for high volatility, whereas the holder of a short straddle desires low volatility. It is more likely, however, that they take positions on changes in market expectations of price volatility rather than on price volatility itself. This requires consideration of profit/loss profiles which take account of time value.

Figure 9.15 incorporates time value into the profit/loss profile of the long straddle illustrated by Figure 9.13. The intrinsic value of an option is the profit (without deduction of premium) to be obtained from immediate exercise of the option. The profit/loss profiles of Figures 9.11 to 9.14 reflect intrinsic value. Option premiums consist of time value as well as intrinsic value. Time value can be looked upon as a payment for the possibility that the intrinsic value might increase prior to the expiry date. When an option is sold, rather than exercised, time value is received in

FIGURE 9.14 Short straddle

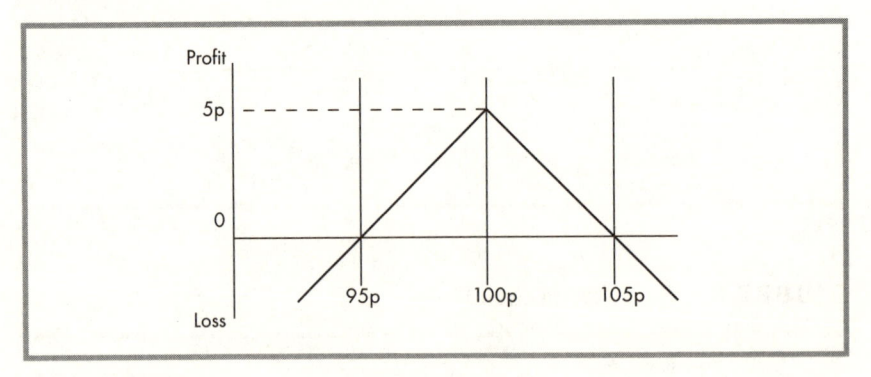

addition to the intrinsic value. Figures 9.11 to 9.14 are based on exercising options, while Figure 9.15 is based on selling them.

The broken line of Figure 9.15 represents the price received upon sale of the options minus the price originally paid for the options, i.e. the new sum of the premiums minus the original sum of the premiums. The vertical distance between the 2 profiles represents the time value.

One of the factors that determine time value is the market expectation of volatility. If it is expected that the price of the stock will be highly volatile in the period up to the expiry date of the option, the time value will be relatively high, reflecting the strong possibility of a substantial increase in intrinsic value.

A trader who takes the view that the market's expectation of future volatility will increase might buy options so as to profit from the increase

FIGURE 9.15 Long straddle profile including time value

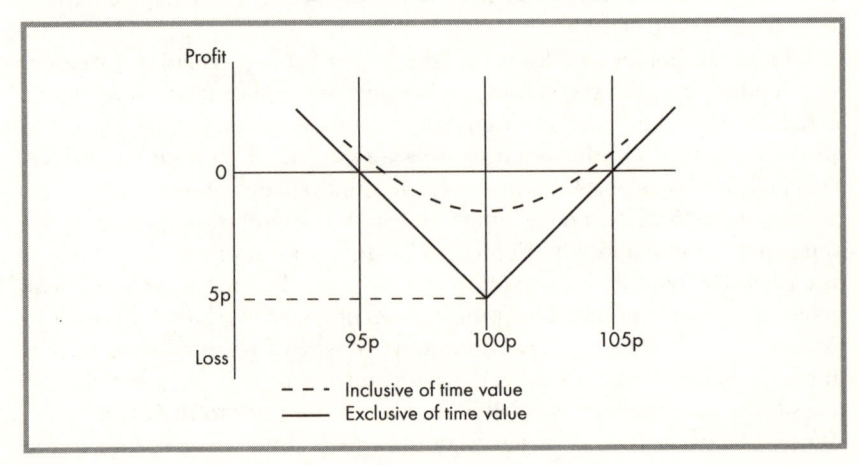

in their prices resulting from enhanced time value. However, buying options individually provides an exposure to direction of price movement as well as to expected volatility. The trader may not wish to take a view as to which way the stock price will move. He would then seek a position that is unaffected by stock price change as such, but which can yield profits from a rise in expected volatility. This objective might be satisfied by a long straddle that is delta neutral.

The delta of an option is the ratio of the change in the price of the option to the change in the underlying stock price. Call options have positive deltas while put options have negative deltas. Call and put option deltas thus tend to offset each other. This offset can produce a situation in which the option premiums, when considered together, show little net response to movements in the underlying stock price.

A straddle therefore allows the trader to take a position on changes in expectations of volatility while providing little exposure to movements of the stock price. Straddles would typically be established so that both options are as close as possible to being at the money. At-the-money call options have deltas of about 0·5 and at-the-money put options have deltas of around –0·5. So if both options are at the money, the net delta is close to zero. The net delta of the options is represented by the gradient of the broken line in Figure 9.15.

The gradient is equal to, or close to, zero when the stock price is equal to the exercise price of 100p. When the gradient of the profit/loss profile is equal to zero, the position is said to be delta neutral. The position illustrated by Figure 9.15, however, is gamma positive. The gamma is a measure of the responsiveness of the delta to stock price movements. The profile in Figure 9.15 moves from being delta negative, to being delta

FIGURE 9.16   Long straddle

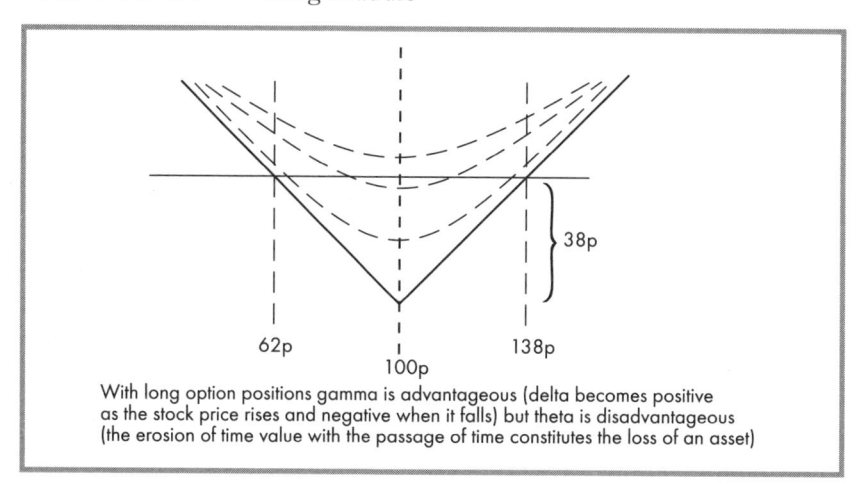

62p   100p   138p   38p

With long option positions gamma is advantageous (delta becomes positive as the stock price rises and negative when it falls) but theta is disadvantageous (the erosion of time value with the passage of time constitutes the loss of an asset)

neutral, to being delta positive as the stock price rises. It is thus termed gamma positive. If the stock price is volatile, this is beneficial to the holder of the options since a rise in the stock price above 100p establishes a delta-positive position, which produces profits from a rising stock price, while a fall in the stock price to below 100p causes the position to become delta negative and thus prone to benefit from falls in the stock price; see Figure 9.16.

ACTIVITY 9.3

The June S&P 500 stock index futures price stands at 200. June S&P 500 stock index futures options prices (deltas in brackets) are as shown in Table 9.3.

Table 9.3 Stock index futures options prices

Strike price	Calls	Puts
195	6.80(0.84)	1.65(–0.16)
200	2.79(0.50)	2.69(–0.50)
205	1.75(0.15)	6.60(–0.85)

Describe a strategy using options and futures that will result in a profit from a movement of the futures price, irrespective of direction, in the event of market expectations of volatility remaining constant. What might cause a loss to be incurred?

Answer

Buy 2 June 200 calls: Delta $= 2 \times 0.5$
Sell 1 June futures   Delta $= -1$
contract:
                          Net delta $= 0$

A fall in the futures price would cause the options delta to decline. The net delta of the position thus becomes negative and the trader benefits from the price fall.

A rise in the futures price would cause the options delta to rise. The net delta of the position thus becomes positive and the trader profits from the price rise. In other words, the position is gamma positive.

Losses could be incurred if market expectations of volatility were to decline and thereby reduce option prices. Also, if time were to pass and the futures price remained stable, there would be a decline in options prices which would render the overall position loss making.

Strangles

Strangles differ from straddles in that the 2 options have different exercise prices. A strangle would typically be constructed using an out-of-the-money call and an out-of-the-money put; see Figures 9.17 and 9.18. (It could be constructed with an in-the-money call and an in-the-money put, or with one option being in the money and the other out of the money. However, in the case of short strangles it must be borne in mind that strategies involving in-the-money options run a relatively high risk of early exercise, i.e. the short option position could be closed out by an option holder choosing to exercise.) The buyer of a strangle takes the view that volatility is going to be high, while the seller of a strangle is taking a position on low volatility.

If shares in Shoddigoods plc are 99p, a long strangle on 1 December might be produced by buying a January 90p put option and a January 110p call option. If the premium of each option is 1p, the profit/loss profile of Figure 9.19 would be the result. The holder of the strangle depicted by Figure 9.19 would make a profit if the stock price moved outside the range 88p–112p. The maximum loss of 2p, the sum of the premiums paid, would be incurred in the event of the stock price remaining in the range 90p–110p. A short strangle, created by writing a January 90p put and a January 110p call, is illustrated by Figure 9.20, which is a mirror image of Figure 9.19.

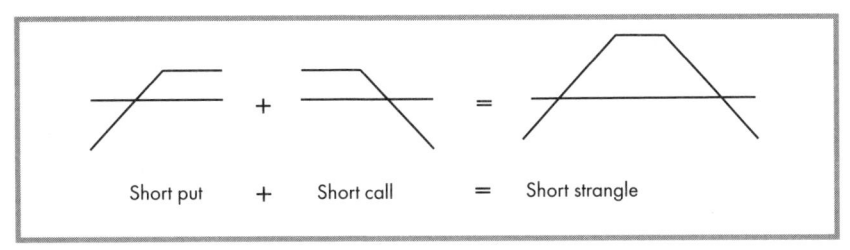

FIGURE 9.17 Long strangle

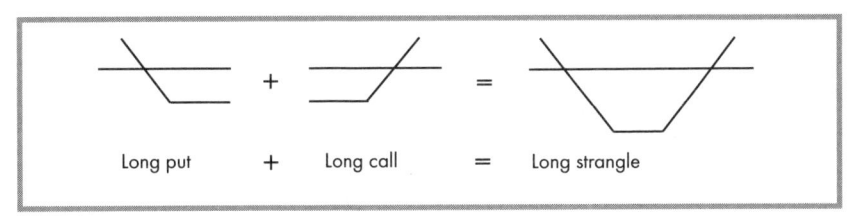

FIGURE 9.18 Short strangle

FIGURE 9.19   Long strangle

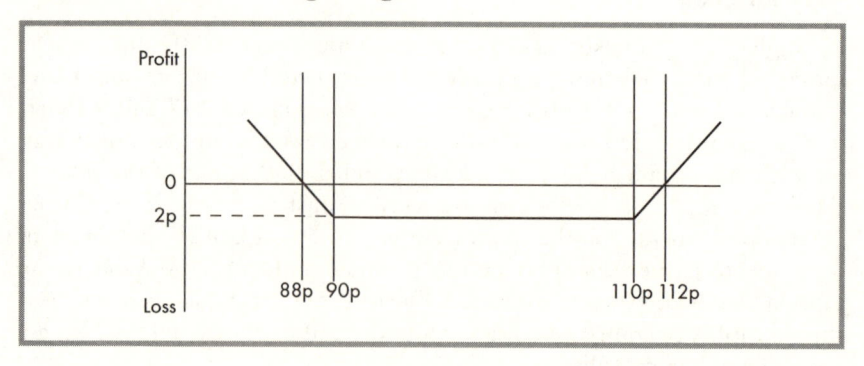

FIGURE 9.20   Short strangle

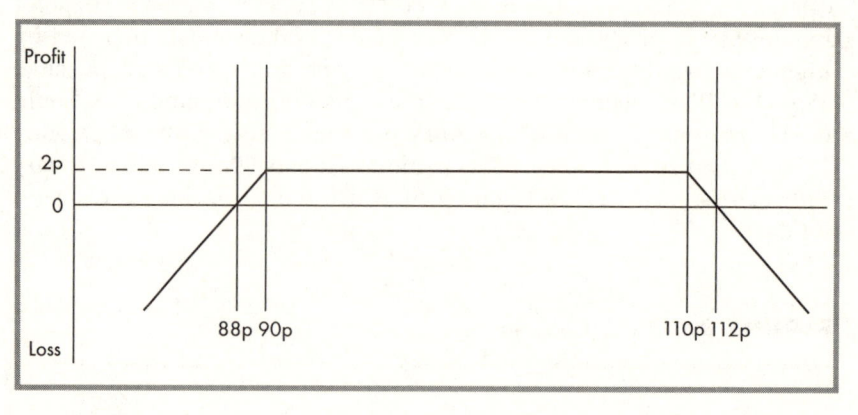

Although the long and short strangles are suitable for taking positions on volatility, they are more likely to be used for taking positions on changes in market expectations of volatility, with the combining of calls and puts being for the purpose of achieving delta neutrality. Figure 9.21 illustrates the profit/loss profile of the short strangle, inclusive of time value, for 2 different market expectations of volatility.

The volatility trader with a short strangle hopes for a reduction in market expectations of volatility so that the time value of both options falls and moves the profit/loss profile closer to the intrinsic value (i.e. straight-line) profile. Such a change would tend to move the position into profit so long as the share price does not simultaneously undergo a substantial rise or fall.

The writer of option contracts can be regarded as having incurred liabilities in exchange for premium receipts. The prices of options represent the extent of the liabilities. The intrinsic value is the sum

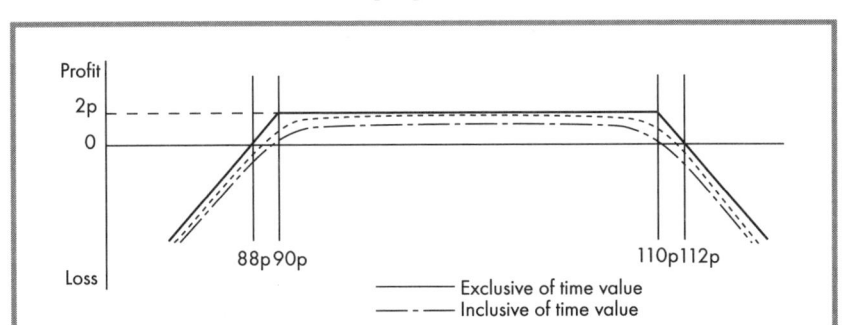

FIGURE 9.21 Short strangle profile including time value

immediately lost in the event of the buyer of the option exercising it; the time value reflects the possibility that this potential loss might increase prior to expiry. A lower expected volatility suggests a diminished likelihood of intrinsic value rising substantially (or coming into being), so if the market expectation of volatility falls, so will the time value paid and received when options change hands. The option writer will enjoy a decline in his liabilities and hence an improvement in his profit/loss position. This will show up as a movement of the profit/loss profile (broken line) towards the profit/loss profile that excludes time value (unbroken line), since the vertical distance between these 2 profiles represents time value.

The buyer of a strangle hopes for an increase in market expectations of share price volatility, which will cause time value to rise and the profit/loss profile to move away from the profile that excludes time value, as illustrated by Figure 9.22.

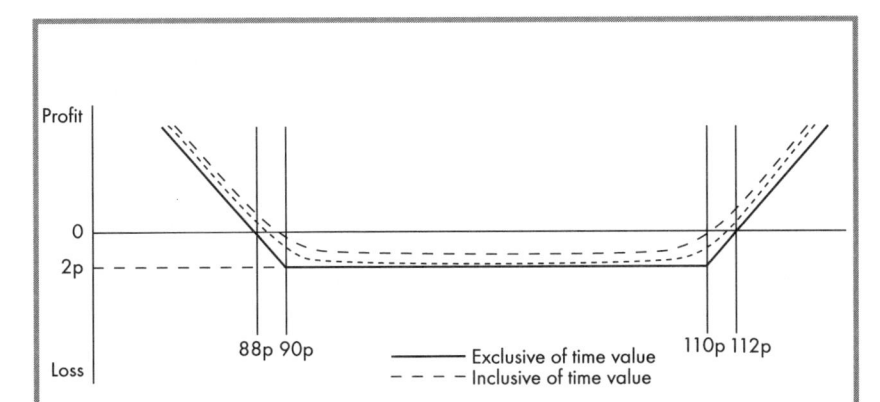

FIGURE 9.22 Long strangle profile including time value

Both Figures 9.21 and 9.22 serve to demonstrate the interrelationship of the 2 dimensions of volatility trading. Both strategies seek to profit from the changes in time value that ensue from variations in the market expectations of future volatility. At the same time, the profit potential is dependent upon the actual volatility of the share price as represented by the extent of movement of the share price from its original value. In the case of the short strangle (Figure 9.21) the share price should remain within a range, whereas in the case of the long strangle (Figure 9.22) profits are enhanced by substantial deviations of the share price from its original level (see also Figure 9.23).

FIGURE 9.23   Short strangle

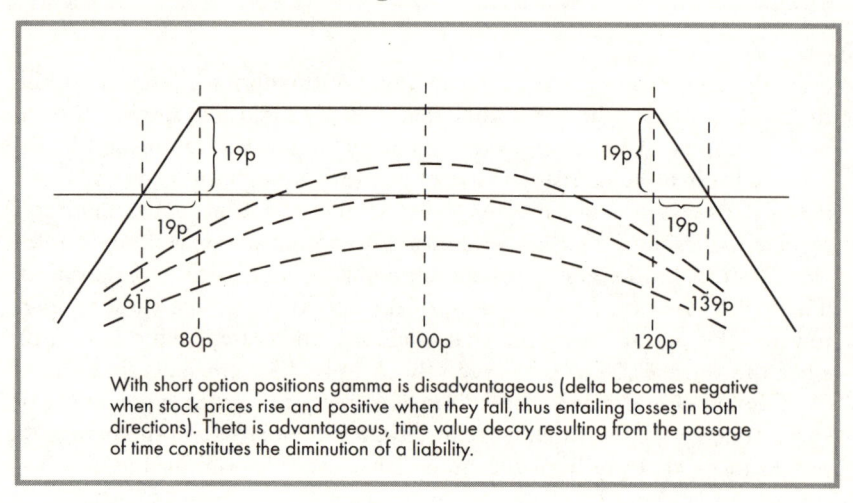

With short option positions gamma is disadvantageous (delta becomes negative when stock prices rise and positive when they fall, thus entailing losses in both directions). Theta is advantageous, time value decay resulting from the passage of time constitutes the diminution of a liability.

Butterflies

Long and short butterflies are illustrated by Figures 9.24 and 9.25 respectively. Butterfly spreads can be constructed in a number of ways. A long butterfly can be formed in the following ways:

1. Buy an in-the-money call, write two at-the-money calls and buy an out-of-the-money call. In the context of Figure 9.24, this means buying a 90p call, writing two 100p calls and buying a 110p call.
2. Buy an in-the-money put, write two at-the-money puts and buy an out-of-the-money put. In the context of Figure 9.24, this means buying a 110p put, writing two 100p puts and buying a 90p put.
3. Buy an out-of-the-money put, write an at-the-money put, write an at-the-money call and buy an out-of-the-money call. In the context of

FIGURE 9.24 Long butterfly

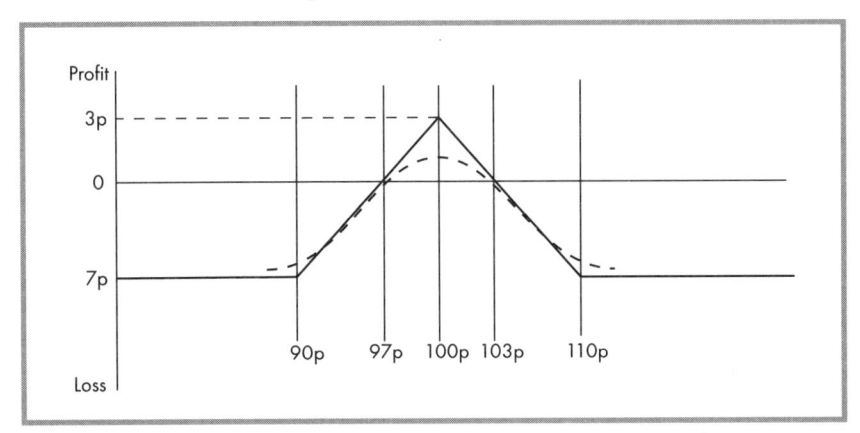

FIGURE 9.25 Short butterfly

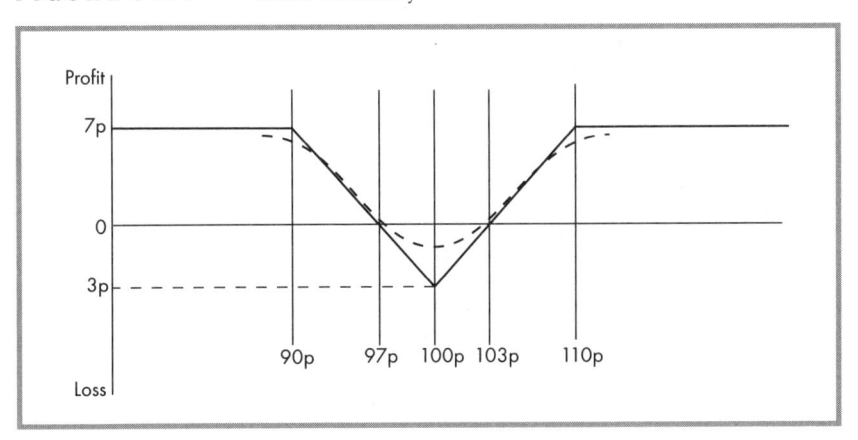

Figure 9.24, this means buying a 90p put, writing a 100p put, writing a 100p call and buying a 110p call. (This is a short straddle and a long strangle; the strangle could alternatively be constructed with in-the-money options.)

A short butterfly can be constructed in the following ways:

1. Write an in-the-money call, buy two at-the-money calls and write one out-of-the-money call. With reference to Figure 9.25, this means writing a 90p call, buying two 100p calls and writing a 110p call.
2. Write an in-the-money put, buy two at-the-money puts and write an out-of-the-money put. In relation to Figure 9.25, this means writing a 110p put, buying two 100p puts and writing a 90p put.

3. Write an out-of-the-money put, buy an at-the-money put, buy an at-the-money call and write an out-of-the-money call. In the context of Figure 9.25, this would involve writing a 90p put, buying a 100p put, buying a 100p call and writing a 110p call. (This is a long straddle and a short strangle; the strangle might alternatively be created with in-the-money options.)

Although all these butterflies ideally involve at-the-money options, it is unlikely in practice that any exchange traded options will be precisely at the money. In reality, traders would use those options that are closest to being at the money.

The reason for using options close to being at the money as the middle options in butterfly spreads is the achievement of a delta that is as close as possible to zero. This reflects the concern with trading on changes in time value that arise from variations in market expectations of volatility, rather than with trading on a direction of change in price. Delta neutrality also provides a position for the short butterfly that allows gains from share price movements in either direction, and a position for the long butterfly that renders share price stability desirable, since losses would accrue from share price movements in either direction.

ACTIVITY 9.4

The June gilt futures price is 119–29. Gilt futures options prices are as shown in Table 9.4.

Table 9.4   Gilt futures options prices

	Calls		Puts	
	June	September	June	September
116	4–49	5–35	0–55	1–51
118	3–18	4–20	1–24	2–36
120	2–18	3–18	2–24	3–34
122	1–22	2–27	3–28	4–43
124	0–52	1–48	4–58	6–00

Design a strategy that would allow a trader to gain from a narrow price range in the gilt futures market while limiting the maximum possible loss. Indicate the maximum profit, maximum loss(es) and break-even point(s). (Note that the futures are priced in 1/32nds, whereas the futures options are priced in 1/64ths; so, for example, 4–49 means £4 $^{49}/_{64}$.)

Answer
The trader might buy a butterfly spread. For example, selling a June 120 call for 2–18 and a June 120 put for 2–24 while buying a June 118 put for 1–24 and a June 122 call for 1–22 would achieve the objective.
The maximum profit is option receipts minus option payments:

$$(2-18 + 2-24) - (1-24 + 1-22) = 1-60$$

(This would be achieved at a futures price of 120, at which price none of the options could be profitably exercised.)
The maximum loss is 2 minus maximum profit:
$$2 - (1-60) = 0-04$$

The break-even points occur at 120 +/– 1–60, i.e. 118–04 and 121–60.

Comparison of volatility trading strategies

Figures 9.26 and 9.27 provide comparisons of profit/loss profiles for straddles, strangles and butterflies. Figure 9.26 shows the profiles exclusive of time value (the profits that would exist on the expiry date of the options). Figure 9.27 illustrates the profiles inclusive of time value.

Straddles tend to provide the highest potential profits, but also the greatest potential losses. Strangles involve a low maximum loss but a greater likelihood of it occurring. Butterflies have small potential losses, but at the cost of limited profit possibilities. The volatility trading strategies thus conform to the general rule that higher potential profits are obtained at the cost of higher risk – a rule applicable to all options strategies and indeed all investments.

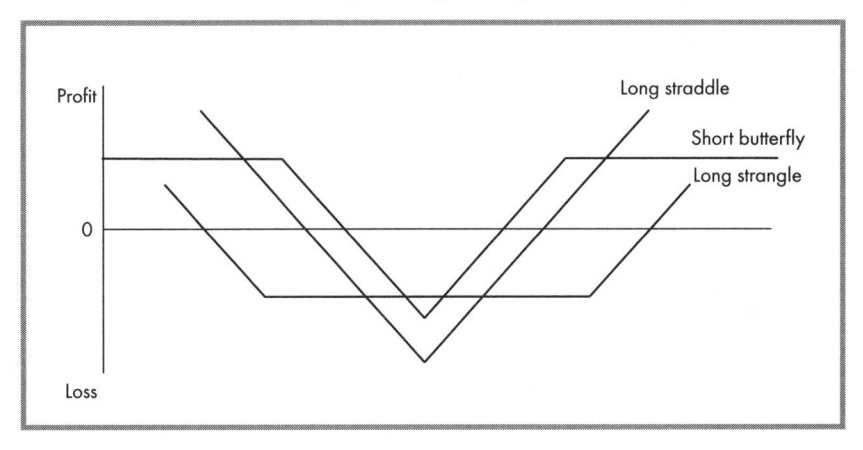

FIGURE 9.26   Volatility trading strategies exclusive of time value

FIGURE 9.27 Volatility trading strategies inclusive of time value

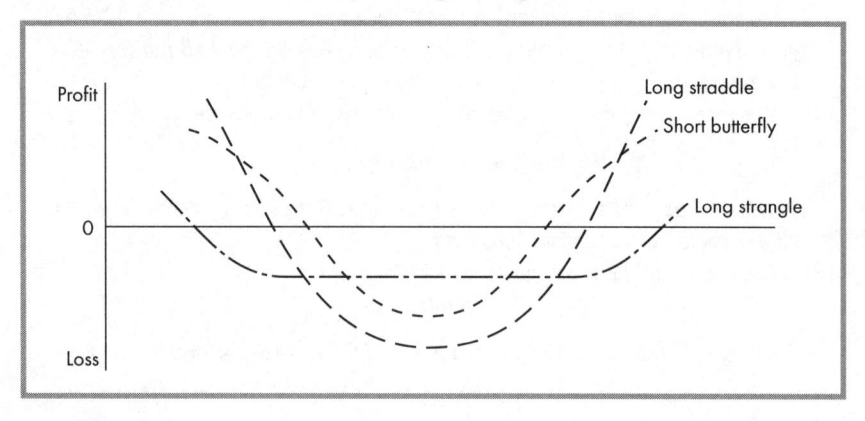

Ratio spreads

Ratio spreads can be looked upon as hybrid volatility trading strategies in that they mirror one of the basic strategies on the up side and another on the down side. Figure 9.28 illustrates the 4 generic possibilities.

Call ratio spreads can be seen as involving a butterfly on the down side and a straddle on the up side. This position is created by buying calls with the lower strike price while writing a greater number of calls at the higher strike price. This strategy might be used by a trader who anticipates stability of the price of the underlying instrument around the higher strike price but is anxious about a possible price fall, against which he seeks protection.

FIGURE 9.28 Ratio spreads: (a) call ratio spread; (b) call ratio backspread; (c) put ratio spread; (d) put ratio backspread

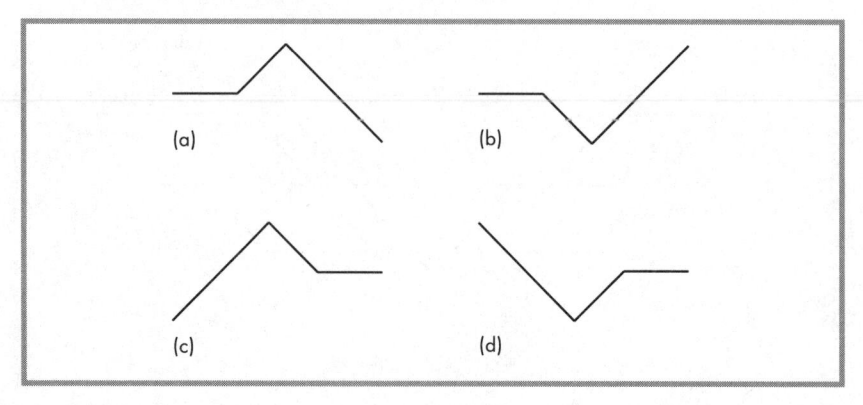

The call ratio backspread can also be seen as a butterfly on the down side and a straddle on the up side. This strategy is established by writing calls at the lower strike price and buying a greater number of calls at the higher strike price. This position might be established by a bullish trader who seeks profits from movement in either direction. He feels that an upward movement is the most likely, but suspects that a downward movement is possible.

The put ratio spread can be looked upon as a straddle on the down side together with a butterfly on the up side. It could be established by buying puts with the higher strike price and selling a greater number of puts at the lower strike price. Maximum profit is achieved if the price of the underlying instrument stabilises at the lower strike price. The position affords protection against a rise in the price of the underlying instrument (perhaps even providing a modest profit for prices above the higher strike price).

The put ratio backspread can also be viewed as a straddle on the down side combined with a butterfly on the up side. It could be established by means of writing puts with the higher strike price and buying a larger number of puts with the lower strike price. This position is a bearish one that is based on an anticipation of high volatility that is most likely to be manifested on the down side.

Figure 9.29 illustrates 2 more volatility trading strategies.

FIGURE 9.29   A condor and a table top

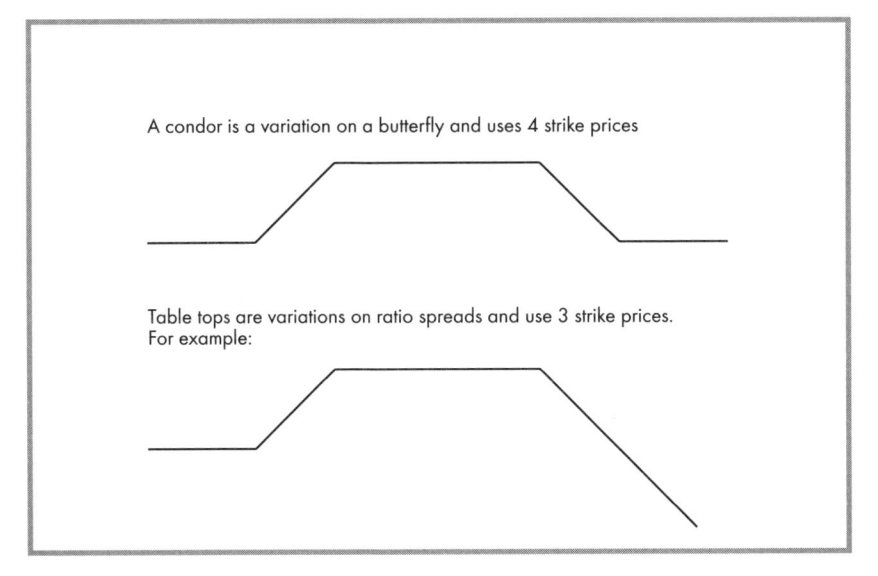

A condor is a variation on a butterfly and uses 4 strike prices

Table tops are variations on ratio spreads and use 3 strike prices. For example:

238 • TRADING WITH OPTIONS

ACTIVITY 9.5

It is 5 October. Amstrad shares are 60p and the option prices are as follows.

Strike price	Calls			Puts		
	Dec	Mar	Jun	Dec	Mar	Jun
50	14	18	21	3	4.5	6
60	7.5	11.5	14.5	7	10	10
70	4.5	9	11	13	16	16

(a) An investor holds Amstrad stock and is bullish about its price. Suggest 2 distinct trading strategies based on the view that the implied volatility is too high.

(b) What dangers are inherent in these strategies? What steps could be taken to counter these dangers?

(c) A week later the share price is 56p and the option prices are as follows.

Strike price	Calls			Puts		
	Dec	Mar	Jun	Dec	Mar	Jun
50	10	10	17	4.5	6	7
60	4.5	9	11.5	9	11	13
70	2	6	8.5	16	18	19

Calculate the profit/loss on the 2 strategies and comment on the reasons for the outcomes.

(Based on the Securities Institute examination in Financial Futures and Options, December 1989, Question 21.)

(a) If the belief is that implied volatility is too high, then any short position in options (and hence short position in time value) will profit from the expected fall in implied volatility (and hence time value). Since long dated at-the-money options contain the greatest amount of time value, they would seem to be appropriate options to write. Writing June 60p calls and June 60p puts would constitute 2 alternative strategies. The resulting profit/loss profiles would be:

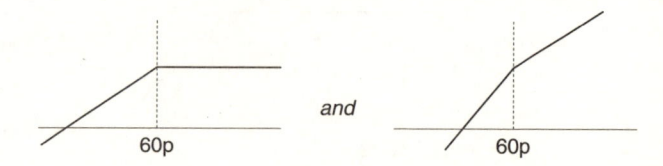

and

for the call and put strategies respectively (i.e. long underlying plus short option).

(b) A danger inherent in the strategy using calls is that there would be an opportunity cost if the share price rose by more than the premium receipt. This might be offset by buying out-of-the-money calls (effectively using a call bear spread rather than a simple short call).

A danger inherent in the strategy using puts is that a fall in the share price could entail heavy losses. This might be ameliorated by buying out-of-the-money puts (effectively using a put bull spread rather than a simple short put).

(c) On both strategies there is a 4p loss on the shares. The strategy that involved the writing of June 60p calls provided a profit of 3p from the options. The strategy involving the sale of June 60p puts provided a loss of 3p from the options.

The net losses, 1p and 7p respectively, resulted from the fall in the share price. The more aggressive strategy – the one with short 60p puts – provided the greater loss. There appears to have been little decline in implied volatility (e.g. the time value of the June 60p puts declined from 10p to 9p).

ACTIVITY 9.6

It is 27 February and Philadelphia Stock Exchange $/$ March option prices include the following (strike prices in dollars per pound, option prices in cents per pound):

Strike price	Calls	Puts
1.530	1.35	0.43
1.540	0.76	0.85
1.550	0.37	1.38

(a) Construct two vertical bull spreads using the 1.53 and 1.55 strike price options. Identify the maximum profit, maximum loss, and (at expiry) breakeven currency price in both cases.

(b) Construct two alternative volatility trading strategies based on a bullish view of volatility (a view that market expectations of volatility will increase). In each case show the maximum profit, maximum loss, and breakeven currency prices in the event of the option positions being retained to expiry.

(c) Construct two trading strategies based on bearish views in relation to both the currency price and volatility.

240 • TRADING WITH OPTIONS

Answer
(a) Buy 1.53 call, write 1.55 call.
Net premium payment 1.35 − 0.37 = 0.98 c/£
Maximum loss (if neither call is exercised) = 0.98 c/£
Maximum profit = 2 − 0.98 = 1.02 c/£ (based on the maximum net intrinsic value of 2 c/£)
Breakeven currency price = 1.53 + 0.0098 = 1.5398
Write 1.55 put, buy 1.53 put
Net premium receipt 1.38 − 0.43 = 0.95 c/£
Maximum profit (if neither put is exercised) = 0.95
Maximum loss = 2 − 0.95 = 1.05 c/£ (based on the maximum net intrinsic value of 2 c/£)
Breakeven currency price = 1.55 − 0.0095 = 1.5405

(b) Long straddle using $1.54 options
Maximum loss = sum of premiums paid, 0.76 + 0.85 = 1.61 c/£
No maximum profit
Breakeven currency prices are 1.54 + 0.0161 = $1.5561 and 1.54 − 0.0161 = $1.5239
Long strangle using $1.53 and $1.55 options
Maximum loss = sum of premiums paid, 0.43 + 0.37 = 0.8 c/£
No maximum profit
Breakeven currency prices are 1.55 + 0.008 = $1.558 and 1.53 − 0.008 = $1.522

(c) Write a $1.54 call option
Construct a call ratio spread; buy a $1.53 call and write two $1.54 calls.

CASE STUDY – BARINGS BANK

In February 1995 Barings Bannk collapsed as a result of the uncontrolled speculation by one trader, Nick Leeson. Most of the problems identified were not specific to derivatives; they could occur in any market. These problems included fraud, concealment and poor management controls. There were, however, some aspects that were specifically derivative related. One aspect was the facility, permitted by the futures margining system, to take a highly geared position. Leeson established a very large exposure to the Nikkei 225 by taking long futures positions in Singapore and Osaka. The fall in the Nikkei 225 (particularly the fall that followed the Kobe earthquake) required variation margin payments that exceeded the capital of the bank.

There was also an options dimension. Leeson had sold option straddles on the Nikkei 225, possibly to help finance the futures margin payments. The straddles reduced upside potential from the index while increasing downside exposure. To the extent that futures, calls and puts were matched in size, the strategy resembled a ratioed short put. The long futures and short calls would have tended to offset each other on the up side (futures profits cancelled by option losses), while the long futures and short puts would have reinforced each other in creating a strong downside exposure. Such a strategy is bullish on the index and bearish on volatility (a decline in market expectations of volatility would have reduced the time value of the options and thereby enhanced profitability, since time value represents a liability to the writer of options).

The market views taken by Leeson turned out to be incorrect. The Nikkei 225 fell, causing huge losses on the futures that had been bought and on the puts that had been sold.

The lessons from the collapse of Barings Bank (which was subsequently bought by ING for the nominal sum of £1) in terms of the need for stronger management controls and regulations have been well documented. There are many other lessons to be learned. These include the need for a better understanding of derivatives at all levels within a bank (there seems to have been inadequate understanding of derivatives within Barings Bank) and the need to avoid excessive confidence in a market view (forecast of market prices). A greater understanding of financial economics should lead to increased caution about the potential accuracy of predictions of market price movements. The 1990s have seen a number of heavy financial market losses by financial institutions and other corporations. Often, the media has ascribed these losses to the use of derivatives (even when no derivatives have been involved). The most common feature of these losses has been overconfidence in forecasts of market price movements.

CONCLUSIONS

For speculators, options have a number of advantages when compared with investing in the underlying instrument (such as a stock, bond or currency). They permit gearing (leverage) in that the cost of the option is much less than the price of the underlying stock. This results in much higher percentage profits (and losses) than would be obtained from buying shares. Since the maximum loss from buying an option is the premium paid for it, and since this is much less than the stock price, options may be looked upon as providing lower risk than stocks. However, options, unlike shares, have expiry dates. If an option expires out of the money, its value would have fallen to zero. So options provide an exposure to the passage of time. The passage of time erodes the time value of an option (but does not cause a corresponding loss on stocks).

Options provide a means of taking a short position on a stock. In many countries most people are not allowed to sell stock short (borrowed stock), so options may provide the only means of profiting from falls in stock prices. Short positions on a stock are obtained from buying puts or writing calls. Conversely, long positions can be taken by buying calls or writing puts. The choice between buying or selling options is influenced by views relating to the effects of volatility and the passage of time on option prices.

Option prices are affected by volatility (specifically, market expectations of stock price volatility) and the passage of time. If a speculator wishes to profit from these dimensions, options constitute a suitable instrument. Indeed, options provide the only practical means of taking positions on these dimensions for most market participants. While stocks (or other underlying instruments) allow speculators to make profits from the direction of stock price movements, options allow speculators to take views on the direction of stock price movements, on the speed and extent of such movements (are they fast and large enough to offset time value decay?), on changes in market expectations of volatility and on actual volatility (the extent of stock price movement irrespective of direction).

Further reading

Classic sources on trading strategies using options are:

Lawrence G. McMillan, *Options as a Strategic Investment*, 3rd edn (New York Institute of Finance, New York, 1992).

Geoffrey Chamberlin, *Trading in Options*, 3rd edn (Woodhead-Faulkner, Cambridge, 1990).

Other informative sources include:

M. Desmond Fitzgerald, *Financial Options* (Euromoney Publications, London, 1987), especially Chapter 4.

John F. Marshall, *Futures and Option Contracting* (South-Western, Cincinnati, 1989), especially Chapters 19 and 20.

ARBITRAGE WITH OPTIONS   10

INTRODUCTION

Arbitrage involves making riskless profits from mispricing; relatively underpriced options are bought and relatively overpriced ones sold. Pure arbitrage requires that none of the arbitrager's own capital is used. If the arbitrager's own capital is used, the process is known as quasi-arbitrage.

Arbitrage with derivatives often takes the form of buying/selling the derivative while simultaneously taking an opposite position in a synthetically constructed (but otherwise identical) derivative. The process of synthetically constructing derivatives, or other financial instruments, is known as financial engineering.

The chapter begins by showing the construction of synthetic futures positions by buying and selling options. For example, buying a call and writing a put on the same stock, the options having identical strike prices and expiry dates, creates a synthetic long futures position in that stock.

This is followed by an examination of reversal, conversion and option box arbitrages. Reversal and conversion arbitrages involve synthetic positions against actual positions in the underlying instrument. Option boxes use a long synthetic, using options with one strike price, against a short synthetic based on options with a different strike price. An example of a reversal arbitrage is provided. The example uses futures options, i.e. options on futures contracts. So the arbitrage involves a synthetic long futures position against an actual short futures position.

The chapter then shows the construction of synthetic options. Simultaneously, it indicates the arbitrage opportunities that would arise from mispricing. As always, the pursuit of arbitrage profits tends to eliminate the mispricing and thereby restore the equilibrium relationship between the various prices.

This is followed by a discussion of the put–call parity relationship. Put–call parity is a price relationship whose breakdown could provide opportunities to profit from some of the arbitrage strategies described earlier in the chapter. Pursuit of arbitrage profits using strategies such as reversal or conversion arbitrage would tend to (via the forces of demand and supply) restore put–call parity.

The next arbitrage illustrated is based on the convexity property of option pricing. This property implies a relationship between the prices of options with differing strike prices (but otherwise identical). If this relationship fails to hold, arbitrage profits may be obtained by the use of an options butterfly.

The chapter ends with a discussion of boundary conditions, in the form of minimum option values. Violation of the boundary conditions can provide opportunities for arbitrage profit. Again, the behaviour of arbitragers will tend to impact on demand and supply so as to remove any violation of the boundary conditions.

SYNTHETICS

A synthetic long position can be created by buying a call option and writing a put option. A synthetic short position is constructed by buying a put option and writing a call. Figure 10.1 illustrates a synthetic long position in Nogood plc stock. (These are synthetic futures.)

The simultaneous purchase of a call option and writing of a put, both at the exercise price of 140p, creates a synthetic purchase at 140p. At prices above 140p it is worthwhile to exercise the option to buy stock at 140p, whereas below 140p the buyer of the put option could profitably exercise the option to sell at 140p. Thus, above 140p the holder of the synthetic chooses to buy at 140p, while below 140p he is obliged to buy at 140p; either way he buys at 140p.

The line depicting the profit/loss profile of the synthetic is obtained by summing the profits or losses on the 2 options at each price. The assumption that the premiums of the 2 options are the same, at 2p, implies that the profit/loss profile of the synthetic crosses the horizontal at 140p. At 140p, the exercise price of the 2 options, the premium received and the premium paid are equal so that there is neither a net gain nor a net loss. This means that the synthetic is equivalent to a purchase of stock at 140p. If the option premiums had differed, the profit/loss profile of the synthetic would have intersected the horizontal at a different price, so that the

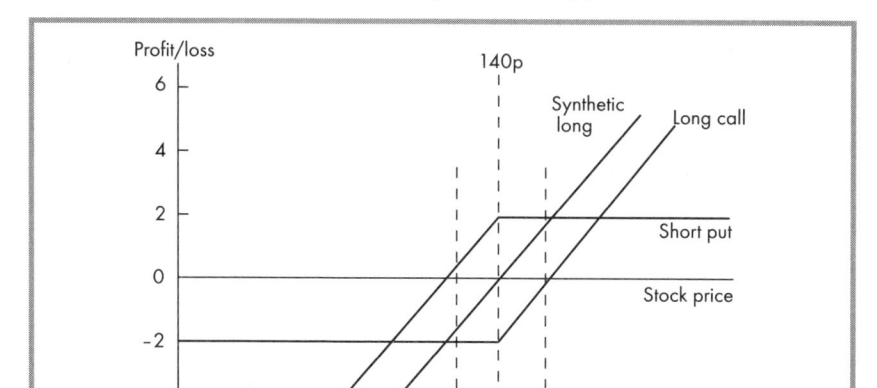

FIGURE 10.1   Creation of a synthetic long position

[Profit/loss chart showing Synthetic long, Long call, Short put, and Stock price lines around strike 140p, with markers at 138p and 142p]

synthetic would have been equivalent to a purchase at a price other than 140p. Suppose that the call option premium were 3p. Then the synthetic price would be 141p, represented by the exercise price of 140p plus the net premium payment of 1p; see Figure 10.2.

Figures 10.1 and 10.2 involve at-expiry profiles. The derivation of the synthetic futures position is, however, essentially the same when prior-to-

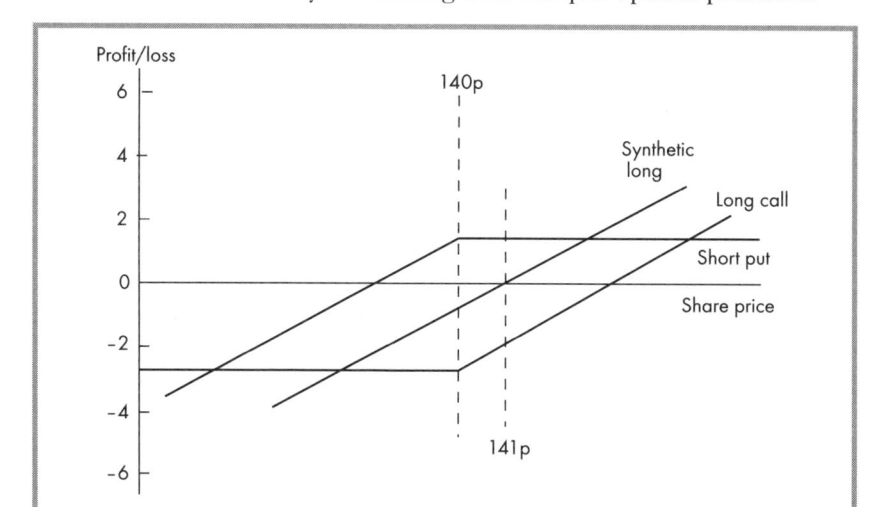

FIGURE 10.2   A synthetic long with unequal options premiums

[Profit/loss chart showing Synthetic long, Long call, Short put, and Share price lines around strike 140p, with synthetic price marker at 141p]

expiry profiles are used. When a long call is combined with a short put with the same exercise price, the sum of the deltas will be approximately 1 (a long put plus a short call with the same exercise price would exhibit a combined delta of about −1). So, in Figure 10.1, any deviation of the stock price from 140p would result in a change in the net value of the options that approximately matches the price change of the stock. In other words, there is a synthetic at about 140p prior to expiry as well as at expiry.

Example 10.1

Busby Bank shares are 459p and the 460p strike price call options are 13p, while the puts are 23p. Central Bank shares are 475p, while the 500p options are 6p and 45p for the calls and puts respectively. If a fund manager holds 20,000 Central Bank shares and wishes to switch immediately into Busby Bank shares while retaining the right to the forthcoming Central Bank dividend, synthetics offer a possible technique.

The fund manager could take a short synthetic position in Central Bank shares (to offset the actual shareholding) and a long synthetic position in Busby Bank shares. The synthetic positions can be unwound, and actual stock transactions undertaken, when the ex-dividend date for Central Bank shares passes.

The synthetic prices would be equal to the strike price plus the call price minus the put price in both cases.

Busby Bank: 460p + 13p − 23p = 450p
Central Bank: 500p + 6p − 45p = 461p

In the case of Busby Bank shares, the cash outflows (if the options were held to expiry) would be 460p + 13p, while 23p would have been received from the sale of the put options. In the case of Central Bank, the cash inflows (if the options were held to expiry) would be 500p + 6p, while 45p would have been paid for the put option.

REVERSALS, CONVERSIONS AND OPTIONS BOXES

A reversal involves the construction of a synthetic long position and the simultaneous holding of a short position in the underlying instrument (which may take the form of a short futures position). The difference between the

REVERSALS, CONVERSIONS AND OPTIONS BOXES • 247

synthetic price obtained and the market price is locked in for the duration of the reversal, since profits/losses on the underlying instrument would be matched by losses/profits on the synthetic. This is a technique for locking in a profit on one or more of the component instruments (since an overall profit must arise from the mispricing of one or more of the components).

ACTIVITY 10.1

The December eurodollar futures price is 93.08, while December eurodollar futures options prices are as shown in Table 10.1.

Table 10.1 Eurodollar futures options

Strike price	Calls	Puts
92.75	0.40	0.07
93.00	0.19	0.18
93.25	0.10	0.28
93.50	0.04	0.46

What is the best arbitrage opportunity?

Answer
The best arbitrage opportunity arises from buying a 93 call, selling a 93 put and selling a futures contract. The buying price of the synthetic is

$$93 \cdot 00 + 0 \cdot 19 - 0 \cdot 18 = 93 \cdot 01$$

while the selling price of the futures contract is 93·08.

A conversion involves the creation of a synthetic short position together with holding a simultaneous long position; see Figure 10.3. An options box

FIGURE 10.3 Conversion arbitrage

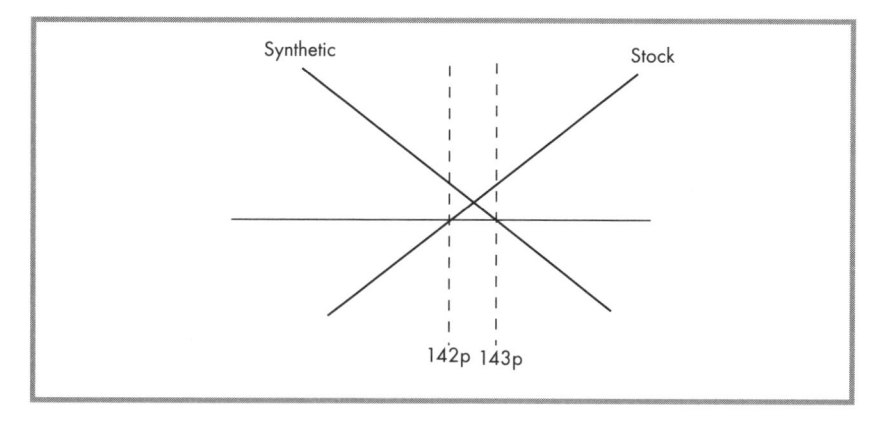

consists of a synthetic long together with a synthetic short (based on 2 different strike prices).

ACTIVITY 10.2

November FTSE 100 option prices include those given in Table 10.2 below.

Table 10.2   FTSE 100 option prices

	Calls	Puts
1800	74	20
1850	39	36
1900	23	72

Do the options provide opportunities for profitable arbitrage?

Answer
The implied FTSE 100 Indices are 1854, 1853 and 1851 from the 1800, 1850 and 1900 options respectively. An options box involving 1800 and 1900 options should yield an arbitrage profit. Buying an 1800 put and writing an 1800 call produces a synthetic short at 1854. Buying a 1900 call and writing a 1900 put produces a synthetic long at 1851. However, this arbitrage opportunity will not be available if bid–offer spreads are not sufficiently fine.

Making riskless profits from mispriced options

Perhaps the first response to the observation that an option is mispriced is to buy if it is cheap and write if it is expensive. Such positions, however, leave the trader exposed to adverse market movements. The profit potential is accompanied by risk; indeed, it is likely that a small profit potential is accompanied by substantial risk. In such a situation, it would make sense to seek to profit from the mispriced option by means of a delta neutral strategy; in other words, a strategy which involves no net exposure to movements in the price of the underlying financial instrument. What follows is based on LIFFE gilt futures options, but most of the principles involved are readily adaptable to other types of option.

Suppose it is 24 May and the prices of September gilt futures options are as shown in Table 10.3. The September gilt futures price is 95–15.

Table 10.3 Gilt futures options

Strike price	Calls	Puts
90	5–38	0–08
92	3–50	0–20
94	2–13	0–47
96	0–49	1–35
98	0–26	2–60
100	0–09	4–43
102	0–06	6–40

An analyst concludes that the 96 calls are underpriced. A valuation trading strategy would involve buying 96 calls while adopting an offsetting position elsewhere so as to achieve zero net market exposure.

A synthetic long futures can be created by buying a call and writing a put. In order to profit from the underpriced 96 call, the trader would buy a 96 call, write a 96 put and sell a futures contract. The effective buying price would be:

96 + (0–49) – (1–35) = 95–14

when expressed in 1/64ths. Although gilt futures options are priced in 1/64ths, the gilt futures are priced in 1/32nds. So the above price is equivalent to a gilt futures price of 95–07.

The synthetic thus generates a buying price of 95–07 when the price of the futures contract is 95–15. So it is possible to buy at 95–07 and simultaneously to sell at 95–15. An arbitrage profit of 8/32nds is generated, which amounts to £125 (8 × £15·625) for each combination of one long call, one short put and one short futures. While holding the reversal, the arbitrager has no net exposure to movements in the price of the futures contract. In other words, the net delta is zero. The short futures position has a delta of –1 and the synthetic long has a delta of 1.

CONSTRUCTING SYNTHETIC OPTIONS

There are 8 basic positions available to a transactor in financial markets, sometimes referred to as the building blocks of financial engineering. They are:

1. Long underlying (buying stocks, currencies, etc.)
2. Short underlying (e.g. selling borrowed stock)

3. Deposits (cash)
4. Debts (cash)
5. Long call (buying call options)
6. Short call (selling call options)
7. Long put
8. Short put

They are referred to as the building blocks of financial engineering because each one can be constructed by a combination of some of the others and because combining them in various ways can produce a virtually infinite variety of financial structures. A vast variety of profit/loss and risk/reward profiles can be created using these building blocks. Investment products that would otherwise be unavailable can be produced by financial engineering.

Synthetic puts

Some of the simplest examples of financial engineering involve the creation of synthetic versions of building blocks using other building blocks. For example, a put option position can be constructed by buying a call option, depositing cash and short selling the stock. Figure 10.4 illustrates the combination of a short position in stock with a long call.

FIGURE 10.4 Short position with long call

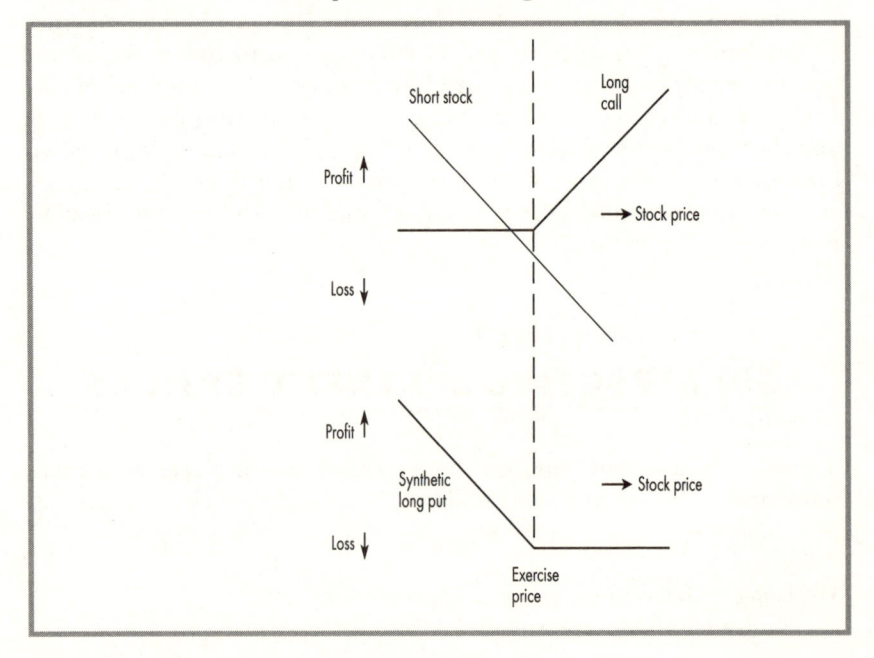

In Figure 10.4, as the stock price rises above the exercise price, gains on the call are offset by losses on the short stock, with the result that there is no change in the net profit or loss. This absence of change in the profit/loss position is illustrated by the horizontal line to the right of the exercise price in the lower part of the figure. As the stock price falls below the exercise price, gains on the short stock are not offset by losses on the call option (ignoring the premium). The result is that as the stock price falls, the profitability of the combined position improves. This is illustrated to the left of the exercise price in the lower part of Figure 10.4.

There remains an important difference between the combination shown in Figure 10.4 and an actual put option. This is the net indebtedness resulting from the short position in stock (stock has been borrowed and sold). The actual put option does not involve such indebtedness. To complete the synthetic construction of a put option, it is necessary to eliminate the net indebtedness. This is achieved by adding a deposit of money (which would wholly or largely come from the proceeds of the short sale of stock). This construction can be expressed as:

Synthetic put = Call + Deposit − Stock

If the net cost of the synthetic put differs (by more than the transactions costs) from the price of the actual put option, there would be an arbitrage opportunity. Arbitragers would buy the cheaper and sell the dearer, and thereby make a profit while being completely hedged (the 2 options would give offsetting exposures to the stock price). The pursuit of the arbitrage profits would, via the forces of demand and supply, tend to restore equality between the 2 put prices; see Table 10.4.

Table 10.4   An arbitrage opportunity

Synthetic put = Call + Deposit − Stock sale
Put price = Synthetic put price
$P = C + K/(1 + r)^t - S$

At expiry
If $S < K$ buy stock at S to close short sale, leaving $K - S$ which equals the value of the put.
If $S > K$ the call is exercised using K from the deposit. The resulting receipt of stock is used to close the short sale. There is zero profit/loss.
If $P \neq C + K/(1 + r)^t - S$ there is an arbitrage opportunity.
The higher priced (of the actual and synthetic puts) is sold and the cheaper is bought, the difference between the prices is the arbitrage profit.

Synthetic calls

In an analogous fashion call option positions can be created synthetically and, similarly, arbitrage should ensure that the price of the actual call should equal the net cost of the synthetic call. A synthetic long call can be created by buying stock, buying a put option and borrowing money. That is:

Synthetic call = Put + Debt + Stock

Figure 10.5 illustrates the construction of a synthetic call option. Below the exercise price, losses on the stock are offset by gains on the put option. Above the exercise price, profits on the stock are not offset by losses on the put option (ignoring the premium). The result is a horizontal line below, and an upward slope above, the exercise price.

The positions illustrated in the top part of Figure 10.5 do not fully describe the synthetic call option. That is because the long position in stock constitutes a net asset position. This needs to be offset by a liability in the construction of the synthetic call. The requisite liability position can be achieved by means of financing the stock purchase with borrowed money. The borrowing will fail to match the purchase price of the stock, to the extent that the premium of the long put fails to match that of the

FIGURE 10.5   A synthetic call option

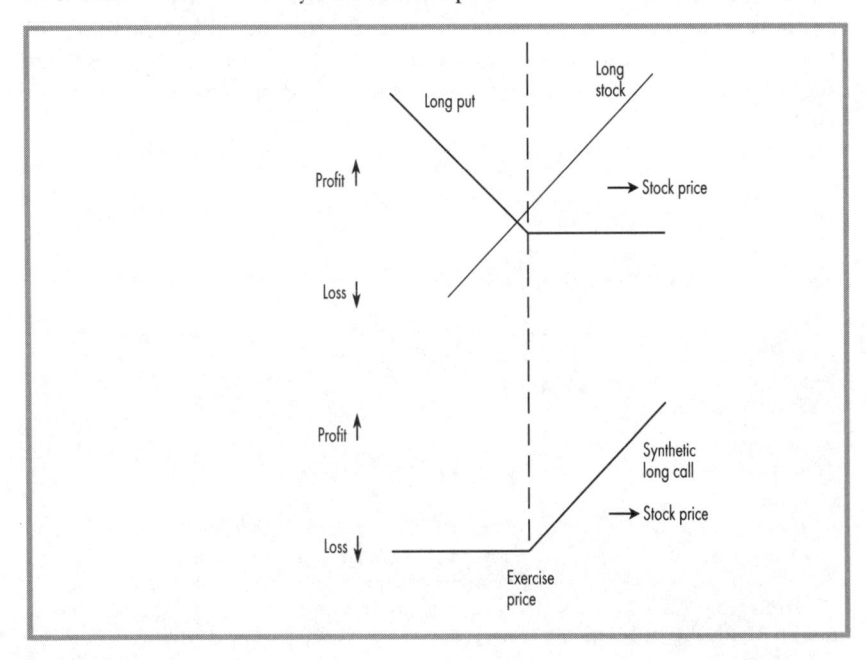

synthetic call. For example, if the price of the put exceeds the value of the call, the sum borrowed will totally finance the stock and partially finance the put. The remaining finance required for the put corresponds to the call option premium; see Table 10.5.

Table 10.5   A synthetic call option

Call price = Price of synthetic call
Long call = Long stock + Long put + Debt
$C = S + P - K/(1 + r)^t$

At expiry   If $S > K$ $C = S - K$
             If $S < K$ $C = (S + P) - K = 0$

t = year before expiry
A debt of K at expiry requires $K/(1 + r)^t$ to be borrowed now. If $S > K$ (and since the volatility values of C and P are equal) the cost of the synthetic exceeds $S + P - K$ by $K - K/(1 + r)^t$. So the price of C should exceed $S + P - K$ by $K - K/(1 + r)^t$ (which is the financing cost component of time value). If $C \neq S + P - K/(1 + r)^t$ there is an arbitrage opportunity from selling the relatively high priced and buying the cheaper.

PUT–CALL PARITY

Like many other relationships in financial markets, put–call parity can be defined as a condition that precludes arbitrage profits. The arbitrage that is precluded is between a long or short position in the underlying (stock, bond, currency or futures) and a synthetic short or long constructed using options. A conversion arbitrage involves buying the underlying and selling it by means of a synthetic short position (long put and short call). A reversal arbitrage involves a long synthetic (buying calls and selling puts) and a short position in the underlying instrument. Put–call parity holds if neither conversion nor reversal arbitrage yields a profit.

The absence of profit from conversion or reversal arbitrage would appear to require the effective price achieved by means of the synthetic to be equal to the actual price of the instrument. The price of the synthetic is the option strike price plus the price of the call minus the price of the put ($K + C - P$), which is the same irrespective of whether one is buying or selling by means of the synthetic. If the absence of arbitrage profits requires the price via the synthetic to be equal to the price of the underlying (so there is no profit potential from buying via one and selling via the other), the following relationship would prevail:

$$K + C - P = S$$

or:

$$C - P = S - K$$

where S is the price of the underlying instrument. This is the simplest form of the put–call parity relationship. Unfortunately, this is (for most underlying instruments) an oversimplification.

When interest rates are taken into account, the effective price, via the synthetic, would be $C - P + K/(1 + rt)$, since $K/(1 + rt)$ is the sum which invested in the present would generate K by the expiry date of the options (r is the rate of interest as a decimal and t is the fraction of a year to the expiry date). The absence of arbitrage profits requires $C - P + K/(1 + rt) = S$. So put–call parity becomes $C - P = S - K/(1 + rt)$.

It is worth noting that $C - P = S - K$ implies that the time values of the calls and puts are equal. Since $S - K$ is the intrinsic value of an in-the-money call option, it follows that $C - P$, which is the excess of the call price over the put price, equals the intrinsic value of the call option. It follows that the time values are equal (the analogous result for $K > S$ can be obtained by multiplying both sides of $C - P = S - K$ by -1). The amended form of put–call parity, i.e. $C - P = S - K/(1 + rt)$, implies that $C - P$ is greater than $S - K$. In other words, the price of the call exceeds the price of the put by more than the intrinsic value of the call option. So the call option has a greater time value than the put option. The excess time value is $K - K/(1 + rt)$, which is the financing cost component of time value (the volatility value component remains equal for the calls and the puts).

The formulation $C - P = S - K/(1 + rt)$ is based on there being no dividend yield from the stock. If dividends were payable on a continuous basis, the put–call parity condition would become $C - P = S/(1 + dt) - K/(1 + rt)$, where d is the rate of dividend yield. The formulation without dividends was based on S being the cash outlay required for the purchase of stock. Comparing the direct purchase of stock with purchase via a synthetic should be based on purchases at the same point of time, which might be the expiry date of the options. If the rate of dividend yield is d, then the acquisition of stock worth $S/(1 + dt)$ in the present would be expected to lead to a stockholding worth S on the expiry date of the options if dividends are invested in further shares of stock.

For individual stocks the assumption of a continuous dividend yield is unrealistic. However, it is not too unrealistic for stock index portfolios that contain a large number of stocks paying dividends at different points in time. So the put–call parity formulation of $C - P = S/(1 + dt) - K/(1 + rt)$ is a reasonably good approximation for stock index options.

In the case of individual stocks that pay dividends at discrete intervals (typically every 6 months or quarterly) a different approach is required.

This involves subtracting the present values of expected future dividends (those dividends relating to ex-dividend dates prior to the option expiry date) from the stock price. The reasoning is that part of the initial cost of the share can be met by borrowing on the basis of future dividend receipts (which would subsequently be used to repay the debt). If D represents the present value of expected future dividends, then put–call parity for an individual stock becomes $C - P = S - D - K/(1 + rt)$.

Stocks are not the only underlying instrument likely to yield a return. Bonds are obvious cases of an underlying with a yield. Currencies are less obvious. However, foreign currency does yield a return whose rate is the interest rate on that currency. In parallel with the case of stock dividends, the put–call parity relationship for foreign currency can be written as $C - P = S/(1 + ft) - K/(1 + rt)$, where f is the rate of interest on the foreign currency and r is the domestic currency rate of interest. The reason for discounting S is that an amount of foreign currency equal to $S/(1 + ft)$ when invested at rate f for time period t (the period to the expiry date of the options) yields S on the expiry date of the options.

Futures are a type of underlying without an income yield. However, since futures are traded on margin they do not involve initial expenditure (except for initial margin payments, which themselves may yield interest returns to the futures trader) and hence the sum of money to which the futures relate can be put on deposit until the contracts are closed out. So the sum of money to which a futures contract relates can earn a rate of return equal to the rate of interest on deposits. So to take delivery on a futures delivery date at a price F requires $F/(1 + rt)$ to be invested in the present. The put–call parity condition for futures options thus becomes $C - P = F/(1 + rt) - K/(1 + rt)$.

An alternative way of interpreting this put–call parity condition for futures options is in terms of discounting the 2 future values, F and K, so as to render them comparable with the 2 current values, C and P. However, when futures options, as well as futures, are traded on a margin system, there will be no initial payment for the options. So C and P will not constitute current values, and hence F and K do not need to be discounted in order to render them comparable with C and P. As a result, for futures options based on a margin system, the put–call parity condition is $C - P = F - K$.

The analysis thus far has considered only European-style options and hence has allowed for only one possible exercise date, namely the expiry date of the options. In the case of American-style options, it is necessary to allow for exercise at any time between the present and the expiry date. Taking the case of a non-dividend paying stock, the put–call parity condition (for European-style options) of:

$$C - P = S - K(1 + rt)$$

needs to be replaced by:

$$S - K \leq C - P \leq S - K/(1 + rt)$$

The extreme of $S - K$ is based on immediate exercise and that of $S - K/(1 + rt)$ on exercise at expiry.

ACTIVITY 10.3

The ASDA share price is 210p and options for October expiry have the following prices:

Strike price	Calls	Puts
200	29	11

There is 6 months to expiry and the six-month interest rate is 7% p.a. Check for put–call parity. How might any apparent deviation from put–call parity be taken advantage of?

Answer
Using the equation

$$C - P = S - K/(1 + rt)$$

then in the absence of arbitrage opportunities

$$\begin{aligned} C - P &= 210 - 200/(1 + 0.035) \\ &= 210 - 193.27 \\ &= 16.73 \end{aligned}$$

However $C - P = 29 - 11 = 18$.

So $C - P > S - K/(1 + rt)$

Either the call price is too high or the put price is too low.

An arbitrage would involve selling the call option and buying the put option. In other words the arbitrage would entail a synthetic short position. A conversion arbitrage could be used. This involves buying the stock and simultaneously constructing a short synthetic position in the stock.

ACTIVITY 10.4

US dollar three-month interest rates are 15% p.a.
Sterling three-month interest rates are 10% p.a.
Spot sterling is $1.95/£1.
Sterling currency options with three-month maturity stand at (c/£).

PUT–CALL PARITY • 257

Strike price	Calls	Puts
$1.90	10	2
$1.95	7	5
$2.00	3	8

Check for put–call parity. How might any discrepancies be taken advantage of?

Answer

$C - P = S/(1 + ft) - K/(1 + rt)$

$ is the base currency, £ is the foreign currency.

$\underline{\$1.90}$ $10 - 2 = 195/(1 \cdot 025) - 190/(1 \cdot 0375)$

$8 \neq 7.1$

$\underline{\$1.95}$ $7 - 5 = 195/(1 \cdot 025) - 195/(1 \cdot 0375)$

$2 \neq 2.3$

$\underline{\$2.00}$ $3 - 8 = 195/(1 \cdot 025) - 200/(1 \cdot 0375)$

$-5 \neq -2.5$

For $2·00 the put is too high relative to the call. An arbitrage strategy should sell puts and buy calls. So reversal arbitrage should be used (sterling sold).

ACTIVITY 10.5

It is 23 January. LIFFE March gilt futures are 123–17 and March gilt futures options have the following prices:

Strike price	Calls	Puts
123	1–12	0–52
124	0–44	1–10
125	0–35	1–55

Check for put–call parity. How could any arbitrage opportunities be exploited?

Answer

LIFFE gilt futures options are traded on margin, so the put–call parity condition is $C - P = F - K$. Taking each strike price in turn (and bearing in mind that since gilt futures options are priced in 1/64ths whilst gilt futures are priced in 1/32nds, the futures price should be restated as 123–34 to render it comparable to the option prices):

123   (1–12) – (0–52) < (123–34) – 123
        (0–24) < (0–34)
124   (0–44) – (1–10) = (123–34) – 124
        –(0–30) = –(0–30)
125   (0–35) – (1–55) = (123–34) – 125
        –(1–20) > –(1–30)

Put–call parity holds for the £124 strike options, but not for the £123 and £125 strike options. This suggests that the £123 and £125 strike options could provide arbitrage opportunities.

The prices of synthetics are equal to K + C – P. The synthetics have the following prices.

Strike price	Price of synthetic
123	123 + (1–12) – (0–52) = 123–24
124	124 + (0–44) – (1–10) = 123–34
125	125 + (0–35) – (1–55) = 123–44

Since gilt futures options are priced in 1/64ths and gilt futures are priced in 1/32 nds, the futures price of 123–17 is comparable to a synthetic price of 123–34. In the following analysis all prices are in 1/64ths.

Three arbitrage possibilities are:

Reversal arbitrage using £123 strike price options.
Long synthetic giving a purchase at 123–24 against a short futures giving a selling price of 123–34.

Conversion arbitrage using £125 strike price options.
Long futures giving a buying price of 123–34 against a short synthetic giving a selling price of 123–44.

Box arbitrage using £123 and £125 strike price options.
Long synthetic based on £123 strike options giving a purchase at 123–24, against a short synthetic based on £125 strike options giving a selling price of 123–44.

Example 10.2

A cap is a succession of interest rate options that establishes a maximum interest rate in relation to a succession of interest rate reassessment dates. A treasurer might look at interest rate futures options in order to estimate the cost of such a cap. The relevant price is that of short-term interest rate futures put options. If put prices are unreliable because of poor liquidity, but call prices are deemed to be reliable, put–call parity can be used to ascertain theoretical prices for the put options.

Suppose that the following data are available:

Maturity month	Futures price	92 call price
June	93·20	1·40
September	93·30	1·60

The treasurer uses this information to estimate the prices of put options with strike prices of 92 (corresponding to a ceiling of 8% p.a. on the interest rate).

For futures options traded on margin (such as the three-month sterling futures options on LIFFE):

$C - P = F - K$

where C is the call price, P is the put price, F is the futures price and K is the strike price. This can be rewritten as:

$P = K + C - F$

So the June futures put options should cost:

$P = 92 + 1·4 - 93·2 = 0·2$ (20 ticks)

The price of September contracts should be:

$P = 92 + 1·6 - 93·3 = 0·3$ (30 ticks)

At £12·50 per tick, the cost of the cap would be (20 + 30) × £12·50 = £625 for each £500,000 covered (£500,000 being the contract size).

OPTION PRICE CONVEXITY

An implication of the curvature of the relationship between the option price and the price of the underlying instrument is that if 3 (otherwise identical) options have different, but equidistant, strike prices, then the option with the middle strike price should be worth less than the average of the other 2 options. This is analogous to the point that if 3 prices of the underlying are used to produce option premiums from the same option, the middle premium will be less than the average of the other 2. This is illustrated by Figure 10.6.

If the option with the middle strike price has a premium higher than the average of the premiums of the options with strike prices either side of, and equidistant from, its strike price, an arbitrage opportunity will be available. This arbitrage opportunity could be exploited by means of a butterfly.

A long butterfly can be constructed by means of buying a low strike price call option, writing 2 middle strike price call options and buying a

FIGURE 10.6 Option price convexity

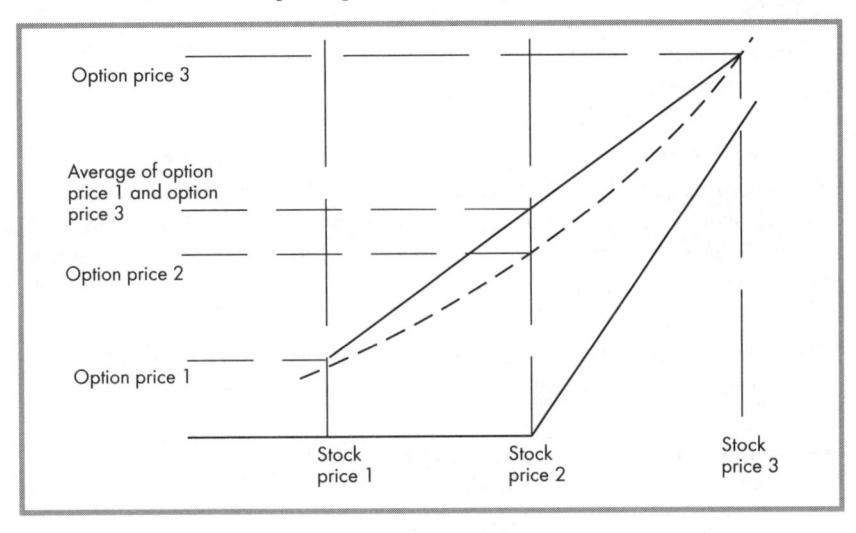

high strike price call option. In this way the relatively underpriced options are bought and the relatively overpriced option is sold. A butterfly can thus be used to profit in the event of the convexity condition being violated; see Table 10.6.

Table 10.6 Arbitrage from breakdown of convexity

Call option strike price	Premiums with convexity	Premiums without convexity
90p	5p	5p
100p	8p	12p
110p	15p	15p

Convexity requires that the premium of the 100p option should be less than the average of the premiums of the 90p and 110p options. When convexity is not present an arbitrage profit can be made with a butterfly spread.

Buy a 90p call, write two 100p calls and buy a 110p call.
The net receipts are

−5p + 12p + 12p − 15p = 4p

4p is the minimum profit from the butterfly
(The profit amounts to the net premium receipts, when all of the options expire unexercised.)

OPTION PRICE CONVEXITY • 261

ACTIVITY 10.6

The rate of interest is 10% and the prices of three-month options on a bond which has no coupon payments in the next 3 months and whose price is 100 are as follows:

Exercise	Call	Put
90	15	3
100	11	6
110	5	10
120	1	18

(a) Identify 3 arbitrage opportunities involving the bond and its options.
(b) What principles of option pricing are violated in each case?

(Based on the Securities Institute examination in Financial Futures and Options, December 1992, Question 11.)

Answer
(a) The intrinsic value of the 120 put is 20. The put is priced at less than its intrinsic value. An arbitrage profit can be made by simultaneously buying the bond and the 120 put for a total outlay of 118 and immediately exercising the put to realise 120, giving a profit of 2.
(b) The 110 series violate put–call parity. For a non-coupon paying bond:

$C - P = S - K/(1 + rt)$
$5 - 10 \neq 100 - 110/(1.025)$
$-5 \neq -7.32$

Either C is too high or P is too low, so the call should be sold and the put bought, creating a synthetic short position. This would be arbitraged against a long position in the bond. The initial expenditure is $100 + 10 - 5 = 105$. The receipt upon exercise is 110. If exercise occurs at expiry, the net profit is $110 - 105 (1·025) = 2·38$. (Note that the difference between 5 and 7·32, i.e. 2·32, relates to the date on which the initial expenditures are made. If this is converted to an expiry date profit, the result is $2·32 (1·025) = 2·38$.)

(c) The 100 calls are overpriced relative to the 90 and 110 calls. Convexity requires that the 100 call price should be less than the average of the 90 and 110 call prices, i.e. less than 10. (The point about convexity can be seen if a rise in the call option exercise price is treated as equivalent to a fall in the bond price. If the exercise price is 100, a decline in the bond price from 110 to 90 would cause a fall in the call option price. A straight line between these option prices would, because of the curvature of the line showing the option price at each bond price, be above all intermediate option prices. So the option price at a bond price of 100 would be less than the average of the option prices at bond prices of 110 and 90.)

To make an arbitrage profit from the overpricing of the 100 calls relative to the 90 and 110 calls, a long butterfly should be constructed. A 90 call is bought, two 100 calls are sold and a 110 call is bought (this allows selling the relatively expensive option series, buying the relatively cheap option series and the maintenance of approximate delta neutrality). The long butterfly involves a net outlay of 15 − 11 − 11 + 5 = −2 (i.e. a net receipt of 2). If the bond price falls below 90, so that none of the call options is exercised, there would be a profit of 2 at expiry. In the event of a bond price between 90 and 110, the profit will be greater than 2.

ACTIVITY 10.7

It is late December. The following prices hold on three-month sterling futures and futures options:

March futures 85.91; June futures 86–87.

Strike	Calls		Puts	
	Mar	Jun	Mar	Jun
8500	90	197	5	10
8550	51	153	10	16
8600	16	120	25	30
8650	9	82	68	45

Describe 3 distinct opportunities for profitable arbitrage which arise from the above prices and estimate the amount of profit in each.

(Based on the Securities Institute examination in Financial Futures and Options, December 1990, Question 21.)

Answer
The first step is to calculate the time values; they are shown in brackets.

Strike	Calls		Puts	
	Mar	Jun	Mar	Jun
8500	90(−1)	197(10)	5(5)	10(10)
8550	51(10)	153(16)	10(10)	16(16)
8600	16(16)	120(33)	25(16)	30(30)
8650	9(9)	82(45)	68(9)	45(45)

(i) The March 8500 calls are clearly underpriced. There is an arbitrage opportunity from purchase and immediate exercise of the option (and closing out of the resulting futures position).

(ii) Since the call is underpriced, the March 8500 series violate put–call parity:

$C - P \neq S - K$
$90 - 5 \neq 8591 - 8500$
$85 \neq 91$

(Note: Since LIFFE futures options are marked to market, there are no initial premium payments and hence no need to discount any values – so $C - P = S - K$ is the appropriate form of put–call parity.)

Since the call is underpriced, the appropriate arbitrage would involve buying the calls. So a long synthetic is created against a short futures position (i.e. a reversal arbitrage). The synthetic purchase price is 85·85, while the futures price is 85·91. A net profit of 6 ticks is available.

(iii) The June calls permit the creation of a butterfly with a positive minimum profit. Buy one 8550 call, sell two 8600 calls, buy one 8650 call:

$-153 + 240 - 82 = 240 - 235 = 5$

So a butterfly can be created to provide a profit that is at least 5 ticks.

BOUNDARY CONDITIONS

Arbitrage possibilities impose minimum and maximum values for options; these values are often referred to as option price boundaries. For practical purposes, only the minimum values are of significance and hence the following account will focus exclusively on them.

It is useful to begin by considering American-style options, which are options that can be exercised at any stage prior to expiry. The prices of such options should not fall below their intrinsic values, otherwise the options could be purchased for less than their intrinsic values and immediately exercised to realise the intrinsic values. The possibility of such arbitrage will tend to prevent option prices being below the intrinsic values by inducing arbitrage-based purchases whenever option prices fall below such levels; see Figure 10.7. Although the intrinsic value constitutes the minimum value in the case of American-style put options, the minimum values of American-style call options tend to be higher. This latter point can be appreciated by considering the case of European-style call options.

FIGURE 10.7 Arbitrage opportunity from the violation of the minimum price boundary of an American-style put option

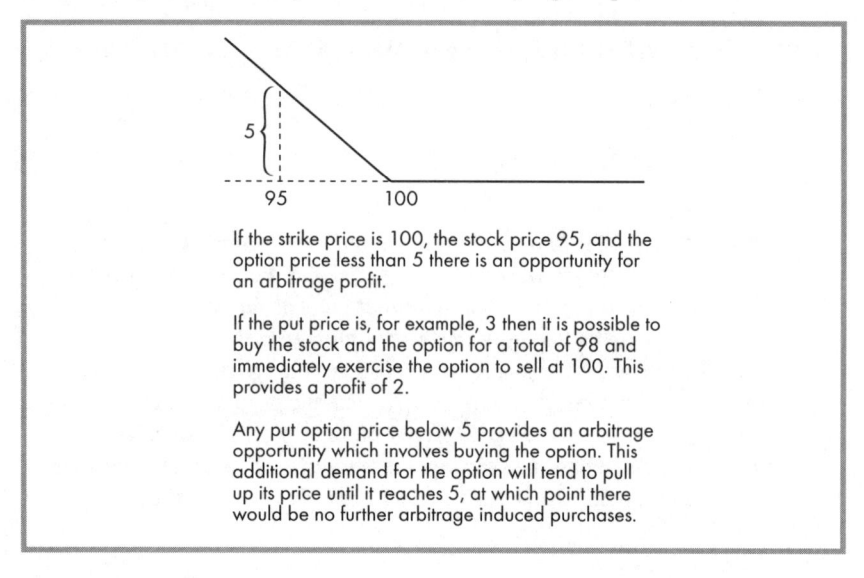

> If the strike price is 100, the stock price 95, and the option price less than 5 there is an opportunity for an arbitrage profit.
>
> If the put price is, for example, 3 then it is possible to buy the stock and the option for a total of 98 and immediately exercise the option to sell at 100. This provides a profit of 2.
>
> Any put option price below 5 provides an arbitrage opportunity which involves buying the option. This additional demand for the option will tend to pull up its price until it reaches 5, at which point there would be no further arbitrage induced purchases.

Example 10.3

A bond is priced at $100 and its $120 strike price put option is priced at $18. The option price is below its intrinsic value, which is $120 − $100 = $20. An arbitrage profit can be made by simultaneously buying the bond and the put for a total expenditure of $100 + $18 = $118 and immediately exercising the put. Upon exercise the bond is sold for the strike price of $120. Receipts exceed expenditures by $2, which constitutes the arbitrage profit.

European-style options can be exercised on only one date: the expiry day. So a European-style option, prior to its expiry date, cannot be exercised to realise the intrinsic value. So it is not possible simply to buy the option and immediately exercise it for an arbitrage profit. Instead, the arbitrage is more complex in that the arbitrage transactions cannot all be completed in the present for an instant profit. Positions need to be held until the option expiry date.

In the case of a call option on a non-dividend paying stock, the arbitrage would involve selling the stock short (borrowing stock and selling it), using most of the proceeds to put money on deposit and buy a call option, and then waiting until the expiry date to exercise the option and return the stock. The arbitrage profit would be the excess of the initial proceeds of the stock sale over the combined amount of the sum on deposit and the cost of the option. Since the sum on deposit can earn interest up to the option expiry date, only the present value of the option strike price needs to be deposited. So an absence of arbitrage opportunities requires that the option price plus the present value of the strike price exceeds (or equals) the initial stock price. So the minimum value of the option should be the stock price minus the present value of the strike price (rather than the American-style case of stock price minus strike price) – but if this is negative, the minimum value is zero; see Figure 10.8.

The excess of the stock price over the present value of the strike price is greater than the intrinsic value of the option (defined as stock price minus strike price). An American-style option should not have a price lower than that of a European-style option since the American-style provides everything offered by the European-style plus the facility of exercise before the expiry date. Consequently, the minimum value of an American-style call option should not be lower than the minimum value of a European-style call option. It follows that the minimum value of an American-style call option is the excess of the stock price over the present value of the strike price (i.e. the same as the minimum value of the

FIGURE 10.8   Arbitrage opportunity from the violation of the minimum price boundary of a call option

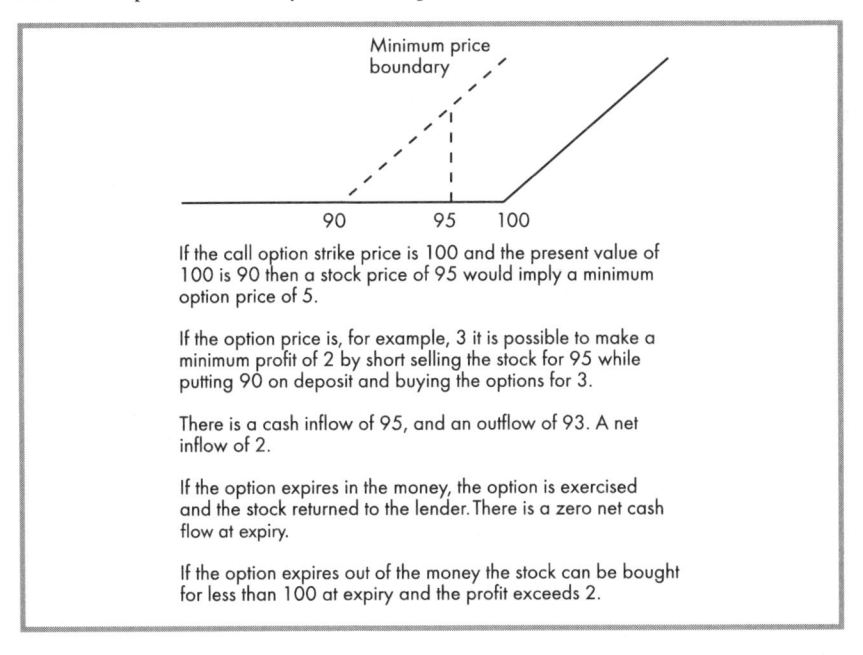

If the call option strike price is 100 and the present value of 100 is 90 then a stock price of 95 would imply a minimum option price of 5.

If the option price is, for example, 3 it is possible to make a minimum profit of 2 by short selling the stock for 95 while putting 90 on deposit and buying the options for 3.

There is a cash inflow of 95, and an outflow of 93. A net inflow of 2.

If the option expires in the money, the option is exercised and the stock returned to the lender. There is a zero net cash flow at expiry.

If the option expires out of the money the stock can be bought for less than 100 at expiry and the profit exceeds 2.

European and greater than the intrinsic value). Again, if this value is negative the minimum option price is zero.

In the case of put options on non-dividend paying stocks, arbitrage possibilities determine a minimum value of a European-style option below the intrinsic value (and hence below the minimum value of the corresponding American-style option). The minimum value of the European-style put option equals the present value of the strike price minus the stock price, and that boundary is below the minimum value of the corresponding American-style put option (the strike price minus the stock price); see Figure 10.9 and Table 10.7. The following activity illustrates a more rigorous approach to the establishment of the lower boundaries of put option prices (similar reasoning can be applied to ascertain the minimum values of call options). It must always be borne in mind that neither call nor put option prices can be negative – negative prices would involve being paid for the opportunity of making a profit without the risk of loss.

FIGURE 10.9   Boundary conditions

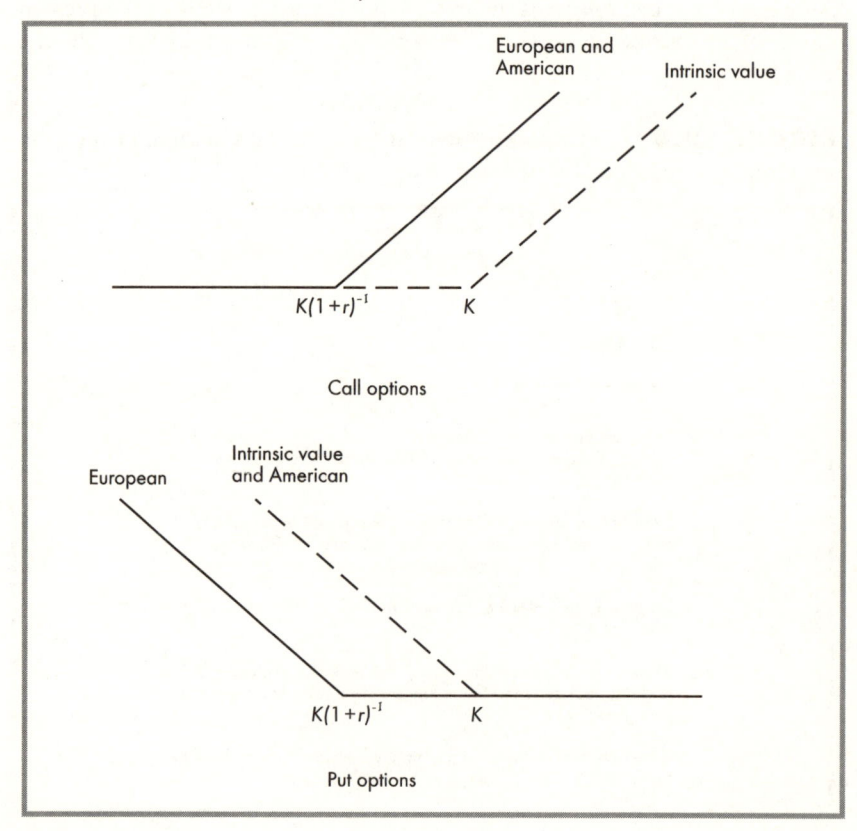

Table 10.7 Lower bounds

The lower bound for calls on non-dividend paying stocks
European calls:

$C \geq \max[0, S - K(1 + r)^{-T}]$

American calls:

$C \geq \max[0, S - K(1 + r)^{-T}]$

(An American call cannot be worth less than a European call, and $[S - K(1 + r)^{-T}] > [S - K]$.)

The lower bound for puts on non-dividend paying stocks
European puts:

$P \geq \max[0, K(1 + r)^{-T} - S]$

American puts:

$P \geq \max[0, K - S]$

where:
C = price of call option
P = price of put option
S = stock price
K = strike price
r = risk-free interest rate
T = time to expiry

ACTIVITY 10.8

In the following equations, P is the put option price, K is the option strike price, r is the risk-free interest rate for the period to expiry, T is the period to expiry, S is the spot price of the stock, D is the dividend expected before expiry, and t is the period to the receipt of that dividend. (Note that the formulation max( ) indicates that the highest value in the brackets should be taken; so, for example, max(0, $S - K$) means that if $S - K$ is positive it is the option price, whereas if $S - K$ is negative the option price is zero.)

The lower bound for puts on non-dividend paying stocks is:

(a) $P \geq \max[0, K(1 + r)^{-T} - S]$ for European puts, and
(b) $P \geq \max[0, K - S]$ for American puts.

The lower bound for puts on dividend paying stocks is:

(c) $P \geq \max[0, K(1 + r)^{-T} - S + D(1 + r)^{-T}]$ for European puts, and
(d) $P \geq \max[0, K - S, K(1 + r)^{-t} - S + D(1 + r)^{-t}]$ for American puts.

268 • **ARBITRAGE WITH OPTIONS**

> What transactions would provide arbitrage profits in the event of these conditions being violated when the options are in the money? Under what circumstances would the minimum profits be exceeded and what would be the maximum profit in each case? Why might apparent arbitrage opportunities not be real ones?

Answer
If (a) is violated when the option is in the money:

$$P < K(1 + r)^{-T} - S$$

This violation implies that the price of the put is too low. So the arbitrage should involve buying the underpriced put. The arbitrager would simultaneously buy the put and the stock with a view to exercising the put at expiry (if it is in the money at expiry) and receiving the strike price for the stock. The arbitrager could borrow the present value of the strike price with a view to repaying the debt when the option is exercised.

The total cost of the stock and the put amounts to less than the sum borrowed. So there is a net cash inflow in the present. If the option expires in the money, it is exercised to sell the stock at the strike price and the proceeds are used to repay the debt. So there would be no net cash flow at expiry and the original net inflow constitutes the arbitrage profit. If the put expires out of the money, the option is worthless but the stock can be sold for more than the strike price, with the result that there is an additional profit equal to the excess of the stock price over the strike price. This additional profit is potentially unlimited.

Apparent arbitrage opportunities might fail to be real ones in the event of the published option and stock prices relating to different points in time (non-synchronous trading), or in the event of the gross arbitrage profits being less than the transactions costs (bid–offer spreads and commissions).

If (b) is violated when the option is in the money, then:

$$P < K - S$$

Again, P is too low and hence the put option should be bought in order to benefit from the mispricing. At the same time, the stock would be bought and the option immediately exercised to realise the strike price (it makes sense to exercise immediately since that way the money is available for use at the earliest possible time). The total cost of the stock plus put option is less than the money to be received upon exercise. The difference is the arbitrage profit.

If (c) is violated when the option is in the money, then:

$$P < K(1 + r)^{-T} - S + D(1 + r)^{-t}$$

This differs from (a) in that a dividend will be received before the option is exercised at expiry. The amount that can initially be borrowed on the basis of future cash inflows is enhanced by the present value of the dividend receipt. If the present value of the strike price plus the present value of the dividend exceeds the total cost of the option plus stock, then the sum that can initially be borrowed exceeds the immediate cash outflow and this excess constitutes an arbitrage profit. If the option expires in the money it will be exercised for the strike price which, together with the dividend, can be used to repay the initial borrowing. If the option expires out of the money, the stock is sold for more than the strike price and the profit will be higher (by the excess of the stock price over the strike price).

If (d) is violated when the option is in the money, then:

$$P < max[K - S, K(1 + r)^{-t} - S + D(1 + r)^{-t}]$$

If $D(1 + r)^{-t} > K - K(1 + r)^{-t}$, the option will be exercised on the ex-dividend day, otherwise it will be exercised immediately. In the event of immediate exercise, case (d) is the same as case (b). If exercise is delayed until the ex-dividend date, time t, there will be scope initially to borrow money that is repayable when the strike price and dividend are received. Thus, $K(1 + r)^{-t}$ plus $D(1 + r)^{-t}$ is borrowed (strictly speaking, the period of discount for the dividend should exceed that for the strike price since the dividend payment date would be later than the ex-dividend date). If the cost of establishing the strategy, P + S, is less than the sum that can be borrowed, there is a net cash inflow that constitutes an arbitrage profit. If exercise is delayed in order to obtain the dividend and the option is out of the money on the ex-dividend day, the stock can be sold at the market price (enhancing the profit by the excess of S over K) and the put can be sold for any remaining time value (thereby further adding to the profit).

CONCLUSIONS

Pure arbitrage is the process of making riskless profits from mispricing without the arbitrager's own resources being used. Although in practice arbitrage is typically not pure in that elements of risk are often present and the arbitrager's own capital is often used (when one's own capital is used, the process is known as quasi-arbitrage), pure arbitrage provides a useful model for determining equilibrium price relationships. Arbitrage (pure or otherwise) operates, via its impact on demand and supply, to maintain particular relationships between prices. In the case of many futures, cash-and-carry arbitrage tends to maintain a particular relationship between the spot price, the futures price, the relevant interest rate and the expected asset yield. Likewise, arbitrage tends to maintain certain option–price relationships. Conversion and reversal arbitrage tend to maintain put–call parity. Arbitrage also tends to ensure that boundary conditions and convexity relationships are adhered to. In the event of these option-price relationships being violated, opportunities for profitable arbitrage will tend to arise. The transactions of arbitragers when seeking to take advantage of these profit opportunities will impact on demand and supply in such a way that the violations tend to be eliminated. Underpriced options are bought, and hence their prices are pulled up. Overpriced options are sold, with the effect that their prices are pushed down. There may also be pressures on the price of the underlying instrument. The overall effect of the arbitrage transactions would be to restore the equilibrium price relationship, and hence remove the opportunity for further arbitrage.

It may seem that since arbitrage provides risk-free profits, the number of arbitragers would be so large that arbitrage profits would always be small and available for very short periods. In very liquid markets this may be the case. In less liquid markets the profit opportunities may be larger and longer lived. Since the number of arbitragers is limited (by factors such as the need for expertise and expensive information technology) and access to funds is also subject to limitations, arbitrage may not always ensure that pricing relationships are constantly maintained. Despite this, arbitrage activity is normally adequate to ensure that the theoretical price relationships are satisfactory models for the analysis of the interrelationships among the prices of various option series, and between the prices of options and the underlying instruments. It is reasonable to suppose that substantial mispricing, in the form of deviations from equilibrium price relationships, will attract arbitragers who will tend to correct the mispricing in the process of making arbitrage profits.

Further reading

A very thorough account of the role of arbitrage in options markets is available in:

David A. Dubofsky, *Options and Financial Futures* (McGraw-Hill, Singapore, 1992), Chapters 4 and 5.

A useful source on boundary conditions and put–call parity is:

Gordon Gemmill, *Options Pricing* (McGraw-Hill, Maidenhead, 1993), Chapter 3.

BLACK–SCHOLES OPTION PRICING MODELS 11

INTRODUCTION

It has been pointed out earlier that option prices can be subdivided into intrinsic value and time value. For call options the intrinsic value is the excess of the stock (or other underlying instrument) price over the option strike price if the option is in the money, or zero if the option is at the money or out of the money. For put options the intrinsic value is the strike price minus the stock price, or zero if the stock price exceeds the strike price. If the option is American-style, then the intrinsic value is the pay off (ignoring the initial premium payment) from immediate exercise of the option.

Time value is the excess of the option price over the intrinsic value. It is time value that poses problems when estimating fair, or theoretical, option prices.

The chapter begins with an attempt to convey an intuitive understanding of the Black–Scholes option pricing model by means of statistical expectations based on normal distributions of returns. It is to be emphasised that this does not constitute a rigorous elucidation of the Black–Scholes model. In particular, the Black–Scholes model uses log normal, rather than normal, distributions. One reason for using log normal distributions is the need to avoid the possibility of negative stock prices; normal distributions allow for the possibility of any stock prices, including negative ones.

An alternative approach to option pricing is to see option premiums as reflecting the expected costs of hedging written options. Following a brief account of this approach, the chapter introduces the Black–Scholes formula.

The emphasis is on the formula and its application. The variations of the formula for options on differing underlying instruments are shown. These underlying instruments are non-dividend paying stocks, dividend paying stocks, stock indices, currencies and futures.

The chapter ends with a consideration of how volatility might be measured. The alternative approaches are referred to as historical volatility, implied volatility and ARCH models. In the process, consideration is given to possible reasons for an apparent systematic tendency for Black–Scholes models to misprice some options.

THE DETERMINANTS OF OPTION PRICES

The most popular way of calculating the 'fair price' of an option is by means of the Black–Scholes model. An intuitive feel for this model can be obtained by regarding it as equating the price (premium) with the expected profit from a naked option. Expected profit is used in the sense of possible profit outcomes weighted by their probabilities of occurrence.

Figure 11.1 illustrates this with respect to options on the FTSE 100 Stock Index. The curve in the upper part of Figure 11.1 is known as a normal distribution curve and indicates the probabilities of the various possible outcomes. The profile ABC in the lower part shows the profit possibilities from buying a call option (ignoring the premium at this stage).

Suppose that the area under the normal distribution curve between 1600 and 1610, as a proportion of the total area under the curve, is 0.19. This means that there is a 19% chance that the index will fall between 1600 and 1610. If the area under the curve between 1610 and 1620 is 0.15 of the total area, there is a 15% probability of the index being between 1610 and 1620. The statistical expectation of the profit from the call option is given by the sum of the possible profits when each possible profit is weighted by its probability of occurrence. The calculation of this expected profit is illustrated by Table 11.1 in which, for the sake of simplification, the possible profits are represented by the mid-points of the respective ranges. (Note that the probabilities are themselves expectations.)

Table 11.1 involves some simplifications that would be avoided in the actual calculation of expected profit. In particular, the mid-point of a range is not the best measure of the average possible outcome within the range. Nevertheless, the table serves to illustrate the principles behind the calculation of the price (premium) of an option using the Black–Scholes

FIGURE 11.1 Probability distribution of possible future index levels (with exercise price equal to mean of the distribution)

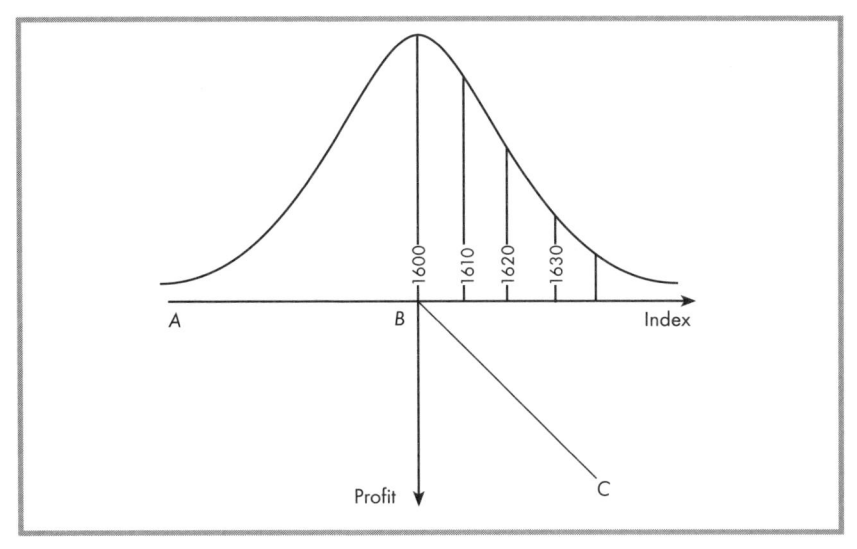

Table 11.1 Calculation of expected profit

Range of index values	Range of profit possibilities	Probability of occurrence	Contribution to expectation of profit
1600–10	0–10	0.19	5 × 0.19 = 0.95
1610–20	10–20	0.15	15 × 0.15 = 2.25
1620–30	20–30	0.09	25 × 0.09 = 2.25
1630–40	30–40	0.05	35 × 0.05 = 1.75
1640–50	40–50	0.01	45 × 0.01 = 0.45
1650–60	50–60	0.01	55 × 0.01 = 0.55
		0.50	Expected profit = 8.20

model. In the example shown, the premium, expressed in index points, is 8.20. At £10 per index point, this would correspond to a money price of £82 per contract. (The FTSE 100 options traded on LIFFE are based on £10 per index point.)

The various factors that affect the premium can be viewed in relation to Figure 11.1. A particularly important determinant is the relationship between the exercise price (index) and the index at the time that the option is purchased. Figure 11.2 illustrates a situation in which the spot index is higher than in the circumstances of Figure 11.1. In this case, the type of calculation illustrated by Table 11.1 would produce an expected profit greater than 8.20 index points.

FIGURE 11.2 Probability distribution of possible future index levels (where exercise price and mean of distribution differ)

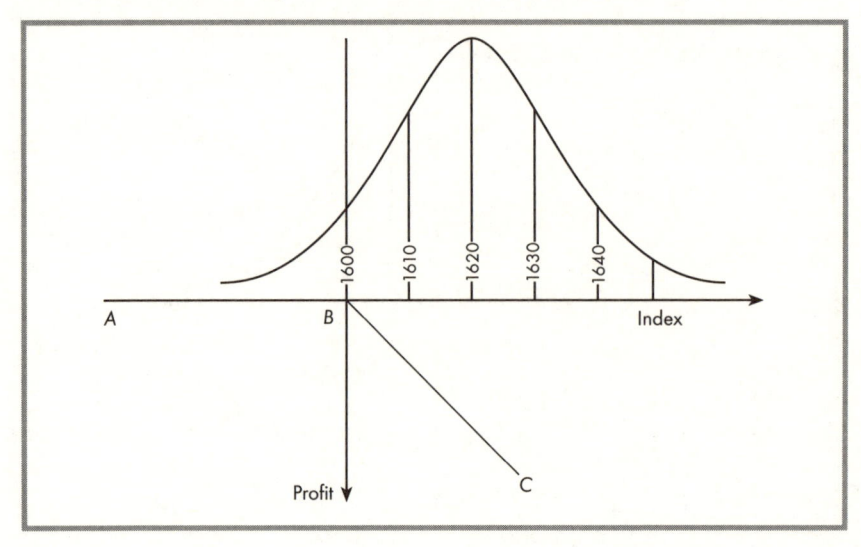

Time value is at its greatest when the option is at the money and declines as the option moves to being either in the money or out of the money. This behaviour of time value can be explained intuitively.

An out-of-the-money option has to reach the at-the-money position before movements of the index can start generating profitable opportunities for exercise. Thus, an option buyer would regard an out-of-the-money option as less valuable than an at-the-money option since some leeway has to be made up before it reaches the threshold of profitability, whereas an at-the-money option is already at this threshold. Consequently, the option buyer is prepared to pay less for an out-of-the-money option. Conversely, the option writer would accept a lower premium because of his reduced chance of loss. (This line of reasoning also underlines the role of the market forces of demand and supply in the establishment of option prices. Black–Scholes calculations merely serve as guidelines to buyers and writers.)

The time value of an in-the-money option would be lower than if that option were at the money because of the possibility of erosion of the intrinsic value. In the case of a call option, a rise in the index would increase the intrinsic value of options that were either in the money or at the money prior to the rise in the index. However, a fall in the index would reduce the intrinsic value of an in-the-money option, whereas an at-the-money option has no intrinsic value to be eroded. This potential for loss of intrinsic value is reflected in a lower time value.

Another determinant of the size of premiums is the expected volatility of the index. A high volatility would mean that the normal distribution of Figures 11.1 and 11.2 would spread out and flatten, indicating an increased chance of extreme values of the index. A calculation similar to that of Table 11.1 but with a normal distribution curve exhibiting a greater variance would produce a higher expected profit. Thus premiums rise as expected volatility increases, since the probability of high profits is enhanced.

The term 'volatility' can be seen as referring to the standard deviation of the distribution of possible spot prices at the end of a particular period of time. This standard deviation depends upon the length of time involved. It is obvious that this standard deviation will increase as the period lengthens (graphically depicted by the normal distribution curve becoming wider and flatter), since the likelihood of substantial movements from the original price becomes greater. What is less obvious is the precise relationship between the standard deviation and time.

The standard deviation is proportional to the square root of the period of time involved. So the volatility over t days is equal to the square root of t times the daily volatility.

This relationship between volatility and the square root of time explains the observed pattern of time value decay. Time value decays at an accelerating rate as the expiry date is approached. In fact, time value is related to the square root of the amount of time remaining before expiry. This pattern of time value decay, slow when expiry is distant but becoming rapid close to expiry, is illustrated by Figure 11.3.

From what has just been said, it is clear that time to expiry also influences the option price. Longer periods to expiry are associated with higher option premiums. A long period to expiry provides more opportunity for the index to move sufficiently above a call option

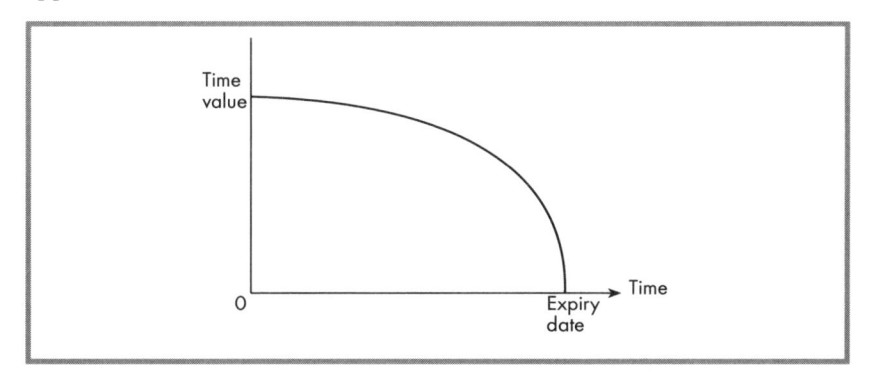

FIGURE 11.3 Time value decay accelerated as the expiry date is approached

exercise price (or below a put option exercise price) to generate a net profit. The enhanced likelihood of profitable exercise would tend to raise the price that a buyer is prepared to pay and that a writer would need to receive. (The point could alternatively be expressed in terms of a longer period leading to a greater variance of the normal distribution curve.)

Interest rates also have an influence on option premiums. The influence of interest rates can be understood by seeing options as a means of changing the timing of transactions in the underlying instrument. An investor can buy call options with the intention of taking delivery of the corresponding shares when the option expires, and in the meantime can receive interest on the money that will be used. The attractiveness of this procedure relative to buying the shares immediately is improved by a rise in interest rates payable on the money held. It follows that when interest rates are high, the demand for call options will be somewhat greater, and option prices will be boosted by this additional demand.

Put options can be used to postpone the sale of shares. Instead of selling shares immediately, the investor might buy put options with the intention of selling in the future. Pending the sale of the shares, the investor would forgo interest on the money that would have been received from an immediate sale. Using puts in this way becomes less attractive as the interest receipts forgone rise. So investors are less likely to buy puts for this purpose when interest rates are high. High interest rates are therefore associated with a somewhat lower demand for put options and hence lower put option premiums.

In the case of stock options, the prospect of an ex-dividend date can have an impact on the premium of an option. When a stock goes ex-dividend its price falls by an amount approximately equal to the anticipated dividend. So an ex-dividend date can be seen as providing a price fall that is anticipated. The price fall will cause a reduction in the premiums of call options and an increase in those of put options. The option premiums would normally discount the anticipated fall in the share price well before the ex-dividend date.

Two points are worth emphasising about the roles of volatility and time to expiry. The first is that whereas increases in these variables would increase potential losses as well as potential profits on the underlying instrument, for example a stock, the asymmetrical nature of options means that potential profits are enhanced more than potential losses. This is because once the stock price is below the strike price of a call option (or above the strike price of a put option), any further stock price falls (increases) would not bring about increased losses in terms of intrinsic value. If an option is at the money or out of the money, there is no potential for loss of intrinsic value.

The second point is that time value can be subdivided into 2 components. One might be regarded as the financing cost component and corresponds to $K - K(1 + r)^{-T}$ in the boundary conditions. This component is not affected by market expectations of volatility and is a linear function of time to expiry. It is the means whereby short-term interest rates have a direct impact on option prices.

The other component of time value might be termed volatility value. It is the part of the option premium that is influenced by market expectations of volatility. It is also the component whose value tends to be (at least according to the Black–Scholes model) a function of the square root of time to expiry.

OPTION PRICES AS THE COSTS OF REPLICATION

Option positions can be replicated by positions in the underlying instrument or the corresponding futures. The positions in the underlying or futures should provide the same profit/loss outcome as the option being replicated. The amount of the underlying or futures should reflect the option delta. For example, an option on £1 million of the underlying with a delta of 0.7 would tend to give the same profit or loss as £700,000 of the underlying (which has a delta of 1). A small price move in the underlying should provide the same profit/loss outcome on £700,000 with a delta of 1 as on £1 million with a delta of 0.7. Replication (simulation) of a call with futures is illustrated by Figure 11.4.

Such replication will involve cash flows. Replicating long option positions involves buying when the price of the underlying rises and selling when it falls. This is because a rise in the price of the underlying causes an increase in delta and hence the need to buy more of the underlying (or futures). Conversely, a fall in price lowers delta and necessitates selling. Buying high and selling low entails a net cash outflow. The theoretical time value of the option equals the expected losses from such transactions. So replicating long option positions results in losses that correspond to the time value of the replicated option. (Specifically, this is the time value resulting from volatility of the price of the underlying rather than from financing costs.) Conversely, the replication of short option positions would be expected to provide profits that correspond to the time (volatility) value.

FIGURE 11.4 Delta hedging a written call option

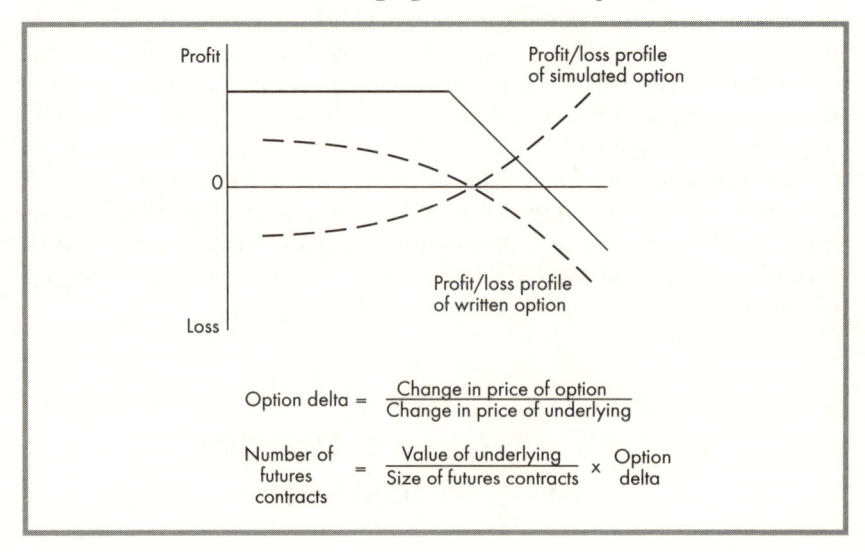

Option delta = Change in price of option / Change in price of underlying

Number of futures contracts = Value of underlying / Size of futures contracts × Option delta

THE BASIC BLACK–SCHOLES OPTION PRICING MODEL

The Black–Scholes model with its variants is probably the most commonly used option pricing model. This is despite its shortcomings, in particular its inability to allow for exercise prior to expiry (this failure to allow for early exercise means that strictly it is applicable only to European-style options). One reason for its popularity is that it allows for an analytical solution; this means that there is a formula into which certain values are input and from which an option price is forthcoming. This formula, when programmed into a computer or calculator, can produce option prices within seconds.

The most basic Black–Scholes model (as published by Black and Scholes in 1973) relates to non-dividend paying stocks. It can be expressed as follows:

$$C = S.N(d_1) - Ke^{-rt}.N(d_2)$$

$$d_1 = \frac{\ln(S/K) + rt}{\sigma\sqrt{t}} + 0.5\sigma\sqrt{t}$$

$$d_2 = \frac{\ln(S/K) + rt}{\sigma\sqrt{t}} + 0.5\sigma\sqrt{t}$$

where C is the call option price, S is the stock price, $N(\ )$ is the cumulative normal distribution function, K is the strike price, e is the exponential (which has the constant value of 2.7182818 and appears on most hand-held calculators), r is the risk-free (annualised) interest rate (as a decimal), t is the time to expiry (in years) and σ is the annualised standard deviation of stock returns (volatility) as a decimal.

The expression e^{-rt} is a discount term similar to $1/(1 + r)^t$ and as such it determines the present value of a future sum of money. The distinct feature of e^{-rt} is that it discounts on a continuous basis. Continuous discounting parallels continuous compounding. To appreciate the significance of continuous compounding, consider the alternatives of receiving 12% payable to an annual basis, 6% six monthly and 1% monthly. The annualised receipts are 1.12, $(1.06)^2 = 1.1236$ and $(1.01)^{12} = 1.1268$ respectively, corresponding to annual interest rates of 12%, 12.36% and 12.68%. The frequency of compounding affects the final outcome. The effective interest rate increases as the frequency of compounding rises. Continuous compounding is based on an infinite number of infinitely small periods (although it can normally be thought of as daily compounding). Likewise, the effect of discounting depends upon the time periods; for example, annual discounting at 12% p.a. gives a discount term of $1/(1.12) = 0.8929$, whereas continuous discounting over a year at 12% p.a. provides a discount term equal to $e^{-0.12} = 0.8869$.

It is also necessary to be aware of the meaning of $N(d)$, the cumulative normal distribution function. This is based on a standardised normal distribution, which is a normal distribution whose horizontal axis is in units of the stock price volatility. In other words, the volatility of stock returns over the period to option expiry, $\sigma \sqrt{t}$, corresponds to the value of 1 on the horizontal axis (hence division by $\sigma \sqrt{t}$ in the expressions for d_1 and d_2). The values of d_1 and d_2 are themselves in units of volatility (because of division by $\sigma \sqrt{t}$) and are points on the horizontal axis of the standardised normal distribution. $N(d_1)$ is the area under the distribution to the left of d_1 and $N(d_2)$ is the area to the left of d_2. Standardised normal distributions have total areas of 1 so that $N(d_1)$ is the probability of d being d_1 or less (likewise for d_2). $N(d_1)$ can be interpreted as the probability of the call option being in the money at expiry. Areas under the standardised normal distribution to the left of particular values can be ascertained from tables (as illustrated by the ensuing exercises) or by means of computer or calculator programs.

In the equations for d_1 and d_2, the term ln (S/K) appears. This is the natural logarithm of the price relative (ratio of stock price to strike price). So the model uses a lognormal rather than a normal distribution. It is a normal distribution of logarithms. One reason for using a lognormal distribution is that the price relative can never be negative, and hence the price relatives cannot be normally distributed. The natural logarithm of the price relative can be negative and will be normally distributed. (It might be noted that the natural logarithm of the price relative is the continuously compounded rate of return on the stock.)

Even this (relatively rudimentary) mathematical analysis of the Black–Scholes model would be a headache for most people. Probably the best way to get a feel for the model is to follow through a worked activity.

ACTIVITY 11.1

It is 24 January and shares in the Burnham Bakery plc stand at 100p. The next option expiry date is 24 March and the next dividend is due in May. The two-month interest rate is 6% p.a. and you estimate the share price volatility to be 10% p.a. Use the Black–Scholes option pricing model to calculate fair prices for at-the-money call options expiring in March. Why might the estimated fair prices for options expiring in September be less reliable?

Standardised cumulative normal probabilities are:

x	$N(x)$
0.0	0.5000
0.1	0.5398
0.2	0.5793
0.3	0.6179

Answer

The Black–Scholes equation for non-dividend paying stocks is:

$$C = S.N(d_1) - Ke^{-rt}.N(d_2)$$

$$d_1 = \frac{\ln(S/K) + rt}{\sigma\sqrt{t}} + 0.5\sigma\sqrt{t}$$

$$d_2 = \frac{\ln(S/K) + rt}{\sigma\sqrt{t}} + 0.5\sigma\sqrt{t}$$

so

$d_1 = [(0.06 \times 0.167)/(0.1 \times 0.408)] + (0.5 \times 0.1 \times \sqrt{0.167})$
$ = 0.2655$ (N.B. $\ln(1) = 0$)
$d_2 = [(0.06 \times 0.167)/(0.1 \times 0.408)] - (0.5 \times 0.1 \times \sqrt{0.167}) = 0.2247$
$C = 100N(0.2655) - Ke^{-0.06, 0.167} N(0.2247)$
$C = 100 \times 0.6046 - (99 \times 0.5888)$
$C = 60.46 - 58.29 = 2.17$

So the fair price of an at-the-money call option is 2.17p per share.

The estimated prices for options expiring in September may be less reliable because (1) there is a need to adjust the share price by the dividend expected

THE BASIC BLACK–SCHOLES OPTION PRICING MODEL • 281

in May, and that dividend may be uncertain; (2) there is a possibility of early exercise and the basic Black–Scholes model does not allow for this; and (3) the assumptions of constancy of interest rates and volatility are more likely to be violated over a long period than over a shorter period.

ACTIVITY 11.2

Shares in Covuni plc are 105p. The six-month interest rate is 6% p.a. Use the Black–Scholes option pricing model to estimate the fair price of a call option with 6 months to expiry and a strike price of 100p based on an expected annual volatility of 20%.
Standardised cumulative normal probabilities are:

x	N(x)
0.0	0.5000
0.1	0.5398
0.2	0.5793
0.3	0.6179
0.4	0.6554
0.5	0.6915
0.6	0.7257
0.7	0.7580

Answer

$$C = S.N(d_1) - Ke^{-rt}.N(d_2)$$

$$d_1 = \frac{\ln(S/K) + rt}{\sigma\sqrt{t}} + 0.5\sigma\sqrt{t}$$

$$d_2 = \frac{\ln(S/K) + rt}{\sigma\sqrt{t}} - 0.5\sigma\sqrt{t}$$

$$d_1 = \frac{\ln(105/100) + 0.06.0.5}{0.2\sqrt{0.5}} + 0.5.0.2\sqrt{0.5}$$

$$d_2 = \frac{\ln(105/100) + 0.06.0.5}{0.2\sqrt{t}} - 0.5.0.2\sqrt{0.5}$$

$$d_1 = \frac{0.04879 + 0.03}{0.2.0.70711} + 0.1.0.70711$$

$$= (0.07879/0.14142) + 0.07071$$

$$= 0.6278$$

$$d_2 = d_1 - 2(0.07071)$$

$$= d_1 - 0.14142 = 0.4864$$

$N(d_1) = 0.7257 + [(0.7580 - 0.7257) \times 0.278]$
$ = 0.7347$
$N(d_2) = 0.6554 + [(0.6915 - 0.6554) \times 0.864]$
$ = 0.6866$
$C = (105 \times 0.7347) - (100e^{-0.06 \cdot 0.5} \times 0.6866)$
$ = 77.1435 - 66.6308 = 10.5127$

So the fair price of the call option is estimated to be 10.51p (to 2 decimal places).

EARLY EXERCISE

Early exercise refers to the exercise of an American-style option before the option expires. In the case of call options, it would never be rational to exercise an option on a non-dividend paying stock prior to expiry, since selling the option would always be preferable. By selling the option both the time and intrinsic values would be received, whereas exercise of the option would provide the intrinsic value only. It follows that American-style options on non-dividend paying stocks are equivalent to European-style options and can therefore be valued using Black–Scholes models.

It may be rational to exercise a call option on a dividend paying stock before expiry. The optimum moment for such early exercise is just before the stock goes ex-dividend. When the stock goes ex-dividend its price falls by the amount of dividend that had been expected. This reduction in the stock price entails a decline in the intrinsic value of a call option. If this potential loss of intrinsic value exceeds the time value that would exist subsequent to the ex-dividend date, it would be rational to exercise the option before it goes ex-dividend. In this case the intrinsic value just before the ex-dividend date exceeds the prospective total value just after it. Another way of looking at the point is in terms of dividend capture. By exercising before the ex-dividend date, the right to the dividend is ensured and, if the value of the expected dividend is greater than the prospective time value subsequent to (or on the) ex-dividend day, the option should be exercised. The optimum time for the early exercise is immediately before the stock goes ex-dividend, because such timing will minimise the financing costs of holding the stock.

In the case of American-style put options, early exercise may be rational whether or not the stock pays dividends. Consider the case in which a holder of stock has bought put options with a view to guaranteeing a minimum selling price. When the option is exercised the proceeds can be put on deposit to earn interest. Early exercise is rational when those prospective interest receipts exceed the time value of the option. Another way of seeing the same point is in terms of the prospective interest receipts exceeding the value of the possible increases in intrinsic value net of possible decreases (time value being the value of possible increases in intrinsic value net of the risk of losses in intrinsic value). Yet another way of interpreting the point is based on the minimum value of a European-style put being $K/(1 + rt) - S$, while that of the equivalent American-style put is $K - S$. If the difference, $K - K/(1 + rt)$, exceeds the time value (specifically volatility value), it would be possible to exercise an American-style put and use the proceeds to buy a European-style put while retaining part of the proceeds of exercise as cash. Again, this is based on a comparison of prospective interest receipts and time value.

In the case of put options on dividend paying stocks, it may be rational to delay exercise until after the stock has gone ex-dividend, particularly if the dividend is expected to be large. By such a delay the dividend is obtained and, since the receipt upon exercise (the strike price) is the same irrespective of whether the stock is cum or ex-dividend, it makes sense to wait until the right to the dividend is secured before exercising the option.

In the case of both call and put options, when it is rational to exercise early, the price of the option should equal its intrinsic value. No one should pay more than the intrinsic value for an option that is about to be exercised. This prospective loss of time value should be reflected in the price of the option at earlier stages; in effect, the date on which early exercise is rational would be treated as the effective expiry date of the option when valuing it prior to that date.

VARIATIONS ON THE BASIC BLACK–SCHOLES MODEL

European-style call options on dividend paying stocks

To use the Black–Scholes model to value call options on dividend paying stocks, it is necessary to adjust the stock price by removing the present value of dividends receivable prior to expiry (more specifically, the dividends that relate to ex-dividend dates falling before expiry). Once the stock price is adjusted in this way, the Black–Scholes model (using the adjusted stock price) can be used in the usual way.

One way of understanding this adjustment process is in terms of the dividend discount model. According to the dividend discount model, the current stock price is the present (i.e. discounted) value of all future expected dividends. However, dividends accruing before the expiry date will be incorporated into the current stock price, but not the stock price on the expiry date. Option pricing requires the use of the stock price on the one day (expiration day) on which exercise of the European-style option can occur. So the stock price used in the Black–Scholes model is the current stock price minus that part of the price that arises from dividends that will not be received by the expiry day stock. In other words, the present value of dividends expected prior to expiry needs to be subtracted from the current stock price in order to ascertain the stock price to be used in the Black–Scholes model.

ACTIVITY 11.3

Shares in Covuni plc are 100p and a 2p dividend is expected in three months. The three-month interest rate is 5% p.a. and the six-month interest rate is 6% p.a. Use a variation of the Black–Scholes option pricing model to estimate the fair price of an at-the-money European style call option with 6 months to expiry based on an expected annual volatility of 20%.

Standardised cumulative normal probabilities are:

x	N(x)
0.0	0.5000
0.1	0.5398
0.2	0.5793
0.3	0.6179

Answer
The stock price to be used in the basic Black–Scholes model is $(100 - 2e^{-0.05 \cdot 0.25}) = 98.025$.

$$C = 98.025\, N(d_1) - 100 e^{-0.06 \cdot 0.5}\, N(d_2)$$

$$d_1 = \frac{\ln(98.025/100) + (0.06 \cdot 0.5)}{0.2\sqrt{0.5}} + 0.5 \cdot 0.2\sqrt{0.5}$$

$$= \frac{-0.01995 + 0.03}{0.14142} + 0.07071$$

$$= 0.07108 + 0.07071 = 0.14179$$

$d_2 = 0.07108 - 0.07071 = 0.00037$
$N(d_1) = 0.5398 + [(0.5793 - 0.5398) \times 0.4179]$
$\qquad = 0.5563$
$N(d_2) = 0.5 + (0.0398 \times 0.0037) = 0.5001$
$C = (98.025 \times 0.5563) - (97.04 \times 0.5001)$
$\quad = 54.5313 - 48.5297 = 6.0016p$

American-style call options on dividend paying stocks (Black's approximation)

Since the Black–Scholes model is strictly applicable only to European-style options, its use in valuing American-style options must be regarded as a relatively crude procedure that merely produces an approximate price. Nevertheless, this crude procedure is frequently employed; it is known as Black's approximation.

Black's approximation is based on the principle that the only time that it is rational to exercise an American-style call option prior to expiry is just before an ex-dividend date (normally it would be rational to sell an option rather than exercise it, since selling would realise both the intrinsic and time values, whereas exercise would realise only the intrinsic value; however, on the ex-dividend date the fall in the stock price would cause a loss in the intrinsic value of a call option and if this potential loss exceeds the time value on that date it would be rational to exercise the option just before the stock goes ex-dividend). In the case of a stock with one ex-dividend date before the option expiry date, there would be 2 possible occasions on which a call option might be exercised, these being immediately before the ex-dividend date and on the expiry date. Two option prices are calculated: one for each time to expiry. The higher of the 2 prices is used as the estimate of the option price.

When using Black's approximation, the stock price is adjusted by removing the present value of dividends expected prior to expiry. In the case of a stock with just 1 ex-dividend date before the option expires, there would be no adjustment to the stock price when the day before the ex-dividend date is used as the expiry date, but an adjustment would be needed when the actual expiry date is used (note that when making such adjustments the expected dividends should be discounted from the prospective date of receipt and not from the ex-dividend date).

> ### ACTIVITY 11.4
>
> On 1 January the price of a share which pays a quarterly dividend of 50p and goes ex-dividend on 1 March and 1 June is £40 and the rate of interest is 9%.
>
> Outline a way of calculating the approximate value of a six-month American call.
>
> (Based on the Securities Institute examination in Financial Futures and Options, July 1992, Question 8.)

Answer
The option could be valued by means of Black's approximation. This approach values the European option expiring at the same time as the American and the European option that expires just before the last ex-dividend date. The higher of the 2 is used as an approximation to the value of the American option.

In both cases the basic Black–Scholes formula for non-dividend paying stock is used, but with the stock price adjusted for expected dividends prior to exercise. Specifically, the present value of all dividends accruing before the exercise date (i.e. all dividends not receivable by the option holder) is subtracted from the current stock price and the resulting figure is used in the Black–Scholes formula. So the value used for the stock price when valuing an option expiring on 1 June would be:

$$£40 - £0.50e^{-0.09 \times 0.167} = £40 - £0.493 = £39.507$$

and the value used when valuing an option expiring on 1 July would be:

$$£40 - £0.50e^{-0.09 \times 0.167} - £0.50e^{-0.09 \times 0.417} = £40 - £0.493 - £0.482 = £39.025.$$

European-style call options on stock indices

Stock index portfolios can usually be treated as producing a continuous income stream, since the various component stocks would be paying dividends at different times. The adjustment that corresponds to subtracting the present value of expected dividends involves discounting the spot stock index by the expected rate of dividend yield. One way of looking at this is in terms of the potential reinvestment of dividends, allowing a discounted amount in the present to correspond to the full amount at expiry, in much the same way as the future strike price is discounted to a present value. In the case of stocks with discrete dividend payments, the adjusted stock price was used in all 3 equations, including the equations for d_1 and d_2. In the case of stock index options, the corresponding amendment to the equations for d_1 and d_2 takes the form of subtracting the expected rate of dividend yield from the risk-free interest rate (i.e. from the discount rate applicable to the strike price). The equations for valuing a European-style call option on a stock index are thus:

$$C = Se^{-dt}.N(d_1) - Ke^{-rt}.N(d_2)$$

$$d_1 = \frac{\ln(S/K) + (r-d)t}{\sigma\sqrt{t}} + 0.5\sigma\sqrt{t}$$

$$d_2 = \frac{\ln(S/K) + (r-d)t}{\sigma\sqrt{t}} + 0.5\sigma\sqrt{t}$$

where C is the call option price, S is the spot stock index, e is the exponential (natural logarithm), d is the expected rate of dividend yield (as a decimal), t is the time to expiry, $N(\ )$ is the cumulative normal distribution function, K is the strike price, r is the risk-free interest rate (as a decimal) and σ is the volatility (annualised standard deviation of returns, as a decimal).

European-style call options on currencies

Currency option pricing parallels stock index option pricing. The rate of interest on the foreign currency takes the place of the expected rate of dividend yield (note that usually the US dollar is the base currency and the option is treated as being on the other currency whose price is expressed in units of the US dollar). Foreign currency interest and stock portfolio dividends are both income yields on the underlying asset and hence play the same role in the option pricing model; in other respects, Black–Scholes-type models are identical for the 2 instruments. So the variant of the Black–Scholes model applicable to currency option pricing is as follows:

$$C = Se^{-ft}.N(d_1) - Ke^{-rt}.N(d_2)$$

$$d_1 = \frac{\ln(S/K) + (r-f)t}{\sigma\sqrt{t}} + 0.5\sigma\sqrt{t}$$

$$d_2 = \frac{\ln(S/K) + (r-f)t}{\sigma\sqrt{t}} + 0.5\sigma\sqrt{t}$$

where S is the spot price of foreign currency in units of the base currency and f is the foreign currency interest rate. Other terms have interpretations similar to those in the previous models.

European-style call options on futures

Although futures themselves do not yield an income return such as dividends or interest, the fact that they are traded on margin means that the cash relating to the futures contract can yield a return. If a futures position is bought, the money relating to the value of that futures contract can be put on deposit, or into other assets, to yield a risk-free interest rate (although part of the value of the futures contract might be accounted for by initial margin, that initial margin may be in a form that permits a yield on the funds used). Consequently, a futures contract can be treated as if it yielded the risk-free interest rate. The variant of the Black–Scholes model applicable to futures options can be expressed as:

$$C = Fe^{-rt}.N(d_1) - Ke^{-rt}.N(d_2)$$

$$d_1 = \frac{\ln(F/K)}{\sigma\sqrt{t}} + 0.5\sigma\sqrt{t}$$

$$d_2 = \frac{\ln(F/K)}{\sigma\sqrt{t}} + 0.5\sigma\sqrt{t}$$

where F is the current futures price. Other terms are defined as in the previous models.

It is to be noted that the discount term in the equations for d_1 and d_2 (i.e. r, $r-d$ or $r-f$) is absent in the model for valuing futures options. That is because the term becomes $r - r$, which equals zero.

There is a further variant of the Black–Scholes model relating to futures options. This other variant is for use when the futures options are traded on margin (as is the case on LIFFE). When futures options are traded on margin, the options do not have to be paid for when they are bought; instead, they are paid for upon exercise (and at the option price ruling at the time of exercise). Such option contracts are subject to initial margin and variation margin in the same way as futures contracts. In the case of margined futures options, the first equation in the Black–Scholes model becomes:

$$Ce^{-rt} = Fe^{-rt}.N(d_1) - Ke^{-rt}.N(d_2)$$

or:

$$Ce = F.N.(d_1) - K.N(d_2)$$

The expressions for d_1 and d_2 are as for non-margined futures options and hence are shown above.

One way of looking at this is to see the equation for non-margined futures options as discounting 2 future values, F and K, to render them comparable to a current value, C. If futures options are traded on margin, even C becomes a future value and hence it is no longer necessary to discount F and K (equivalently, C, F and K should all be discounted).

PRICING PUTS AND AMERICAN-STYLE OPTIONS

All of the foregoing discussion of the Black–Scholes model and its variations has focused on pricing call options and most of it has dealt with European-style options. For pricing puts it is possible to derive equations for put valuation, but it is probably more usual to calculate the call option price and then to use the relevant put–call parity condition to ascertain the corresponding put option price. (It might be noted that the variations on the Black–Scholes model closely mirror the corresponding variations in the put–call parity expression.)

As for the valuation of American-style options, Black's approximation for dividend paying stocks has been outlined. In the cases of stock index options, currency options and futures options, the Black–Scholes models for European-style options are frequently used to value American-style options on the grounds that early exercise is unlikely. If an American-style option is unlikely to be exercised prior to expiry, then it may be a reasonable approximation to treat it as if it were European-style. (It is particularly necessary to be wary of assuming that early exercise is unlikely in the case of put options. An American-style put option may be exercised prior to expiry if the time value is exceeded by the prospective interest returns, net of foregone asset yield, on the funds receivable upon exercise.)

VALUING OPTIONS ON BONDS

There are particular problems that arise in relation to the use of Black–Scholes models to value options on fixed interest securities, to the extent that Black–Scholes-type models may be inapplicable to the pricing of such options. This is because bonds may seriously violate some of the assumptions underlying the Black–Scholes model.

First, the Black–Scholes model assumes that the price of the underlying asset follows a diffusion process (Brownian motion or Wiener process), which is a random walk process in which each period's price change is independent of the price changes of previous periods. The result is that the range, or variance, of possible prices increases over time. This generates a lognormal distribution of possible future prices with a standard deviation that increases over time (and is a function of the square root of time). Since the distribution is lognormal rather than normal, the possibility of negative values is allowed for.

Bonds usually have maturity dates on which their nominal, or par, values will be repaid. Since the bond will be valued at par on its maturity date, its price will tend towards the par value as maturity is approached. This is sometimes known as the pull to par. It implies that as maturity is approached the range, or variance, of possible bond prices decreases. This is in direct contradiction to the diffusion process assumed by the Black–Scholes model. However, if the bond has a very long period to maturity, the pull to par may not be too great a problem.

The diffusion process could also lead to bond prices so high that the redemption yields become negative (the prospective capital loss as the bond price is pulled to par exceeds the coupon yield on the bond). Since interest rates (redemption yields) cannot be negative, the diffusion model could generate an impossible situation. However, this problem can be overcome by using interest rates as the underlying (since bond prices and interest rates are related, they are alternative state variables).

Second, the Black–Scholes model assumes constant short-term interest rates (for the period to the expiry date of the option). Variations in bond prices arise from changes in long-term interest rates. Use of the Black–Scholes models for pricing bonds requires the assumption that short-term interest rates are constant, while long-term rates can vary in a stochastic fashion (i.e. vary randomly in a random walk process that tends to generate a normal or lognormal distribution of possible outcomes). This is a difficult assumption to justify in the light of evidence that short-term interest rates tend to be more volatile than long-term rates.

Third, Black–Scholes models assume constant price volatility of the underlying asset for the period to the expiry date of the option. Quite apart from the evidence that volatility is itself volatile, bond price volatility is based on duration which changes with the passage of time and interest rate variations.

ACTIVITY 11.5

Consider a one-year maturity at-the-money CBOT Treasury bond futures option when the underlying futures price is 100 and the price volatility is 10%; the interest rate is 5%.

(a) Using the table below, calculate the delta of the call and the put.
(b) Calculate the price of the call and the put.

Table of standardised cumulative normal probabilities $N(x)$:

x	N(x)	x	N(x)
0.0	0.5000	0.5	0.6915
0.1	0.5398	0.6	0.7257
0.2	0.5793	0.7	0.7580
0.3	0.6179	0.8	0.7881
0.4	0.6554	0.9	0.8159

Answer

The Black–Scholes equation for futures options is:

$$C = Fe^{-rt}N(d_1) - Ke^{-rt}N(d_2)$$

$$d_1 = \frac{\ln(F/K)}{\sigma\sqrt{t}} + 0.5\sigma\sqrt{t}$$

$$d_2 = \frac{\ln(F/K)}{\sigma\sqrt{t}} + 0.5\sigma\sqrt{t}$$

(a) The delta of the call is $N(d_1)e^{-rt}$:

$d_1 = 0.5 \times 0.1$ (since $\ln(F/K) = 0$)
$N(d_1) = N(0.05) = 0.52$ (approximately)
$0.52e^{-0.05} = 0.495$ (approximately)
A call delta of 0.495 implies a put delta of $-(1 - 0.495) = -0.505$

(b) The price of the call is:

$C = 100e^{-0.05} N(0.05) - 100e^{-0.05} N(-0.05)$
$= (95.123 \times 0.52) - (95.123 \times 0.48)$
$= 49.464 - 45.659$
$= 3.805$

Put–call parity for (non-margined) futures options is:

$$C - P = Fe^{-rt} - Ke^{-rt}$$

In this example:

$3.805 - P = 100e^{-0.05} - 100e^{-0.05} = 0$
∴ $P = 3.805$

So the price of the put is also 3.805.

ACTIVITY 11.6

Using the Black–Scholes model, estimate the price of an at-the-money eurodollar futures call option when the eurodollar futures price is 92.00, volatility is estimated at 3% p.a., the option has 6 months to expiry and is traded on LIFFE. How would the answer differ if it were traded on the Chicago Mercantile Exchange? (Assume that the spot six-month rate is the same as the futures interest rate.)

Standardised cumulative normal probabilities are:

x	N(x)
0.0	0.5000
0.1	0.5398
0.2	0.5793
0.3	0.6179

Answer

The Black–Scholes formula for margined futures call options is:

$$C = F \cdot N(d_1) - K \cdot N(d_2)$$

$$d_1 = \frac{\ln(F/K)}{\sigma\sqrt{t}} + 0.5\sigma\sqrt{t}$$

$$d_2 = \frac{\ln(F/K)}{\sigma\sqrt{t}} + 0.5\sigma\sqrt{t}$$

Since $F/K = 1$ $\quad \ln(F/K) = 0$

$d_1 = 0.5\sigma\sqrt{t} = 0.5(0.03)\sqrt{0.5} = 0.0106$
$d_2 = -0.5\sigma\sqrt{t} = -0.0106$
$N(d_1) = N(0.0106) = (0.0398 \times 0.106) + 0.5 = 0.5042$
$N(d_2) = N(-0.0106) = 1 - 0.5042 = 0.4958$

So:

$C = 92(0.5042) - 92(0.4958)$
$\quad = 46.388 - 45.612 = 0.78$

At $25 per tick, the money value of the call option, per contract, is 78 × $25 = $1950.

On the Chicago Mercantile Exchange, the futures options would not be margined. So the Black–Scholes pricing equation would be:

$$C = F e^{-rt} \cdot N(d_1) - K e^{-rt} \cdot N(d_2)$$

$$d_1 = \frac{\ln(F/K)}{\sigma\sqrt{t}} + 0.5\sigma\sqrt{t}$$

$$d_2 = \frac{\ln(F/K)}{\sigma\sqrt{t}} + 0.5\sigma\sqrt{t}$$

$N(d_1)$ and $N(d_2)$ are unchanged from the previous calculation.

$C = 92 e^{-(0.08)(0.5)} \, 0.5042 - 92 e^{-(0.08)(0.5)} \, 0.4958$
$C = 44.568 - 43.825 = 0.74$

At $25 per tick, the money value of the call option, per contract, is 74 × $25 = $1850.

VOLATILITY

Volatility might be defined as a measure of the expected variability (irrespective of direction) of the price of an instrument over a given time period. It is often calculated as the annualised standard deviation of daily percentage price changes, where the natural logarithm of the ratio of two successive prices is used to compute the percentage price change. The standard deviation of daily percentage price changes is converted to an annualised volatility through being multiplied by the square root of the number of trading days in the year. Volatility is an important input into option pricing models and, unlike most of the other inputs, it is not directly observable since it relates to expectations of future price behaviour. High volatility is associated with high time value and hence high option prices (intuitively, this might be explained in terms of high volatility enhancing the likelihood of substantial intrinsic value being acquired by the expiry date of the option, thereby making the option more attractive to potential buyers).

Estimation

There are 2 main ways of estimating volatility. One is based on historical observations of price movements and the other on contemporaneous option prices.

To estimate the volatility of the price of an instrument (e.g. a stock price) using historical data, it is necessary to obtain price observations at fixed intervals; typical intervals of time would be (trading) days or weeks. The continuously compounded rate of price change during the ith interval is given by u_i in the equation:

$$u_i = \ln(S_i/S_{i-1})$$

where S_i is the observed price at time i and S_i-1 is the observed price one time interval earlier. The standard deviation of these rates of price change is given by σ in the equation.

$$\sigma = \left[(1/n - 1) \left(\sum_{i=1}^{n} (u_i - \bar{u})^2 \right) \right]^{0.5}$$

where n is the number of time intervals (and hence number of values of u_i) and bar u is the average of the u_i's. This is the standard textbook formula that calculates the standard deviation as the square root of the mean of the squares of the deviations of the u_i's from their average value.

This standard deviation is then annualised through multiplication by the square root of the number of days in the year. Empirical research suggests that the number of trading days is more appropriate than the number of calendar days.

The question arises as to how many observations of price changes should be used. Since more data would normally be expected to enhance accuracy, it might seem that the longest possible series of observations should be used. However, volatility changes over time and observations in the distant past may not be good indicators of current and future volatility. Many regard data from the most recent 90 to 180 trading days as providing a satisfactory compromise. Unfortunately, the estimate of volatility tends to vary with the time period chosen.

An alternative technique for ascertaining market expectations of volatility is to work out what volatility is implied by current option prices. Implied volatility is ascertained by reversing option pricing models. Instead of calculating the theoretical option price using the stock price, strike price, volatility, time to expiry, interest rates and expected dividend yield, the observed option price becomes an input and the volatility the output. The method is to find the level of volatility that is consistent with an observed option price. The objective becomes one of finding the value of volatility that generates a theoretical option price equal to the observed option price.

Unfortunately, the Black–Scholes model cannot be rearranged to provide an analytical solution for volatility. Instead, a numerical method must be employed. This involves an iterative search process. This can be likened to a trial and error process in which various values of volatility are put into the model and the resulting theoretical option values are compared with the observed option price.

It may be that the observed option price is 5. The first step might be to input a volatility value of 20%. If this gives a theoretical option price of less than 5, then a higher volatility is tried. It may be that a volatility of 25% produces a theoretical option price of 5.5. This tells us that the implied volatility lies between 20% and 25%. The next step may be to take an intermediate value such as 22.5%. If this produces a fair option price less than 5, we then know that volatility lies between 22.5% and 25%. Again, an intermediate value is taken (e.g. 23.75%) and the theoretical option price is calculated. If the fair option price is above 5, it follows that volatility lies between 22.5% and 23.75%. This iterative process progressively narrows down the range of possible values of volatility and can be continued until implied volatility is estimated to the desired degree of accuracy.

A difficulty with the implied volatility approach is that different option series may provide different implied volatilities, despite relating to the same underlying instrument (e.g. the same stock or same currency) and having the same expiry date. The question arises as to which value of implied volatility to choose.

One approach is to use a weighted average of the implied volatilities, with the weights being based on the sensitivities of the option prices to changes in volatility (i.e. based on their vegas). This would be similar to weighting the implied volatilities according to the option time (volatility) values, on the grounds that high time values contain more information than low time values. Another approach might be to use relative liquidity, on the grounds that the more liquid contracts would provide more reliable information about market expectations of volatility. However, some take the view that it is not possible to improve on simply using the option series that are closest to being at the money.

THE SMILE EFFECT

The variation of implied volatilities across different option series is not random. In particular, there is a relationship between implied volatility and the closeness of the option series to being at the money. At-the-money options tend to exhibit relatively low implied volatilities, whereas deep in-the-money and deep out-of-the-money options are prone to exhibit relatively high implied volatilities.

This smile effect appears to arise from the tendency of the Black–Scholes option pricing model systematically to misprice options. It seems to overprice at-the-money options and interprets the lower observed prices as indicative of low volatility. Conversely, it appears to underprice in-the-money and out-of-the-money options, and interprets the higher observed prices as being the result of high volatility. The smile effect is illustrated by Figure 11.5.

The question arises as to why Black–Scholes models tend systematically to misprice options. One explanation arises from the existence of leptokurtosis, better known as fat tails. Probabilities of extreme values are often greater than supposed by normal distributions, and probabilities of values near to the mean are often lower. This is illustrated by Figure 11.6.

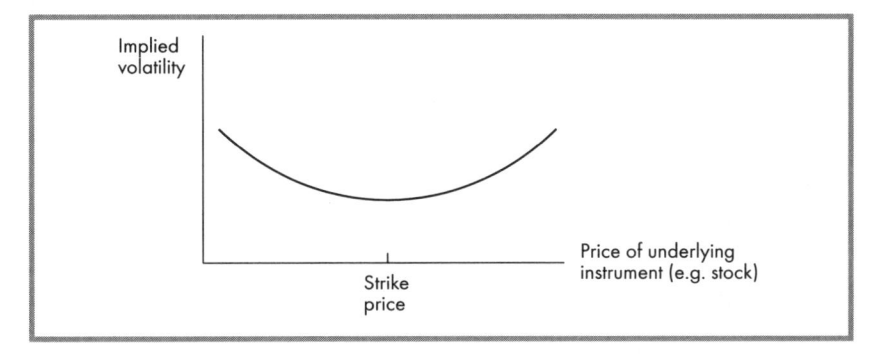

FIGURE 11.5   The smile effect

FIGURE 11.6 Leptokurtosis

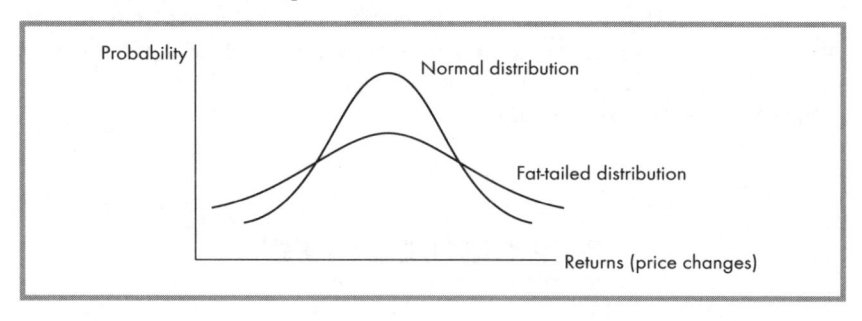

[Figure: Probability distribution showing a normal distribution curve overlaid with a fat-tailed distribution curve, plotted against Returns (price changes)]

There is general agreement that fat tails exist, but there is no such agreement as to why. One view is that the preference for normal distributions is wrong and that fat-tailed distributions are more appropriate. Another explanation suggests that what is actually observed is a mixture of normal distributions with different variances. According to this view, the observed distribution consists of a sequence of normal distributions, each with a different variance. When combined, such distributions lead to fat tails. A third explanation of fat tails lies in the possibility that while prices follow a smooth diffusion process most of the time, there is an occasional jump.

An alternative to fat tails as an explanation of the smile effect lies in the possibility that volatility is stochastic (i.e. volatility itself has volatility). It has been shown that when the volatility is uncorrelated with the stock price, the Black–Scholes formula overprices options that are at the money or near the money, and underprices options that are deep in or deep out of the money.

However, when stock prices and volatility are correlated, different results emerge. When the correlation is positive, the Black–Scholes model appears to underestimate the price for out-of-the-money call options and to overestimate the price for out-of-the-money put options. An increase in the stock price raises volatility so that very high stock prices become more likely, and hence call options are more valuable. A lower stock price is accompanied by lower volatility so that very low stock prices are less likely, and hence put options are less valuable than would be the case in the absence of the positive correlation.

When the correlation between stock prices and volatility is negative, Black–Scholes tends to overestimate the price of out-of-the-money call options and underestimate the price of out-of-the-money put options. When the stock price increases, volatility declines, reducing the likelihood of very high stock prices and rendering call options less valuable than the Black–Scholes model would predict. A fall in the stock price tends to raise volatility, enhancing the likelihood of very low stock prices.

So put options are more valuable than would be suggested by Black–Scholes.

Whether volatility is uncorrelated or correlated with stock prices, Black–Scholes appears to generate errors. The Black–Scholes model assumes constant volatility and provides inaccurate option prices when volatility is stochastic. However, for options with lives of less than a year, the biases arising from stochastic volatility appear to be small in absolute terms (although they can be large in percentage terms for deep out-of-the-money options). The biases become larger as the lives of the options increase.

Another way in which the Black–Scholes assumption of constant volatility may be undermined by systematic variation in volatility is through volatility exhibiting reversion to the mean. If volatility is very high or very low, it is likely to be less extreme in the next period.

If changes in volatility are not systematic, their impact on option prices appears to be small and the Black–Scholes assumption of constant volatility is not a great problem. However, systematic changes may have more significance. If volatility changes, then the volatility to use in the model should be an average of the expected values during the life of the option. That average should reflect mean reversion of volatility.

Historical volatility and implied volatility are now well-established methods of measuring volatility for the purpose of option pricing. A more recent approach addresses itself to the matter of systematic variation in volatility. This approach takes the form of ARCH and GARCH models.

ARCH AND GARCH MODELS

ARCH stands for autoregressive conditional heteroscedasticity. ARCH models provide recognition of the view that the variance of the returns on a security is likely to be distorted in any time period by shocks.

The returns on a security might be divided between a predictable component and an unpredictable part. The unpredictable part may be designated by e_t (e for error) and can be seen as the difference between the observed return and predicted return in period t. This unpredictable component of the return has an expected value of zero and its variance during period t can be designated as v_t.

The squares of the unpredictable components are, in ARCH models, treated as following an autoregressive process. The first order ARCH model can be written as:

$$v_t = a + be^2_{t-1}$$

where $a > 0$ and $b \geq 0$. In any period the conditional variance v_t is a function of the squared errors of the previous time period e^2_{t-1}. So today's volatility depends upon yesterday's unexpected price change, but it does not matter whether the error was positive or negative.

GARCH stands for generalised autoregressive conditional heteroscedasticity. GARCH models differ from ARCH models in using previous conditional variances. A simple GARCH model might be written as:

$$v_t = a + be^2_{t-1} + cv_{t-1}$$

The estimate of next period's conditional variance would be given by:

$$E(v_{t+1}) = \hat{a} + \hat{b}e^2_t + \hat{c}v_t$$

where $E(v_t+1)$ represents the expected period $t+1$ variance, while $\hat{a}$, $\hat{b}$ and $\hat{c}$ represent estimates of a, b and c.

The basic principle underlying ARCH measures of volatility is that large changes tend to be followed by large changes, of either sign, and that small changes tend to be followed by small changes (of either sign). This is sometimes known as the clustering effect.

So in the methodology of ARCH and GARCH, volatility is modelled as conditional on past information and as time varying. An interesting property of such models is that they allow the series distribution to exhibit fat tails without violating the normality assumption.

CONCLUSIONS

The Black–Scholes model was the first option pricing model to receive widespread acceptance. The original version was developed for European-style options on non-dividend paying stocks. Subsequently, the basic model was extended to cover European-style options on other underlying instruments such as dividend paying stocks, stock indices, currencies and futures. Black–Scholes models have major drawbacks, particularly when early exercise is likely. Since they specifically relate to European-style options, they can be unreliable tools for valuing American-style options when early exercise (exercise before expiry) is a possibility. They have particular deficiencies in the valuation of bond options. Two of the attractions of binomial models are that they can deal with the possibility of early exercise and the complicating features of bond options.

Despite the deficiencies of the Black–Scholes model and its variants, these models remain very popular. They are probably still the most widely used option pricing models. This is probably because they offer analytical solutions. In other words, they provide equations that produce values very quickly from personal computers or programmable calculators. Binomial models often require substantial computer time.

The widespread use of the Black–Scholes models by operators in the option markets could mean that the Black–Scholes models, as theories of option pricing, become self-fulfilling prophecies. They could provide good predictions of option prices simply because they are widely used for pricing options. For market participants this might be seen as a further advantage of Black–Scholes models. If the accuracy of an option valuation is judged by its consistency with actual market prices, then use of the same valuation model as that used by everyone else enhances the likelihood of accurate valuations.

Further reading

For informative accounts of the Black–Scholes model, see:

Gordon Gemmill, *Options Pricing* (McGraw-Hill, Maidenhead, 1993), Chapters 5 to 7.

John Hull, *Introduction to Futures and Options Markets*, 2nd edn (Prentice Hall, Englewood Cliffs, 1995), Chapter 11. Also see Chapter 16 for a discussion of deficiencies in the Black–Scholes model.

Peter Ritchken, *Options* (Scott, Foresman, Glenview, 1987), Chapter 8.

For a rigorous account that makes some demands on the mathematical ability of the reader, see:

John Hull, *Options, Futures and Other Derivative Securities*, 2nd edn (Prentice Hall, Englewood Cliffs, 1993), Chapters 10 and 11.

SWAPS 12

INTRODUCTION

The term 'swap' has 2 major meanings in the context of financial markets. According to one definition it is a purchase and simultaneous forward sale (or vice versa). The other meaning defines it as the agreed exchange of future cash flows (possibly, but not necessarily, with a spot exchange of cash flows). The second definition can encompass the first but is much broader.

The term 'swap' is most commonly used in the second sense: an agreement to the future exchange of cash flows. This is the meaning we use here.

The cash flows exchanged may have a wide variety of bases. In the case of interest rate swaps the typical exchange is of cash flows arising from a fixed rate of interest (fixed for the period to the maturity of the swap) for cash flows arising from a floating interest rate (perhaps a rate changed every 6 months reflecting movements in a market rate such as LIBOR). For example, the parties may agree that one pays 5% and the other pays eurodollar LIBOR every 6 months on a principal sum of $10 million in a swap arrangement that is to last 5 years. At six-month intervals 5% is compared with LIBOR and the difference is paid over. A difference of 1% would entail a cash flow of $50,000 ($1,000,000 × 0.01 × 0.5). The cash flow occurs at the end of the six-month period rather than the beginning. This is because interest payments are made at the end of the borrowing/lending period.

Currency swaps involve exchanging interest flows in one currency for interest flows in another (typically the US dollar is one of the currencies). Equity swaps tend to involve cash flows based on the returns from a stock

302 • **SWAPS**

index portfolio being exchanged for the cash flows based on an interest rate.

This chapter begins with an examination of interest rate swaps. Most interest rate swaps involve cash flows in the same currency but on different interest bases. The 'plain vanilla' swap involves the exchange of fixed rate interest flows for floating rate interest flows. One possible motivation is that of hedging.

After examining the hedging use of interest rate swaps the chapter goes on to consider swaps as a technique for reducing interest costs (by exploiting comparative advantage in capital markets).

It then moves on to currency swaps and shows how such swaps can be used for hedging and reducing interest costs. Throughout the descriptions of currency swaps it is useful to keep in mind that since currency swaps (when based on fixed interest rates in the 2 currencies) involve future exchanges of predetermined amounts of currency, they are equivalent to series of forward contracts. Such a currency swap is similar to a succession of forward foreign exchange contracts with progressively more distant maturity dates. Currency swaps are followed by a brief account of equity swaps.

The chapter ends with an account of swap pricing. Swaps can be valued by treating fixed rate interest flows as equivalent to a conventional bond and floating rate interest flows as equivalent to a floating rate note (FRN). The chapter provides a description of FRNs before analysing the processes of valuing interest rate and currency swaps.

HEDGING INTEREST RATE RISK

Floating rate loans expose the debtor to the risk of increases in the interest rate. A debtor may wish to avoid this risk by taking out a fixed rate loan but, owing to insufficient credit standing, is unable to borrow at fixed rates or can do so only at a particularly high rate of interest. The borrower could attempt to swap the floating rate liability for a fixed rate liability, thereby obtaining fixed rate funds.

The swap may be carried out directly between the 2 liability holders or may involve a bank as intermediary. In the latter case, the bank might take the role of counterparty to both participants, thereby bearing the risk of default by either party and eliminating the need for the participants to investigate the creditworthiness of the other. This has the additional advantage of allowing anonymity of the parties. It also facilitates swapping by debtors of relatively low creditworthiness.

Figure 12.1 illustrates a case in which a bank operates as intermediary. Borrower A has taken a loan from lender A at a floating rate of interest but

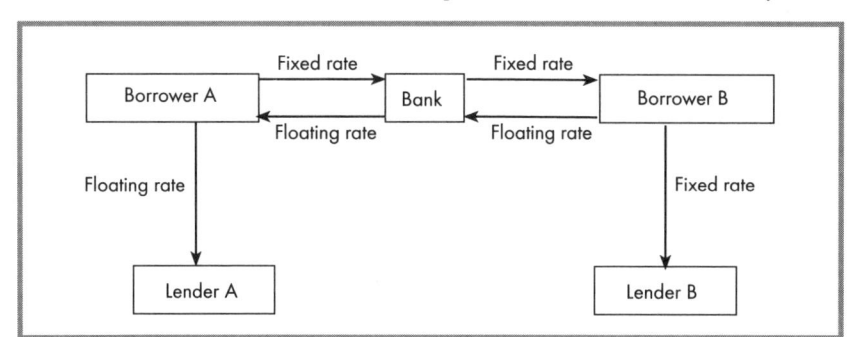

FIGURE 12.1   Interest rate swap with a bank as intermediary

Figure: Diagram showing Borrower A paying Fixed rate to Bank and receiving Floating rate from Bank; Bank receives Fixed rate from Borrower B and pays Floating rate to Borrower B. Borrower A pays Floating rate to Lender A. Borrower B pays Fixed rate to Lender B.

would prefer the certainty provided by a fixed rate loan. The bank agrees that it will provide borrower A with the funds required to pay the interest on the floating rate loan and accept interest payments at a fixed rate. Lender A is unaffected, their debtor continues to be borrower A and interest payments continue to be received from that source. Lender A need never know that the swap has taken place. Meanwhile, borrower A has simulated a fixed rate liability.

The bank seeks to match its commitment by finding a fixed rate borrower wanting a floating rate loan. Borrower B agrees to pay floating while receiving fixed and thereby simulates a floating rate loan, while lender B retains both fixed rate receipts and the original debtor. (Borrower B may be expecting a fall in interest rates. A floating rate debt would allow it to benefit from such a fall, whereas a fixed rate debt would not.)

When acting as counterparty to both borrowers, the bank faces the risk that a borrower could default. This leaves the bank exposed to an interest rate risk; the remaining customer may be receiving a high rate of interest and paying a low one. The original matching allowed losses from transactions with one customer to be offset by the corresponding gains from the deal with the other customer. Once 1 of the 2 counterparties defaults, the bank is exposed to the possibility of losses, and indeed the customer from whom the bank is making gains is the one most likely to renege on its agreement.

Example 12.1

A construction company embarks on a private house-building project for which it raises £2 million working capital. Interest is payable on a floating rate basis. Prospective profit margins are tight and could be erased by a substantial

304 ● **SWAPS**

increase in interest rates on the loan. The company anticipates that the project will take 2 years and takes out a two-year fixed for floating swap with a bank. The bank is prepared to act as counterparty and undertakes to meet the floating rate interest payments of the company in return for a fixed rate of 12% p.a. There would be a cash flow between the company and the bank to reflect the difference between the 2 interest rates.

The interest on the floating rate debt is determined at the beginning of each quarter and paid at the end of the quarter. The resulting cash flows are shown in Table 12.1.

Table 12.1 Cash flows resulting from the swap agreement (from company to bank)

Quarter	Floating rate interest payments	Fixed rate interest payments	Cash flow from company to bank
	£	£	£
1	52,867	57,475	4,608
2	52,867	57,475	4,608
3	52,867	57,475	4,608
4	57,475	57,475	0
5	57,475	57,475	0
6	62,052	57,475	−4,577
7	66,599	57,475	−9,124
8	66,599	57,475	−9,124
			−9,001

Interest rates on the floating rate loan rise progressively. The construction company initially makes payments to the bank but towards the end of the period receives cash flows from the bank. The cash flows between the company and the bank offset the fluctuations in interest rate on the floating rate loan so as to produce a constant quarterly net payment of £57,475.

(Note that the construction company raises a loan from one bank and enters a swap agreement with another bank. A treasurer should not assume that one bank will satisfy all the requirements.)

Example 12.2

A building society raises £5 million by issuing a eurobond at a fixed interest rate of 11% p.a. over 2 years, payable six-monthly, for the purpose of providing mortgages on a floating rate basis. It is exposed to the risk that interest rates might fall with the effect that interest receipts from the mortgages are inadequate to meet the interest payments on the eurobond. The building society could eliminate its exposure by swapping its fixed rate liability for one on a floating rate basis. It finds a bank prepared to enter a floating for fixed swap on the basis of receiving LIBOR +¾% p.a. in exchange for paying 11% p.a. Initially LIBOR stands at 10¼% p.a. Interest payments to the bank under the swap arrangement, as shown in Table 12.2, are on a six-monthly basis.

LIBOR rises by 0.5% between the first and second years, with the result that the building society makes a net payment of £25,000 to the bank.

Table 12.2 Cash flows resulting from the swap agreement (from building society to bank)

Period	Floating rate interest payments	Fixed rate interest payments	Cash flow from building society to bank
	£	£	£
1	275,000	275,000	0
2	275,000	275,000	0
3	287,500	275,000	12,500
4	287,500	275,000	12,500
			25,000

This example underlines the fact that a hedger could either gain or lose from the hedging instrument used. The essential point of hedging is that the gains/losses offset losses/gains on the positions being hedged. In this case the gain from higher mortgage receipts, arising from higher mortgage interest rates, is offset by a loss on the swap. If interest rates had fallen, thereby reducing mortgage interest receipts, there would have been an offsetting gain from the swap.

USING SWAPS TO REDUCE INTEREST COSTS

Investors in fixed rate instruments may be more sensitive to differences in creditworthiness than the banks lending on a floating rate basis. In consequence, borrowers of relatively low creditworthiness may face a higher interest rate differential in the fixed rate than in the floating rate market. Such borrowers stand to gain by borrowing on a floating rate basis and then swapping into a fixed rate basis with a borrower of higher credit standing. Suppose that borrower A, with a high credit standing, and borrower B, with a lower one, face the following interest charges:

	Borrower A	*Borrower B*	*Interest differential*
Floating rate	LIBOR +¼%	LIBOR +½%	¼%
Fixed rate	11% p.a.	12½% p.a.	1½%

The difference in credit standing causes different interest rate differentials in the 2 markets. If borrower A wanted floating rate funds and borrower B needed fixed rate funds, each could reduce interest costs by borrowing in the market in which it had the comparative advantage and then swapping its liability. This is illustrated by Figure 12.2 where the difference between the 2 interest differentials is 1¼% and this is shared between the 3 participants in the swap transaction. Borrower A receives 11¼% p.a. fixed while paying 11% p.a. fixed to its creditor plus LIBOR to the intermediating bank. The net outcome for A is a floating rate liability at LIBOR −¼%. This represents a gain of ½% p.a. relative to borrowing floating rate funds at LIBOR +¼%. Borrower B receives LIBOR while paying LIBOR +½% to its creditor and 11½% p.a. fixed to the bank. The net effect is equivalent to paying 12% p.a. fixed, which represents a ½% gain relative to the alternative of borrowing at a fixed rate of 12½% p.a. The intermediary bank receives 11½% p.a. fixed and pays 11¼% p.a. fixed thus making a net ¼% p.a. in payment for arranging the swap.

FIGURE 12.2 Using a swap to exploit comparative advantage

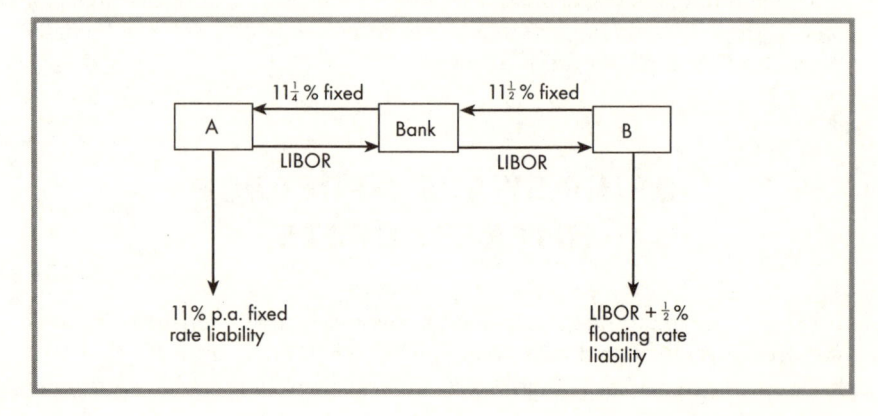

ACTIVITY 12.1

Company A wishes to borrow £10 million at a fixed rate for 5 years and has been offered either 11% fixed or six-month LIBRO +1%. Company B wishes to borrow £10 million at a floating rate for 5 years and has been offered either six-month LIBOR + 0.5% or 10% fixed.

(a) How may they enter into a swap arrangement in which each benefits equally?
(b) What risks may this arrangement generate?

(Based on the Securities Institute examination in Financial Futures and Options, December 1992, Question 8.)

Answer

(a) *By directly borrowing on the required basis, the total interest paid by A and B is:*

£10 million × (11% + LIBOR + 0.5%)

By borrowing according to comparative advantage, the total interest paid is:

£10 million × (10% + LIBOR + 1%)

Borrowing according to comparative advantage provides a total saving of £10 million × ½% to be shared between A and B. Equal sharing means that both have a ¼% reduction in interest charge.

FIGURE 12.3 Two possible swap arrangements

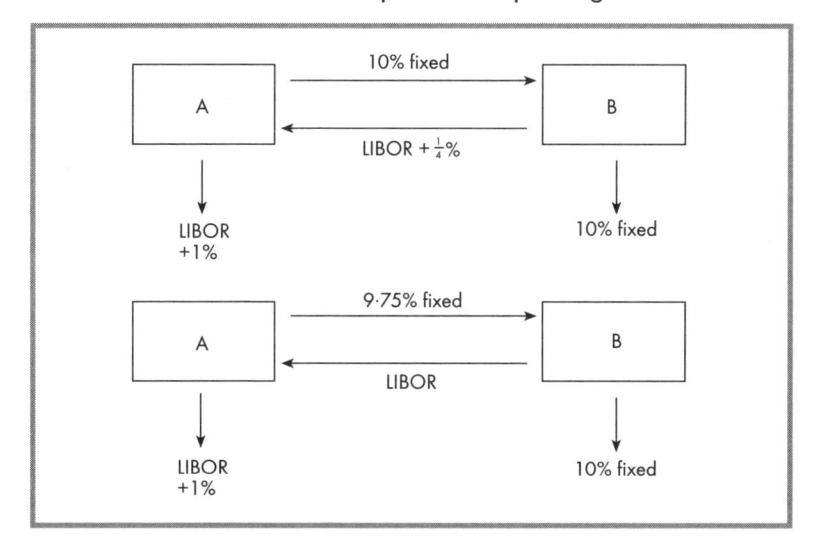

```
              10% fixed
         ┌──────────────────→
    A                              B
         ←──────────────────┐
              LIBOR + ¼%
    ↓                              ↓
  LIBOR                        10% fixed
   +1%

              9·75% fixed
         ┌──────────────────→
    A                              B
         ←──────────────────┐
                LIBOR
    ↓                              ↓
  LIBOR                        10% fixed
   +1%
```

There is a number of alternative swap arrangements that would be consistent with this distribution of the interest rate benefit of borrowing according to comparative advantage. Two possibilities are illustrated by Figure 12.3.

In both cases A synthesises a fixed rate borrowing at 10¾% (a saving of ¼% relative to borrowing directly at 11%) and B effectively obtains a floating rate loan at LIBOR + ¼% (an improvement of ¼% relative to borrowing directly). It may be noted that, conventionally, swaps are quoted in terms of the fixed rate to be exchanged for LIBOR.

(b) B is at risk from LIBOR rising.
A is at risk from an opportunity loss in the event of a fall in LIBOR.
Both are at risk from default by the other.

HOW BANKS MAKE PROFITS FROM SWAPS

Banks offers swaps even when they do not have identical opposing swaps with which to match them. A bank might hold a large portfolio of swaps with a wide range of characteristics in terms of interest rates, settlement periods, maturities, and principal amounts. To the extent that swaps bought do not fully offset swaps sold in terms of interest rate risks the net exposure of the portfolio would be hedged. Hedging instruments are likely to include fixed interest securities (particularly bonds) and interest rate derivatives.

The ability to manage the risks of a new swap by means of diversification within an existing portfolio of swaps or by means of employing hedging instruments enables banks to make a market in swaps. Banks stand ready to buy and sell swaps. They will seek to profit by using a bid/offer spread.

A bank may quote, for example, 5.30/5.25 for a five-year US dollar swap. One swap counterparty is called the payer, and the other is referred to as the receiver. The swap payer is the party making the fixed rate payments, the receiver is the party in receipt of the fixed rate cash flows. Since from the customer's viewpoint the fixed rate payments exceed the fixed rate receipts, this corresponds to ordinary borrowing/lending transactions in which customers that borrow pay a higher rate (the offer rate) than that received by customers who deposit money (the bid rate). Figure 12.4 illustrates swap cash flows.

WAREHOUSING

Warehousing by a bank consists of doing a swap and hedging it. When a suitable swap counterparty appears the hedge is undone. One way in

FIGURE 12.4   Swap cash flows

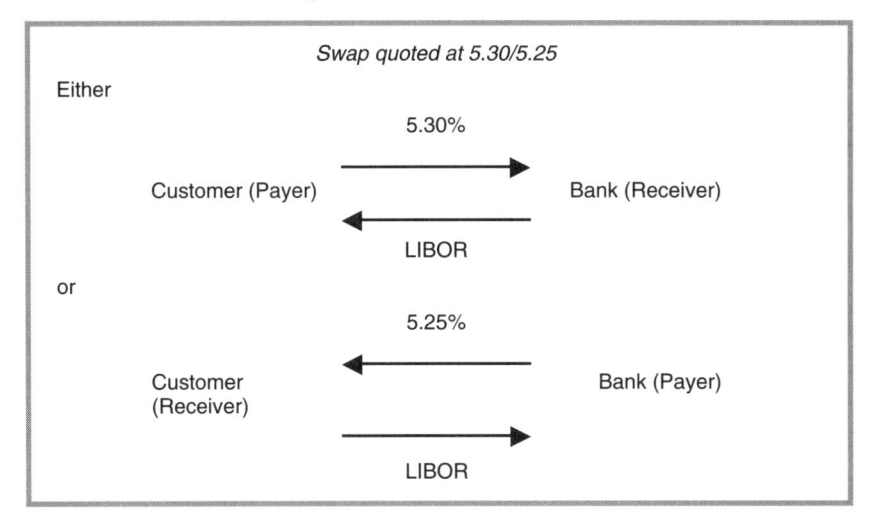

```
                    Swap quoted at 5.30/5.25
Either
                           5.30%
                           ────▶
         Customer (Payer)              Bank (Receiver)
                           ◀────
                           LIBOR

or
                           5.25%
                           ◀────
         Customer                      Bank (Payer)
         (Receiver)
                           ────▶
                           LIBOR
```

which the hedging might be carried out is by the use of financial futures. For example, a bank might agree to pay fixed against receiving floating and covers the risk of a fall in interest rates by buying financial futures.

By buying three-month interest rate futures contracts the bank can lock in interest rates. If interest rates fall the price of futures contracts will rise providing the bank with a gain that compensates for the interest rate fall.

The willingness to make a market in swaps has considerably increased the speed with which swaps are provided. Deals are available on demand without requiring simultaneous availability of a matching counterparty.

Indeed a bank is likely to have a large portfolio of swaps, many of which tend to offset one another. Only the net exposure needs to be hedged. The hedging may be undertaken with short-term interest rate futures, long-term interest rate (bond) futures, and bonds (it will be seen that swaps can be valued as the difference between 2 bond prices).

ACTIVITY 12.2

XYZ Bank is seeking fixed-rate funding. It is able to finance at a cost of six-moth LIBOR +¼% for £100 million for 5 years. The bank is able to swap into a fixed rate at 8.50% versus six-month LIBOR. Treating 6 months as exactly half a year:

(a) Set out the cash flows involved. What will be the all-in cost of funds to XYZ Bank?

310 ● **SWAPS**

> (b) Another possibility being considered is the issue of a 'hybrid' instrument which pays 8.50% for the first 3 years and LIBOR −¼% for the remaining 2 years. Given a three-year swap rate of 9% indicate in general terms the method by which the bank would achieve fixed-rate funding.
> (c) In principle, without calculating the cash flows involved, does this deal seem attractive?
> (d) Briefly outline the risks which would be involved for the bank in such a funding operation.
>
> (Based on the Securities Institute examination in Financial Futures and Options, July 1995, Question 10.)

Answer
(a) XYZ Bank pays LIBOR +0.25% p.a. for 5 years. The swap involves payment of 8.5% p.a. and receipts of LIBOR.

Interest rates
Inflow   Outflow
LIBOR   LIBOR + 0.25% + 8.5%
Net interest payment 8.75% p.a.

Cash flows per six-month period
Inflow   Outflow
(LIBOR/2) × £100 million   (LIBOR/2) × £100 million + £125,000 + £4,250,000

Net outflow £4,375,000 (= all-in cost of funds)

(b) Issue hybrid and enter both the five-year and three-year swaps.

First 3 years
Bank pays 8.5% p.a. on hybrid.
Bank pays 8.5% p.a. on five-year swap.
Bank receives 9% p.a. on three-year swap.
Bank receives LIBOR on five-year swap.
Bank pays LIBOR on three-year swap.

Net interest payment 8% p.a.

Final 2 years
Bank pays LIBOR −0.25% on hybrid.
Bank receives LIBOR on five-year swap.
Bank pays 8.5% p.a. on five-year swap.

Net interest payment 8.25% p.a.

(c) The arrangement in (b), compared with that in (a), saves 0.75% p.a. over the first 3 years and 0.5% p.a. over the final 2 years.

(d) *The risks would include default risk on the part of the 2 swap counterparties. There may also be liquidity risk in the event that one or both of the swaps may need to be reversed. There could also be legal risk; the legality of one or both swaps may be challenged. Taxation risk means that a change in the tax regulations may adversely affect the benefits from the arrangements. There may be country risk if a counterparty is based overseas: payments may be inhibited by an overseas government.*

CURRENCY SWAPS

The term swap has 3 different, but related, meanings in the context of international finance:

1. the spot purchase and simultaneous forward sale of a currency;
2. simultaneous loans in 2 currencies;
3. the exchange of debt servicing liabilities or the exchange of beneficial ownership of assets.

What follows is concerned with currency swaps in the third sense. A company, or other body, may wish to exchange a liability in one currency for a liability in another in order to reduce currency exposure. For example, a company with easier access to the UK capital market than to the US market might seek to finance an investment in the United States by raising sterling in Britain and selling it for US dollars which are invested in the United States. It then has a sterling liability and a US dollar asset. It is vulnerable to a strengthening of sterling against the dollar and would have an interest in swapping its sterling liability for a dollar one.

The currency swap may be carried out by direct negotiation between the counterparties or by means of a bank acting as intermediary and effectively becoming the counterparty to each participant. Figure 12.4 illustrates the latter case. Borrower A acquired a sterling liability and sold the sterling raised for dollars in order to acquire assets in the United States. Borrower B, facing easier access to the US capital market than the UK one, borrowed dollars and sold them in order to purchase assets in the United Kingdom. Both borrowers have an exchange rate exposure, having assets in one currency and liabilities in another. Borrower A would find that, in the event of a strengthening of the pound against the dollar, both the interest payments and the sum to be repaid at maturity rise in dollar value. Conversely, borrower B is vulnerable to a strengthening of the dollar.

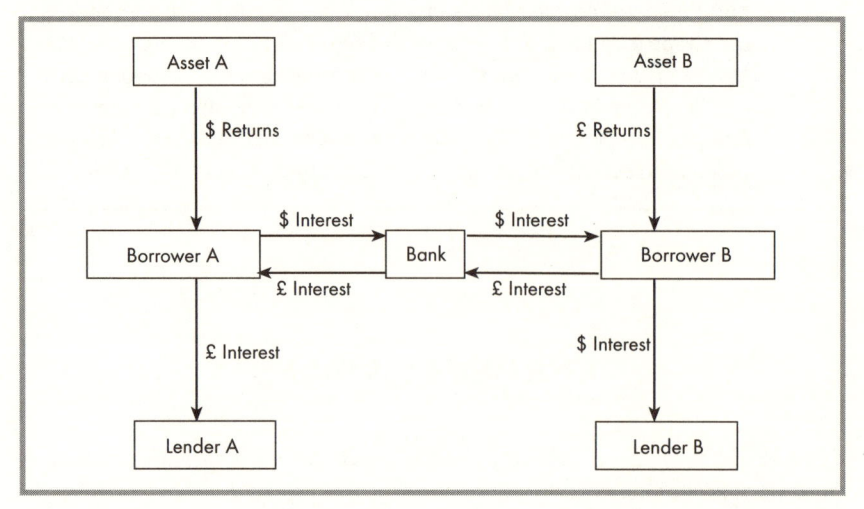

FIGURE 12.5   Currency swap with a bank as intermediary

They enter the swap agreement depicted by Figure 12.5. Borrower A simulates a dollar liability while borrower B simulates a sterling liability. This is achieved by means of borrower A undertaking to meet the interest and principal payments on borrower B's dollar liability by making the dollar payments to borrower B via the bank, while borrower B makes a similar commitment to service borrower A's sterling debt. The bank operates as counterparty to both, and borrowers A and B need not know the other's identity. Borrower A remains the debtor of lender A, similarly for borrower and lender B. The lenders may not know of the swap.

The bank runs the risk of losses arising from default by one of the parties. If, for example, the dollar strengthens against sterling, the bank will be gaining from its transactions with borrower A but losing with B. Normally these gains and losses would cancel each other out but if A were to renege on its obligations, the bank would be left with its loss-making commitments to B. The bank is committed to paying both interest and principal in the relatively strong dollar while receiving the same in the weakened sterling.

Swaps allow advantage to be taken of the relatively advantageous terms that some borrowers might obtain in particular markets. In Figure 12.5 borrower A may be able to borrow sterling more cheaply than borrower B, while borrower B obtains a lower rate of interest than A when borrowing dollars. It is mutually advantageous for each to borrow in the more favourable market and then exchange the currencies borrowed (in practice they could buy the desired currency in the spot market rather than exchange currencies with each other – the effect is the same) and the liabilities acquired. Swaps may arise from different motives and need not involve an exchange of spot currency: there may merely be an agreement to service each other's debt. See Example 12.3.

Example 12.3

	Interest rates available	
	$	DM
US Co	7% p.a.	6% p.a.
German Co	8% p.a.	5% p.a.

If US Co borrows DM and German Co borrows $ the borrowing costs are:

US Co 6% p.a. (DM), German Co 8% p.a. ($)

The 2 interest rates total 6 + 8 = 14%.

If the companies borrow according to comparative advantage then interest rates are:

US Co 7% p.a.($), German Co 5% p.a. (DM)

The 2 interest rates total 7 + 5 = 12%.

By borrowing according to comparative advantage and then exchanging currencies and agreeing to finance each other's liabilities there is a net gain of 2% p.a. to be shared between the 2 companies. If the US Co pays the German Co 5% p.a. (DM) it saves 1% p.a., while if the German Co pays the US Co 7% ($) it also saves 1% p.a.

ACTIVITY 12.3

A British company can borrow sterling at 8.5% p.a. and Deutschmarks at 5.75% p.a.

A German company can borrow sterling at 9.5% p.a. and Deutschmarks at 4.75% p.a.

(a) If the British company needs to borrow Deutschmarks, and the German company needs to borrow sterling, show how they can construct a swap that allows them to share equally in reduced interest costs.

(b) How might the swap arrangement change if a bank is used as an intermediary and takes 0.5% p.a.?

314 ● SWAPS

Answer
(a)

```
                    DM 4.75%
       British  ─────────────►  German
       company  ◄─────────────  company
                    £ 8.5%
         │                         │
   £ 8.5%│                         │DM 4.75%
         ▼                         ▼
```

(b)

```
              DM 5%          DM 4.75 %
    British  ──────►        ──────►   German
    company          Bank             company
             ◄──────        ◄──────
              £ 8.5%         £ 8.75%
       │                                  │
 £ 8.5%│                                  │DM 4.75%
       ▼                                  ▼
```

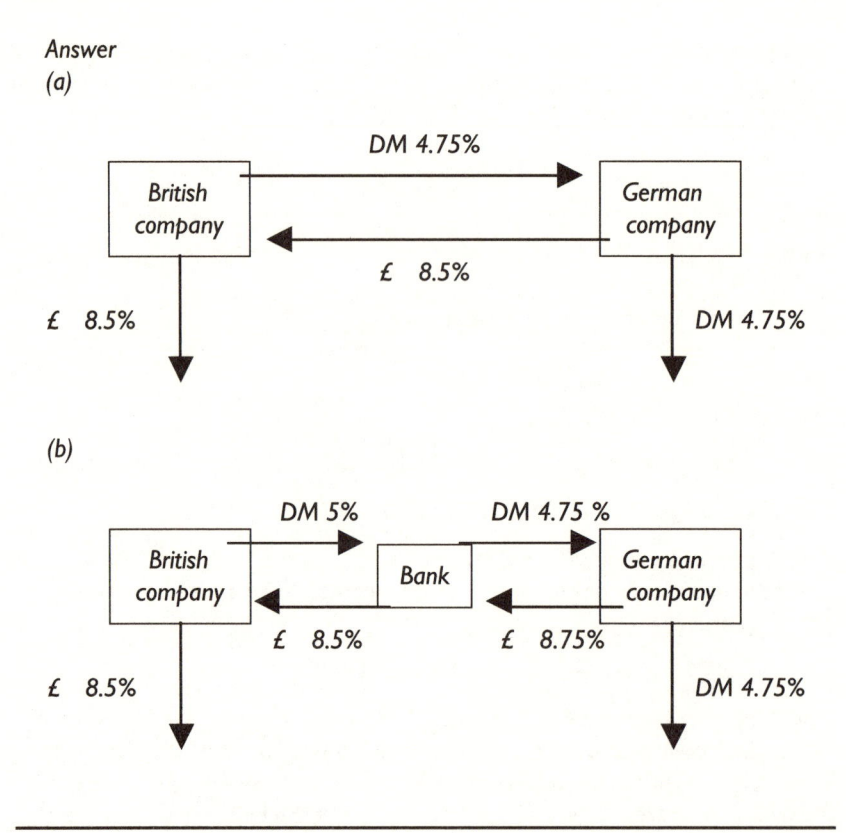

Variations in the terms on which different borrowers can obtain funds in particular currencies can arise for a number of reasons. Exchange controls may inhibit borrowing by non-nationals, a company may be little known outside its own country and hence may have a low credit rating in foreign capital markets, or a market may be saturated with a particular borrower's debt. This latter situation is illustrated by the World Bank's borrowing of Swiss francs in the early 1980s. The Swiss franc market was so saturated with World Bank debt that the Bank was faced with increasing interest rates. It circumvented this problem by borrowing dollars and entering a swap with IBM. There were relatively few US corporates borrowing Swiss francs, so such corporates could borrow them at relatively low interest rates. IBM could thus borrow Swiss francs more cheaply than the World Bank. Thus IBM borrowed Swiss francs and entered a Swiss franc/US dollar swap with the World Bank, to their mutual advantage.

The forward premium or discount is implicit in the interest flows. Different rates of interest on the 2 currencies have the same effect as a forward premium/discount. So although the exchange of principal upon maturity of the swap takes place at the same exchange rate as the original exchange of principal, the interest rate differential renders the swap equivalent to the use of forward currency contracts.

EQUITY SWAPS

An equity swap involves an agreement to exchange the returns on a stock index portfolio for a flow of interest payments. Such swaps could be arranged for any of the major stock indices, e.g. the S&P 500, FTSE 100, Nikkei 225, C and C 40 and DAX. Figure 12.6 illustrates an equity swap.

FIGURE 12.6   An equity swap

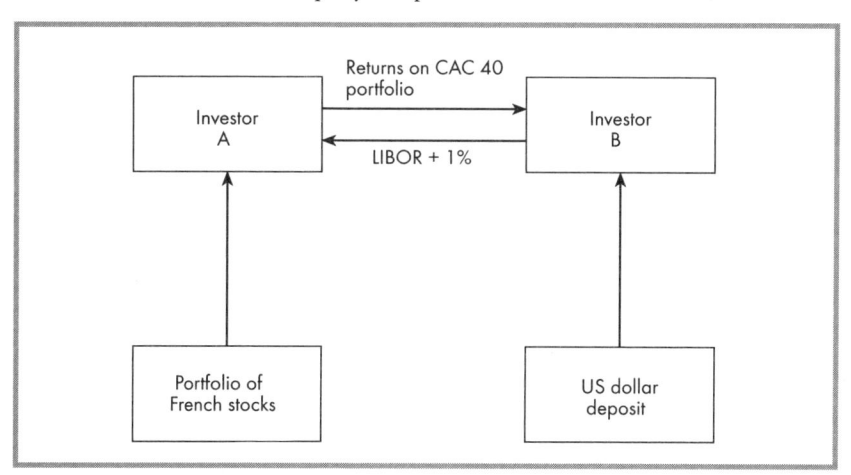

```
                    Returns on CAC 40
                       portfolio
        ┌──────────┐ ─────────────→ ┌──────────┐
        │ Investor │                │ Investor │
        │    A     │ ←───────────── │    B     │
        └──────────┘    LIBOR + 1%  └──────────┘
             ▲                            ▲
             │                            │
        ┌──────────┐                 ┌──────────┐
        │Portfolio │                 │ US dollar│
        │of French │                 │  deposit │
        │  stocks  │                 │          │
        └──────────┘                 └──────────┘
```

Investor A has a balanced portfolio of French stocks but is bearish about the French stock market. As an alternative to selling the portfolio, the investor could enter an equity swap. The swap illustrated by Figure 12.6 would be suitable if the investor were bullish on the US dollar and US dollar interest rates.

Investor B might be an American fund manager who wants an exposure to the French stock market but does not have the expertise to evaluate alternative French stocks. By entering the equity swap of Figure 12.6 the American fund manager simulates a balanced investment in French stocks without getting involved in the analysis of individual French stocks. (Note that stock returns include capital gains or losses as well as dividends).

FLOATING RATE NOTES (FRNS)

Before turning to swap valuation it would be useful to examine floating rate notes. A floating rate note is a bond the coupons of which are not fixed but instead varied at points in time, e.g. after six-month intervals. The interest rate would be reassessed in the light of a reference rate. Such a bond might, for instance, pay 1% p.a. over LIBOR (the rate of interest at which major banks in London will lend to each other). Once determined, the rate would then be fixed for the appropriate time interval, e.g. 6 months.

In many ways, FRNs are similar to short-term money market instruments, such as bank deposits, in that the interest rate is variable. However, the rate is not quite as variable, because once determined it is fixed for a period. As a result of this incomplete variability, a small amount of capital risk persists (as opposed to bank deposits which exhibit no capital risk). If interest rates rise subsequent to an interest fixing date, the fixed rate will seem unattractive and the bond price will fall below par. Conversely, a fall in rates would cause a small enhancement in the value of the bond. This might be looked upon in terms of the yield until the next interest reassessment date being subject to discounting. Of course, the price variations would be much smaller than in the case of conventional fixed coupon bonds.

Unlike conventional bonds, floating rate notes (FRNs) have variable coupons. The coupon will be realigned with market interest rates at predetermined points in time (e.g. every 6 months). Since at each coupon adjustment date the rate of coupon yield would be equated to the required rate of return, and hence rate of discount, the FRN will equal its par value on that date.

Since the value of an FRN will be equal to par on the coupon adjustment date, the valuation of an FRN can be carried out as if there were only 2 future cash flows. These cash flows are the next coupon payment and the par value on the coupon adjustment date. If the coupon payment date coincides with the coupon adjustment date the equation for the value of an FRN will be:

$$P = C/(1 + r)^T + B/(1 + r)^T$$

where P is the price of the floating rate note, C is the next coupon, B is the par value of the FRN, r is the rate of discount, and T is the period in years (normally a fraction of a year) to the next coupon payment (and adjustment) date.

As the period for discounting (i.e. T) is short, normally less than 6 months, the price of a floating rate note will have only limited sensitivity to changes in the rate of discount, and hence to changes in the interest rate. This is in contrast to a conventional bond whose fixed coupons and repayment of principal involve long discount times and hence high sensitivity to interest rate movements.

SWAP PRICING

Interest rate swaps

One way in which an interest rate (fixed for floating) swap can be valued is to treat the fixed rate payments as being equivalent to the cash flows on a conventional bond and the floating rate payments as being equivalent to a floating rate note (FRN). Although an interest rate swap does not entail an exchange of principal at maturity, the correspondence to a bond and FRN can be completed by evoking a hypothetical exchange of principal at maturity whereby the 2 counterparties give each other the same amount of money in the same currency.

The value of the swap could be expressed as the value of the bond minus the value of the FRN. That is:

$$V = B_1 - B_2$$

where V is the value of the swap, B_1 the value of the bond, and B_2 the value of the floating rate note. The value of the bond is given by:

$$B_1 = \sum_{i=1}^{n} k e^{-r_i t_i} + Q e^{-r_n t_n}$$

where k is the periodic fixed payment in the swap, Q is the principal sum, the r's are the discount rates, and the t's the corresponding time periods to the cash flows. The value of the floating rate note is:

$$B_2 = k^* e^{-r_1 t_1} + Q e^{-r_1 t_1}$$

where k^* is the next interest payment and Q is the principal sum, while r_1 and t_1 are the (annualised) interest rate and length of time to the next interest payment (next interest reassessment date). Only the next interest reassessment date is relevant for discounting purposes since FRNs tend to revert to their par values on the interest reassessment dates. This is because rates of interest are set equal to the required rates of return which are also the relevant discount rates (this might be extended to the term structure of interest rates to the maturity date of the swap; the term structure of interest yields would tend to be the same as the term structure of discount rates).

Currency swaps

Taking the example of a currency swap that entails fixed rate payments in one currency being exchanged for fixed rate payments in the other currency, the swap can be valued as the difference between the current values of 2 conventional bonds. The value of the foreign currency interest flows, priced as the value of a foreign currency bond, and the corresponding value of a domestic currency bond would be used in the following way:

$$V = SB_F - B_D$$

where S is the current exchange rate, B_F the value (in foreign currency) of the foreign currency bond, and B_D is the value of the (bond equivalent to) the domestic currency interest flows. The (bond equivalent to) the foreign currency interest flows has the value of:

$$B_F = \sum_{i=1}^{n} k_F e^{-r_i^F t_i} + Q e^{-r_n^F t_n}$$

where k_F is the constant foreign currency interest payment, r_i^F the foreign currency discount rates, and t_i the corresponding periods to the interest payments. The principal sum, in foreign currency, is shown as Q. The bond equivalent to the domestic currency cash flows is:

$$B_D = \sum_{i=1}^{n} k_D e^{-r_i^D t_i} + S'Q e^{-r_n^D t_n}$$

where k_D is the constant foreign currency interest payment, r_i^D are the discount rates for the various periods to the cash flows, and t_i is the length of those periods to cash flows. S is the exchange rate at the time that the swap was agreed; it converts the foreign currency principal sum Q into the equivalent domestic currency principal sum (note that at maturity Q is exchanged for SQ; this means that the exchange rate at the beginning of the swap is also used for the exchange of principal upon maturity of the swap).

ACTIVITY 12.4

An American company has an existing swap agreement with a British company. The original exchange rate was $1.50/£1 (when the swap was agreed) and the current exchange rate is $2/£1. The fixed interest rates for the swap are 10% for sterling and 5% for the US dollar. Interest payments are annual and such payments have just been exchanged. The swap has a remaining life of 3 years. The American company is the recipient of sterling and the payer of dollars. The original sums were $15 million and £10 million. Interest rates are now equal at 5% p.a. What is the value of the swap to the American company?

Answer

$B_F = £1m/(1.05) + £1m/(1.05)^2 + £11m/(1.05)^3 = £11.36m$
$B_D = \$0.75m/(1.05) + \$0.75m/(1.05)^2 + \$15.75m/(1.05)^3 = \$15m$
$V = \$2 B_F - B_D = \$22.72m - \$15m = \$7.72m$

ACTIVITY 12.5

For a value date of 1 July 1991 a company entered into a five-year interest rate swap with its bank, under which it has contracted to pay 10% and receive six-month LIBOR, settled semi-annually, on a notional principal amount of £10,000,000. It is 1 July 1993 and the swap payments have just settled, so the swap now has exactly 3 years to run. The bank offers to unwind the swap at a rate of 8%. If the company agrees, the transaction will be cancelled by means of a settlement today.

(a) Set out the underlying fixed-rate cash flow that would take place, if, instead of cancelling the existing deal, a new deal were made and the 2 deals were to run to maturity. You may assume each interest period has 182.5 days and ignore leap years.
(b) What sum of money would be paid today to cancel the transaction?
(c) To whom?
(d) What assumptions are implicit in the above calculations?

(Based on the Securities Institute examination in Financial Futures and Options, December 1993, Question 8.)

Answer

(a) £100,000 per six-month period from the company to the bank. This is based on £10,000,000 × (0.05 − 0.04), where 0.05 and 0.04 are the old and new unannualised six-month interest rates in decimal form.

(b) The sum of money to be paid to cancel the transaction would be the current equivalent of the future cash flows in (a), i.e. the present value of those cash flows. If the bank offers to unwind the swap at 8% p.a. (i.e. 4% per six-month period) then that would appear to be an appropriate discount rate. The sum would thus be:

$£100,000[1/(1.04) + 1/(1.04)^2 + 1/(1.04)^3 + 1/(1.04)^4 + 1/(1.04)^5 + 1/(1.04)^6] = £524,213.69$

(c) By the company to the bank.
(d) A key assumption in the foregoing calculation is that the yield curve is flat. In other words the same rate of discount (4% per six-month period) is applicable to all 6 future cash flows. If the yield curve were not flat

> then different discount rates should be applied to each cash flow (although in practice the yield to maturity, 4% per six-month period in this case, is often used to discount all the prospective cash flows).

CONCLUSIONS

Whereas futures and options are often exchange traded, swaps are never exchange traded. Swaps are the result of direct negotiations between counterparties, and one of the counterparties may be a bank that makes a market in swaps. Often a bank will be a counterparty to many swaps, and the market risks arising from those swaps will tend to offset each other. There would be some residual risk which the bank may wish to hedge. The hedging may attempt to achieve a net duration that approximates to zero. Hedging instruments are likely to include bonds, bond futures and short-term interest rate futures. In the cases of currency and equity swaps, currency futures and stock index futures are likely to be used.

Since swaps are not marked to market, losses can accumulate and default risk is present. In the 1980s some British local authorities, notably Hammersmith and Fulham, used swaps to speculate on interest rate movements. Substantial losses were incurred, but the courts ruled that since the local authorities were not legally entitled to trade swaps they were not obliged to pay their debts arising from the swaps. So the local authorities defaulted on their swap agreements. Fortunately defaults in the swaps markets have been rare.

Swaps are longer-term instruments than forwards, futures and options. Periods in excess of 10 years are not unusual. In many cases they are equivalent to a succession of forward contracts stretching into the future.

In addition to the various forms of swap described in this chapter there are also swaptions. Swaptions are options on swaps. In return for the payment of a premium the buyer of a swaption obtains the right, but not the obligation, to enter a swap agreement in the future on terms agreed when buying the swaption.

Further reading

Introductions to swaps are available from:
Robert W. Kolb, *Financial Derivatives* (Kolb Publishing, Miami, 1993), Chapter 4.

David Winstone, *Financial Derivatives* (Chapman & Hall, London, 1995), Chapters 18 and 19.

S. Eckl, J. N. Robinson and D. C. Thomas, *Financial Engineering* (Blackwell, Oxford, 1990), Chapter 6.

John Hull, *Introduction to Futures and Options Markets*, 2nd edn (Prentice Hall, Englewood Cliffs, 1995), Chapter 6.

Keith Redhead, *Introduction to the International Money Markets* (Woodhead-Faulkner, Hemel Hempstead, 1992), Chapter 7.

For more detail see:

S. DeCovny, *Swaps* (Woodhead-Faulkner, Hemel Hempstead, 1992).

FORWARDS AND FUTURES IN CURRENCY RISK MANAGEMENT

13

INTRODUCTION

Forward foreign exchange contracts are agreements between 2 parties (e.g. a bank and its client) for the exchange of 2 currencies on a future date at an exchange rate agreed in the present (the forward exchange rate). Currency futures are similar but with important differences; in particular, currency futures are tradable.

For the purposes of hedging foreign exchange exposures (particularly by non-financial sector corporates), forward contracts dominate and this dominance is particularly marked in Europe. This is reflected in an absence of currency contracts on European futures exchanges. However, the use of currency futures in North America is sufficiently widespread to generate a very successful currency futures market, particularly on the Chicago Mercantile Exchange. Of course, the global nature of financial markets means that users outside North America have ready access to the currency futures markets of North America.

This chapter begins with an account of the operation of the underlying currency markets, including the determinants of exchange rates (currency prices) and the conventions for quoting exchange rates. Following some description of the forward markets, the chapter looks at the determination of forward and futures prices. It will be shown that interest rate parity and covered interest arbitrage are central to the relationship between spot and forward prices. Since currency is carryable, the pricing of futures and forwards is based (like bond and stock index futures) on a cash-and-carry arbitrage mechanism, this mechanism being known as covered interest arbitrage. As with other futures contracts, this arbitrage can be seen as being between a synthetic futures (or forward) and the actual futures (or forward).

The chapter then looks at the issue of cause and effect between the spot and futures markets. This provides a reminder that cash-and-carry arbitrage (including covered interest arbitrage) establishes a relationship between spot and futures (or forward) prices, but does not indicate whether the spot price determines the futures price, or vice versa. It may be that price sensitive information first affects futures or forward prices and that cash-and-carry arbitrage then transmits the price effects to the spot market.

The chapter then focuses specifically on currency futures and their use in the hedging of currency risk. The chapter continues with a comparison between forward and futures contracts, and an indication of the circumstances in which forward and futures prices may not be identical. The chapter ends with an examination of the role of the corporate treasurer.

CURRENCY MARKETS

The foreign exchange markets trade currencies for both spot and forward delivery. They do not have a specific location and take place primarily by means of telecommunications both within and between countries. There are a number of major financial centres in which the markets are particularly active – New York, London, Tokyo, Frankfurt, Singapore, Hong Kong and Bahrain among others. Much of the market involves trades between banks, whether acting as agents for customers or on their own behalf. Central banks (such as the US Federal Reserve, Bank of Japan, Bundesbank, and Bank of England) tend to be particularly active participants in the foreign exchange markets, often acting in concert with each other.

Exchange rates are determined by demand and supply (see Figure 13.1). The purchases and sales of currencies stem partly from the need to finance trade in goods and services, although this accounts for only a small percentage of the total (typically, much less than 5%). A very substantial proportion is for the finance of investment and, in particular, the temporary investment in short-term money market instruments such as bank deposits, that might be regarded as speculation on currency movements (buying and investing the currencies that are expected to appreciate in value). A third source of demand or supply arises from the participation of central banks: a participation that would emanate from a desire to influence the direction, extent or speed of exchange rate movements.

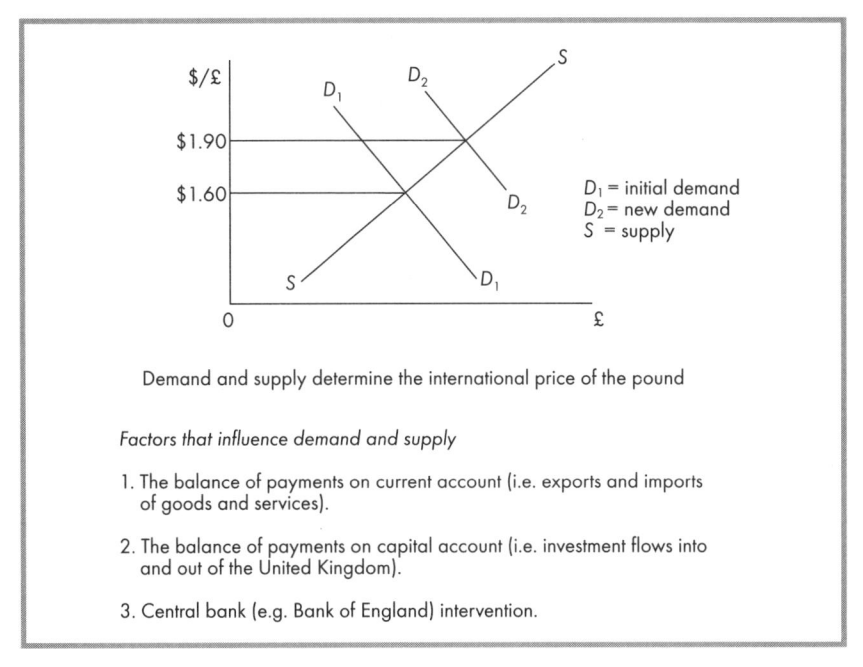

FIGURE 13.1 Determination of exchange rates

```
$/£
         D₁      D₂         S
$1.90 ─────────────────
$1.60 ─────────────────
                    D₂      D₁ = initial demand
                            D₂ = new demand
         S                  S = supply
              S    D₁
  0                          £
```

Demand and supply determine the international price of the pound

Factors that influence demand and supply

1. The balance of payments on current account (i.e. exports and imports of goods and services).

2. The balance of payments on capital account (i.e. investment flows into and out of the United Kingdom).

3. Central bank (e.g. Bank of England) intervention.

Although short-term speculative movements account for the bulk of currency deals, the more fundamental factors of trade in goods and services, long-term investment and government policy are crucial to currency price movements. Not only do these more fundamental factors have a direct impact, but also they are in large part the basis for the speculative flows.

Figure 13.1 shows the determination of the price of sterling, in terms of the US dollar, by the interaction of demand and supply. The demand for sterling can come from foreign residents paying for UK exports, from foreign residents wishing to invest in the UK, or from the Bank of England (or other central banks) buying sterling in order to support its value. Figure 13.1 illustrates a case in which, as a result of an increase in demand from one or more of these sources, the demand curve for sterling shifts to the right and raises the US dollar value of the pound.

The supply of sterling can arise from UK importers selling pounds in order to obtain the currency required to pay for the imports. It can stem from UK investors wishing to acquire foreign currency in order to invest abroad. Alternatively, one or more central banks may be selling sterling in order to depress its value. Rightward or leftward shifts (reflecting increased or decreased supply) of the supply curve would generate declines or rises respectively in the price of sterling. (On a day-to-day basis, speculative trading constitutes the main source of demand and supply changes.)

QUOTATION OF EXCHANGE RATES

There are 2 ways of quoting exchange rates: the direct and the indirect. Most countries use the direct method, which involves stating the number of units of domestic currency per 1 unit of foreign currency. For example, the Deutschmark–US dollar rate might be quoted in Germany as:

$1 = DM1.4890–1.4900

The indirect method of quotation takes the form of stating the number of units of foreign currency per unit of domestic currency. This method is used in the United Kingdom and the Republic of Ireland. The United States uses the indirect method for all currencies except the British pound, the Irish punt and the ecu, for which the direct method is used. So in the United States, the DM/$ rate would also be quoted as:

$1 = DM1.4890–1.4900

Two prices are always quoted. There is the price at which the customers could buy from a bank, known as the offer or ask price. The other is the price at which the customer could sell to the bank, known as the bid price. The offer price is always greater than the bid price, i.e. the bank sells at a higher price than that at which it buys. The difference between these 2 prices is known as the bid–offer spread or bid–ask spread. In the example above, the bid–offer spread is ten points. Buying Deutschmarks from a bank would realise DM1.4890 per dollar (the smallest number of Deutschmarks), while selling Deutschmarks to the bank would require DM1.4900 per dollar received (the larger number of Deutschmarks has to be given).

THE FORWARD FOREIGN EXCHANGE MARKET

A forward purchase is an agreement to buy foreign currency on a specified future date at a rate of exchange determined in the present; likewise, a forward sale. This technique removes uncertainty as to how much future payables or receivables will be worth in terms of domestic currency.

If the forward price of a currency exceeds the spot price, that currency is said to be at a premium. For example, if the spot price of sterling in terms of US dollars is £1 = $1.40, while the six-month forward price is £1 = $1.45, then sterling is said to be at a premium against the dollar. Conversely, if the forward price is less than the spot price, the currency is said to be at a discount. With a spot exchange rate of £1 = $1.40, a forward price of £1 = $1.35 means that sterling is at a discount against the US dollar (correspondingly, the dollar is at a premium against sterling).

The premiums and discounts are reported in terms of per cent per annum. This percentage is ascertained from the following formula:

$$\frac{\text{Premium} \times 365 \times 100}{\text{Spot rate} \times \text{Number of days to maturity}}$$

This formula can be more readily understood by rewriting it as:

$$\text{Percentage} = \frac{\text{Premium}}{\text{Spot rate}} \times \frac{365}{\text{Number of days to maturity}} \times 100$$

The first component, premium/spot rate, expresses the premium as a proportion of the spot rate. The second component, 365/number of days to maturity, annualises the figure. It alters the first ratio to produce the number that would be found for the 12-month premium if the 12-month forward premium was proportional to the three-month (or whatever) premium. So in the case of three-month forwards, this adjustment would multiply the first ratio by 4, while in the case of one-month forwards the multiplication would be by about 12. Finally, the resulting figure is multiplied by 100 in order to convert the decimal into a percentage. Example 13.1 illustrates the calculation of the rate of dollar premium against sterling (sterling discount against the dollar).

The bid–offer spread (the difference between the buying and selling prices) is always larger for forward foreign exchange than for spot.

Table 13.1 illustrates London exchange rates, both spot and forward, at the close of business on 13 December 1995. The first column shows closing mid-points. Since sterling is priced on the indirect quote basis, each figure is a number of units of foreign currency per pound. There would be an offer rate (for buying sterling) and a bid rate (for selling). The offer rate is always higher than the bid rate, and the mid-point is the average of the offer and bid rates. The third column indicates the offer and bid rates. The numbers normally refer to the last 3 places of decimals. For example, the bid price of sterling is 15.6260 Austrian schillings, while the offer price is 15.6419 schillings.

There are columns showing the forward (mid-point) exchange rates for delivery 1 month, 3 months, and 1 year in the future. There are also annualised percentage premiums or discounts. So in the market for three-

328 • FORWARDS AND FUTURES

Table 13.1 Pound spot forward against the pound on 13 December 1995

		Closing mid-point	Change on day	Bid/offer spread	Day's mid High	Day's mid Low	One month Rate	One month % p.a.	Three months Rate	Three months % p.a.	One year Rate	One year % p.a.	Bank of England index
Europe													
Austria	(Sch)	15.6340	+0.0272	260–419	15.6576	15.5889	15.5905	3.3	15.5465	2.2	–	–	106.5
Belgium	(BFr)	45.7130	+0.1025	719–541	45.9800	45.5730	45.598	3.0	45.428	2.5	44.703	2.2	109.1
Denmark	(DKr)	8.6139	+0.0158	096–182	8.6231	8.5864	8.6022	1.6	8.5849	1.3	8.5264	1.0	109.3
Finland	(FM)	6.6632	−0.0104	567–697	6.6810	6.6450	6.6588	0.8	6.6507	0.7	–	–	87.7
France	(FFr)	7.6975	+0.0454	942–008	7.7044	7.6561	7.6984	−0.1	7.6864	0.6	7.645	0.7	109.3
Germany	(DM)	2.2219	+0.0036	208–229	2.2263	2.2151	2.2171	2.6	2.2087	2.4	2.1689	2.4	111.4
Greece	(Dr)	367.980	+1.393	796–163	368.284	365.866	–	–	–	–	–	–	66.2
Ireland	(I£)	0.9684	−0.0009	675–692	0.9705	0.9675	0.9674	1.2	0.9663	0.9	0.9628	0.6	97.5
Italy	(L)	2450.92	+3.21	906–279	2455.23	2442.88	2459.77	−4.3	2475.97	−4.1	2550.37	−4.1	71.3
Luxemburg	(LFr)	45.7130	+0.1025	719–541	45.9800	45.5730	45.598	3.0	45.428	2.5	44.703	2.2	109.1
Netherlands	(FL)	2.4883	+0.006	869–896	2.4930	2.4684	2.4818	3.1	2.4719	2.6	2.4283	2.4	109.1
Norway	(NKr)	9.8220	+0.0383	159–280	9.8311	9.7541	9.8119	1.2	9.7904	1.3	9.7092	1.1	98.0
Portugal	(Es)	233.392	+0.543	262–522	233.722	232.591	233.817	−2.2	–	–	94.9	–	–
Spain	(Pta)	188.959	+0.206	877–040	189.301	188.444	189.444	−3.1	190.389	−3.0	194.614	−3.0	81.9
Sweden	(SKr)	10.2884	−0.0088	795–972	10.3213	10.2795	10.2903	−0.2	10.2939	−0.2	10.3091	−0.2	86.8
Switzerland	(SFr)	1.8041	+0.0043	030–052	1.8067	1.7983	1.7974	4.5	1.7854	4.1	1.732	4.0	115.0
UK†	(£)	–	–	–	–	–	–	–	–	–	–	–	–
83.0													
Ecu	–	1.2130	+0.0034	123–136	1.2142	1.2081	1.212	1.0	1.2105	0.8	1.2031	0.8	–
SDR	–	1.033900	–	–	–	–	–	–	–	–	–	–	–

THE FORWARD FOREIGN EXCHANGE MARKET • 329

Americas												
Argentina	(Peso)	1.5322	+0.0009	318–326	1.5340	1.5282	–	–	–	–	–	–
Brazil	(R$)	1.4814	+0.0017	809–818	1.4828	1.4770	–	–	–	–	–	–
Canada	(C$)	2.1083	−0.0018	074–091	2.1133	2.1039	2.1068	0.8	2.1056	0.5	2.1014	0.3	83.1
Mexico	(New Peso)	11.9225	+0.0618	044–405	11.9405	11.8741	–	–	–	–	–	–
USA	($)	1.5325	+0.0011	321–328	1.5342	1.5282	1.5316	0.7	1.53	0.6	1.5215	0.7	94.4
Pacific/Middle East/Africa												
Australia	(A$)	2.0577	−0.0097	565–588	2.0700	2.0549	2.0592	−0.9	2.063	−1.0	2.0795	−1.1	86.1
Hong Kong	(HK$)	11.8535	+0.0088	500–570	11.8661	11.8219	11.8464	0.7	11.8384	0.5	11.8118	0.4	–
India	(Rs)	53.5592	+0.1822	316–867	53.6130	53.3760	–	–	–	–	–	–
Israel	(Shk)	4.7767	+0.0003	717–817	4.7817	4.7660	–	–	–	–	–	–
Japan	(Y)	155.812	−0.092	738–886	156.020	155.240	154.917	6.9	153.477	6.0	147.172	5.5	142.5
Malaysia	(M$)	3.8994	+0.0086	977–010	3.9022	3.8854	–	–	–	–	–	–
New Zealand	(NZ$)	2.3713	+0.0002	698–728	2.3780	2.3690	2.3742	−1.5	2.3813	−1.7	2.4054	−1.4	100.3
Philippines	(Peso)	40.1885	+0.0428	410–360	40.2360	40.1410	–	–	–	–	–	–
Saudi Arabia	(SR)	5.7476	+0.0039	460–492	5.7537	5.7317	–	–	–	–	–	–
Singapore	(S$)	2.1708	+0.0038	695–720	2.1721	2.1642	–	–	–	–	–	–
South Africa	(R)	5.6180	+0.0011	159–200	5.6282	5.6089	–	–	–	–	–	–
South Korea	(Won)	1179.45	−0.72	910–980	1181.33	1176.26	–	–	–	–	–	–
Taiwan	(T$)	41.8596	+0.0401	462–730	41.9036	41.7474	–	–	–	–	–	–
Thailand	(Bt)	38.5335	+0.0264	170–499	38.5750	38.4240	–	–	–	–	–	–

† Rates for 12 December. Bid/offer spreads in the pound spot table show only the last 3 decimal places. Forward rates are not directly quoted to the market but are implied by current interest rates. Sterling index calculated by the Bank of England. Base average 1990 = 100. Index rebased 1 February 1995. Bid, offer and mid-rates in both this and the dollar spot tables derived from the WM/Reuters closing spot rates. Some values are rounded by the *Financial Times*.

Source: *Financial Times*, 14 December 1995.

Example 13.1

Spot £1 = $1.9510–1.9520
Three-month forward rate is £1 = $1.9257–1.9270
Three-month forward premium = 2.53 – 2.50 cents (spot minus forward)

Rate of premium (% p.a.)
For seller of sterling

$$\frac{0.0253}{1.9510} \times 4 = 0.0519 \text{ (5.19\% p.a.)}$$

For buyer of sterling

$$\frac{0.0250}{1.9520} \times 4 = 0.0512 \text{ (5.12\% p.a.)}$$

Mid-price quote

$$\frac{0.02515}{1.9515} \times 4 = 0.0516 \text{ (5.16\% p.a.)}$$

---

month forward contracts, the Austrian schilling is at a 2.2% p.a. premium against the pound (fewer schillings are needed forward than spot, so each schilling buys more forward sterling than spot sterling; hence the schilling is more valuable forward than spot). On the other hand, Italian lire were at a 4.1% p.a. discount against the British pound.

The last column is a Bank of England index that shows how each currency has moved against an average of other currencies since a 1990 base date. It can be seen that the British pound had fallen to 83% of its 1990 value, while the corresponding fall for the Greek drachma was to 66.2% of its 1990 value. At the other extreme, the Japanese yen had risen by 42.5%.

PRICING CURRENCY FORWARDS AND FUTURES

As with other forwards and futures, arbitrage plays a crucial role in the determination of the prices of forward and futures contracts on foreign exchange. The arbitrage may be looked upon as a cash-and-carry arbitrage, but is more usually referred to as covered interest arbitrage. As with other arbitrage pricing mechanisms, the arbitrage can be seen as being between the forward or futures contract on the one hand and a synthetic forward or futures contract on the other. The arbitrage involves buying the cheaper of the two and simultaneously selling the more expensive. The fair forward or futures price is the price that provides no opportunity for arbitrage profits. In other words, the price of the forward or futures should equal that of the synthetic forward or futures.

To illustrate the general principle for the case of currencies, consider futures contracts on sterling using the US dollar as the base currency (the US dollar is normally the base currency in foreign exchange futures contracts). The synthetic long forward involves borrowing dollars and simultaneously buying spot sterling which is put on deposit. There is no initial cash outlay but on the maturity date a sum of sterling is held and a dollar debt has to be repaid. So the transactions that occur on the maturity date are equivalent to those under a forward contract (dollars are paid and sterling is received as the sterling deposit matures). If sterling futures (or forwards) are overpriced relative to the synthetic, an arbitrage profit can be made via a synthetic long forward position together with a short futures position.

If the price of buying forward sterling by means of the synthetic is lower than the futures price of sterling, the receipts from selling sterling via the (overpriced) futures will exceed the dollar debt to be repaid. The difference constitutes the arbitrage profit. Conversely, a futures price below the synthetic price offers an arbitrage profit from buying the (underpriced) futures and simultaneously taking a short position in the synthetic.

The short synthetic position is established by means of borrowing the foreign currency (sterling) and using the proceeds to buy the base currency (US dollars) which is then deposited. On the maturity date the debt is repaid with sterling and the dollar deposit matures to provide US dollars (so on the maturity date there is an outflow of sterling and an inflow of dollars, just as in the case of a forward contract to sell sterling for US dollars). If the futures price is below the price provided by the synthetic, it would be possible for an arbitrager to construct the synthetic forward and use the dollar proceeds to buy sterling through the futures contract. The dollars from the synthetic would exceed the amount required to buy sterling via the futures. The excess would be the arbitrage profit.

These arbitrage processes are illustrated by Figures 13.2 and 13.3. They would tend to bring the futures (or forward) price into line with the synthetic price. In the first case, the sale of futures would tend to reduce the futures price towards the price of the synthetic forward. Simultaneously, the purchase of spot sterling would tend to raise the spot price, with the consequence that more dollars need to be borrowed. So the ratio of dollars to be repaid to pounds received would rise; in other words, the price of sterling provided by the synthetic would rise. So the actual futures price would fall and the synthetic price rise, and the two would tend to equality, at which point there would be no further arbitrage profits available (transactions costs may prevent complete equality, a point that will be returned to). There may also be effects on the two interest rates; again, such effects would tend to bring about equality between the 2 prices. In the second case described above (underpriced futures or forwards and relatively overpriced synthetics), the opposite transactions would take place and tend to restore equality between the two prices.

FIGURE 13.2   Long synthetic and short forward (or futures)

```
Deposit £  ─────────▶  Receive £          Sell £ forward
      ▲                                   (or via futures)
      │                                          │
      │ Buy                                      │
      │ £ spot                                   │
      │                                          ▼
Borrow $  ─────────▶  Repay $          Receive $ forward
                                          (or via futures)
Synthetic long forward to buy £       Short forward (or futures) to sell £
```

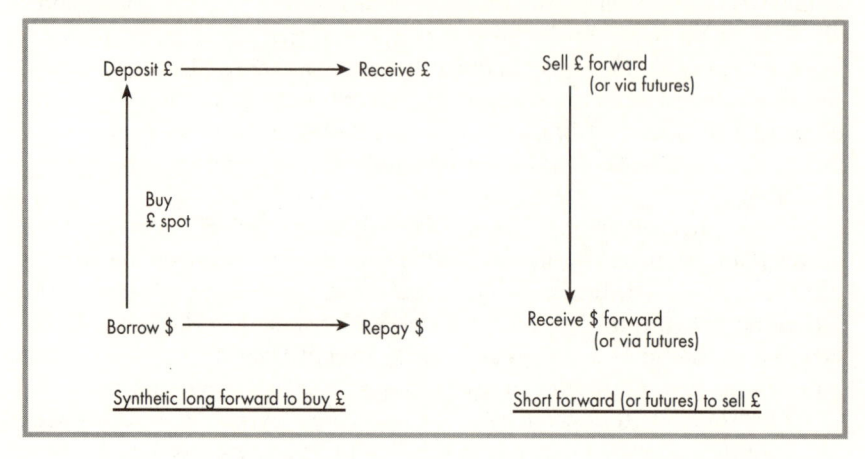

FIGURE 13.3   Short synthetic and long forward (or futures)

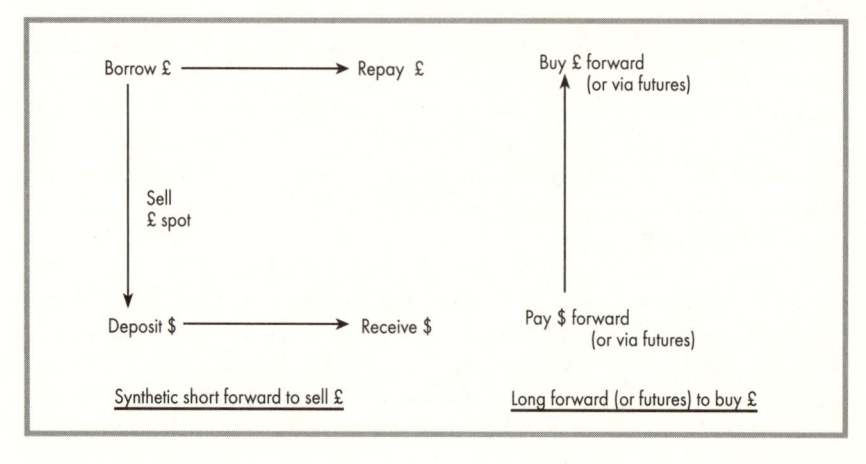

```
Borrow £  ─────────▶  Repay £          Buy £ forward
      │                                   (or via futures)
      │                                          ▲
      │ Sell                                     │
      │ £ spot                                   │
      ▼                                          │
Deposit $  ─────────▶  Receive $         Pay $ forward
                                          (or via futures)
Synthetic short forward to sell £     Long forward (or futures) to buy £
```

Interest rate parity

Equality between the synthetic forward price and the actual forward (or futures) price is often referred to as interest rate parity. An alternative way of looking at the relationship is in terms of equality between the forward premium or discount on the one hand and the difference between the 2 interest rates on the other. The premium or discount offsets the difference in interest rates. For example, if sterling yields the higher interest rate it would trade at a discount to the US dollar. This means that the forward (futures) price of sterling would be below the spot price so that, from the perspective of dollar-based traders, there would be a guaranteed capital loss from holding sterling that matched the additional interest from sterling deposits. Conversely, if sterling interest rates are below US dollar rates, sterling should trade at a premium in the forward and futures markets, i.e. the forward (futures) price of sterling would be greater than the spot price so that there is a capital gain that compensates for the lower interest returns. Seen from this perspective, the interest rate parity relationship can be described by the following equation:

$$\frac{R_\$ - R_£}{1 + R_£} = \frac{F - S}{S}$$

where $R_\$$ is the (euro-)dollar interest rate for the period to the maturity of the forward or futures contract, $R_£$ is the (euro-)sterling interest rate for the same period, F is the forward or futures price of sterling, and S is the spot price of sterling.

More generally, this can be expressed as:

$$\frac{R_B - R_F}{1 + R_F} = \frac{F - S}{S}$$

where R_B is the base currency (eurocurrency) interest rate, R_F the foreign (euro-) currency interest rate, F the forward or futures price of the foreign currency in units of the base currency, and S is the spot price of the foreign currency. The point about the prices of the foreign currency being in units of the base currency is significant. The equation as expressed relates to a direct price quotation, i.e. the number of units of the home currency per unit of the foreign currency. The United States uses the direct quote system against sterling (but not against most other currencies) and hence the formulations above are appropriate.

If a country uses the indirect quote system, i.e. number of units of the foreign currency per unit of the home currency (as the United Kingdom does), the equation needs to be rewritten as:

$$\frac{R_F - R_B}{1 + R_B} = \frac{F - S}{S}$$

334 • FORWARDS AND FUTURES

In the case of the US dollar/sterling rate, this becomes:

$$\frac{R_\$ - R_£}{1 + R_£} = \frac{F - S}{S}$$

It is to be noted that this is identical to the specific form of the equation when viewed from the US perspective. This is to be expected since both quote the rate as US dollars per pound sterling and the actual rate is the same for both countries; see Figure 13.4.

The interest rate parity relationship can alternatively be expressed as:

$$F = \frac{(1 + R^B)}{(1 + R_F)} \cdot S$$

for direct price quotes (units of home currency per unit of foreign currency), and:

$$F = \frac{(1 + R^F)}{(1 + R_B)} \cdot S$$

for indirect price quotes (units of foreign currency per unit of base currency).

FIGURE 13.4   Covered interest arbitrage

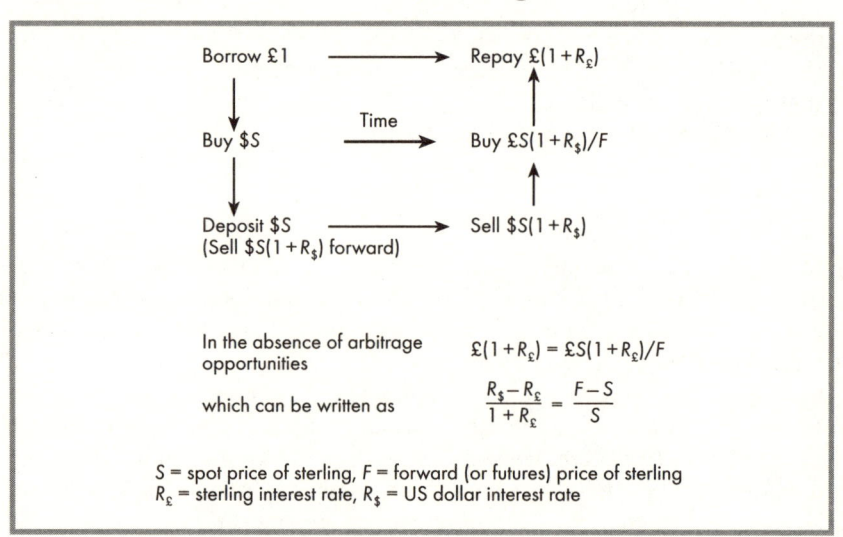

```
Borrow £1  ──────────►  Repay £(1+R_£)
   │                         ▲
   ▼          Time           │
Buy $S     ──────────►  Buy £S(1+R_$)/F
   │                         ▲
   ▼                         │
Deposit $S ──────────►  Sell $S(1+R_$)
(Sell $S(1+R_$) forward)
```

In the absence of arbitrage opportunities $£(1+R_£) = £S(1+R_\$)/F$

which can be written as $\dfrac{R_\$ - R_£}{1 + R_£} = \dfrac{F - S}{S}$

S = spot price of sterling, F = forward (or futures) price of sterling
$R_£$ = sterling interest rate, $R_\$$ = US dollar interest rate

The significance of bid–offer spreads

The gross returns from arbitrage must exceed transactions costs, otherwise arbitrage would not occur. In ascertaining the synthetic forward price, account must be taken of the fact that currency is bought at an offer and sold at a bid price (and that the offer price is higher than the bid price). Likewise, money is borrowed at the offer (high) interest rate and deposited at the bid (low) rate. As a result, synthetic long and short positions have different prices. Specifically, synthetic purchases will be at a relatively high price and synthetic sales at a lower price. The difference between the prices will reflect the bid–offer spreads on currencies and interest rates. The following activities illustrate covered interest arbitrage and the effects of bid–offer spreads.

ACTIVITY 13.1

A UK company has been invoiced in Deutschmarks and has been quoted a forward exchange rate of DM2.8400/£. The following data is available:

Spot exchange rate: DM2.8713–2.8703

Three-month interest rates:

DM3.625–3.5% p.a.
£7.5–7.375% p.a.

Should the company accept the forward exchange rate of DM2.8400/£? Would the answer be different if the company were due to receive, rather than pay, Deutschmarks?

Answer
The interest rate parity equation can be expressed as:

$$\frac{R_{DM} - R_£}{1 + R_£} = \frac{F - S}{S}$$

If the UK company is buying Deutschmarks, the forward price would be expected to be as given by F in the following calculation:

$$\frac{0.00875 - 0.01875}{1.01875} = \frac{F - 2.8703}{2.8703}$$

F = 2.8421

The company should reject the offer of a forward rate of DM2.8400/£ since it could expect to receive DM2.8421 for each pound.

If the company were due to be selling, rather than buying, Deutschmarks the forward exchange rate to be expected would be given by the following calculation:

$$\frac{0.0090625 - 0.0184375}{1.0184375} = \frac{F - 2.8713}{2.8713}$$

$F = 2.8449$

The company should accept the forward rate of DM2.8400 per £1 since it involves giving up fewer Deutschmarks for each pound than the forward rate of DM2.8449/£, which is the rate that would normally be expected.

ACTIVITY 13.2

The spot DM/£ exchange rate is £1 = DM2.5000–2.4990. Six-month interest rates are:

DM   £
$7\frac{7}{8}$–8% p.a. $5\frac{7}{8}$–6% p.a.

(a) Within what range should the six-month forward exchange rate fall?
(b) If a 1% rise in sterling interest rates causes a DM0.1 rise in the spot price of the pound, what should happen to the forward price of the pound?

Answer
(a) Borrow DM, sell DM, deposit £, buy DM forward:

$$\frac{0.04 - 0.029375}{1.029375} = \frac{F - 2.5}{2.5}$$

$(0.010322 \times 2.5) + 2.5 = F = 2.5258$

Borrow £, buy DM, deposit DM, sell DM forward:

$$\frac{0.039375 - 0.03}{1.03} = \frac{F - 2.499}{2.499}$$

$(0.009102 \times 2.499) + 2.499 = F = 2.5217$

The range is DM2.5258–DM2.5217/£

(b) The spot exchange rate becomes £1 = DM2.6000–2.5990 with interest rates at:

DM   £
$7\frac{7}{8}$–8% p.a. $6\frac{7}{8}$–7% p.a.

Borrow DM, sell DM, deposit £, buy DM forward:

$$\frac{0.04 - 0.034375}{1.034375} = \frac{F - 2.6}{2.6}$$

$$(0.005438 \times 2.6) + 2.6 = F = 2.6141$$

Borrow £, buy DM, deposit DM, sell DM forward:

$$\frac{0.039375 - 0.035}{1.035} = \frac{F - 2.599}{2.599}$$

$$(0.004227 \times 2.599) + 2.599 = F = 2.61$$

The new range should be DM2.6141–DM2.61/£

ACTIVITY 13.3

$ 12–11⅞% p.a. (for one-month money)
£ 6⅛–6% p.a. (for one-month money)
£/$ spot $1.7990–1.8000

Calculate the no-arbitrage range of futures prices for contracts maturing in one month. If the futures were trading at £1 = $1.82, how could an arbitrage profit be made?

Answer
Borrow $, buy £, invest £, sell £ futures:

$$\frac{0.01 - 0.005}{1.005} = \frac{F - 1.8000}{1.8000}$$

$$\left[\frac{0.005}{1.005} \times 1.8 \right] + 1.8 = F = 1.8090$$

Borrow £, sell £, invest $, buy £ futures:

$$\frac{0.0099 - 0.0051}{1.0051} = \frac{F - 1.7990}{1.7990}$$

$$\left[\left(\frac{0.0099 - 0.0051}{1.0051} \right) \times 1.7990 \right] + 1.7990 = F = 1.8076$$

At a price of £1 = $1.82, the sterling currency futures would be overpriced. The arbitrage strategy would therefore involve selling futures. So the appropriate arbitrage is:

borrow $, buy £, invest £, sell £ futures

Example 13.2

Using forwards to restructure debts

A company has purchased equipment from an American firm for $6,000,000, payable in 4 annual instalments. The first instalment is payable immediately. The US company allows credit at 6% p.a. The purchaser, whose revenues are in sterling, is at risk from an appreciation of the US dollar against sterling. The purchaser shops around for forward contracts and finds that the UK subsidiary of a US bank is prepared to offer one-, two- and three-year forward contracts at £1 = $1.47, £1 = $1.44 and £1 = $1.41 respectively. The spot rate is £1 = $1.50. The purchaser agrees to buy forward dollars as follows:

1 year hence $1,590,000 for £1,081,632
2 years hence $1,685,400 for £1,170,416
3 years hence $1,786,524 for £1,267,038

The future sterling cash flows are thus predetermined and exchange rate risk is eliminated. Effectively, the 6% p.a. dollar liability is converted to a sterling liability of about 8% p.a.

Example 13.3

A company wishes to borrow 10 million Finnish markka for 2 years, but can only borrow on a six-month floating rate basis. Forward contracts can be used to create a liability on a fixed rate basis.

The company borrows 2 million eurodollars for 2 years at 6% p.a. The spot exchange rate is $1 = 5 markka and the two-year forward rate is $1 = 5.10 markka. The company buys 10 million markka spot and agrees to a forward sale of markka as follows:

2 years hence   11,460,720 markka for $2,247,200

To repay the 2 million eurodollar loan, US$2,247,200 is required. The company has guaranteed that 11,460,720 markka will be required at the end of the 2 years. This sum is equivalent to a fixed annual rate of about 7% on the initial 10 million markka.

CURRENCY FUTURES

A currency futures contract provides a simultaneous right and obligation to buy or sell on a specific future date a standard amount of a particular currency at a price that is known at the time of entering the contract. These commitments are tradable. A contract can be closed out (i.e. cancelled) by buying or selling an opposite contract. If a futures contract is bought, that contract can be closed out by means of selling another contract, the 2 contracts cancelling each other out.

It is desirable that the markets in such contracts are liquid so as to ensure easy trading conditions. Financial futures contracts are highly standardised so as to enhance the quantities of each contract and thereby generate market liquidity. The contracts traded on financial futures exchanges have a limited number of maturity dates each year. The contract sizes are also standard; e.g. for sterling currency contracts they are £62,500 on the Chicago Mercantile Exchange (CME). This standardisation limits the number of different contracts available and correspondingly increases the volume traded in each case.

HEDGING CURRENCY RISK WITH FUTURES

Sterling futures will be discussed in the following exposition. Fluctuations in exchange rates produce risk. Suppose a UK exporter sells goods to a US importer and the transaction is priced in US dollars. The British exporter is thus due to receive a sum of US dollars some time after the transaction is agreed upon. The exporter is then exposed to foreign exchange risk. A fall in the value of the US dollar relative to the pound sterling would reduce the sterling value of the receipts. This would reduce the profitability of the exports, and perhaps even render them loss making. If the exporter wishes to avoid such a risk he can hedge. By hedging with financial futures he seeks to guarantee the rate of exchange at which he will buy the sterling. He wants to know in advance how much he will receive in terms of sterling. The guaranteed exchange rate might be less favourable than the current rate, but at least he is free of the risk that it might be so unfavourable as to render the sale unprofitable.

A hedger transfers his risk. If he buys futures, someone else must sell them, i.e. his acquisition of the simultaneous right and obligation to buy currency on a specified date in the future at a price agreed upon in the present is matched by another user's right and obligation to sell that currency at that date and price. In the above example, the risk that the US dollar may fall in value is transferred to the seller of sterling futures. If the dollar falls (and hence sterling rises against the dollar), this seller finds that he has committed himself to selling sterling at a price that is lower than the spot rate available at the time that the currency actually changes hands. The seller of sterling futures would be either a hedger wanting to avoid the opposite risk – i.e. a rise in the US dollar relative to sterling – or a futures trader willing to take on the risk in the expectation of making a profit.

In Example 13.4 it is assumed that a British exporter anticipates receipt of $1 million on 1 May. The sale of goods is agreed upon on 3 February and the exporter wants to hedge against the risk that the dollar will depreciate against the pound before 1 May, thus reducing the sterling value of the dollar receipts. The exporter might actually anticipate a fall in the dollar or might simply want to insure against the possibility of a weakening of the dollar. In either case the exporter could hedge by buying sterling futures.

Example 13.4

Cash market

Futures market

3 February
Exporter anticipates receipt of $1 million on 1 May. The spot exchange rate is £1 = $1.50 ($1 million = £666,666).

Buys 10 June sterling futures contracts, at £62,500 per contract, at an exchange rate of £1 = $1.50. Total value is £625,000, notionally committing the exporter to a payment of $937,500 for £625,000.

1 May
The dollar has fallen so that the exchange rate stands at £1 = $1.60. The sterling value of the $1 million is now £625,000.

Sells 10 June sterling futures contracts at £1 = $1.60. This gives the exporter the notional right to the receipt of $1,000,000 (625,000 × 1.60) in exchange for £625,000.

Loss is £666,666 – £625,000 = £41,666 ($66,666).

Profit is $62,500 ($1,000,000 – $937,500).

The loss in the cash market, arising from the weakening of the dollar, is largely offset by the profit in the futures market. The offset is not perfect since the £666,666 in the cash market is coupled with only £625,000 in the futures market. Such a mismatch arises from the denomination of sterling futures contracts in units of £62,500 – perfect matching is impossible. Fortunately, there is no change in basis. The exchange rate in the futures market moves in line with that in the cash market, and is indeed equal to it.

The exchange rate for futures need not be equal to, or move to the same extent as, the spot exchange rate. If the spot and futures rates change by different amounts, there is a change in basis and a degree of imperfection enters the hedge. This possibility is illustrated by Example 13.5, which differs from Example 13.4 only in the assumption that the rate of exchange for the June sterling futures moves to £1 = $1.58 rather than £1 = $1.60. Basis thus changes from zero to $0.02 and, as a result, the hedge is imperfect.

The change in basis results in a net loss of $16,666 ($66,666 – $50,000). The hedge is only partially successful. The hedger replaces outright risk with basis risk and consequently replaces a loss of $66,666 with a loss of $16,666.

Example 13.5

Cash market

3 February
Exporter anticipates receipt of $1 million on 1 May. The spot exchange rate is £1 = $1.50 ($1 million = £666,666).

1 May
The dollar has fallen so that the exchange rate stands at £1 = $1.60. The sterling value of the $1 million is now $625,000.

Loss is £666,666 – £625,000 = £41,666 ($66,666).

Futures market

Buys 10 June sterling futures contracts at an exchange rate of £1 = $1.50. Notionally $937,500 is to be paid for £625,000.

Sells 10 June sterling futures contracts at £1 = $1.58. This yields $987,500 (625,000 × 1.58) in exchange for £625,000.

Profit is $50,000 ($987,500–$937,500).

342 ● **FORWARDS AND FUTURES**

> ### ACTIVITY 13.4
>
> *International asset reallocation*
> A UK fund manager decides to increase exposure to the US stock market at the expense of UK equity investment. It is desired that £1 million of exposure be reallocated immediately with stock selection (for both sales and purchases) to take place during the following 2 weeks. It is 20 March and the current price data include:
>
> > June FTSE 100 futures = 2500
> > $/£ exchange rate = $2.00/£1
> > June S&P 500 futures = 200
>
> Design a strategy that might be followed and calculate the numbers of futures contracts involved.

Answer
The UK equity exposure is reduced by selling FTSE 100 futures. The US stock exposure is increased by buying S&P 500 futures. The US dollar currency exposure implicit in a US stock holding is obtained by selling sterling currency futures. The futures positions are progressively closed out as the cash market transactions take place.

Numbers of futures contracts

£1,000,000/(£25 × 2500) = 16 FTSE 100 *futures contracts*
£1,000,000/£62,500 = 16 *sterling currency futures contracts*
$2,000,000/($500 × 200) = 20 S&P 500 *futures contracts*

The 'guaranteed' exchange rate

The exchange rate that a hedger obtains will lie between the spot rate and the futures rate, and will be dependent upon the timing of closing out. If the futures position is closed out immediately after being opened, the exchange rate obtained will be the initial spot rate, e.g. £1 = $1.50. If the contract is held to maturity, the rate obtained will be the futures rate ruling on the date of entering the contract, e.g. £1 = $1.485. Closing out on an intermediate date would attain an exchange rate between these 2 extremes, as indicated by Figure 13.5. The exchange rate obtained is a function of time. So, for example, if the futures contract is agreed at time t and closed out after 4 months, the exchange rate obtained might be £1 = $1.49.

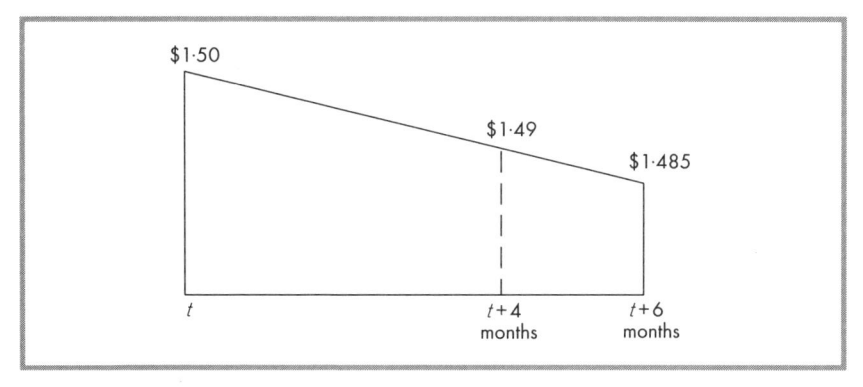

FIGURE 13.5 Variation of the effective exchange rate with time

```
$1·50
         $1·49
                $1·485


 t       t+4    t+6
         months months
```

The variation of the realised exchange rate with the passage of time can be explained in terms of changes in basis. Basis is initially $0.015 ($1.50 – $1.485), but after 6 months it will have eroded to zero: at maturity of a contract the futures and spot prices are identical. The difference between the spot and futures prices can be regarded as the rate of depreciation/appreciation required to offset the interest rate differential. As the time period shortens, the cash value of the interest rate differential falls proportionately and the corresponding depreciation/appreciation declines to match. So with just 2 months to maturity the cash value of a 2% p.a. interest rate differential is one-third its level when 6 months remained and, correspondingly, the depreciation prior to maturity is $0.005 rather than the original $0.015.

Figure 13.6 shows that basis changes over time, beginning at $0.015 and declining to zero. This change in basis renders hedging imperfect; and the greater the period of time that elapses, the more imperfect is the hedge. A contract that is closed out very quickly would entail little change in basis, the hedge would be nearly perfect and the exchange rate guaranteed would be very close to the spot rate when the contract was agreed. The more time that elapses before closing out, the greater is the change in basis and the larger is the divergence between the realised exchange rate and the spot rate ruling when the contract was entered into, as is illustrated by Figure 13.5.

Suppose, for example, that the spot exchange rate remained at $1.50 for the whole six-month period. As the futures price converged towards the spot price, a buyer of the futures contract would receive variation margin payments. These receipts would be proportionate to the period of time that elapsed, amounting to virtually zero after one day but to $0.015 at expiry. Sterling would be purchased at $1.50, but this would be offset by variation margin receipts varying from near zero after one day, so that the effective purchase price is $1.50, to $0.015 at expiry, so that the effective purchase price is $1.485 ($1.50 – $0.015); see Figure 13.6.

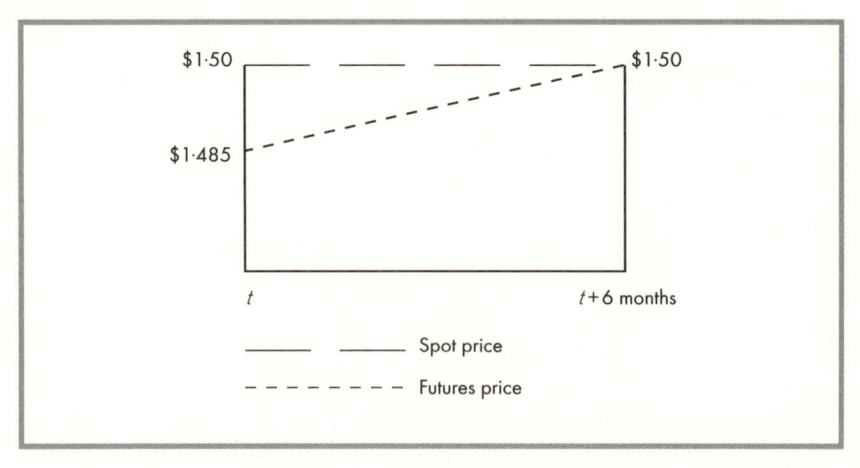

FIGURE 13.6   Convergence of the futures price and spot price

(Chart: Spot price constant at $1·50 from t to t+6 months; Futures price rising from $1·485 at t to $1·50 at t+6 months.)

— Spot price
- - - - Futures price

The foregoing might give the impression that if a hedger knows the date upon which the futures position will be closed out, he knows by how much basis will have changed and can take this into account when designing the hedging strategy. He would appear to lock in a known profit or loss. However, basis would be deflected from the path suggested by the figures if the interest rate differential were to change. For example, if at the date $t + 4$ months the interest rate differential had doubled to 4% p.a., then the basis would be $0.01 rather than $0.005. So if basis risk were to be defined in terms of the possibility of unexpected (i.e. excluding the predictable element) changes in basis, it can be seen to emanate from the possibility of changes in the interest rate differential between the 2 currencies concerned.

The 'guaranteed' exchange rate is not dependent on constancy of the spot rate. Changes in the spot rate would tend to be compensated for by parallel changes in the futures exchange rate.

Futures hedge ratio

When using currency futures, the appropriate hedge ratio is the generic one applicable to all futures:

$$H = \rho \sigma_S / \sigma_F$$

where H is the hedge ratio, ρ the coefficient of correlation between changes in the spot price and changes in the futures price, σ_S is the standard deviation of changes in the spot price, and σ_F is the standard deviation of changes in the futures price.

The size of the exposure (e.g. DM10 million) should be divided by the size of the futures contract (DM125,000) and the result (80 contracts) multiplied by the hedge ratio. When an exposure in a currency is hedged with futures on the same currency, the hedge ratio should be close to one. However, when an exposure in one currency (e.g. Danish krone) is hedged with futures on another currency (such as Deutschmarks), the coefficient of correlation would be less than one and the two standard deviations would not be equal. So the application of the hedge ratio would be particularly important when cross hedging.

Table 13.2 shows some currency futures data. All of these contracts are traded on the IMM (International Monetary Market, part of the Chicago Mercantile Exchange). Sizes of contracts are also shown, e.g. the Deutschmark contracts are each for DM125,000. The prices quoted are on a direct basis, i.e. the price of a unit of the foreign currency in US dollars (e.g. $0.6936 per DM, $1.5322 per £). In the case of the Japanese yen, the quote is in US dollars per 100 yen.

A latest figure is presented rather than a closing figure because the contracts were still being traded when the *Financial Times* went to press. Otherwise, the columns have the same meanings as for other futures contracts (the final 2 columns being the estimated number of contracts traded the previous day and the open interest, which is the number of contracts outstanding at the close of business on the previous day).

Table 13.2 Currency futures

	Open	Latest	Change	High	Low	Estimated volume	Open interest
■ Deutschmark futures (IMM) DM125,000 per DM
Dec	0.6936	0.6891	−0.0016	0.6910	0.6882	12,218	40,921
Mar	0.6955	0.6921	−0.0016	0.6933	0.6912	21,797	40,131
Jun	0.6971	–	–	–	–	39	2,087
■ Swiss franc futures (IMM) SFr 125,000 per SFr
Dec	0.8569	0.8499	−0.0013	0.8514	0.8481	6,192	23,854
Mar	0.8640	0.8571	−0.0016	0.8588	0.8555	13,818	30,134
Jun	0.8640	0.8651	−0.0010	0.8651	0.8638	129	729
■ Japanese yen futures (IMM) Y12.5 per Y100
Dec	0.9899	0.9837	+0.0008	0.9847	0.9830	10,361	34,487
Mar	1.0028	0.9971	+0.0008	0.9982	0.9965	20,888	43,165
Jun	1.0092	1.0095	+0.0007	1.0095	1.0092	3	635
■ Sterling futures (IMM) £62,500 per £
Dec	1.5322	1.5322	+0.0010	1.5328	1.5302	6,438	34,116
Mar	1.5318	1.5298	+0.0010	1.5306	1.5280	9,203	31,917
Jun	–	–	–	–	–	8	18

Source: *Financial Times*, 14 December 1995.

A COMPARISON OF FUTURES AND FORWARDS

Futures and forwards are similar instruments whose prices tend to be very close. There are, nonetheless, important differences. Forwards are actual commitments to future transactions, whereas futures are notional commitments. Forward contracts are used to effect the end transaction; the parties to the forward contract are the same as the parties to the subsequent exchange of currencies. Futures rarely go to the point of delivery of the underlying financial instrument and, if they do, the counterparties involved are not the same as the counterparties to the original futures deal. Futures are financial instruments that are independent of the underlying position, albeit with prices that normally correlate with those of the underlying instrument. Futures positions are normally closed out by taking an opposite futures position (e.g. someone who initially sells closes out the short position by buying an equal number of contracts of the same maturity as those sold).

Secondly, forwards are over-the-counter (OTC) instruments whereas futures are exchange traded. OTC products take the form of an agreement between two parties (e.g. the client and a bank). This agreement is not visible to other parties – the market is not transparent. This lack of transparency means that it is not possible to know the prices at which others are transacting. Different clients may obtain different prices from the banks. Futures markets are transparent. Everyone can see the prices available. The most transparent markets are the face-to-face markets in which all transactors occupy the same trading area (known as a pit). Everyone can see what quantities are being traded and at what prices. Everyone can obtain the same prices: there is no discrimination between different transactors.

Thirdly, forwards can be tailor-made to the specific requirements of a client. The client can specify dates and amounts to be transacted. Futures are highly standardised. Each futures contract relates to a standard quantity of the underlying instrument. Furthermore, only a limited number of maturity dates are available at any time. A high degree of standardisation is necessary for market liquidity, i.e. for ensuring that the volumes traded are sufficiently high for buyers and sellers to experience no difficulty in conducting their desired transactions. If the standardisation were less, for example, through a greater number of maturity dates or a variety of contract sizes, the number of different contracts would be greater and each variety of contract might experience few and infrequent trades. Such inadequate liquidity could reduce the ability of users, such as hedgers, to establish and subsequently close out futures positions.

Fourthly, the profit or loss from a forward is realised, in its entirety, when the contract matures. Profits and losses on a futures contract are realised on a daily basis (via the marking to market process).

The relationship between futures and forward prices

It is tempting to think that since both futures and forward prices of currency are determined by the same process – covered interest arbitrage – they should be equal. However, there is reason to believe that they may not be equal. This arises from one of the key differences between futures and forwards: futures are marked to market, whereas all of the profits or losses from a forward contract are incurred on the maturity date of the contract.

The daily cash flows that arise from the marking to market will entail interest payments or receipts. If interest rates on receipts do not differ systematically from interest rates on payments, the marking to market should not render futures any more or less attractive than forward contracts, and hence should not imply any difference between futures and forward prices. The conclusion that futures and forward prices should be equal would cease to hold if there were a correlation between the base currency (normally US dollar) interest rate and the futures price.

A correlation between the futures price and the interest on the daily cash flows could mean that inflows and outflows have a consistent tendency to entail different interest rates. There tends to be a negative correlation between US dollar interest rates and the prices of non-US dollar currencies (and hence futures on those currencies). A rise in the US dollar interest rate tends to strengthen the US dollar against other currencies, and hence weaken other currencies relative to the dollar. So a rise in the US dollar interest rate would be associated with falling currency futures prices (note that this process is different from the interest rate parity relationship and the effect may be somewhat reduced by the restoration of interest rate parity).

A consequence of this negative correlation is that someone with a long position in currency futures would have to make payments when (US dollar) interest rates are relatively high, but would receive money when interest rates are low. So marking to market is to the disadvantage of the buyer of futures and would therefore tend to reduce demand.

The seller of futures would receive money when interest rates are high and pay when rates are relatively low. So marking to market benefits those with short futures positions and would therefore tend to encourage people to sell futures. The reduction of demand and enhancement of supply would tend to cause futures prices to fall below the corresponding forward prices. However, the empirical evidence suggests that if there is such an effect it is very small.

THE ROLE OF THE CORPORATE TREASURER

Traditionally corporate treasurers have had the function of ensuring sources of funds to finance both the day-to-day running costs of a business and its longer-term cash flow requirements. They have also performed the role of investing any surplus funds with a view to maximising returns subject to the constraints of the time span involved and the acceptable level of risk.

Since the 1970s risk management has become part of the treasury function, in particular with respect to exchange rate and interest rate risk. Corporate treasurers are now expected to protect cash flows, assets, and liabilities from adverse currency and interest rate movements.

The nature of currency risk

Exchange rate risk, or exposure, is often divided into three types. These are transactions exposure, translation (or accounting) exposure, and economic exposure.

Transactions exposure relates to possible losses on known future cash flows arising from exchange rate movements. An importer who has been invoiced in a foreign currency would lose if that foreign currency rose relative to the domestic currency. Take the example of a British company invoiced in euros. The British company would face a future payment in euro without knowing how much those euros will cost in pounds. If the euro were to become more expensive in terms of pounds sterling the cost of the imports would rise. Since the future exchange rate is uncertain the sterling cost of the imports is uncertain. The British company is exposed to currency risk.

The uncertainty about the sterling cost of the imports poses problems for the British company. If the imports are to be used in the production of goods for the export market, problems would arise in relation to the pricing of the exports. Uncertainty about the euro cost of imported components or materials makes it difficult to quote a price in sterling to potential customers. A rise in the euro against the pound could cause import costs to rise to the point that the exports become loss making at the quoted sterling prices. The problem is further compounded if the export prices are quoted in a foreign currency. The determination of the appropriate US dollar prices is complicated by the possibility of adverse movements in the sterling/US dollar exchange rate.

Uncertainty as to the sterling value of export revenues in foreign currency provides another example of transactions exposure. A fall in the value of the US dollar relative to the pound sterling could turn a profitable dollar priced export into a loss-making one. If the US dollar becomes less valuable in terms of the pound then dollar receipts from exports would become less valuable. Such a fall in the sterling value of US dollar receipts would reduce the profitability of the exports, perhaps even causing them to be loss making.

Transactions exposure relates to any known or foreseeable future cash flow whose value might be adversely affected by exchange rate movements. As well as foreign currency cash flows arising from international trade, transactions exposure would arise from international investment. The purchase of productive capacity overseas, whether by the takeover of an existing enterprise or by the establishment of a newly created subsidiary, would require foreign currency. The cost of the overseas investment would increase if the price of the foreign currency rose relative to the currency of the home country.

Income flows from overseas investment would also be vulnerable to exchange rate movements. Profits generated by a foreign subsidiary would normally be in the respective foreign currency. A fall in the value of that currency would reduce the domestic currency value of the profits repatriated from the subsidiary. The returns from portfolio investment would also be subject to currency risk. Dividends from shareholdings in foreign companies would be in the foreign currency and hence would be vulnerable to a fall in the value of the currency. The situation would be similar in respect of interest earnings on bank deposits in foreign currencies. Income from intellectual property rights, such as royalties, could also be subject to exhange rate exposure. Any payments due to be made in foreign currencies to overseas resident organisations or individuals would also be subject to exchange rate risk.

Translation exposure refers to changes in value of foreign assets and liabilities (rather than the cash flows from those assets and liabilities). This relates to both physical assets, such as plant and premises, and to financial instruments such as shares, bonds and deposits. Translation exposure is alternatively known as accounting exposure, in accounting terms it relates to balance sheet items.

It is sometimes argued that translation exposure is unimportant and that firms should not attempt to hedge this form of exchange rate risk. The reasoning underlying this view is that the exchange rate movement, relative to the currency of the home country, does not reduce the foreign currency profitability of the overseas investment. The asset remains intact as a going concern and the exchange rate change does not hinder the economic peformance of the foreign investment.

However, there are two situations in which translation gains or losses can impact on the performance of the domestic company that owns the overseas investment. First, if there is an intention to sell the foreign investment an adverse movement in the exchange rate would reduce the domestic currency value of the prospective foreign currency sale receipts. Secondly, a fall in the domestic currency value of a foreign asset could adversely affect the terms on which new capital could be raised (or the ability to raise new capital at all).

Prospective lenders would look at the balance sheet of a company seeking to borrow from the money or capital markets. Currency movements could reduce the balance sheet value of foreign currency assets and/or increase the balance sheet value of foreign currency liabilities when those foreign currency assets and liabilities are translated into home currency terms for the balance sheet, The balance sheet would appear weaker and in consequence any loan might seem to be riskier. The greater perceived risk could cause lenders to require higher interest rates on bank loans or bonds, or to offer lower prices in the event of a share issue.

Economic exposure

Economic exposure is a less precise concept than transactions and translation exposure. Consequently it is more difficult to measure, and the risks are more difficult to manage. It encompasses any effect of exchange rate movements on potential future cash flows. The measurement and risk management problems posed by economic exposure can be appreciated by observing that a firm that does not buy imports, does not export and has no foreign currency assets or liabilities may be subject to considerable economic exposure.

Economic exposure can be illustrated by an indication of some of the possible sources of risk. One medium for economic exposure would be through exchange rate impacts on consumer demand. An exchange rate movement that makes holidays abroad cheaper would have an adverse effect on the domestic holiday industry. A currency movement that causes a fall in the price of imported brandy might adversely affect the scotch whisky industry if some consumers switch from whisky to brandy as a result of the price change.

A related source of economic exposure concerns the impact of exchange rate movements on the competitiveness of domestic rivals. If a company has a competitor that imports components or materials, an exchange rate movement that reduces the costs of those imports would give the competitor a cost advantage. A firm may not import any material, components or services itself but if it faces competition from imports or from producers who use imported inputs, then exchange rate changes could affect the firm's sales by means of an effect on the prices that those competitors offer to customers.

Economic exposure could also arise from potential effects of exchange rate movements on the prices charged by a firm's suppliers. If suppliers use imports and an exchange rate movement causes those import prices to rise, the suppliers may pass on the higher costs to their customers. So a firm that does not directly import may suffer the effects of higher import prices indirectly through its suppliers.

These forms of economic exposure are not exclusive. There are many ways in which future currency price changes can affect the cash flows of a company. Economic exposure is problematical for organisations, but cannot be easily measured or managed.

Measuring currency exposure

Measuring transactions exposure is not simply a matter of adding up all the money values of future foreign currency cash flows. A number of possible complications need to be considered.

There is the possibility of currency matching. If an enterprise has simultaneous exports and imports priced in Japanese yen, the net exposure will be the difference between the two cash flows rather than their sum. There may not only be matching in a single currency but also matching via parallel currencies. Some currencies are strongly linked such that they move up and down together. Sometimes the link is formalised, for example the Belgian franc and the Dutch guilder within the exchange rate mechanism of the European Monetary System. Sometimes the link arises from close trading ties (in which case it will be less than perfect), for example the US dollar and the Canadian dollar. Cash inflows in one of the pairing currencies can be offset against cash outflows in the other. An exchange rate movement that causes a loss in one of the currencies would tend to provide an offsetting profit in the other.

The measure of currency exposure would need to be reduced to reflect currency matching, whether it is direct or via parallel currencies. The measure may also need to be reduced to reflect the effects of diversification. Just as the holding of a diversified portfolio of shares is less risky than holding just one share, exposure to a range of different currencies is likely to entail less risk than exposure to a single currency. There will be a tendency for losses on some currencies to be offset by profits on others. Such risk reduction by diversification should be reflected in a reduced measure of currency risk.

Not only does diversification affect the extent of risk, so does the volatility of the currencies concerned. Exposure to volatile currencies is more risky than exposure to stable currencies. To reflect this, as well as the other influences mentioned above, a form of composite measure of risk is necessary. One such measure is VAR (Value At Risk). This involves estimating a distribution of possible gains and losses, with each possible gain or loss being associated with a probability of occurrence. The standard deviation (a measure of dispersion) of the distribution can be used as the measure of currency exposure. Alternatively VAR could be measured as the value of a predetermined number of standard deviations. For example the chances of a loss exceeding two standard deviations is 2.5%. By using the value of two standard deviations as the measure of exposure a company would be stating the level of loss that has only a 2.5% chance of being exceeded. This measure of exposure could be adapted to take account of the above factors, and of any other consideration relevant to the measurement of exposure to exchange rate risk.

Risk management decisions

A corporate treasurer needs to decide on whether to hedge risk, and if so how much of it to hedge. There is also the need to decide how to hedge.

The decision as to whether to hedge would depend on a number of factors. One of those factors could be the view that the treasurer takes as to the future direction of the direction of exchange rate movement. The treasurer might attempt to forecast the movement of an exchange rate (a procedure which itself is very risky, and which has an approximately 50% likelihood of arriving at the wrong answer). If the treasurer takes the view that the exchange rate movement will be favourable, and is confident in that view (a confidence that would be in contravention of all the existing evidence on the unreliable nature of exchange rate forecasting) then the treasurer would choose not to hedge.

Not only might the treasurer take a view on the direction of the movement of an exchange rate, a view might be taken as to the future volatility of the exchange rate. Indeed a view on volatility could be taken without taking a view on the direction of movement. Taking such a view would be laudable in certain circumstances. For example there may be a government policy of maintaining a close relationship between the domestic currency and a particular foreign currency, or historical evidence might indicate little volatility in the exchange rate. If low volatility is expected the treasurer may choose not to hedge against possible future exchange rate changes. If the expectation turns out to be correct then, even if the direction of exchange rate movement is unfavourable, the extent of that movement would not be such as to cause substantial losses.

The decision as to whether to hedge could be influenced by the prospective costs of the hedging. Perhaps the most obvious example of a hedging cost is the premium to be paid for an option. An option gives the right, but not the obligation, to exchange currencies at a specified exchange rate. This feature renders options particularly suitable for hedging uncertain cash flows. Tendering for contracts in foreign currency involves uncertainty as to whether the cash flow will occur. The need to exchange currencies in the future will only arise if the tender is successful. Options are suitable for hedging any exposure that is uncertain in amount, whether it is a tender for a specific project or a foreign currency price list that will lead to an unpredictable volume of sales. The use of options involves the payment of premiums. A corporate treasurer may decide that the cost of the premiums is too high and that some, or all, of the exposure will remain unhedged. The dilemma could be especially acute when a large number of foreign currency tenders are involved, and each has a low probability of success.

Another source of hedging cost is the need to employ people with the expertise necessary to carry out this corporate treasury function. However the only way to avoid this cost is to ignore foreign exchange risk and leave currency exposure unhedged. For many firms, especially those heavily involved in international trade, ignoring foreign exchange exposure would be a very risky strategy.

How much to hedge

If a corporate treasurer has decided to hedge the next decision relates to the extent of the hedging. The view might be taken that a certain level of risk can be accepted and that only exposure in excess of the acceptable level needs to be hedged. There could be a perceived trade off between the expected benefits and costs of hedging. The optimal level of hedging might be seen as falling between the extremes of complete hedging and zero hedging. It may be the case that the treasurer merely wants a form of disaster insurance. In such a case hedging would be employed only if the success (or survival) of the firm would be significantly jeopardised by an adverse exchange rate movement.

The view might be taken that only large transactions should be hedged since the administrative, or other, costs of hedging small orders would be disproportionate to their value. Indeed the minimum size of some hedging instruments may exceed the size of some export or import orders. Another criterion could be the predictability of an exposure. If a treasurer wants to avoid the cost of buying options, the approach might be to hedge only the cash flows that can be forecast with certainty. If a future cash flow is known with certainty, it can be hedged with instruments that do not entail the payment of a premium. Such instruments include forward contracts, futures and swaps.

Some exposures have more than one dimension. A treasurer might choose to hedge some dimensions but not others. For example a British company may have borrowed Swiss francs, but no longer has any assets denominated in Swiss francs. The company has exposure both to the Swiss franc interest rate and to the exchange rate between the Swiss franc and the pound. Losses could arise both from a rise in Swiss franc interest rates and from a rise in the sterling value of Swiss francs. The treasurer could decide to hedge one dimension, say the exchange rate, whilst leaving the interest rate dimension unhedged.

Another means of avoiding complete hedging of all exposures is to leave positions unhedged until some adverse exchange rate movement has occurred. An advantage of this approach is that unnecessary hedging is avoided. If the exchange rate moves in a favourable direction the position remains unhedged. The costs of hedging are avoided and the company is able to benefit from the favourable currency movement since it is not locked into a predetermined exchange rate. A disadvantage of this strategy is that adverse currency movements could be so rapid that the treasurer does not have time to implement a hedging strategy. History indicates that large exchange rate movements tend to take place within short time intervals.

So a corporate treasurer needs to identify and measure currency risk. Then decisions need to be taken as to whether to hedge, and if so how much to hedge. If hedging is to be undertaken, the next step is to determine how to hedge.

Risk management techniques

Risk management techniques can be divided between internal and external approaches. There are a number of internal strategies that firms can use to reduce currency risk. One obvious one is to insist on pricing goods and services in the firm's home currency. Such a procedure imposes the currency risk on the trade counterparty. This could deter the counterparty from entering the trade. Exporters who insist on pricing in their own currency are likely to lose export orders since they impose exchange rate risk on their potential customers.

A popular internal technique is netting. This is used by firms with subsidiaries. Some of the subsidiaries will have inflows in currencies in which other subsidiaries will have outflows. One British-based subsidiary may receive US dollars from exports whilst another UK subsidiary needs to make payment in US dollars. The US dollar exposure of the corporation is the difference between the two exposures. It is only the difference between the two exposures that provides risk. Except for this difference the two exposures hedge each other, an exchange rate movement that causes a loss for one subsidiary will produce an offsetting gain for the other.

Another internal technique is matching. This involves a firm in seeking to match inflows and outflows in a particular currency. For example a company that needs to pay for imports in euros may choose to invoice its exports in euros. In this way the currency exposure from future payments in euros would be offset by the opposite exposure arising from the future euro receipts. The payments and receipts will hedge each other to the extent that they match in amount and timing. This could be viewed in terms of the euros received from exports being used to pay for the imports priced in euros. The exchange rate exposure that remains is the net amount that arises from mismatching between the inflows and outflows.

Even after a firm has used internal techniques, there is likely to be some exchange rate exposure remaining. The remaining exposure could be hedged by means of external techniques. These techniques employ instruments that are acquired from sources outside the firm. The instruments available include forwards, futures, options, swaps, currency accounts, and forfaiting. Forwards, futures, options and swaps have been discussed in previous chapters. Before carrying out an assessment of the relative merits of the external techniques the nature of currency accounts and forfaiting will be outlined.

Currency accounts and forfaiting

Currency accounts are bank deposits, or overdrafts, that provide an opposing exposure to that arising from expected cash flows. Expected currency payments would be hedged with currency deposits. A rise in the value of the foreign currency relative to the home currency makes the payments more expensive in the home currency, but this is offset by a rise in the home currency value of the foreign currency deposits. This can alternatively be seen in terms of the foreign currency deposit being available to meet the foreign currency payment. As soon as the import deal is agreed the company could buy the requisite currency (thereby ensuring the exchange rate) and put it on deposit. However, this does tie up funds until the payment is actually made. Those funds could have other uses, and may not even be available.

Conversely a company expecting foreign currency receipts could borrow the foreign currency with a view to repaying the debt when the money is received. The borrowed foreign currency could immediately be converted into domestic currency, thereby guaranteeing the exchange rate. The foreign currency debt would give an opposite exposure to the prospective foreign currency receipts. A decline in the value of the foreign currency would entail a fall in the value of the future receipts but this would be offset by a reduction in the value of the foreign currency liability.

Forfaiting is similar to factoring. An exporter with future foreign currency receipts sells the right to receive the money to a bank. In this way the exporting company receives money immediately. Furthermore this will be a receipt in the firm's home currency. Exchange rate risk is thus avoided.

The sum of money received in the present will be less than the projected future sum to be received. In the event that the bank can cover the exchange rate risk at little cost, and in the absence of other risks such as default risk, the difference between the sum immediately received and the future sum will be based on interest rates. The exporting company is effectively borrowing from the bank pending the future receipt of foreign currency and should expect a present sum that falls below the future sum by the amount of the interest payable.

In the presence of exchange rate risks that are difficult to hedge (such as those involving currencies that are not fully convertible), or in the presence of the risk that the foreign importer might default on the payment, the immediate sum will be reduced further. The greater the risks that the bank has to accept, the greater will be the compensation that it requires. Consequently the greater will be the difference between the future sum that the bank hopes to receive and the amount that it is willing to pay in the present. This is equivalent to charging the exporter a higher interest rate to reflect the higher risks involved.

The relative merits of external hedging techniques

A corporate treasurer intending to use external instruments to manage exchange rate risk needs to be aware of the relative advantages and disadvantages of each. The risk management operation is likely to use several of the techniques in conjunction with one another.

Currency forwards are particularly useful for exposures that are short to medium term, and whose timing is known with certainty. Although the most frequently used maturities tend to be 1, 3 and 6 months, forward contracts can be obtained for up to 5 years into the future. The market for forward foreign exchange, particularly for maturities of a year or less, is a liquid one. There is little difficulty in finding a bank to offer a contract, so long as the desired contract exhibits conventional characteristics. Conventional characteristics would include maturities of whole months. Contracts involving fractions of months, known as broken date forwards, can be more difficult to negotiate. Contracts are conventionally in large sums (millions of pounds, dollars, euros, etc). A treasurer needing to deal in tens, or even hundreds, of thousands may face difficulties.

Uncertainty as to the date on which the currency would need to be bought or sold would also pose problems. Normally forward contracts relate to a specific future date. Option date forwards allow the exchange of currency to occur between two dates, but there is a cost. The exchange rate guaranteed by an option date forward is the least favourable of the forward rates available for the future period involved. As a result the exchange rate guaranteed could be significantly inferior to the one that would have been obtained if the date had been known with certainty.

Forward contracts are problematical in cases in which there is uncertainty as to the size of the future transaction, or as to whether it will occur at all. If the currency exchange turns out to be unnecessary the corporate treasurer is left with a forward contract that must be honoured, possibly at an unfavourable exchange rate. If the treasurer enters a forward contract to buy yen on a future date, and the purchase turns out to be unnecessary, the treasurer would lose in the event of a fall in the value of the yen. The treasurer is committed to buying at a price that is higher than that at which it can be sold. The unnecessary forward contract entails a currency exposure.

Currency futures are superior to forwards in some respects, but inferior in others. One of the advantages of futures is that they allow for flexibility in timing. A futures contract can be closed out at any time. So futures may be superior to forwards when there is uncertainty as to the date on which the exchange of currencies will take place. Another relative merit of futures is that, unlike forwards, they do not tie up lines of credit from a bank. Since a forward contract increases a bank's exposure to the possibility of default by a particular customer the potential for loans to that customer, within an overall exposure limit, is reduced. A third advantage of futures, when compared to forwards, is that they can be used to hedge relatively small sums. For example, the size of a sterling futures contract on the Chicago Mercantile Exchange is £62,500. A related point is that users of futures all get the same exchange rate, irrespective of the size of their transactions.

Futures have some disadvantages in comparison to forwards. They can be subject to liquidity constraints. If a hedger needs to trade futures, either to establish a futures position or to close one out, the hedger will be unsuccessful if there is no counterparty willing to trade. A hedger cannot buy if no one is willing to sell, alternatively the hedger may have to offer an exceptionally high price in order to induce someone to sell. This problem can be significant if distant maturity futures, or particularly large numbers of contracts, are involved. Nearby (close) maturities and small numbers of contracts would not normally entail liquidity problems. One implication is that futures are most suitable for the hedging of short-term, and relatively small, exposures.

Another relative disadvantage of futures is that they can be administratively difficult. Futures are marked to market, which means that profits and losses are received and paid on a daily basis as they arise. The administration can be simplified by establishing a margin account from which payments can be made, or into which money is paid, on a daily basis. However a margin account ties up funds that could be used for other purposes. Also futures, and their operation, are more difficult to understand than forwards.

Although swaps usually entail commitments for periods ranging from 3 to 10 years, swaps with lives well in excess of 10 years have been negotiated. So swaps are particularly suitable for hedging long-term exposures. Like forwards there is no flexibility, after the swap has been agreed, as to the timing of the exchanges of currency. Also swaps pose problems if the cash flows being hedged do not continue for as long as was initially expected. The holder of the swap is committed to the future exchanges of currency. Closing out a swap can be expensive. Either the original counterparty has to be compensated, or an opposite swap has to be entered into. Whichever approach is taken, the costs will at least equal the present value of expected future losses (although there could be a receipt upon closing out if markets have moved such that the swap is expected to generate profits).

Like forwards, but unlike futures swaps involve a counterparty risk. There is a risk that the swap counterparty will default on the swap payments. Counterparty risk is a feature of OTC (Over The Counter) derivatives. OTC derivatives are negotiated directly between a bank and its customer. In the case of exchange traded derivatives, such as futures, there is a clearing house that guarantees that contracts will be honoured. (Ultimately the guarantee stems from the marking to market which ensures that losses cannot accumulate over time, they must be paid on a daily basis.)

Options differ from forwards, futures and swaps in that they do not oblige the holder to exchange currencies at the predetermined exchange rate. The holder has the right to simply ignore the option, and will do so if it becomes possible to exchange currencies at a more favourable rate than the predetermined one. An option protects the holder against an adverse movement in the exchange rate whilst preserving the ability to profit from a favourable movement. For this facility a premium has to be paid. This is another way in which options differ from forwards, futures and swaps. Options have to be paid for whatever subsequently happens to the exchange rate. Forwards, futures and swaps do not have to be paid for, cash outflows only occur in the event of exchange rate movements in a particular direction.

Options can be preferable to forwards or futures in three situations. The first situation is the one in which there is uncertainty as to whether the hedged cash flow will take place. Since an option can be simply ignored if it is not needed it is useful for such a situation. Even if it is not required for hedging an option would be exercised if it is profitable to do so, the essential point is that there is no commitment to exchange currencies at the predetermined rate whereas forwards, futures and swaps entail commitments to such an exchange of currencies.

The second situation is the one in which the corporate treasurer has a view as to the future direction of the exchange rate. If the treasurer believes that the exchange rate is more likely to move in the favourable direction than in the adverse direction, the treasurer will seek to preserve the ability to benefit from an exchange rate movement in the favourable direction. Options would be preferred to forwards or futures. Forwards and futures eliminate the possibility of profits as well as losses. If profits are thought to be more likely than losses, forwards and futures would be more likely to prevent profits than protect against losses. On balance forwards and futures would be expected to be disadvantageous. Options can provide the same protection against loss as forwards and futures without removing the facility of making profits.

The third situation is the one in which there is uncertainty as to whether competitors are hedging. The treasurer may have no view as to future exchange rate movement but could feel that it is necessary to preserve any possibility of benefiting from a favourable exchange rate movement lest competitors have not hedged. An unhedged competitor would benefit from a favourable exchange rate movement and hence gain a competitive advantage. If an importer of Australian wine has hedged with forwards and the Australian dollar falls then that importer's costs fail to fall with the Australian dollar. Unhedged competitors would benefit from the exchange rate movement. Competition could push down the price of Australian wines, undermining the profitability of the importer who had hedged with forwards.

Options are available on both OTC and exchange traded bases. OTC options generally exhibit the relative merits of forwards. They can be tailor made to the specific requirements of the customer. They can be negotiated for any amount of any currency at any predetermined exchange rate. However once negotiated they may be difficult or expensive to withdraw from, and there is a risk that providers (sellers) of the options will default on their obligations.

Exchange traded options tend to exhibit the relative merits of futures. They are standardised so users have limited choice as to currencies, amounts of currency and guaranteed exchange rates. However they can be closed out by being sold at any time (subject to buyers being found), and default risk is minimal since they are guaranteed by a clearing house.

Currency accounts, unlike the preceding instruments, involve immediacy of cash flows. This is an advantage when the cash flow is a receipt. The company borrows foreign currency against future foreign currency receipts and immediately exchanges it for domestic currency. The company has the use of the present home currency equivalent of the future foreign currency receipt. In this way the exporting company can realise payment for the exports as soon as the export deal is made.

When payment is to be made, the immediacy of the cash flow can be a disadvantage. As soon as an import deal is agreed the importing company buys foreign currency and puts it on deposit. This sum, together with the interest on it, should equal the sum required for the future payment for the imports. Hedging with instruments such as forwards or futures delays the purchase of the foreign currency until it is needed to pay for the imports. The use of a currency account ties up funds for a period during which those funds might have other uses.

Currency accounts are unsuitable if there is uncertainty as to whether a future cash flow will occur. If the cash flow fails to materialise the currency account provides a currency exposure. A currency loss could have developed on the currency account during the period until the fate of the cash flow is known. However currency accounts may provide flexibility as to timing to the extent that deposit, or borrowing, periods can be shortened or lengthened.

Forfaiting also has the advantage of providing immediacy of cash flows for exporters. An advantage that it enjoys relative to other techniques is that it provides a hedge against other risks as well as exchange rate risk. These other risks would include the risk of default by the importer. However the hedge against the various risks comes at a cost. As the risks get greater, the sum of money to be received by the exporter from the bank gets smaller. Forfaiting is only suitable when the future cash flow is expected to occur with certainty. There are likely to be difficulties arising if there is uncertainty as to the timing of the future cash flows. Forfaiting is only applicable to future receipts, it is not applicable to future payments.

CONCLUSIONS

In the case of currencies, successful forward and futures markets coexist. This coexistence is most marked in North America. Elsewhere, particularly in Europe, forward markets are predominant. A balanced coexistence might in time become the norm throughout the world since forwards and futures have their relative merits. Futures have a considerable advantage in that they allow flexibility as to the date of closing out (futures can be closed out on any trading day up to maturity), whereas forwards tend to involve a commitment to an exchange of currencies on a specific date. If there is doubt as to the timing of the cash flow being hedged, futures may be the more attractive hedging instrument. On the other hand, futures can be more complex to administer because of the daily cash flows arising from marking to market. Typically, a futures margin account would be held, possibly with the futures broker, from which and into which daily cash flows would occur. The hedger would only be involved in making payments (or receiving money) if the balance in the margin account were to fall below (or exceed) a predetermined limit. Margin accounts do have the disadvantage of tying up liquidity. There is also the risk that losses from daily marking to market accumulate to a problematic extent and, although there would be offsetting future profits from the underlying transaction (the transaction being hedged), significant liquidity problems could arise prior to the date on which the cash flow from the underlying transaction takes place (Metalgesellschaft encountered this type of problem when using commodity derivatives).

Currency forwards and futures involve 2 simultaneous prices: the price of each currency in terms of the other. In the case of futures contracts, possible confusion from this is reduced since the major contracts price currencies in US dollars use US dollars for the daily marking to market cash flows, and stipulate contract sizes in amounts of the foreign (non-US dollar) currency, e.g. £62,500, DM125,000. So the foreign (non-US dollar) currency is the underlying asset on which the futures contract is based and prices are in US dollars (the Brazilian futures exchange provides an exception to this).

Since currencies can be carried, forward and futures prices can be determined by cash-and-carry arbitrage. In the cases of bonds and stock index portfolios, the underlying assets provide returns in the form of coupons and dividends respectively. In the case of currencies, the return takes the form of interest on the foreign currency. Cash-and-carry arbitrage with currencies is alternatively known as covered interest arbitrage.

Covered interest arbitrage, like other forms of cash-and-carry arbitrage, can be interpreted as an arbitrage of an actual forward or futures contract against a synthetic forward or futures position. This highlights the point that if derivatives were not available they could be synthetically constructed.

If futures or forward contracts can be replicated synthetically, the question arises as to why these instruments should exist. The explanation is in terms of immediacy. Derivative instruments can be transacted more cheaply, more quickly and (at least in the case of futures) with less default risk. Also, when constructing a synthetic position there is market risk while the position is being constructed, when it is not possible to establish all components of the synthetic simultaneously. So the speed of acquiring a derivatives position gives the derivatives, particularly futures, a strong advantage relative to synthetics. The role of a futures market is not just the provision of a hedging capability, but one that can be applied very quickly. The immediacy provided by futures is just as important in explaining their existence as their usefulness in the hedging of risk.

Currency forwards and futures provide important opportunities for overlay and asset reallocation strategies in investment. A foreign investment provides exposure to the specific security, exposure to the foreign stock or bond market, and an exposure to the foreign currency. Currency forwards or futures can be used to remove the currency exposure (remove the currency overlay), just as stock index or bond futures can be used to reduce the stock or bond market exposure. Just as stock index and bond futures can be used to expedite asset reallocation between shares and bonds, currency forwards and futures can be used to achieve exposure to foreign markets quickly and cheaply. For example, combining stock index futures relating to the foreign stock market with currency futures provides an exposure that is equivalent to holding a balanced portfolio of foreign stocks.

Further reading

Readable introductions to currency markets, including currency forwards and futures, are provided by:

Adrian Buckley, *The Essence of International Money*, 2nd edn (Prentice Hall, Hemel Hempstead, 1996).

David Winstone, *Financial Derivatives* (Chapman & Hall, London, 1995), Chapters 2 to 6 and Chapter 12.

Keith Redhead and Steward Hughes, *Financial Risk Management* (Gower, Aldershot, 1988), Chapters 1 to 5 and Chapter 8.

Case studies illustrating the use of currency forwards and futures can be found in:

Paul Stonham and Keith Redhead (eds.), *European Casebook on Finance* (Prentice Hall, Hemel Hempstead, 1995), Part 3.

APPENDIX 13.1: CALCULATING NUMBERS OF FUTURES CONTRACTS REQUIRED FOR HEDGING

Basis is the difference between a spot (cash market) price and the corresponding futures price. Changes in basis reduce the efficiency of hedging with futures. One source of basis change arises directly from price movements. Futures prices tend to stand at premiums (or discounts) to cash market prices. This relationship between futures and cash prices, which is based on cost of carry, extends to the relationship between changes in futures prices and changes in cash prices. In the absence of a change in cost of carry, a futures premium would entail the extent of movement in the futures price exceeding that of the cash price. This means that basis changes as a result of price changes. The analysis that follows demonstrates that this source of basis change can be eliminated by an appropriate calculation of the number of futures contracts, a calculation that may seem to be counter-intuitive.

The requisite number of contracts depends on the currency of the sum to be hedged (e.g. sterling or US dollars, against which the derivatives are quoted) and upon the expected point in time at which closing out will occur. This analysis uses the Chicago Mercantile Exchange sterling currency contracts and assumes an awareness that the locked-in rate depends on the closing-out date – the spot rate if contracts are closed out immediately, the initial futures rate if contracts are held to maturity, or an average of the 2, weighted according to the period of time for which the contracts are held.

Suppose that there is a need to hedge £10 million against $US and that the pound is trading at a 2% premium against the dollar. Spot £1 = $1.50 and six-month futures £1 = $1.53. Further suppose that the £10 million is covered by 160 sterling currency contracts (160 × £62,500 = £10 million).

Now consider 2 scenarios:

1. An immediate rise in the pound to £1 = $2.00, followed immediately by closing out (with no change in relative £/$ interest rates).
2. A rise in the pound to £1 = $2.00 by the futures maturity date, with closing out on the futures maturity date.

In the first case, the futures price would rise to $2.04. The cash market loss would be $0.50/£, whereas the futures profit would be $0.51/£ (because the futures profit includes the premium). So the initial number of contracts should ideally be margined down to an extent that offsets the premium. This could be achieved by dividing the initial US dollar value of the hedged sterling by the futures price:

$15,000,000/$1.53 = £9,803,922

In principle, futures contracts corresponding to £9,803,922 (in practice, probably 157 contracts) should be entered into.

In the second scenario, the futures price reaches $2, providing a futures profit of $0.47/£. The effective price of sterling is thus $1.53 – the number of contracts does not need to be margined. In other words, a number of contracts equivalent to the initial dollar value of the hedged sterling divided by the initial spot exchange rate would be appropriate:

$15,000,000/$1.50 = £10,000,000.

So 160 futures contracts (£10 million/£62,500) are required. If contracts are to be closed out before maturity, the requisite number of contracts would lie between 157 and 160 and be a direct function of time to closing-out (approaching 160 as the closing-out date approaches the maturity date of the contract).

In order to ascertain the number of contracts needed to hedge a dollar sum, a sterling equivalent must be found. Consider 2 possibilities:

1. Hedging $15,000,000 with a view to closing out almost immediately (i.e. hedging an imminent sum of $15,000,000).
2. Hedging $15,300,000 with a view to holding the futures contracts to maturity (i.e. hedging a sum of $15,300,000 anticipated for 6 months hence).

In both cases, suppose that the initial spot rate is £1 = $1.50 and the initial (six-month) futures price is £1 = $1.53. Suppose, further, that the spot price moves immediately to £1 = $2 in the first case, and to £1 = $2 by the futures maturity date in the second.

In the first case, the sterling value of the dollars falls from £10,000,000 to £7,500,000. At £1 = $2 the requisite dollar profit from futures would be $5,000,000. This would be obtained from contracts relating to £9,803,922 ($15,000,000/$1.53) since the futures profit per £1 would be $0.51, bearing in mind the 2% premium. So the appropriate number of contracts would be based on dividing the dollar sum to be hedged by the initial futures exchange rate.

In the second case, the dollar profit from the futures required to ensure that the $15,300,000 is worth £10,000,000 (i.e. to ensure that the $15,300,000 is converted at the original futures price) is $4,700,000. This would be obtained from futures based on £10,000,000, since the futures profit would be $0.47 per £1. Again, the appropriate number of contracts is based on dividing the dollar sum to be hedged by the initial futures exchange rate.

So whether the futures are to be closed out almost immediately, or are to be held to maturity, the dollar sum should be divided by the initial futures price of sterling in ascertaining the sterling value to be covered by futures. It follows that whenever the contracts are to be closed out, the dollar sum should be divided by the initial futures rate. So the number of contracts is independent of the point in time at which the exposure is due to appear (the date on which the currency flow is expected).

This conclusion conflicts with the intuitive idea that the exchange rate at which conversion takes place should be the forward rate relating to the closing-out date, which would be a weighted average of the initial spot and futures exchange rates.

The role of basis

The reason for ascertaining the appropriate number of sterling contracts to cover a dollar-denominated exposure by dividing the dollar sum by the futures exchange rate (relating to the futures maturity date), rather than by the implied forward rate (relating to the date of the exposure), can be seen in terms of avoiding part of the basis risk. If the interest rate structure between the two currencies remains unchanged, movements in the general level of exchange rates would cause changes in basis. With futures prices at a discount (or premium) against the spot, futures price movements would be smaller (or larger) than the spot price changes. As a result basis changes, and hedges would tend to be imperfect.

To compensate for such changes in basis, numbers of futures contracts need to be factored up or down. In the case of a futures discount, the number of contracts needs to be factored up by the same percentage as the discount. In the presence of a premium, factoring down by the same percentage as the premium would be appropriate. Dividing the dollar sum to be hedged by the futures price, rather than by an implied forward price for the exposure date, would provide the factoring required. A futures discount leads to an increase in the number of contracts by the required percentage; vice versa for a premium.

An illustration

The points raised can be illustrated by means of a hypothetical example. It is 28 October and prices for sterling currency futures are as outlined below:

December futures $1.7595 (18 December maturity)
March futures $1.7475 (18 March maturity).

A treasurer anticipates that $20 million will be received on 18 January and decides to hedge the exposure using the March futures.

The implied forward rate for 18 January can be obtained by interpolating between the December and March futures prices; it is $1.7555.

The number of contracts suggested by the implied forward rate for 18 January is:

(20,000,000/1.7555)/62,500 = 182 (to the nearest whole number)

whereas the number of contracts suggested by using the March futures price as the divisor is:

(20,000,000/1.7475)/62,500 = 183 (to the nearest whole number).

On 18 January the new spot (offer) rate is $1.90. There has been no change in the interest rate structure between the currencies, so that the futures discount remains at the same percentage. The January–March discount was $0.008/$1.7555 = 0.004557. The new money value of the futures discount will be $1.90 × 0.004557 = $0.0087, which implies a new March futures price of $1.90 − $0.0087 = $1.8913.

The profit from each March futures contract is therefore ($1.8913 − $1.7475) × 62,500 = $8,987.5. The 2 hedging strategies generate futures profits of:

$8,987.5 × 182 = $1,635,725 (£860,907.9)

and:

$8,987.5 × 183 = $1,644,712.5 (£865,638.2).

Meanwhile, the loss on the underlying exposure was ($20,000,000/$1.7555) − ($20,000,000/$1.90) = £866,449.8.

The hedging strategy using the March futures price for determining the number of contracts produces the more efficient hedge. The factoring up of the number of contracts largely compensates for the 0.07 cent ($0.0087 − $0.008) change in basis, though the compensation was less than complete since some rounding down was required in order to ascertain the nearest whole number of futures contracts.

FINANCIALLY ENGINEERED INVESTMENTS

14

INTRODUCTION

The chapter begins with a description of some forms of futures funds. Despite the name, these funds often employ options. The chapter goes on to examine some other popular investment strategies that employ options, namely covered writing and switching between stock exposures.

The chapter then examines the construction of synthetic bond portfolios and of options funds. This is followed by a discussion of the potential benefits of holding a portfolio of options funds.

Credit derivatives are then examined, together with their potential uses for a fund manager. The chapter concludes with an examination of a particular portfolio strategy, the constant ratio fund, in the light of the options that are implicit within the strategy.

Financial futures, options and swaps can be used to produce a vast range of investment opportunities that are not available (or at least not easily available) from deposits, bonds and equities. This chapter illustrates some out of the huge number of possibilities.

FUTURES FUNDS

Futures funds are collective investments that operate by means of keeping most of their assets in a liquid form such as short-term bank deposits while the remainder is used to finance the margin requirements of futures trading. The gearing offered by futures provides an opportunity for such funds themselves to be highly geared. The market exposure of a futures fund might be several times the value of the fund. Obviously such highly geared funds are very risky.

Futures funds often contain a wide variety of futures contracts. Multi-sector funds would not only contain a range of financial futures but also commodity futures. Furthermore the contracts are likely to derive from exchanges in a number of different countries. Such diversification helps to reduce the risk inherent in the futures funds. They may be particularly attractive to fund managers since they are likely to exhibit little or no correlation with the assets (such as stocks and bonds) that constitute the major part of investment portfolios. An asset that has low correlation with the other elements of a portfolio will tend to reduce the risk of the portfolio.

Taking views on market movements can normally be achieved more quickly and cheaply via using futures than by means of the spot instruments. Futures bid–offer spreads and commissions are often much lower than in the spot markets and time need not be spent on deciding between specific securities. It follows that a fund that is likely to shift frequently between sectors would benefit from the use of futures rather than spot instruments.

Not only do futures allow quick and cheap movement between types of assets, such as equities and gilts, but also between national markets. The time and expense of researching foreign stocks can be avoided by means of using stock index futures relating to the foreign stock markets. Furthermore only margin payments are subject to currency exposure; the bulk of the fund can remain in the home currency.

A futures fund would involve most of the fund being invested in short-term money-market assets such as bank deposits or Treasury bills, the remainder being used for the margin requirements arising from futures positions. The futures may relate to a sum of securities equal to the value of the fund, but not necessarily. Futures provide the flexibility to gain exposure to a quantity of assets in excess of the value of the fund, or to take a short position on the underlying instrument.

The margin system

The margin system is central to futures markets. There are three types of margin: initial margin, maintenance margin and variation margin. The *initial margin* is a sum of money to be provided by both the buyer and the seller of a futures contract when they make their transaction. This is a small percentage of the face value of the contract (perhaps 1 per cent). The initial margin is subject to variation (by a clearing house) and will be dependent upon the volatility of the price of the underlying instrument concerned. (Initial margins might be as little as 0.1 per cent or as much as 10 per cent of the value of the instrument to which the futures contract relates and are returnable deposits.)

The *maintenance margin is* the minimum sum of money (or other security) that must remain in a contract holder's margin account with the clearing house. On some futures exchanges this is equal to the initial margin, whereas on others the maintenance margin is less than the initial margin.

Variation margin is payable on a daily basis and reflects futures price movements. It is the means whereby futures profits and losses are realised on a daily basis. Someone whose futures contract shows a loss on a day must pay the amount of the loss to the clearing house by the following morning. Correspondingly, a futures position showing a profit on a day will result in a cash payment to the contract holder's account by the following morning. The process whereby profits and losses are realised on a daily basis via variation margin payments and receipts is known as *marking to market*.

One implication of the margin system is that futures are highly geared investments. For example, an initial margin of 1 per cent of the underlying means that the exposure acquired is one hundred times the initial money outlay.

Bull futures fund

The money in the fund is held on deposit (or in other money market instruments) whilst stock index futures are purchased. The value of the stock underlying the futures may match the sum on deposit (which includes the margin balance).

Bear futures fund

Similar to the bull futures fund except that stock index futures are sold rather than bought. This provides profits from a falling market but losses from a rising market.

Geared bull futures fund

Similar to the bull futures fund except that the value of stock underlying the futures contracts exceeds the sum on deposit. This provides more than proportionate profits from market rises, but a heavy fall in the market could reduce the fund to zero.

Geared bull futures fund with downside protection

This is similar to the geared bull futures fund except that there is disaster insurance in the form of heavily out-of-the-money put options. For example, the purchase of put options with a strike price 20 per cent below the current market index would prevent the fund from losing more than 40 per cent of its value (the 40 per cent is based on a 2 to 1 ratio between the futures and the deposits).

Controlled-risk index fund

This might be looked upon as a fund that uses derivatives to reduce downside risk at the cost of sacrificing some upside potential. It is a useful vehicle for demonstrating that even within a class of strategy there is a tremendous variety of different structures and hence different payoff profiles. One possible structure is illustrated by Figure 14.1.

The investor holds a portfolio of stock together with a cylinder. The cylinder involves buying a put option with a low strike price whilst selling (writing) a call option with a high strike price. The put option provides some protection against a fall in the market but the call option attenuates the profit potential from a rise in stock prices.

Figure 14.2 illustrates the payoff profile that arises from the structure of Figure 14.1. The unbroken line shows the possible outcomes at the expiry date of the options. The broken line shows the profit or loss at different stock indices prior to the expiry date of the options. The profile of Figure 14.2 is obtained by adding together the profits and losses on the

FIGURE 14.1 One possible structure for a controlled-risk index fund

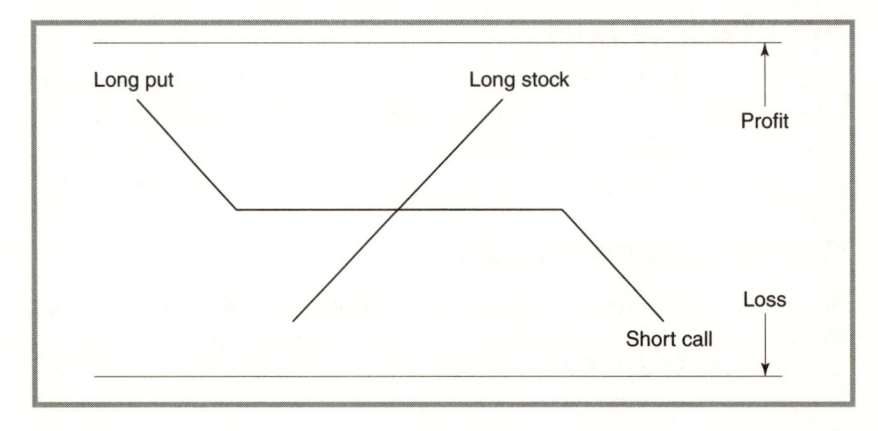

FIGURE 14.2 Payoff profile resulting from the structure in Figure 14.1

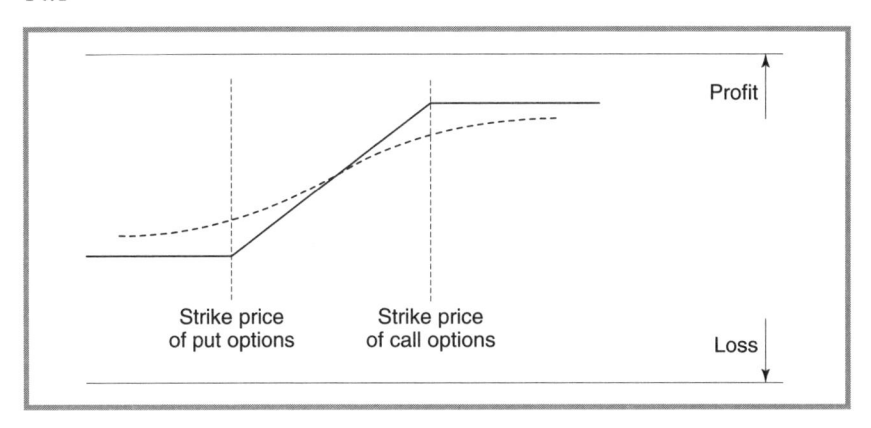

stock and options of Figure 14.1 (this includes, in the case of the prior-to-expiry profile, taking account of the time value of the options).

If options are held to expiry the result is the prevention of a fall in the value of the portfolio below a minimum value at the cost of sacrificing possible gains above a maximum level. If one considers the position before the option expiry date (shown by the broken-line profile), the effect of the cylinder can be seen to be that of moderating the market movements. This structure can be varied in a number of ways:

1. The stock index may coincide with one of the strike prices rather than falling between the option strike prices.
2. The value of stock underlying the options need not match the value of the stock held in the portfolio.
3. The put options and call options need not be in equal numbers.
4. A futures position (or synthetic futures position) may be held instead of a portfolio of shares.
5. More than two option strike prices may be used.

This list of variations is far from exhaustive but hopefully gives a feel for the range of alternatives available.

Figure 14.3 illustrates a case in which the lower strike price coincides with the actual stock index. (A close alternative is for the lower strike price to coincide with the futures stock index.)

A fund manager with a mildly bullish view might choose to write a number of call options that exceeds the number of put options purchased. This could have the result that there is a net premium receipt to add to the portfolio dividend yield so as to produce a high-yield fund. However, this risks losses in the event of a substantial market rise if it involves

372 • **FINANCIALLY ENGINEERED INVESTMENTS**

FIGURE 14.3   Lower strike price coincides with actual stock index

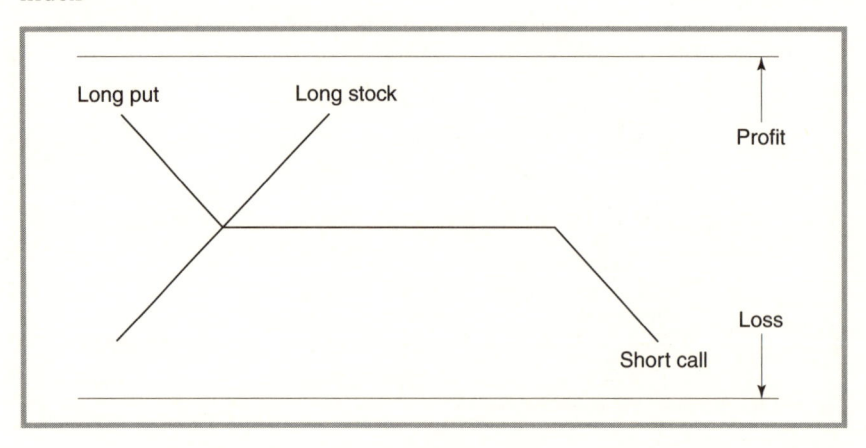

writing call options that relate to a quantity of stock in excess of that held in the portfolio. Diagrammatically the result could be as shown in Figure 14.4.

The profile depicted by Figure 14.4 is that of a call ratio spread. To avoid the risks arising above the higher strike price while preserving the ability to be a net recipient of option premiums, the fund manager could match the number of short calls to the size of the portfolio while buying a smaller number of put options. Such a strategy would lessen the downside protection of the put options.

A fund manager may seek to remove the unlimited loss potential of the call ratio spread in Figure 14.4 by means of buying call options at a third, higher, strike price. The result might be as depicted in Figure 14.5. This profile is that of a butterfly. Strike price 1 is the put option strike price (and also the stock index). Strike price 2 is the strike price of the written calls. Calls are bought at strike price 3.

FIGURE 14.4   Profile of a call ratio spread

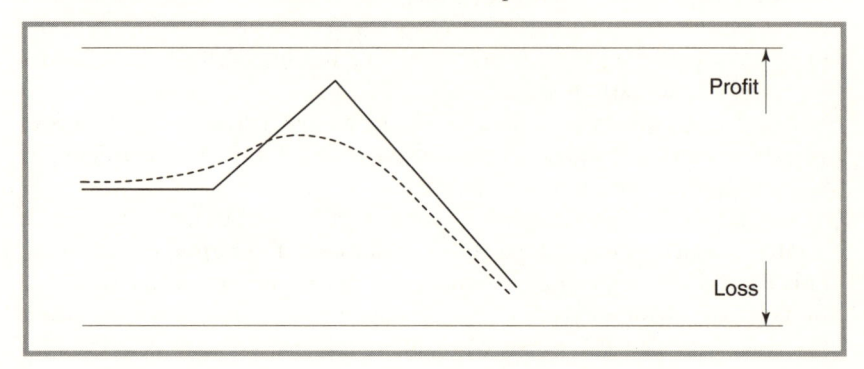

FIGURE 14.5 Buying call options at a third strike price: profile of a butterfly

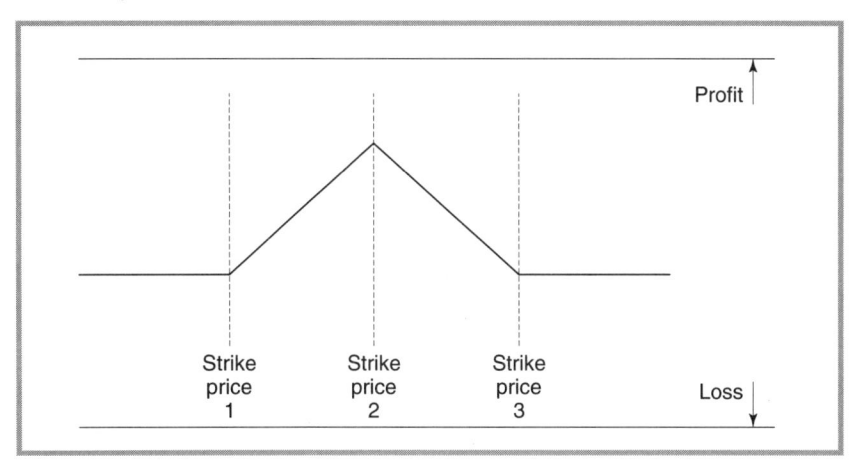

Instead of holding a portfolio of stocks the investor could buy stock index futures (or synthetic stock index futures) while holding the fund in the form of deposits (or other short-term money market instruments). In such a case the fund would consist entirely of bank deposits and derivatives (options and/or futures). It is worth noting that the use of derivatives allows for a short position in the underlying portfolio (by selling futures). Such a short position would profit from a falling stock market while losing from a rising one.

Synthetic futures are created by combining long and short option positions. A synthetic long futures position would be created by buying a call option and selling a put option with the same strike price and expiry date. A synthetic short' futures position involves buying the put and writing the call. These constructions; are illustrated by Figures 14.6 and 14.7.

An investor could choose to create synthetic futures positions while holding the fund in the form of deposits instead of holding stock. Arbitrage would tend to ensure that the synthetic futures price is close to the actual futures price (otherwise arbitragers could profit by buying the cheaper and selling the dearer). Cash and carry arbitrage would tend to maintain a close relationship between the stock index and the futures price (index). If investors hold futures or synthetic futures it does not mean that stocks are not being held. The stocks themselves would be held by arbitragers who simultaneously buy stocks and sell futures (to the investors), a process known as cash and carry arbitrage. The investor using futures or synthetic futures has an indirect exposure to the stocks themselves.

374 • **FINANCIALLY ENGINEERED INVESTMENTS**

FIGURE 14.6   A synthetic long futures position

Long call
+
Short put

= Long futures

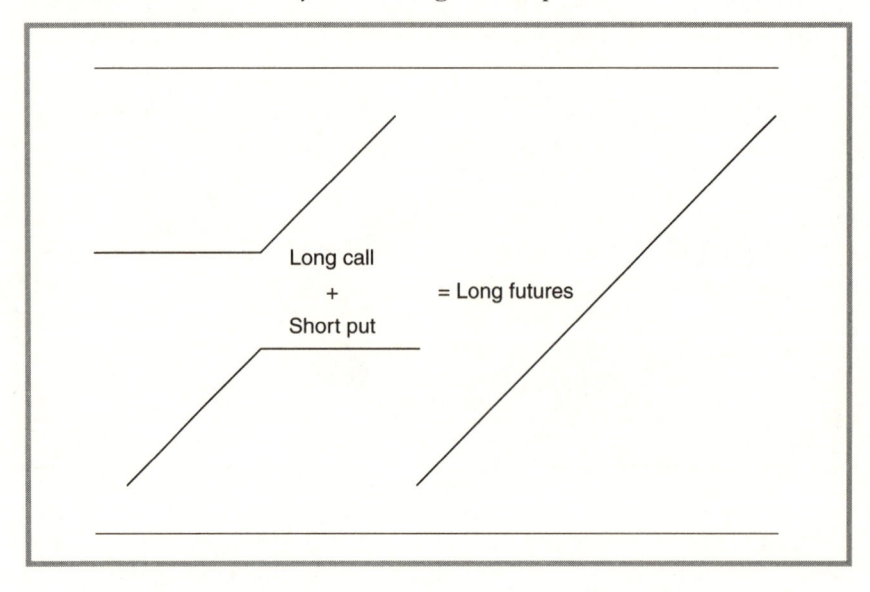

FIGURE 14.7   A synthetic short futures position

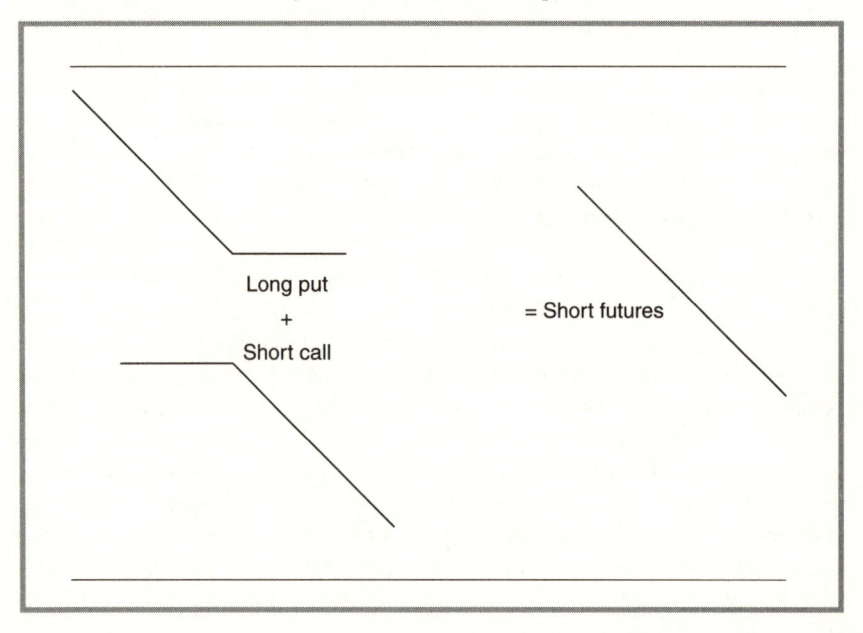

Long put
+
Short call

= Short futures

Covered writing (very high income funds)

These funds involve writing call options against the stock portfolio that is being held. The premium receipts from writing the options provide an addition to the stock dividends in producing an income yield for the investor. A drawback with such a strategy is that the potential to profit from rising stock prices is largely lost, since profits on the portfolio would be offset by losses on the short call. Indeed there is a danger that the capital value of the fund will fall over time because market declines might be locked in by written call options at the lower market prices (a downward ratchet effect).

Some investors might write puts as well as calls against a portfolio of stocks. While this considerably enhances the income yield from the fund it adds to the risks. A falling market leads to losses from the put options as well as from the portfolio. To limit this loss potential, out-of-the-money put options might be purchased.

SWITCHING BETWEEN STOCKS WITHOUT TRADING IN STOCKS

There may be occasions when a switch between stocks is intended to be very temporary, needs to be carried out extremely quickly, or without affecting expected dividend receipts. In such circumstances there may be advantages in using an options strategy either as a replacement for, or as a means of changing the timing of, the switch. The options strategy would entail constructing a synthetic short position in the stock to be sold and simultaneously establishing a synthetic long position in the stock to be purchased. The synthetic short position eliminates the exposure to the stock that is currently held, whilst the synthetic long position creates an exposure to the stock that the fund manager wants to own.

A synthetic short position is created by buying put options and writing (selling) an equal number of call options with the same strike price and expiry date. Delta measures the profit (or loss) on a strategy arising from a 1p change in the stock price. The delta of the short synthetic would be –1, which is the delta of a short position in the stock The delta of the synthetic, –1, neutralises the +1 delta of the stock being held The construction of a synthetic short position is illustrated by Figure 14.8.

A synthetic long position is constructed by buying call options and writing (selling) an equal number of put options with the same strike price and expiry date. The delta of the long position would be +1, which is the

FIGURE 14.8

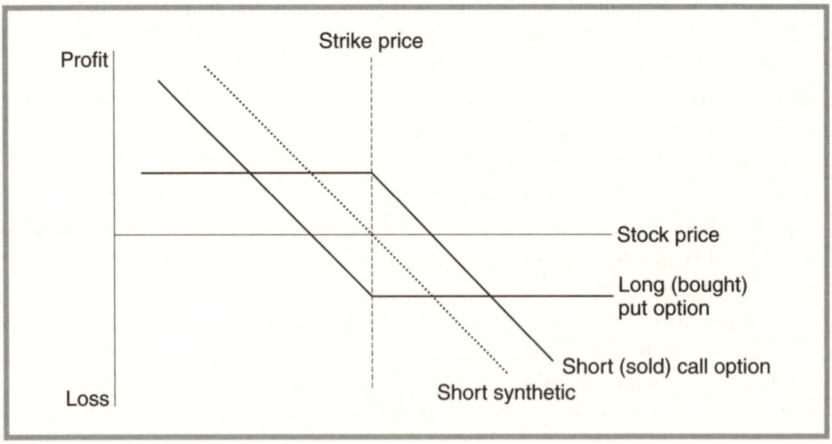
Strike price
Profit
Loss
Stock price
Long (bought)
put option
Short (sold) call option
Short synthetic

delta of a long position in the stock (i.e. a stockholding). In terms of market exposure the synthetic long position can be regarded as equivalent to buying the stock. The construction of a synthetic long position is illustrated by Figure 14.9.

FIGURE 14.9

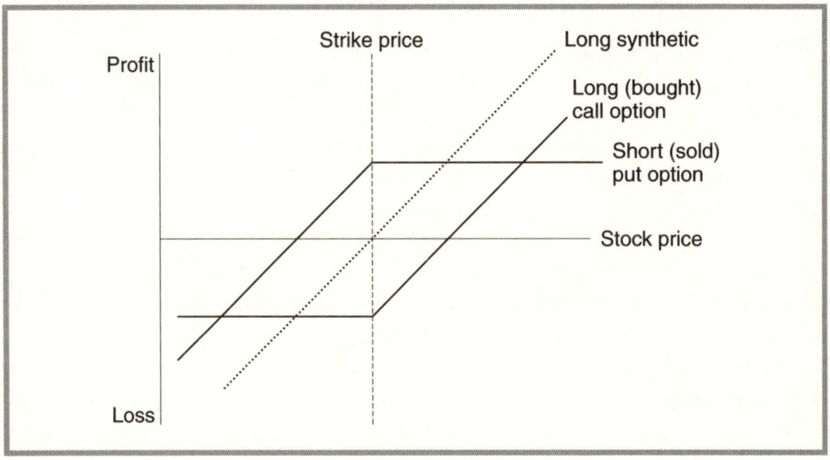
Strike price
Long synthetic
Profit
Long (bought)
call option
Short (sold)
put option
Stock price
Loss

An example

Suppose that a fund manager wants to switch from Sainsbury shares to Tesco shares when Sainsbury shares stand at 521p and Tesco shares at

563p. The Sainsbury option prices for the nearby month (earliest expiry date) are as shown in Table 14.1.

Table 14.1

Strike price	Calls	Puts
500	36	19
550	17	46.5

The Tesco option prices for the nearest expiry month are as shown in Table 14.2.

Table 14.2

Strike price	Calls	Puts
550	21	6
600	2	38.5

The price of a synthetic position in shares is equal to:

(PV) Strike price + Call price − Put price.
The present value of the strike price [(PV) Strike price] is given by

$K/(1 + rt)$

where K is the strike price, r the interest rate, and t the time to expiry of the option as a fraction of a year. Interest rates at the time were close to 7.5%. Sainsbury options had 58 days to expiry, Tesco options had 13 days to expiry.

The synthetic price of Sainsbury shares was (based on the 550p options):

[550/(1 + 0.075.0.159)] + 17 − 46.5 = 514 p.

The synthetic price of Tesco shares was (based on the 550p options):

[550/(1 + 0.075.0.036)] + 21 − 6 = 563.5 p.

The fund manager could construct a synthetic short position in Sainsbury shares, thereby removing the exposure to Sainsbury shares. Simultaneously a synthetic long position in Tesco shares is created, thereby obtaining an exposure to Tesco shares.

Whilst the price of the Tesco synthetic is close to the actual share price (563.5p as against 563p), the price of the Sainsbury synthetic is significantly lower than the actual share price (514p as against 521p). This could be explained in terms of a dividend on Sainsbury shares, prior to the option expiry date, being expected. Indeed this could provide the reason for using the synthetics rather than immediately trading in shares. Switching exposure by means of the synthetic enables the fund manager to retain the right to the forthcoming Sainsbury dividend. Subsequent to the receipt of the dividend Sainsbury shares might be sold, Tesco shares purchased, and the synthetics unwound. The synthetics would have been used to effect the switch between the stocks whilst retaining the right to the forthcoming dividend.

Conclusion

The possibility of constructing synthetic positions in stocks using options is potentially a source of considerable flexibility for fund managers. Switches between stocks can be achieved very quickly. The synthetics may subsequently be unwound as actual stock trades are undertaken, or as the need for a short-term switch disappears. Effecting a switch without affecting dividend receipts in the near future would be another potential motivation for using the synthetics strategy. The construction of a short synthetic position in a stock also allows a trader to take a view on a decline in the stock price, and the construction of a long synthetic can be a means of acquiring a highly leveraged exposure to a stock.

SYNTHETIC BOND PORTFOLIOS

Government bond futures, together with a corresponding sum in money market investments, can be used to create a portfolio with the same characteristics as a portfolio of government bonds. Although this is unlikely to confer significant advantage when used to synthesise a portfolio of domestic bonds, it can be highly beneficial as an alternative to the holding of a portfolio of bonds issued by a foreign government. This benefit arises from the avoidance of currency risk. A portfolio of foreign currency bonds entails a currency exposure equal to the full value of the portfolio. A synthetic portfolio has a foreign exchange exposure only to the extent of money in margin accounts, and that will normally be a small fraction of the total value of the portfolio.

When replicating a bond portfolio it is necessary to reproduce two characteristics of the portfolio being synthesised. One of these characteristics is the exposure to capital gain or loss from changes in interest rates.

The other characteristic is the stream of income, which would take the form of a series of coupon payments in the case of the actual portfolio of bonds.

Creating the interest rate exposure (price volatility) characteristic

To simplify the exposition it will be assumed that the bond portfolio to be replicated consists of one bond. Suppose that it is a German government bond with a coupon of 6.75% and remaining term to redemption of 10 years. Further suppose that its clean price is DM102, its redemption yield is 6.5%, and that accrued interest amounts to DM3. If a fund manager has DM10.5 million to invest the nominal value that can be purchased is:

$$\frac{DM10,500,000}{102 + 3} \times 100 = DM10,000,000.$$

To replicate the interest rate risk exposure of this bondholding with futures it is necessary to ascertain the PVBP (Price Value of a Basis Point) of the portfolio, and of a futures contract. The PVBP of a bond is the change in its price resulting from a basis point (0.01%) change in a relevant interest rate. It is thus a measure of volatility. The PVBP can be calculated by multiplying the modified duration of the bond by its price. For present purposes it will be assumed that the computations to ascertain modified duration and hence the PVBP have already been carried out.

Suppose that the PVBP of the bond being held has been found to be DM0.00071 per DM1 nominal. Since DM10 million nominal is held the PVBP for the whole bondholding will be

DM10,000,000 × 0.00071 = DM7,100.

The next step is to estimate the PVBP of a bond futures contract. This is carried out in two stages. First the PVBP of the CTD (Cheapest To Deliver) is calculated. The CTD is the most profitable bond for sellers of futures contracts to deliver. Since sellers of futures contracts have the choice of which bond to deliver if a contract reaches maturity it is the CTD that will be delivered. In consequence it is the CTD that is used in the arbitrage processes that determine futures prices, and the futures contract tends to reflect the characteristics of the CTD. These characteristics include the PVBP.

However one characteristic in which the futures will differ from the CTD is in the underlying market value. The futures contract is based on a notional bond with a specific coupon rate. In the case of the German

Government Bond (Bund) futures traded on LIFFE the coupon rate of the underlying notional bond is 6%. If the CTD has a different coupon it will have a different market value. Conventionally price factors, published by exchanges, are used to convert bond prices into their futures equivalents. By dividing a bond price by the price factor of that bond, the effects on its price from having a coupon other than 6% can be eliminated. For example a CTD with a coupon greater than 6% will have a market price that is higher than that of a bond with a coupon of 6%. Such a CTD would have a price factor greater than 1 such that division of the price of the CTD by the price factor would remove the effect of the coupon being greater than 6%. Division of the price of the CTD by the price factor generates a futures price that reflects the price of the CTD. Further, dividing the PVBP of the CTD by the price factor produces an estimate of the PVBP of a futures contract.

Suppose that the PVBP of the CTD has been found to be DM0.0007 per DM1 nominal, and that the price factor of the CTD is 1.1. Dividing the PVBP of the CTD by the price factor, and multiplying by the size of the futures contract gives an estimate of the PVBP of a futures contract. The size of the German government bond contract traded on LIFFE is DM250,000

$$\frac{0.0007}{1.1} \times DM250,000 = DM159.09$$

With a desired interest rate exposure of DM7,100 and each futures contract providing a volatility of DM159.09 the number of futures contracts to be bought in order to create the desired exposure is given by:

$$\frac{DM7,100}{DM159.09} = 44.63$$

Since futures contracts are indivisible the fund manager would choose either 44 or 45 contracts.

Creating the income component

The more obvious income component is the interest from depositing the underlying sum of money. Since a futures contract costs nothing the money that would otherwise have been used to buy bonds is available to be put on deposit (that part of the money that is held in margin accounts can also earn interest).

There is another source of cash flow. This arises from variation margin receipts, or payments, as the futures price moves over time. Cash and carry arbitrage tends to ensure that the returns from a bondholding, hedged by the sale of futures, match the interest cost on money borrowed to finance that bondholding. An implication of this is that the futures price should be such as to ensure a capital gain, or loss, that offsets the difference between the coupon receipts on the bond and money market interest rates.

Take the case in which coupon receipts on the bond exceed the interest flows on the corresponding cash. Equalising the two cash flows requires that the futures price is such as to provide a capital gain. This entails a futures price below the bond price. In the event of a constant bond price the futures price would rise over time so as to converge on the bond price by the maturity date of the futures contract. The variation margin receipts received over time, when added to the interest receipts on the money market deposit, will tend to provide an income flow that matches the flow of coupons from the bond.

Changes in the bond price will not affect the conclusions. Bond price movements were dealt with by means of the replication of the interest rate exposure characteristic. The replication means that bond price movements are paralleled by futures price movements.

Conclusion

Futures funds can be used as alternatives to actual bond portfolios. Futures funds replicate major characteristics of bond portfolios, particularly in relation to interest rate exposure (price volatility) and income flows. Other characteristics would not normally be replicated. The currency exposure (exchange rate risk) of a portfolio of foreign currency bonds would not be replicated by a futures fund. Other characteristics may also differ between the two alternatives. For example, the convexity (changes in volatility arising from variations in interest rates) of a bond portfolio will differ from that of a futures fund.

OPTIONS FUNDS

An options fund is characterised by upside exposure to a stock index (or other underlying price) together with a lower limit to the value of the fund. This profile of returns can be achieved in two main ways (see Figure 14.10). One is the fiduciary call (another name for 90/10 fund) which involves investment in risk-free assets and call options. The risk-free assets, such as Treasury bills, provide the guaranteed minimum value while the call options provide the upside exposure to the stock market.

FIGURE 14.10 Alternative means of constructing options funds

1. *Fiduciary call (90/10)* Investment in risk-free assets to provide the guaranteed sum plus purchase of call options to give upside exposure.
2. *Protective put* Equity investment to provide upside exposure. Purchase of put options plus investment in risk-free assets to produce the guaranteed sum.

   (a) $M = X(1 + r)^T$
       $N = (V - X)/C$

   (b) $M = X(1 + r)^T + NK$
       $N = (V - X)/(S + P)$

where M = guaranteed minimum fund value, X = investment in risk-free assets, r is the interest rate on risk-free assets, T is the maturity of the fund, N is the number of options V is the initial value of the fund, C is the price of a call option, K is the strike price, P is the price of a put option, S is the value of stock relating to one option.

The other main approach is that of the protective put. This consists of a holding of stock to give the upside exposure together with put options that guarantee a minimum value of that shareholding. Protective put strategies (sometimes referred to as portfolio insurance) also tend to involve some investment in riskless assets in order to guarantee the minimum value. The minimum value is ensured by a combination of an investment in assets such as Treasury bills, or bank deposits, and a lowest possible value of the shareholding based on the strike price of the put options.

The fiduciary call (90/10) approach involves calculating the present value of the guaranteed sum and investing it in risk-free assets. This generates the minimum value upon maturity of the fund. The remainder is used to buy call options. The cost of the downside protection is reduced profit on the upside. Potential returns from a rising stock market are less than would be obtained if the entire fund were to be invested in shares. The proportion of market returns accruing to the fund in the event of a market rise is dependent upon the guaranteed minimum value and the strike price of the options. A greater guaranteed sum requires relatively substantial investment in risk-free assets and hence relatively low expenditure on options. This would entail a low potential to profit from a market rise. Acceptance of a high option strike price, and hence high market index beyond which market exposure begins, involves cheaper options and hence a greater number that can be purchased for a given money outlay. So a high strike price allows the fund to obtain a higher proportion of the stock market returns above the strike price.

An options fund created using the protective put approach also involves the trade-offs between the proportion of a market rise that is obtained, the guaranteed minimum value, and the index level at which exposure begins. However, since the guaranteed minimum value is provided from two sources – the investment in risk-free assets, and a shareholding combined with put options – it is necessary to use simultaneous equations to calculate the amounts of the constituent components.

If M is the guaranteed minimum value, X is the amount to be invested in risk-free assets, K is the option strike price, r is the interest rate on risk-free assets, T is the maturity of the fund and N is the number of put options (which matches the amount of stock purchased), then:

$$M = X(1 + r)T + NK$$

that is, the guaranteed minimum fund value equals the maturity value of the investment in risk-free assets plus the minimum value of the shareholding guaranteed by the put options.

The value of N can be calculated as:

$$N = (V - X)/(S + P)$$

where V is the value of the fund, S is the value of stock covered by one option, and P is the price of a put option. N is thus the number of combinations of stock and put option that can be purchased after X has been allocated to the purchase of risk-free assets.

The two equations can be simultaneously solved for X and N. In this way the amount to be invested in risk-free assets can be ascertained together with the number of matched combinations of stock and put option.

ACTIVITY 14.1

The FTSE 100 stands at 3000. Two-year European style at-the-money call options are priced at 600 and the corresponding put options are priced at 250. The two-year riskfree interest rate is 10 per cent p.a. How might a fund manager construct an options fund that guarantees the return of the initial £1 million at the end of a two-year period while providing upside exposure to the FTSE 100 index? What proportion of the return on the FTSE 100 portfolio would be obtained?

Answer
If the fiduciary call approach were to be used the sum to be invested in risk-free assets would be £1,000,000/(1.1)2 = £826,446 which leaves £1,000,000 – £826,446 = £173,554 to be used to buy call options. The number of call options that could be purchased is £173,554/£6,000 = 28.9 (29 to nearest whole number).

The number of units of the FTSE 100 that could be bought if a unit equals £10 per index point (corresponding to the option size) would be £1,000,000/ £30,000 = 33.33. The option fund would obtain (29/33.33) × 100 per cent =

87 per cent of the capital appreciation of the FTSE 100 portfolio but would receive none of the dividend return.

If the protective put approach were to be used it is necessary to solve the equations:

$$M = X(1 + r)T + NK$$
$$N = (V - X)/(S + P)$$

for X and N when M = £1,000,000, r = 0.1, T = 2, K = 3000 × £10, V = £1,000,000, S = £30,000, and P = 250 × £10:

$$£1,000,000 = X (1.1)2 + N £30,000$$
$$N = (£1,000,000 - X)/£32,500$$

so:

$$£1,000,000 = X\ (1.1)2 + (£1,000,000 - X)$$
$$ £30,000/ £32,500$$
$$£1,000,000 - £923,077 = X(1.21 - 0.923077)$$
$$X = £76,923/0.286923$$
$$X = £268,096$$
$$N = (£1,000,000 - £268,096)/£32,500 = 22.52$$

Ignoring the problem of the indivisibility of option contracts, the strategy would appear to involve a deposit of £268,096, the purchase of stock to the value of £30,000 × 22.52 = £675,603 and the purchase of 22.52 put options at £2,500 per contract. In practice the number of put options bought would be 22 or 23. The proportion of the return on the FTSE 100 portfolio that would be obtained would be (£675,603/£1,000,000) × 100% = 67.56 per cent.

Variations on the theme

An options fund need not necessarily be bullish. It is possible to create funds that profit in the event of a market decline. In the case of a fiduciary (i.e. 90/10) strategy this would involve an investment in risk-free assets plus a purchase of put options. The alternative would be a short position in stock (selling borrowed stock) and the purchase of calls as a protective strategy (against a rise in the market).

Taking a short position in stock is not always possible. An alternative would involve a short position in stock index futures, which would be accomplished much more easily. Indeed options funds that require long stock positions may, as an alternative, use stock index futures in order to obtain the market exposure.

Another variation might be to use vertical spreads in combination with an investment in risk-free assets. Vertical bull spreads involve buying call options at a low strike price and writing an equal number of calls at a high strike price (they could also be constructed using put options). The lower net cost of the option position allows the number of vertical spreads to exceed the number of options that could alternatively be bought. As a result, upside capture would be enhanced as far as the higher strike price. However, there would be no further gains from stock market rises beyond the higher strike price.

Costs of options funds

When considering the costs of options funds it is appropriate to view it from two perspectives: that of the constructor of the fund, and that of the investor in the fund. Costs also need to be measured against the two alternative benchmarks: full investment in stocks, and total investment in risk-free assets such as Treasury bills or bank deposits with a maturity matching that of the options fund. A further dichotomy is between the costs involved in the fiduciary call and the protective put approaches.

From the point of view of the creator of the fund the cost of a fiduciary call compared to total investment in risk-free assets is the call option premiums, whereas the cost of a protective put relative to the risk-free assets is the option premium plus the net income flow foregone (excess of interest rate over expected dividend yield). For the costs to be identical the call price must equal the put price plus interest on risk-free assets minus expected dividends, which would be the case if put–call parity holds.

Again from the perspective of fund construction but using complete investment in stocks as the alternative, the cost of a protective put would be the option premium, whereas the cost of a fiduciary call would encompass the net expected income flow as well as the option premium. Compared with an investment in stocks the fiduciary call approach provides interest income while foregoing dividend receipts; as a result the cost amounts to the call premiums plus dividends foregone minus interest receipts. If the cost of the protective put and that of the fiduciary call are to be equal then the put price must equal the call price minus the excess of prospective interest receipts over expected dividends. As before, this would be the case if put–call parity holds.

From the point of view of the investor in the fund the distinction between the fiduciary call and protective put approaches is of no concern- indeed the investor may not even know which has been used. The investor has a profile of possible returns from the fund which entails some exposure to upward movements in stock prices together with a guaranteed minimum fund value at maturity; whether this arises from a fiduciary call or protective put is of no significance to the investor.

An investor in the fund is interested in how the fund compares with the alternatives of investment in risk-free assets and of investment in stocks. When comparing an options fund with risk-free assets the potential to profit from a rising stock market is obtained at the cost of a reduced interest return on the investment. Upside exposure and interest return would be inversely related; more of one involves less of the other. When comparing the payoffs from an options fund with those from investment in stocks, the protection against stock price falls below a particular level is obtained at the cost of foregoing dividend receipts and perhaps obtaining less than the full benefit of market rises. For example, the fund may provide just 80 per cent of market rises above the guaranteed minimum level.

Some points relating to fiduciary call (90/10) funds

These funds provide security together with upside exposure. As with other funds, increased profit potential is obtained at the cost of increased risk. The greater the proportion of the fund in options, the lower is the capital certainty. Raising the proportion of the fund that is used to buy options will raise the delta of the fund (the delta being the relationship between changes in the value of the fund and changes in the prices of the stocks that underlie the options). The proportion of the fund in options can be raised either by buying a greater number of options or by buying deeper in-the-money (or fewer out-of-the-money) options, either way the delta of the fund would be increased.

If the wish is to obtain exposure to the stock market in general rather than specific stocks, then stock index options would be better than options on individual stocks. Such an approach spreads the risk, so that adverse developments that are specific to particular stocks can be diluted (and offset by favourable developments in other stocks). The avoidance of stock-specific risk reduces option premiums. Volatility is an important determinant of option premiums. Since a stock index avoids the risks that are specific to individual stocks (and bears only the general market risk that is common to all stocks), it tends to be less volatile than individual stock prices. Consequently, option premiums for stock index options tend to be lower than those for individual stocks. This is a good reason for using stock index options rather than individual stock options.

Finally, it might be noted that 90/10 funds provide a means of reducing the currency risk that normally accompanies investment in overseas stock markets. A fund that is 90 per cent invested in sterling deposits and

10 per cent invested in US options has considerably less exposure to the risk of a fall in the value of the US dollar than a fund that is 100 per cent invested in US stocks, although they might have identical exposures to the US stock market.

CONSTRUCTING A PORTFOLIO OF CAPITAL PROTECTED FUNDS

A top–down approach to portfolio construction involves determining an optimal allocation of funds between asset classes; for example between money market deposits, bonds and equities. The choice of individual assets within each class (security selection) occurs after the allocation between asset classes has been decided upon.

The use of derivatives allows for an avoidance of the security selection stage. Futures funds can be used as the constituent investments. Instead of a portfolio of equities the fund manager could construct a futures fund by putting money on deposit and simultaneously buying stock index futures. Similarly a gilt futures fund could replace a portfolio of gilts.

The employment of options allows the fund manager to go one step further. Instead of a portfolio of futures funds, a portfolio of options funds with capital protection could be held. An options fund could be constructed by depositing sufficient money to ensure the return of capital at the end of the investment period, together with using the remaining money to gain exposure to the stock market by buying call options. Stock index options could be purchased to provide an exposure to a well-diversified portfolio of equities.

Diversification with options funds

The problem of obtaining the optimal mix of money market investments, bonds and equities is often solved by employing the principles of Markowitz diversification. However the equations and computer programmes used to ascertain the optimum mix of asset classes assume that expected returns and risk can be expressed in terms of the mean and standard deviation of normal distributions. The distribution of returns from options funds are not normally distributed. Options funds preclude the possibility of fund values below the protected sum. The value of an options fund at the end of the investment period cannot be less than the sum placed on deposit plus interest.

Although the expected returns from an options fund do not conform to a normal distribution during a single investment period (for example, 3 months) the average return from a succession of options funds over a longer investment horizon would be close to being normally distributed. Taking the example of a three-year investment horizon, the (compound) average of returns over 12 successive three-month investment periods would approximate to a normal distribution.

It is thus possible to estimate the expected returns (distribution means), risks (distribution standard deviations), and correlation coefficients required by the Markowitz analysis. These values would be estimated for deposit funds, gilt options funds, and stock index options funds to produce the efficiency frontier of Markowitz diversification. Such an efficiency frontier may take the following form:

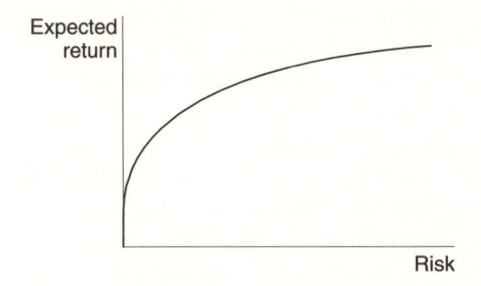

The fund manager can then choose the mix of the deposit fund, the gilt options fund and the stock index options fund that best meets the preferred trade off between expected return and risk. It is thus possible to combine the risk reduction effects of portfolio diversification with the capital protection provided by options funds.

CREDIT DERIVATIVES AND THEIR POTENTIAL ROLE IN FUND MANAGEMENT

Credit derivatives originate from the early 1990s. They are derivatives on credit risk and can be used to hedge credit risk on a specific bond. The pay off from a credit derivative might be based on the relationship between the price of a reference asset and a risk-free (normally government) bond. This relationship would be affected by credit events.

The reference asset would be an actively traded bond (corporate or government) or a portfolio of such bonds. Alternatively it could be a widely syndicated loan or a portfolio of loans. Credit events would include bankruptcy, insolvency or payment default on the part of the issuer of the bond whose credit risk is being hedged. Other credit events would include rating changes for the hedged bond or the reference asset, or a predetermined price decline on the part of either the bond being hedged or the reference asset.

A forward contract might be based on a specified bond's yield spread over a benchmark asset (such as a government bond). At maturity of the forward contract a payment would be made based on the difference between the spread agreed in the contract and the spread at maturity.

In the case of a credit swap, prior to maturity the net cash flows could be based on the relative cash flows arising from the reference asset and those generated by a reference rate. The reference rate would typically be an agreed fixed interest rate or a LIBOR-based floating rate. At maturity there would be a final net cash flow. The final net cash flow between the counterparties might be similar to the cash flow arising when a forward contract matures, for example in being based on the difference between an agreed spread between yields and the spread at maturity.

Option structures take a number of different forms. A common form is the default put. If there is a credit event the writer (seller) of the option pays the buyer a sum of money. In this way the option buyer obtains protection from credit events. The credit event that triggers the payment could arise in relation either to the specific asset being hedged or to a reference asset.

Using credit derivatives in fund management

Credit derivatives allow fund managers to include in their portfolios assets and positions that would not otherwise be available. As a result the potential for diversification is enhanced. The increased ease of taking short positions and of gearing, along with easier and cheaper access to some classes of asset, add to the range of possibilities available to fund managers.

The purchase of a liquid bond with stable risk characteristics together with appropriate derivative positions can simulate a bond with different risk characteristics. For example the purchase of a UK government bond could be combined with a derivative position based on the credit risk of a corporate bond issued in Poland. This combination simulates a holding of the Polish bond but without most of the currency risk that would otherwise be present (since most of the investment is in a sterling denominated asset). This financially engineered asset also circumvents any foreign exchange or other restrictions that could inhibit the purchase of the Polish bond. It is also likely to save on transactions costs. Furthermore by combining derivative positions it is possible to simulate assets that do not otherwise exist, for example bonds that reflect an average of the risk characteristics of the 3 Baltic states.

In a parallel fashion illiquid bonds within the portfolio can have their risk characteristics changed by means of credit derivatives. For example a fund manager may hold the above-mentioned Polish bond but want to sell it in order to buy a UK gilt. If the fund manager is unable to find a buyer for the Polish bond an alternative would be to take a derivatives position that converts the risk characteristics of the Polish bond into those of a UK gilt (currency derivatives may also provide the choice as to whether exposure to the Polish Zloty is maintained).

By combining credit derivatives with bond derivatives it is possible to hold geared positions in various bonds. It is also possible to construct short positions. A money market debt together with a short position in government bond futures and appropriate credit derivatives can simulate a short position in a specified bond or bond portfolio.

A related issue is the potential for increased efficiency in the origination and holding of loans. For example, consider a bank loan to a Spanish firm. A Spanish bank is likely to be the most efficient originator of the loan since the Spanish bank will possess relevant local knowledge. The Spanish bank, however, may not be the best holder of the credit risk arising from the loan since it probably already holds considerable Spanish debt in its loan portfolio. Additional Spanish debt adds little to the diversification of the loan portfolio. On the other hand, a British bank, or investing institution, is likely to have little credit risk exposure to Spanish borrowers. The Spanish debt might provide useful diversification to the institution's portfolio of credit exposures. The Spanish bank is the more efficient lender but the British institution is the more efficient holder of the debt. Credit derivatives provide a means whereby the credit risk can be transferred from the Spanish bank to the British institution.

A second use of credit derivatives involves forward credit spread curves. Use of yield curves to estimate forward interest rates, and hence forward yield curves, is well known. By producing forward yield curves for different risk classes of bonds (for example, government bonds and A-rated corporate bonds) an implied forward credit spread curve can be derived. A credit derivative transaction can be used to seek profits from a view that the future default rate will differ from the default rate implied by the forward credit spread curve.

Prior to the emergence of credit derivatives, nothing guaranteed that two equivalent credit markets (for example, a bond market and a syndicated loan market) had the same implied future default probabilities. If they are not the same, profits can be made by arbitraging between the two markets using credit derivatives.

A third use of credit derivatives arises from the facility they provide for separating credit risk from other types of risk. In particular since credit derivatives allow credit exposure to be isolated from interest rate exposure, bond portfolio managers can take views on credit risk without simultaneously taking a position on interest rates. This can be particularly important in the light of evidence to the effect that, in bond markets, interest rate risk tends to be much higher than credit risk.

Conclusions

It is now widely recognised that the use of derivatives in fund management can provide opportunities for return enhancement, risk reduction, operational efficiency and increased flexibility. The arrival of credit derivatives adds to the range of possibilities available to fund managers.

THE IMPLICATIONS OF IMPLICIT OPTIONS IN CONSTANT RATIO FUNDS

Option positions can be replicated by positions in the underlying instrument or the corresponding futures. The positions in the underlying or futures should provide the same profit/loss outcome as the option being replicated. The amount of the underlying or futures should reflect the option delta. For example, an option on £1 million of the underlying with a delta of 0.7 would tend to give the same profit or loss as £700,000 of the underlying (which has a delta of 1). A small price move in the underlying should provide the same profit/loss outcome on £700,000 with a delta of 1 as on £1 million with a delta of 0.7. Replication of a call with futures is illustrated by Figure 14.11 and replication of a short call with the underlying stock is demonstrated by Activity 14.2.

Such replication will involve cash flows. Replicating long option positions involves buying when the price of the underlying rises and selling when it falls. This is because a rise in the price of the underlying causes an increase in delta and hence the need to buy more of the underlying (or futures). Conversely, a fall in price lowers delta and necessitates selling. Buying high and selling low entails a net cash outflow. The theoretical

FIGURE 14.11   Delta hedging a written call option

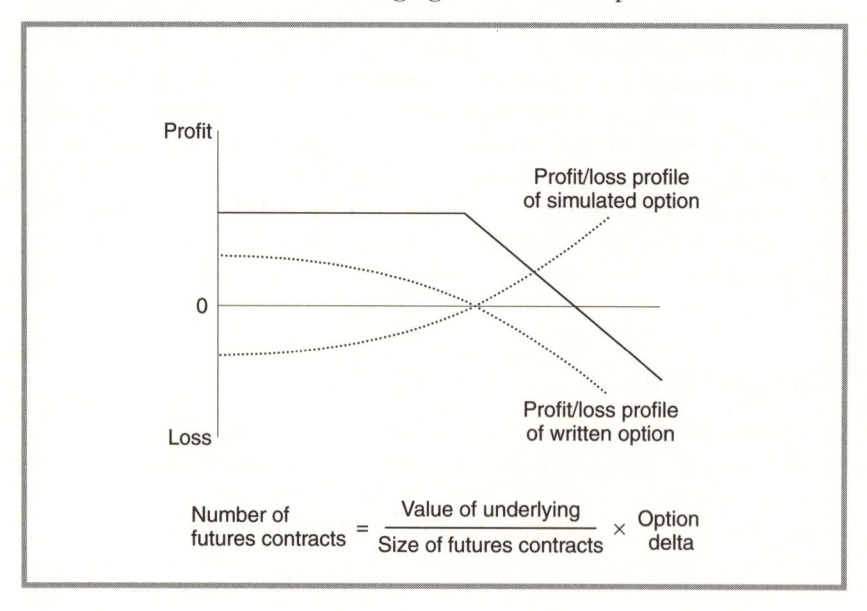

$$\text{Number of futures contracts} = \frac{\text{Value of underlying}}{\text{Size of futures contracts}} \times \text{Option delta}$$

time value of the option equals the expected losses from such transactions. So replicating long option positions results in losses that correspond to the time value of the replicated option. (Specifically this is the time value resulting from volatility of the price of the underlying rather than from financing costs.) Conversely the replication of short option positions would be expected to provide profits that correspond to the time (volatility) value.

ACTIVITY 14.2

An equity options trader sells an at-the-money call option on 1,000 shares of the equity of XY:L plc for a 28-day period. The trade is hedged in the equity market using delta weighted hedging until 7 days before expiry, when the position is closed by buying back a similar call in the market. Assuming that the trader always deals at the market's price, and neglecting the funding of interim cash flows, calculate the net profit or loss on the transaction, given the following information about the underlying share price and the option's delta:

Week	Share price (p)		Option price (p)		Option delta	Days remaining
	Bid	Offer	Bid	Offer		
1	98.5	101.5	2.5	4.0	0.54	28
2	103.5	106.5	5.5	7.0	0.78	21
3	105.5	108.5	6.5	8.0	0.89	14
4	108.5	111.5	9.5	11.0	1.00	7

Answer
Week 1. Sell call option for £25. Buy 540 shares at £101.5 = £548.10
Week 2. Buy 240 shares at £1.065 = £255.60
Week 3. Buy 110 shares at £1.085 = £119.35
At close. Buy call option for £110. Sell 890 shares at £1.085 = £965.65
Net loss: £25 − £548.10 − £255.60 − £119.35 − £110 + £965.65 = £42.40

The analysis will consider three constant ratio funds: (i) 50 per cent in equities and 50 per cent in short term deposits; (ii) 50 per cent in equities and 50 per cent in bonds with a positive correlation of returns; and (iii) 50 per cent in equities and 50 per cent in bonds with a negative correlation of returns. The funds are rebalanced to the 50 per cent split once a year.

1. Suppose that the fund has just been rebalanced and that over the following five years the rate of return on equities is constant at 8 per cent p.a. and the rate of interest on deposits is constant at 4 per cent p.a. What is the overall rate of return on the fund? What would the rate of return have been in the absence of rebalancing over the five-year period?

   Suppose that the fund initially consists of £100 in equities and £100 on deposit. The progress of the fund is as follows:

Year	Initial value (£)		Value after return (£)		Value after rebalancing (£)	
	Equities	Deposit	Equities	Deposit	Equities	Deposit
1	100.00	100.00	108.00	104.00	106.00	106.00
2	106.00	106.00	114.48	110.24	112.36	112.36
3	112.36	112.36	121.35	116.84	119.10	119.10
4	119.10	119.10	128.63	123.87	126.25	126.25
5	126.25	126.25	136.35	131.30	133.82	133.82

The total fund value after five years is:

$$£133.82 + £133.82 = £267.64$$

394 • **FINANCIALLY ENGINEERED INVESTMENTS**

In the absence of rebalancing the fund value would have been:

$$£100(1.08)s + £100(1.04)s = £268.60$$

2. What fund values would have emerged if deposits had consistently yielded 4 per cent p.a. while equities yielded 28, – 12, 28, – 12 and 15.8 per cent in successive years? (Note that these equity yields provide the same average compound rate of return as a constant 8 per cent p.a.)

Year	Initial value (£)		Value after return (£)		Value after rebalancing (£)	
	Equities	Deposit	Equities	Deposit	Equities	Deposit
1	100.00	100.00	128.00	104.00	116.00	116.00
2	116.00	116.00	112.64	120.64	116.64	116.64
3	116.64	116.64	149.30	121.31	135.30	135.30
4	135.30	135.30	119.07	140.71	129.89	129.89
5	129.89	129.89	150.41	135.09	142.75	142.75

The total value of the fund after five years is £285.50. In the absence of rebalancing the fund value would have been £100 (1.28) (0.88) (1.28) (0.88) (1.158) + £100(1.04)s = £268.59.

There is a dynamic replication of a short call option position. Rising stock prices lead to a sale of shares, producing a decline in delta; falling share prices lead to buying, thereby raising the delta of the implicit option. The implicit option sale should enhance returns, with the enhancement rising with share price volatility and the length of time for which the investment is made.

The difference between the fund values of £267.64 in (1) and £285.50 in (2) represents the time value of the implicit short option. In (1) there is zero volatility of returns on equities whereas in (2) there is a non-zero volatility. It will be seen from (3) that an increase in the volatility of equity returns causes an increase in the time value of the implicit option and hence a further enhancement of the return on the fund.

3. Carry out (2) with equity returns of 56, – 24, S6, – 24, and 4.5 per cent in successive years. (These equity returns provide the same average compound rate as in (1) and (2)).

Year	Initial value (£)		Value after return (£)		Value after rebalancing (£)	
	Equities	Deposit	Equities	Deposit	Equities	Deposit
1	100.00	100.00	156.00	104.00	130.00	130.00
2	130.00	130.00	98.80	135.20	117.00	117.00
3	117.00	117.00	183.52	140.61	161.56	161.56
4	161.56	161.56	122.79	168.02	145.41	145.41
5	145.41	145.41	151.95	151.22	151.59	151.59

The total value of the fund after five years is £303.17. This compares to £268.59 without rebalancing and £293.87 with 100 per cent investment in equities.

4. Carry out (3) but instead of the deposit use an investment in bonds with returns of 28, −12, 28, −12, and −4.1 per cent. (The average compound rate of return on bonds is thus the same as that produced by a constant 4 per cent p.a.)

Year	Initial value (£)		Value after return (£)		Value after rebalancing (£)	
	Equities	Deposit	Equities	Deposit	Equities	Deposit
1	100.00	100.00	156.00	128.00	142.00	142.00
2	142.00	142.00	107.92	124.96	116.44	116.44
3	116.44	116.44	181.65	149.04	165.34	165.34
4	165.34	165.34	125.66	145.50	135.58	135.58
5	135.58	135.58	141.68	130.02	127.85	127.85

The total fund value after five years would be £255.69. In the absence of rebalancing, the fund value would have been £268.59. The implicit short call on the equities is accompanied by an implicit long call on the bonds. The enhancement from the short option is offset by the implicit payment of an option premium.

5. Carry out (4) but with bond returns of −12, 28, −12, 28, and 4.1 per cent (again producing an average compound rate of return equal to that from a constant 4 per cent p.a.).

Year	Initial value (£)		Value after return (£)		Value after rebalancing (£)	
	Equities	Deposit	Equities	Deposit	Equities	Deposit
1	100.00	100.00	156.00	88.00	122.00	122.00
2	122.00	122.00	92.72	156.16	124.44	124.44
3	124.44	124.44	194.13	109.51	151.82	151.82
4	151.82	151.82	115.38	194.33	154.86	154.86
5	154.86	154.86	161.82	148.51	155.17	155.17

The total fund value after five years would be £310.33. In the absence of rebalancing, the fund value would have been £268.59. In this case both equities and bonds are subject to a 'buy low, sell high' strategy so that there are implicit short options on both equities and bonds, and hence yield enhancements on both corresponding to the option premiums.

Evaluation

When using a fixed ratio between equities and deposits total fund returns are greater when the volatility of equity returns rises. This is consistent with the yield enhancement from the implicit sale of an option rising with increased volatility, as would be expected given the relationship between option prices and the volatility of the underlying instrument.

When comparing fixed ratio strategies it can be seen that if bond returns negatively correlate with equity returns, then combining equities with bonds provides the highest returns, whereas if bond returns positively correlate with equity returns, then combining equities with deposits is the superior strategy. Empirically, bond returns tend to positively correlate with equity returns, whereas returns on deposits tend to have a lower (possibly even negative) correlation with equity returns. Such observations suggest the superiority of equity-deposit funds over equity-bond funds.

This superiority of equity-deposit funds could be overturned if bond returns, on average, sufficiently exceeded returns on deposits. This implies that higher correlation with equity returns should be compensated for with higher expected returns on bonds. Such an inference is consistent with the increased expected returns required to compensate for increased systematic risk (usually measured by beta) in the Capital Asset Pricing Model.

CONCLUSIONS

Financial derivatives can be used to change the characteristics of portfolios. Furthermore they can be used to construct investment products that would not otherwise be available. Every investment has its own expected return and risk features. Derivatives can be used to modify these features to create risk/return profiles that would not be available without financial engineering.

Further reading

A useful text on financial engineering is:

S. Eckl, J. N. Robinson and D. C. Thomas, *Financial Engineering* (Blackwell, Oxford, 1990).

REFERENCES

Black, F., Derman, E. and Toy, W., 'A one-factor model of interest rates and its application to treasury bond options', *Financial Analysts Journal*, 11, 1990.

Black, F. and Scholes, M., 'The pricing of options and corporate liabilities', *Journal of Political Economy*, 81, 1973.

Buckley, A., *The Essence of International Money*, 2nd edn, Prentice Hall, Hemel Hempstead, 1996.

Campbell, T. S. and Kracaw, W. A., *Financial Risk Management*, Harper Collins, New York, 1993.

Carpenter, A., *Inside the International Financial Futures Markets*, Woodhead-Faulkner, Cambridge, 1991.

Chamberlin, G., *Trading in Options*, 3rd edn, Woodhead-Faulkner, Cambridge, 1990.

Chance, D. M., *An Introduction to Options and Futures*, Dryden, Orlando, 1989.

Cox, J., Ross, S. and Rubinstein, M., 'Option pricing: a simplified approach', *Journal of Financial Economics*, 7, 1979.

Daigler, R. T., *Financial Futures Markets*, Harper Collins, New York, 1993.

DeCovny, S., *Swaps*, Woodhead-Faulkner, Hemel Hempstead, 1992.

Dixon, R. and Holmes, P., *Financial Markets*, Chapman & Hall, London, 1992.

Dubofsky, D. A., *Options and Financial Futures*, McGraw-Hill, Singapore, 1992.

REFERENCES

Eales, B. A., *Financial Risk Management*, McGraw-Hill, Maidenhead, 1995.

Eckl, S., Robinson, J. N. and Thomas, D. C., *Financial Engineering*, Blackwell, Oxford, 1990.

Edwards, F. R. and Ma, C. W., *Futures and Options*, McGraw-Hill, Maidenhead, 1992.

Fitzgerald, M. D., *Financial Futures*, Euromoney Publications, London, 1983.

Fitzgerald, M. D., *Financial Options*, Euromoney Publications, London, 1987.

Gemmill, G., *Options Pricing*, McGraw-Hill, Maidenhead, 1993.

Heath, D., Jarrow, R. and Morton, A., *Bond Pricing and the Term Structure of Interest Rates: A New Methodology for Contingent Claims Evaluation*, Cornell University, 1989.

Heath, D., Jarrow, R. and Morton, A., 'Bond pricing and the term structure of interest rates: a discrete time approximation', *Journal of Financial and Quantitative Analysis*, 1991.

Ho, T. and Lee, S., 'Term structure movements and the pricing of interest rate claims', *Journal of Finance*, 41, 1986.

Hull, J., *Options, Futures and Other Derivative Securities*, 2nd edn, Prentice Hall, Englewood Cliffs, 1993.

Hull, J., *Introduction to Futures and Options Markets*, 2nd edn, Prentice Hall, Englewood Cliffs, 1995.

Hull, J. and White, A., 'Pricing interest-rate-derivative securities', *Review of Financial Studies*, 3, 1990.

Kolb, R. W., *Financial Derivatives*, Kolb Publishing, Miami, 1993.

McMillan, L.G., *Options as a Strategic Investment*, 3rd edn, New York Institute of Finance, New York, 1992.

Mandell, L. and O'Brien, T. J., *Investments*, Maxwell Macmillan, Singapore, 1992.

Marshall, J. F., *Futures and Option Contracting*, South-Western, Cincinnati, 1989.

Redhead, K., *Introduction to the International Money Markets*, Woodhead-Faulkner, Hemel Hempstead, 1992.

Redhead, K., *Introduction to Financial Investment*, Prentice Hall, Hemel Hempstead, 1995.

Redhead, K. and Hughes, S., *Financial Risk Management*, Gower, Aldershot, 1988.

Ritchken, P., *Options*, Scott, Foresman, Glenview, 1987.

Rutterford, J., *Introduction to Stock Exchange Investment*, 2nd edn, Macmillan, Basingstoke, 1993.

Sharpe, W. F. and Alexander, G. J., *Investments*, 5th edn, Prentice Hall, Englewood Cliffs, 1995.

Stonham, P. and Redhead, K. (eds.), *European Casebook on Finance*, Prentice Hall, Hemel Hempstead, 1995.

Sutcliffe, C. M. S., *Stock Index Futures*, Chapman & Hall, London, 1992.

Watsham, T. J., *Options and Futures in International Portfolio Management*, Chapman & Hall, London, 1992.

Webber, A., *Dictionary of Futures and Options*, Probus, Cambridge, 1994.

Winstone, D., *Financial Derivatives*, Chapman & Hall, London, 1995.

GLOSSARY

Accrued interest The amount of interest accumulated on a bond since its last coupon payment date.

AFOFs Authorised futures and options funds (UK).

All-or-nothing options Digital options that pay out a set amount if the underlying asset is above or below the strike price at expiry. (The amount the option is in the money is irrelevant since it is a fixed amount that is paid out). See also Digital options.

American option An option that can be exercised at any time before expiration.

Amortising option An interest rate or swap option whose notional amount (underlying value) decreases during the life of the option. This includes amortising caps, collars and swaptions.

Anticipatory hedge A transaction in which hedger expects to make a transaction in the spot market at a future date and is attempting to obtain protection against a change in the spot price.

APT LIFFE's Automated Pit Trading System It operates from terminals in members' offices from 4.30 to 6.00 p.m. after the floor has closed. Its displays replicate floor trading.

Arbitrage The simultaneous purchase and sale of similar financial instruments to benefit from an expected change in relative prices.

Arbitrage(u)r An individual who engages in an arbitrage transaction.

Asian option (average rate option) An option that gives the holder the right to deal at the average price of the underlying asset over the life of the option. At the expiry of the option, the average spot rate is calculated and compared with the strike price. If in the money, a cash payment is then made to the buyer representing the difference between the 2 rates times the face value of the option. The volatility of the average rate is lower than that of the price of the underlying. So these options are cheaper than standard options.

Ask price The price at which a market maker offers to sell. Also known as offer price.

Assignment Notice to an option writer that an option has been exercised by an option holder. An assignment notice is generally issued by the clearing house for exchange traded options.

Atlantic option The name given to an option where the exercise style, American or European, can vary over the life of the option depending on the value of the underlying.

At-the-money option An option whose exercise price is equal to the market price of the underlying asset.

Automatic exercise A procedure for exchange-listed options whereby the clearing house automatically exercises in-the-money options at expiration.

Backwardation A condition in financial markets in which the forward or futures price is less than the spot price. Alternatively defined as a condition in which the fair forward or futures price is below the expected price (the spot price that the market expects to hold on the maturity date of the forward or futures contract).

Barrier option There are various forms of barrier option. It is a path dependent option that becomes cancelled, or alternatively becomes activated, if the underlying asset attains a certain level (out-strike, in-strike). Up-and-out options are puts that become cancelled if the underlying rises above a certain level. Up-and-in options are worthless unless the underlying rises above a certain price. Down-and-out options are calls that are cancelled if the underlying falls below a certain price, while down-and-ins are activated only when the underlying asset price falls to a certain level.

Basis The difference between the spot price of a financial instrument and the price of a futures contract on that instrument.

Basis point A measurement of the change in yield levels for fixed-income securities. One basis point equals 0.01%.

Basket option An option that gives the holder the right to buy or sell a basket of assets (usually currencies) against a base asset (currency).

Bear call spread A spread designed to take advantage of falling asset prices by selling a call option with low exercise price and buying one with a high exercise price.

Bear put spread A spread designed to take advantage of falling asset prices by purchasing a put option with a high exercise price and selling one with a low exercise price.

BED spread The spread obtained from US Treasury bill and eurodollar futures. This is a trade based on quality margins.

Bermuda option An option that is part-way between an American and a European option. Typically, it can be exercised on a number of predetermined occasions as stated in the option contract. It is a limited exercise or quasi-American option.

Beta A measure of the relative volatility of stock price movements and market movements.

Better-of-two-assets option An option that pays out on the better performing of 2 underlying assets: one that pays out the better performing of 2 stock indices.

Bid An offer to purchase a specified quantity of a contract at a specified price.

Bid–offer spread The difference between the offer price and the bid price. Also known as the bid–ask spread.

Bid price The price at which a market maker offers to buy a currency, security, option or futures.

Binomial model An option pricing model based on the assumption that at any point in time the price of the underlying asset or futures can change to one of only 2 possible values.

Black's model A pricing model for an option on a forward or futures contract.

Black–Scholes model A pricing model for an option on an asset.

Board of Trade Clearing Corporation An independent corporation that settles all trades made at the Chicago Board of Trade acting as a guarantor for all trades cleared by it, reconciles all clearing member firm accounts each day to ensure that all gains have been credited and all losses have been collected, and sets and adjusts clearing member firm margins for changing market conditions. Also referred to as the Clearing Corporation. See Clearing house.

Boundary condition A statement specifying the maximum or minimum price or some other limitation on the price of an option.

Box spread A combination of a horizontal, or calendar, call spread and a horizontal put spread. Both spreads have the same expiration dates on their long and short positions, and have the same strike prices. One would be a bull spread and the other a bear spread.

Breakeven point The underlying price at which a given options strategy is neither profitable nor unprofitable.

Break forward A forward contract which the purchaser can break at a predetermined rate. This allows advantage to be taken of any favourable rate movements. It usually relates to currencies. It is also known as a Boston option, cancellable forward and a forward break.

British Bankers' Association Interest Settlement Rate The rate used by LIFFE to settle its three-month interest rate contracts.

Broker A person paid a fee or commission for acting as an agent in making sales or purchases. A floor broker is a person who actually executes someone else's trading orders on the trading floor of an exchange.

BTP Italian government bond.

Bull call spread A spread designed to take advantage of rising asset prices by buying a call option with a low exercise price and selling one with a high exercise price.

Bull put spread A spread designed to take advantage of rising asset prices by selling a put option with a high exercise price and buying one with a low exercise price.

Bunds German government bonds. Usually issued with maturities of 10 years. They pay an annual coupon.

Butterfly spread (futures) A spread taken out in 2 adjacent contracts together with an opposite spread in the later contract and the next maturity contract. It is the placing of 2 inter-delivery spreads in opposite directions with the centre delivery month common to both spreads.

Butterfly spread (options) A combination of a bull and bear spread, either put or call, using 3 different exercise prices. A volatility trading strategy.

Buy–writes Strategies that involve the purchase of stock and the simultaneous writing of call options against it. They reduce the cost of the stock purchase to the extent of the premium received.

CAC 40 The principal French equity index. Futures trade on MATIF and options on MONEP.

Calendar spread A spread involving the simultaneous sale of an option with a nearby expiration date and the purchase of an option with a more deferred expiration date. Both options have the same exercise price. Also known as a horizontal spread or a time spread.

Call option An option giving the buyer the right to purchase the underlying asset at a fixed exercise price at or before expiration.

Cap An option agreement that puts a ceiling or cap on an interest rate or on rates of reference in foreign exchange or equity markets. The cap is a strip of interest rate guarantees. If, on prescribed reference dates, a standard rate is above a rate agreed between the seller of the cap and the buyer, then the seller pays the buyer the extra interest costs until the next reference date.

Capped option An option where the holder's potential profit from a favourable change in the underlying asset is capped off at a specific limited amount.

Caption An option to buy a cap. A form of compound option giving the holder the right, but not the obligation, to enter into a cap contract at a predetermined rate on a predetermined date.

Carry The cost of holding an asset including the cost of borrowing to purchase it.

Carry basis The difference between the cash price and the fair futures price. It reflects the net carrying cost. Actual basis is the sum of carry basis and value basis.

Cash and carry A theoretically riskless transaction consisting of a long position in the spot asset and a short position in the futures contract that is designed to be held until the futures contract expires.

Cash market The underlying currency, money or capital market in which transactions for the purchase and sale of cash instruments to which futures contracts relate are carried out. Also known as the spot market.

Cash settlement A procedure for the settlement of futures contracts where, at delivery, instead of the physical transfer of the underlying asset, there is a final marking to market at the existing cash price and the positions are closed.

CBOE Chicago Board Options Exchange.

CBOT Chicago Board of Trade.

Certificate of deposit (CD) A tradeable time deposit with a specific maturity evidenced by a certificate.

CFTC   Commodity Futures Trading Commission. The federal agency that regulates the futures markets in the United States.

Charm   A measure of the change in delta as time passes while other variables remain the same.

Chooser option   An option that offers the holder the choice during a predetermined period to designate the option to be a call or a put.

Class of options   All call options or put options on the same underlying asset.

Clean price   The price of a bond or gilt exclusive of accrued interest.

Clearing   The process by which a clearing house maintains records of all trades and settles margin flow on a daily mark-to-market basis for its clearing members. Also the procedure through which the clearing house or association becomes buyer to each seller of a futures contract, and seller to each buyer, and assumes responsibility for protecting buyers and sellers from loss by assuring the financial integrity of each contract open on its books.

Clearing house   The organisation which registers, monitors, matches and guarantees trades on a futures or options market, and carries out financial settlement of transactions.

Clearing member   A member firm of the clearing house. Each clearing member must also be a member of an exchange, but not all members of an exchange are also members of the clearing house. All trades of a non-clearing member must be registered with, and eventually settled through, a clearing member. Also known as a clearing firm.

Close, the   The period at the end of the trading session, officially designated by the exchange, during which all transactions are considered to be made 'at the close'.

Close out   Undertake a transaction that cancels an existing position (e.g. a purchase to eliminate a short position).

Closing price   The price at which transactions are made at the close on a given day. Frequently there is not just one price, but a range of prices at which transactions were made at the close.

Closing purchase   The purchase of an option identical in exercise price and expiration date to an option originally sold to liquidate an open option position. Likewise buying a futures contract to cancel an existing short position.

Closing range   The high and low prices at which transactions took place during 'the close'.

Closing sale The sale of a derivative that cancels an open purchased position.

CME Chicago Mercantile Exchange.

Collar This is the simultaneous purchase of a cap and sale of a floor used with interest rates. It thus establishes a desired band in which buyers of the collar want their interest rate costs to be held.

Colour A measure of the rate of change of gamma as time passes and other variables remain the same.

Combination A position created either by purchasing a put and a call or by writing a put and a call, on the same underlying asset but with different exercise prices and/or expiry dates. Also any options strategy formed from calls and puts.

Combo A bought put with a short call at a higher strike price. In other words a short cylinder.

Commercial paper A short-term promissory note issued by a large, creditworthy corporation.

Compound option An option on an option.

Contango A condition in financial markets in which the forward or futures price is greater than the spot price. Alternatively a condition in which the fair futures price exceeds the expected spot price.

Contingent option An option where the premium, while higher than usual, is paid only if the value of the underlying asset reaches a specified level. Also known as a contingent premium option.

Continuously compounded return A rate of return in which the asset value grows continuously, as opposed to interest being paid at discrete intervals.

Contract month The month in which futures contracts may be satisfied by making or accepting delivery.

Convergence The movement to equality of spot and futures prices as the delivery date approaches.

Corner Secure such relative control of a commodity or security that its price can be manipulated. In the extreme situation, obtaining contracts requiring delivery of more commodities or securities than are available for delivery.

Counterparty risk The exposure of one party to the risk that a trade counterparty might default or fail to deliver his or her obligations with no form of insurance or contract guarantee available to offset or mitigate such an occurrence.

Coupon   The interest paid on a bond or gilt.

Coupon yield   The coupon of a bond divided by the (dirty) price of the bond and expressed as an annualised percentage. Also known as flat yield, interest yield or running yield.

Covered call write   A strategy of writing call options against a long position of the underlying asset.

Covered option   A written option is covered if it is matched by an opposing cash or futures position in the underlying asset, or by an opposing option position.

Covered put write   A strategy of writing put options while simultaneously shorting an identical amount of the underlying asset.

Covered warrant   A warrant issued by a company or securities house that enables the holder to buy shares in another company. It is referred to as covered because the issuer should have made arrangements to hold or obtain the underlying shares at the time the warrant may be exercised. Alternatively known as a third party warrant.

Cox–Ingersoll–Ross option pricing model   A model for pricing interest rate options. It does not guarantee consistency with the initial term structure, has mean reversion, and an analytic solution for European options.

Cross-currency cap   A cap where the payout to the holder is the spread between 2 currency base rates (say sterling LIBOR and dollar LIBOR) minus a strike spread, where this exceeds zero. It can thus be considered as a strip of options on forward spread agreements.

Cross hedging   The hedging with a futures contract of a different, but related, cash instrument.

Cross rates   The exchange rate between 2 currencies implied by their exchange rates with a third currency, e.g. the £/DM rate implied by the £/$ and DM/$ rates.

Cum   Cum-dividend means a security is sold such that the buyer will obtain the next dividend or coupon.

Currency contract   A futures or options contract for a currency, quoted in terms of another. The major world currency futures market is the IMM division of the Chicago Mercantile Exchange, while the premier options market is the Philadelphia Stock Exchange.

Currency option   The option to buy or sell a specified amount of a given currency at a stated rate at or by a specified date in the future.

Currency warrant   A warrant giving the holder the right to purchase a currency, at a particular exchange rate.

Current delivery The futures contract that will become deliverable during the current month.

Current yield The bond's annual coupon payment divided by that bond's current market price. Also known as coupon yield, interest yield or running yield.

Cylinder The purchase of a call and writing of a lower exercise put, or purchase of a put and writing of a higher exercise call.

Daily price limits The maximum and minimum prices at which a futures contract can trade. These are established by the clearing house and are expressed in relation to the previous day's settlement price.

Daily settlement The process in a futures market in which the daily price changes are paid by the parties incurring losses to the parties making profits.

DAX The German stock index on 30 blue-chip equities. A future on the index is available on the DTB.

Day trading Refers to establishing and liquidating the same futures position or positions within one day's trading.

Debt warrant A warrant enabling the holder to buy a bond or debt at a fixed price over a given period of time.

Deferred futures The contracts maturing in the more distant delivery months in which futures trading is taking place.

Deferred pay out option An American option where settlement is at expiry.

Deferred start option An option purchased before its life commences. This might be used by investors who want to lock into current prices for options they know they will need some time in the future.

Deferred strike option An option, usually on foreign exchange, where the exercise or strike price is established at a future date from a prescribed formula based on the spot exchange rate on that future date.

Delivery The tender and receipt of an actual financial instrument or cash in settlement of a futures contract.

Delivery date The date on which the underlying financial instrument must be delivered to fulfil the terms of a futures contract.

Delivery month A calendar month during which delivery against a futures contract can be made.

Delivery notice The written notice given by the seller of his intention to make delivery against an open, short futures position on a particular date.

Delivery price The price fixed by the clearing house at which deliveries on futures contracts are invoiced.

Delta A measure of the amount the option price will change for a one-unit change in the price of the underlying asset (the derivative of the option price with respect to the asset price).

Delta hedge An options hedge in which the number of contracts is ratioed up by the reciprocal of the option delta in order to achieve complete cover for the hedged position.

Delta neutral A position is said to be delta neutral if it has a delta of zero. Such a position will not change in value if the price of the underlying moves, so long as the move is small.

Derivatives Instruments derived from securities or physical markets, essentially forwards, futures, options and swaps. Thus options on equities or futures on bonds are derived from the underlying cash markets and hence may be termed derivatives.

Deutsche Terminbörse (DTB) Located in Frankfurt, it lists contracts on the DAX, Bunds and individual stock options.

Diagonal spread A spread in which the options differ with respect to both strike price and expiry date.

Difference option An option whose payout is based on the difference between the prices of 2 underlying assets.

Digital options Pay out of a fixed amount if the underlying reaches a predetermined level. These options can be cheaper than conventional options because the payout is restricted and not open ended.

Dirty price The price of a bond including accrued interest.

Distant months The far-dates delivery (or expiry) months in a futures (or options) contract.

Dividend That part of a company's post tax profits distributed to shareholders. It is a discretionary payment, not a fixed amount, except in the case of preference shares.

Dividend protection A feature associated with some over-the-counter options in which the exercise price is reduced by an amount of any dividend paid on the underlying stock.

Dividend yield The ratio of the dividend to the stock price.

Double option   An option to buy or sell but not both. Exercise of the right to buy causes the right to sell to expire and vice versa.

Down-and-out call   A call option that expires if the asset price falls below a predetermined level.

Dual-currency option   An option that allows the holder to buy either of 2 currencies.

Dual-strike option   An interest rate option, usually either a cap or a floor, with one rate for part of the option's life and another for the rest of its life. Essentially it is 2 options running back to back, one being a deferred start option.

Duration   The sensitivity of a bond's price to a change in its yield.

Early exercise   Exercise of an option before its expiration date.

EDSP   Exchange delivery settlement price, the price at which futures contracts are settled for delivery, the balance being paid over by way of margin to achieve the price of the contract (if cash settled).

Eligible margin   The cash or other collateral which the exchange specifies that members may accept from their customers to satisfy initial and variation margin requirements.

Epsilon   The change in the price of an option associated with a 1% change in implied volatility (the derivative of the option price with respect to volatility). Also referred to as eta, vega, omega and kappa.

Equities   Common stocks or ordinary shares.

Equity option   An option on a stock.

Equity warrant   A warrant, usually attached to a bond but capable of being separated, entitling the holder to purchase shares. The shares are usually those of the warrant issuing company but not always.

Eurodollar   A dollar deposited in a bank outside the United States.

European currency unit   A combination of European currencies.

European option   A call or put option that can be exercised only on the expiration date.

Ex   The opposite of cum. A share bought ex-dividend will not entitle the purchaser to obtain the next dividend.

Exchange rate   The rate at which a given amount of one currency converts to another currency.

Exchange rate agreement   A synthetic agreement for forward exchange. In contrast to a forward agreement it is settled without reference to the spot rate and does not reflect changes in the spot market. It guarantees a particular premium or discount.

Exchange rate futures   Futures contracts for currencies.

Ex-dividend date   A date after which an investor purchasing a stock does not become eligible to receive the upcoming dividend. The seller will receive the dividend.

Exercise   The action taken by the holder of an option contract to exercise his right. When a call is exercised, the holder acquires the underlying asset at the option exercise price. When a put is exercised, the holder sells the underlying asset at the option exercise price.

Exercise limit   A limit on the number of option contracts a holder may exercise within a specific period.

Exercise notice   A notice in writing delivered to a clearing house on or by a specific time giving notice of intent from an option holder (buyer) that they wish to make or take delivery of the underlying instrument.

Exercise price   The price at which the option holder may buy or sell the underlying asset, as defined in the option contract. Also known as the strike, or striking, price.

Expiry   The date after which an option can no longer be exercised (the date on which it ceases to exist).

Extinguishable option   An option where the holder's right to exercise is cancelled if the value of the underlying passes a specified level.

Extrinsic value   That part of the premium of an option which is not intrinsic value. Usually known as time value.

Fair value   The option value derived from an option valuation model. The theoretical futures price (the price that would offer no arbitrage profits in the absence of transactions costs).

Financial instrument   The actual currency, security or deposit which is specified in a financial futures or options contract.

Fixed hedge   A hedge in which the quantity being hedged is matched by the quantity that the options give the right to buy or sell.

Fiva   Forward or futures contract on implied volatility.

Floating rate note (FRN)   A bond that pays a coupon that is set off a reference rate, e.g. LIBOR + x%. In other words, it does not carry a fixed rate of interest: the interest rate is changed at fixed intervals, e.g. every 6 months.

Floor   A series of European exercise interest rate put option contracts whereby the seller will refund to a holder the difference between current interest rates and an agreed strike rate should rates fall below the floor. Like caps, with which they may be combined to form collars, they are based on a reference rate such as three-month or six-month LIBOR.

Floortion An option on a floor.

Forward band A zero-cost collar, i.e. one in which the premium paid for the cap is offset by the premium gained from selling the floor.

Forward An agreement between 2 parties – a buyer and a seller – to buy an asset or currency at a later date at a fixed price.

Forward/forward rate The rate agreed upon in a forward contract for a loan or the rate implied by the relationship between interest rates for different maturities. Alternatively known as the forward interest rate.

Forward market A market in which forward contracts are traded.

Forward rate agreement (FRA) A contract to provide a given interest rate, for a given maturity, from a date in the future. Quotations are made on the basis of bid and offer yield levels for the period of the FRA. They are labelled on the basis of the number of months to the start and end of the FRA. For example, a three-month FRA starting one month forward, would be termed a 1 × 4 FRA. It starts in one month and ends after 4 months.

Forward spread agreement The counterparties contract into a spread between 2 forward rate agreement (FRA) rates applied to a nominal amount of one currency. The settlement amount is the spread between prevailing LIBOR rates minus the contracted spread.

Forward start option An option that provides the purchaser the right, after a contracted period of time, to hold a standard put or call option with an at-the-money exercise price at the time the option is granted rather than when it is activated.

FRA Forward rate agreement. Alternatively known as a future rate agreement.

Front month The nearest maturity contract month trading.

FTSE 100 Index Index of 100 major UK shares listed on the London Stock Exchange. It was drawn up specifically to be used for a futures contract and trades on LIFFE as a future and as a European- and American-style option.

Fugit The probability of early exercise on an American-style option. It is measured either in per cent, or on a comparable scale of zero to ten. It is a product of the delta and the theta.

Fungibility The characteristic of interchangeability. Futures contracts for the same instrument and delivery month are fungible due to their standardised specifications for quality, delivery date and delivery locations. The homogeneity of contracts means that a contract can be closed out with any counterparty. In some cases a contract established on one exchange can be closed out on another.

Future rate agreement A forward rate agreement (FRA).

Futures butterfly See Butterfly spread (futures).

Futures contract A contract traded on a futures exchange for the (possibly notional) delivery of a specified quantity of a specified commodity or financial instrument at a future time.

Futures fund A mutual fund that specialises in trading futures contracts.

Futures option An option written on a futures contract rather than a cash or spot instrument.

Gamma The amount by which the delta of an option changes for a one-unit change in the price of the underlying asset (the second derivative of the option price with respect to the asset price).

Gearing The ability to gain exposure to a larger monetary value of a financial instrument with a comparatively small amount of capital. Futures and options, where margin or premium form the initial down payment, offer high gearing. Also known as leverage.

GFOFs Geared futures and options funds (UK).

Gilts Gilt-edged securities, British government bonds.

GLOBEX Global Electronic Exchange jointly developed by the CME, CBOT, Reuters and MATIF. It is an electronic trading system which displays prices of various contracts around the world. Bids and offers are shown, together with market size. Deals can be done on screen and confirmation is shown almost instantaneously.

Grantor The maker, writer, or seller of an option contract.

Gut A strangle formed from in-the-money options, i.e. buy a call and buy a put at a higher exercise price when the underlying's price lies between the 2 exercise prices.

Haircut The discount applied by the clearing house to assets such as government bonds deposited as margin collateral.

Hang Seng index The Hong Kong equity index on about 30 stocks representing 70% of market turnover.

Hedge A transaction in which an investor seeks to protect a position or anticipated position in the spot market by using an opposite position in derivatives.

Hedged portfolio A portfolio being hedged, often used in the context of a long stock, short call or long stock, long put in which the hedge ratio is continuously adjusted to produce a risk-free portfolio.

Hedger A person who hedges.

Hedge ratio The ratio of options or futures to a spot position that achieves an objective such as minimising or eliminating risk.

Hi–low option A combination of 2 look-back or path-dependent options. Such an option pays the difference between the high and low during a specified period of an underlying asset. If the difference between the high and low levels is greater than the premium, the holder makes a profit.

Historical volatility The standard deviation of a security, futures or currency obtained by estimating it from historical data over a recent time period.

Horizontal spread See Calendar spread.

IMM The International Monetary Market of the Chicago Mercantile Exchange, listing currency and interest rate futures.

Implied delta Delta calculated from the implied volatility of the option rather than the volatility estimate input to the option pricing model. This delta is also known as the price delta.

Implied volatility The value of asset price volatility that will equate the fair value of an option with the market price of that option.

Index option An option written on an underlying stock index as opposed to a specific asset.

Initial margin The deposit a customer must make on purchasing or selling a futures contract.

Inter-delivery spread The purchase of one delivery month of a given futures and simultaneous sale of another delivery month of the same futures on the same exchange. Also known as intra-market spread or futures straddle.

Interest rate guarantee (FRAption) An option on a forward rate agreement. Purchasers have the right, but not obligation, to take an FRA at an agreed strike price or interest rate level. A strip of interest rate guarantees forms a cap.

Interest rate option Option to pay, or receive, a specified rate of interest on or from a predetermined date.

Interest rate parity The equality of the forward (or futures) premium/discount between 2 currencies and the interest rate differential between those currencies.

Intermarket Clearing Corporation A subsidiary of the OCC clearing futures for the AMEX Commodities Corporation, New York Futures Exchange and the Philadelphia Board of Trade. OCC provides operations, processing, system development and risk management services to ICC. Cross-margining of hedged positions exists with OCC.

Inter-market spread The sale of a given delivery month of a futures contract on one exchange and the simultaneous purchase of the same delivery month and a related futures contract on another exchange. See TED spread and BED spread.

International Commodities Clearing House (ICCH) Organisation owned by the major UK banks that, through its London clearing house division, clears both futures and options contracts for the London exchanges.

Interval The standard differential or interval between the exercise or strike prices of traded options contracts.

In-the-money option An option having intrinsic value. A call option is in the money if its strike price is below the current price of the underlying asset. A put option is in the money if its strike price is above the current price of the underlying asset.

Intra-contract spread A futures transaction consisting of a long position in a futures expiring in one month and a short position in an otherwise identical futures expiring in another month. Also known as a futures straddle, inter-delivery spread, or intra-market spread.

Intrinsic value The amount of profit that would be realised if the option were immediately exercised (ignoring the premium paid). Also known as parity value.

Inverted market A futures market in which the nearer months are selling at a premium to the more distant months.

Invoice amount The cash amount paid and received upon delivery against a government bond futures contract.

Irish Futures and Options Exchange (IFOX) Located in Dublin, this lists contracts on Irish gilts, three-month DIBOR, and the ISEQ index.

ISDA International Swap Dealers Association.

Jelly rolls (options) An arbitrage strategy comprised of a long synthetic asset position in one month and a short synthetic asset position in a different month, where both synthetic positions are done at the same exercise price.

JGB   Japanese government bond. Most JGBs are of 10-year maturity and pay coupons semi-annually.

Kappa   See Vega.

Ladder   A table top, i.e. buy a call, sell a higher strike call and sell an equally higher strike call, or sell a put, sell a higher strike put and buy an equally higher strike put.

Last trading day   The final day during which trading may take place in a particular delivery month. Futures contracts outstanding at the end of the last trading day must be settled by delivery of the specified financial instrument, or settlement may be made in cash in certain contracts.

LEAPS   Long-term Equity AnticiPation securities. These are long-dated options listed on CBOE and PHLX among others.

Leg   One side of a spread position.

LEPOs   Low exercise price options that trade on SOFFEX.

Leverage   The ability to control large monetary amounts of a financial instrument or commodity with a comparatively small amount of capital. Also known as gearing.

LIBID   The London inter-bank bid or deposit rate, or the rate at which banks will bid for funds (deposits).

LIBOR   The London Inter-Bank Offered Rate, or the rate at which banks will offer funds. Rates exist for overnight, one month, three months, six months, etc., up to five years, and for eurocurrencies.

LIFFE   London International Financial Futures and Options Exchange.

Lifting a leg   Closing-out one half of a spread position. The trader is now uncovered to the extent of the remaining (open) commitment.

LIMEAN   The average of LIBID and LIBOR.

Limit order   A request to purchase or sell a security, option or futures that specifies the maximum price to pay or the minimum price to accept.

Linkage   The ability to buy (sell) contracts on one exchange (such as the Chicago Mercantile Exchange) and later sell (buy) them on another exchange such as the Singapore International Monetary Exchange), i.e. mutual offset. A form of fungibility.

Liquid   A characteristic of a market with enough units outstanding to allow large transactions without a substantial change in price. Institutional investors are inclined to seek out liquid investments so that their trading activity will not influence the market price.

Liquid market   A market where buying and selling can be accomplished with ease, due to the presence of a large number of interested buyers and sellers prepared to trade substantial quantities at small price differences.

Local   A trader on the floor of the futures exchange who executes trades for his or her personal account.

LOCH   London Options Clearing House. The former clearing house for LTOM. It was a wholly owned subsidiary of the London Stock Exchange responsible for registering and settling all Stock Exchange options transactions.

London Clearing House (LCH)   The clearing house for LIFFE. It is owned by the major UK banks as a division of the ICCH. It provides a comprehensive service to members including registration, clearing, settlement, central banking and treasury, the administration of physical delivery and risk management.

London Inter-Bank Offered Rate (LIBOR)   The interest rate at which major London banks will lend to one another.

London International Financial Futures and Options Exchange (LIFFE)   A UK exchange which lists futures on long-term interest rates (bonds), short-term interest rates, and the FTSE 100 Index. It lists options on its futures, on the FTSE 100 Index and on individual UK equities.

London Stock Exchange   The UK Stock Exchange, listing UK gilts and fixed interest, domestic equities, international equities and traditional options.

Long   The position which is established by the purchase of an asset if there is no offsetting position. A position that benefits from price rises and loses from price falls.

Long hedge   The purchase of a futures contract in anticipation of actual purchases in the cash market.

Long of the basis   The position of a person who has purchased the cash instrument and hedged it with sales of the corresponding futures contract.

Long-term interest rate contracts   Futures and options contracts on long-term interest rates are contracts on bonds. The futures contracts are for notional bonds of a stated coupon and maturity range, such as LIFFE's long gilt future, which is based on a 9% notional gilt of 10–15 years' maturity.

Long-term interest rate futures These are bond futures on instruments such as long gilts, Treasury bonds, Bunds, BTPs, JGBs. The contracts are on notional instruments, but delivery is effected with actual bonds that meet eligibility requirements as set by the exchange in terms of maturity, liquidity, coupon, etc.

Lookback option An option that gives the holder the right to buy (call) at the lowest price or sell (put) at the highest price the underlying has traded at during the option's life.

Lookback strike options These set the strike rate for calls as the lowest, or for puts as the highest, level of the underlying asset over a period of time less than the final option maturity.

Macro hedging A strategy in which a firm hedges the combined exposure of all of its assets and liabilities.

Maintenance margin The minimum margin which a customer must keep on deposit with a member at all times.

Marché à Terme International de France (MATIF) Located in Paris, the exchange listing contracts on long- and short-term interest rates and stock indices.

Marché des Options Négociables de Paris (MONEP) The Paris options exchange listing contracts on individual equities and the CAC 40 stock index.

Margin calls Additional funds which a person with a position may be called upon to deposit if there is an adverse price change or if margin requirements alter.

Market-if-touched (MIT) Also called a board order. This order becomes a market order if the contract trades, or is offered at or below the limit price in the case of a buy order, or if the contract trades or is bid at or above the limit price in the case of a sell order.

Market maker An individual or organisation which, in exchange for reduced dealing fees and other concessions, commits in certain securities, contracts or markets to continuously make two-way prices (i.e. bids and offers) at an agreed maximum spread differential and for an agreed minimum volume, during market hours.

Market order An order to buy or sell a contract that is to be executed at the best possible price and as soon as possible.

Marking to market The process by which daily price changes are reflected in payments by parties incurring losses to parties making profits. Also known as daily settlement.

Matching system The system operated by or on behalf of an exchange for the matching and confirmation of contracts. Contracts are paired sellers to buyers in order to be confirmed by each before registration with the clearing house. They are then separated into contracts between each party and the clearing house alone.

MATIF Marché à Terme International de France.

Micro hedging A strategy in which a firm hedges only specific assets, liabilities or transactions as opposed to hedging the aggregate net exposure.

Minimax A collar with a tight range or, in foreign exchange markets, a strategy for reducing cost by forgoing some gain. An option buyer also sells an option at a different strike price.

MONEP See Marché des Options Négociables de Paris.

Money market The market for short-term securities.

Money spread An option transaction that involves a long position in one option and a short position in an otherwise identical option with a different exercise price. Also known as a vertical spread.

Multi-index option An option that gives the holder the right to buy the asset that performs best out of a number of assets, e.g. a call on the best performing index.

Mutual offset The ability to open a contract on one exchange and close it out on another, e.g. Treasury bond futures on CME and SIMEX. A form of fungibility.

Naked call writing Writing a call on an underlying asset which is not owned by the writer.

Nearby The nearest delivery or expiry month.

Nikkei 225 The Nikkei Stock Average on 225 Japanese equities traded on the Tokyo Stock Exchange. Derivatives contracts are available on Osaka, CME and Simex.

Nominal price Price quotation on a futures contract for a period in which no actual trading took place.

Nominal value The face value of a financial instrument. In the case of bonds this is usually 100 and all price quotes are expressed against this, i.e. 96 meaning 96% of the nominal value. Also known as par value or redemption value.

Non-clearing member A member of an exchange that is not a clearing member of the exchange's clearing house. All non-clearing member trades must clear through a clearing agent that is a clearing member of the clearing house.

Note futures Futures on US Treasury notes. They operate the same way as long-term interest rate or bond futures.

Notice day A day on which notices of intent to deliver, pertaining to a specified delivery month, may be issued.

Novation The principal of operation of a clearing house whereby it becomes the counterparty to each trade.

OCC Options Clearing Corporation. A clearing body for exchange traded options in the United States.

Offer A willingness to sell at a given price.

Offer price The price at which a market maker offers to sell.

OMLX, The London Securities and Derivatives Exchange The Swedish options market operating in London. It lists contracts on Swedish equities, the OMX Index, Treasury bills, government bonds and mortgage bonds.

OM Swedish options market listing equity, equity index, and interest rate futures and options. It is linked in to OMLX to form a single market.

One touch (all-or-nothing) options Digital options that pay out a fixed amount ('all') if, at any time during the life of the option, the underlying asset reaches a defined level.

Open contracts Contracts which have been bought or sold without the transactions having been completed or offset by subsequent sale or purchase, or actual delivery or receipt of the underlying financial instrument.

Opening The period at the beginning of the trading session officially designated by the exchange during which all transactions are considered to be made 'at the opening'.

Opening price (or range) The price or price range of transactions recorded during the period designated by the exchange as the official opening.

Opening purchase An order that establishes a new long position (rather than closing out a short one).

Opening sale An order that establishes a new short position (rather than closing out a long one).

Open interest The total of outstanding contracts.

Open outcry Method of dealing on futures and options markets involving verbal bids and offers (supported by hand signals) that are audible

422 • **GLOSSARY**

(visible) to all the other market participants in the trading pit, or on the trading floor.

Option   The right to buy or sell a specific quantity of a specific asset at a fixed price at or before a future date.

Option box   A long option box is a synthetic long asset at the low exercise price and a synthetic short asset at the higher exercise price. It is a long call and a short put at one exercise price and a short call and a long put at a higher exercise price. It is also equivalent to a bull call spread and a bear put spread. Conversely for a short option box.

Option forward   A forward foreign exchange contract with an option to select the date of the exchange.

Option premium   The going (market) price for an option.

Original margin   The initial deposit of margin money required to cover a specific new futures position.

Ordinary share   The most common form of shares or equity. The ordinary shareholders are the owners of a company. Holders receive dividends the amount of which will vary with the profitability of the company. Also known as common stock.

Osaka Securities Exchange (OSE)   Located in Osaka, Japan, this lists Nikkei 225 options and Osaka 50 futures.

OTC   Over-the-counter.

Out-of-the-money option   An option that has no intrinsic value – because for a call the exercise price is above the asset price, and for a put the exercise price is below the asset price.

Outperformance option   See Rainbow option.

Outright or outright forward   A forward.

Over the counter   A contract not made on a listed exchange. There is a direct link between buyer and seller, and no standardisation of contract terms.

Par   100% of the nominal value of a debt security.

Participating cap   The simultaneous purchase of an out-of-the-money cap and sale of a lesser amount of in-the-money floors. Since the floors are worth more than the caps a zero-cost combination can be purchased.

Participating option   An option where the buyer forgoes a certain percentage of potential profits in return for a reduced premium.

Path dependent option   An option with a payout directly related to movements in the price of the underlying asset during the life of the option, rather than the price at a point in time before expiry (American) or at expiry (European). As such the category includes average rate (Asian) options, barrier options and lookback options.

Perpetual bond (perpetuity) A bond with no predetermined redemption date. Many have a date after which they may be redeemed by the issuer. Effectively, they have an open-ended issuers' call.

Perturbation A measure of volatility based upon the change in the price of a bond in response to a specific change in the relevant interest rate.

Philadelphia Stock Exchange (PHLX) A US exchange which lists options on currencies, equities, and a number of stock indices.

Physical delivery Settlement of a contract by the delivery or receipt of a financial instrument.

Pit An octagonal area on the trading floor of an exchange, surrounded by a tier of steps upon which traders and brokers stand while executing futures trades.

Pitch Conventionally an options trading area, analogous to a futures pit.

Portfolio insurance An investment strategy employing combinations of securities, options or futures that is designed to provide downside protection of the portfolio.

Position An interest in the market, either long or short, in terms of open contracts.

Position limits The maximum number of puts and calls on the same side of the market (e.g. long calls and short puts) that can be held in a single account.

Position trading A type of trading involving the holding of open futures contracts for an extended period of time.

Premium (1) The excess of one futures contract price over that of another, or over the cash market price.

Premium (2) The price of an option – the sum of money which the option buyer pays and the option writer receives for the rights granted by the option.

Price factor The relative value of an actual deliverable bond when the actual bond has the same yield as the notional bond trading at par. Price factors are established for all deliverable bonds for each futures contract, calculated off the relative prices for the first day of the delivery month. This value, when multiplied by the settlement price, provides the price for the principal invoice amount. When accrued interest is added, this forms the invoice amount.

Price limits The maximum price advance or decline from the previous day's settlement price permitted for a contract in one trading session by the regulations of the exchange.

Price sensitivity hedge ratio The number of futures contracts used in a hedge that leaves the value of a portfolio unaffected by a change in an underlying variable, such as an interest rate.

Prime rate Interest rate charged by major banks to their most creditworthy customers (US).

Principal invoice amount The initial amount first calculated when calculating the invoice amount to a buyer for the delivery of a bond against a notional bond futures contract. It is the EDSP × price factor of each bond deliverable at delivery of LIFFE long-term interest rate contracts on long bonds.

Programme trading The use of computers to detect and trade upon mispricing in the relationship between the prices of stocks and stock index futures.

Protective put An investment strategy involving the use of a long position in a put and a stock to provide a minimum selling price for the stock.

Pure discount bond A bond, such as a Treasury bill, that pays no coupon but sells for a discount from par value.

Put–call parity A relationship between put and call prices that implies an absence of arbitrage opportunities.

Put option An option which gives the buyer the right to sell the underlying asset at a fixed price at or before the expiration date.

Pyramiding The practice of margining additional futures trades using accrued profits from previous futures transactions.

Rainbow option An option that offers the best performance of two or more selected markets, such as a call option on the greatest appreciation of the FT-All share or S&P 500. Also called an outperformance option.

Random walk A theory that price movements in the futures and securities markets are unrelated to previous price movements.

Range The high and low prices, or high and low bids and offers, recorded during a specified period.

Ratio hedging In financial futures trading, ratio hedging usually refers to the calculation of the proper ratio of futures to cash.

Ratio spread A spread in which the component options are not equal in number.

Ratio write Buying stock and selling options on a larger amount of stock.

Redemption value The value at which a financial instrument is redeemed by the issuer at maturity. For bonds, this is the par value or nominal value, usually 100.

Repo (repurchase agreement) The selling of a security by one party to another at the same time that the other party enters into an agreement to resell the security to the first party at a predetermined price and date.

Reversal A synthetic long position combined with a short position in the underlying instrument.

Rho A measure of the sensitivity of option prices to interest rate changes. The relevant interest rates are those relating to the period to expiry and which determine financing costs.

Riding the yield curve Trading in interest rate futures according to the expectation of a change in the yield curve.

Risk aversion The characteristic of an investor who dislikes risk and will not assume more risk without an additional return.

Risk premium The additional return risk-averse investors expect for assuming risk.

Risk–return trade off The concept in which additional risk must be accepted to increase the expected return.

Rolling hedge A futures hedging strategy that constantly uses only contracts with the nearest delivery month.

Roll-over Substitute a futures or options contract with a more distant expiry/delivery date for a previously established position.

Roll-over loan A loan for a fixed period during which there are regular specified intervals at which the interest rate is re-established.

Round turn A complete futures transaction in which a long or short position is established and subsequently closed out by an opposite futures transaction, or by making or taking delivery. Also known as a round trip.

Running yield The coupon of a bond divided by its (dirty) price and expressed as an annualised percentage. Also known as coupon yield, interest yield or flat yield.

Sandwich spread Butterfly spread.

Scalp Trade for small gains. Scalping usually involves establishing and liquidating a position quickly, always within the same trading day.

Seat A membership of a futures or options exchange.

Second currency options These pay out in a currency different from that of the underlying asset, based on a notional principal amount. For example, the percentage performance of the CAC 40 payable in sterling, based on a notional amount of pounds.

Secondary market The market for assets that were issued previously and are now trading among investors.

Securities Financial instruments such as bonds, shares, bills, CDs.

Securities and Investments Board (SIB) The body which oversees the UK financial services industry.

Series All options of the same class having the same exercise price and expiration date.

Settlement price The daily price at which the clearing house clears all trades. The settlement price is determined by reference to the closing range, and is used to determine margin calls and invoice prices for deliveries.

SFA Securities and Futures Authority. The UK self-regulatory organisation for these areas of the financial industry.

Short The position created by the sale of an asset or option if there is no offsetting position. A position that profits from price falls and loses from price rises.

Short add-on An additional amount of margin call applied to the writers of options which are traded on a margin system.

Short hedge The sale of a futures contract to lock in the current price and thereby eliminate or lessen the possible decline in value of ownership of an approximately equal amount of an actual financial instrument.

Short of the basis The position of a person who has sold the cash financial instrument and hedged it with a purchase of financial futures contracts.

Short sale A transaction in which securities are borrowed and sold.

SIMEX Singapore International Monetary Exchange.

Simple return A rate of return that is not compounded.

S&P 100, S&P 500 Indexes Standard and Poor's US equity indexes based on 100 stocks and 500 stocks, respectively.

SPAN Standard Portfolio Analysis of Margin. The system used for assessing margin levels on exchanges in the UK and USA, originally introduced by the CME. The London clearing house version is referred to as London SPAN.

Speculator A person who buys or sells contracts in the hope of profiting from subsequent price movements.

Speed A measure of the change in gamma in relation to a change in the underlying asset price.

Spot The actual instrument as distinguished from futures. The same as actuals or cash.

Spot market The market for assets that involves the immediate delivery of an asset.

Spot price The price of an asset on the spot market.

Spreads Options or futures transactions involving a long position in one contract and a short position in another, similar contract.

Spread margin The margin required for a spread. Because a spread reduces risk, the margin requirement may be lower than for each contract involved separately.

Standard deviation A measure of the dispersion of a variable around its mean, equal to the square root of the variance.

Stock index An indicator of the general level of stock prices.

Stock index future A future on a stock index such as the FTSE 100 Index (UK), Standard and Poor's 500 (S&P 500) (US). The futures trade the index at a fixed sum per point. The FTSE 100 Index contract is valued at £25 a point and the S&P 500 contract at $500 a point.

Stop loss order An order to sell at the market when a definite price is reached. Usually used as a method of limiting losses by traders with open positions.

Straddle A combination of a long put and a long call (or a short put and a short call) on the same underlying asset, each with the same exercise price and expiration date. An intra-contract futures spread.

Straddle calendar spread (options) The sale of a straddle in a near month and purchase of a straddle in a far month at the same strike.

Strangle This is where an investor buys both a put and a call option, or writes both a put and a call option on an underlying security, at different exercise prices.

Strap A combination of 2 calls and one put, with the same exercise price and expiration date.

Strike price   The same as exercise price.

Strip   A combination of 2 puts and one call, with the same exercise price and expiration date. A strip hedge uses futures contracts of differing maturities in order to approximate the maturities of the exposures being hedged.

Swap   A contractual agreement to exchange a stream of periodic payments with a counterparty. These may be fixed for floating interest rate commitments (plain vanilla swap), one currency for another (currency swap), both of these (cocktail swap), and there are many other varieties too, such as basis swaps, and asset swaps.

Swaption   An option on a swap.

Sydney Futures Exchange (SFE)   An Australian exchange which lists contracts on Treasury bonds and the All-Ordinaries Share Price Index.

Synthetic stock   A combination of a put and a call option which is equivalent to a futures contract on the stock.

Systematic risk   The risk associated with the market as a whole. As opposed to non-systematic risk which characterises specific sectors or stocks.

Taker   The buyer of an option contract.

T-bills, T-bonds   Treasury bills, US Treasury bonds.

TED spread   The spread obtained from US treasury bond and eurodollar futures.

Term structure of interest rates   The relationship between interest rates and maturities of money market instruments and bonds.

Texas 'hedge'   Long the underlying geared up with the addition of a long call, or short the underlying together with a long put. The directional view is much more geared. It is not a hedge at all.

Theoretical edge   The price difference between the theoretical price of an option position or strategy and its market price.

Theta   The change in the price of the option associated with a one-period reduction in the time to expiration (the derivative of the option price with respect to time).

Tick   The minimum possible change in price, either up or down.

Time spread   The same as calendar spread and horizontal spread.

Time value   The amount by which an option's premium exceeds its intrinsic value.

Time value decay The erosion of an option's time value as expiration approaches.

TIMS Theoretical Indicative Margin System. A system that has been used by some US exchanges for margining options as an alternative to SPAN.

Tokyo International Financial Futures Exchange (TIFFE) A Japanese exchange which lists contracts on currencies and interest rates.

Tokyo Stock Exchange A Japanese exchange which lists contracts on Japanese government bonds, US T-bonds and the TOPIX stock index.

TOPIX Tokyo Stock Price Index.

Traded options Options that can be bought and sold on the floor of an exchange.

Trade out A brief period of time at the end of official trading hours in which unsatisfied orders can be settled at the closing price or within the closing range.

Trading hours The hours when a particular contract is open for trading.

Traditional options A London Stock Exchange quasi-American-style option. Puts, calls and double options are available from option dealers but there is no secondary trading market. They may be sold back to the original counterparty.

Treasury bill A short-term government debt instrument with a maturity of one year or less. Bills are sold at a discount from par with the interest earned being the difference between the face value received at maturity and the price paid.

Treasury bond A coupon-bearing bond issued by the US government with an original maturity of at least 10 years.

Treasury note A coupon-bearing bond issued by the US government with an original maturity of 1 to 10 years.

Trigger option The same as limit option. A form of barrier option.

Tunnel The same as cylinder.

Underlying instrument The instrument to which an option relates.

Up-and-in option A form of barrier option that becomes activated when the price of the underlying reaches a particular level.

Up-and-out option A form of barrier option that ceases to exist when the price of the underlying reaches a particular level.

Value basis   The difference between the theoretical and actual futures prices.

Variation margin   The gains or losses on open positions which are calculated by marking to market at the end of each trading day, and credited or debited by the clearing house to each clearing member's account, and by members to their customers' accounts.

Vega   A measure of the rate of change in the theoretical option price due to changes in the volatility of the underlying asset price.

Vertical bear spread   The purchase of an option with a high exercise price and the sale of an option with a lower exercise price. Both options will have the same expiration date and could be puts or calls.

Vertical bull spread   The sale of an option with a high exercise price and the purchase of an option with a lower exercise price. Both options will have the same expiration date and could be puts or calls.

Volatility   A measure of the amount by which an asset price is expected to fluctuate over a given period. Normally measured by the annual standard deviation of daily price changes.

Volatility surface   A three-dimensional surface created by plotting option implied volatility (vertical axis) against exercise prices (horizontal axis) over time (third axis).

Volume   The number of transactions in a contract made during a specified period of time.

Warrant   A stock market security with a market price of its own that can be converted into a specific share at a predetermined price and date. The value of the warrant is thus determined by the premium (if any) of the share price over the conversion price of the warrant. They are effectively long term (usually call) options. They are also available on stock indices and currencies.

Writer   The seller of a call or a put option in an opening transaction.

Yield   A measure of the annual return on an investment.

Yield curve   The relationship between yields on money market instruments and bonds and their maturities.

Yield to maturity   The rate of discount that equates the future coupons and principal repayment with the current price of a bond or gilt. Also known as the redemption yield.

Zero-cost option   Any strategy where the premium income on written options matches the premium expenditure on bought options.

Zero-coupon bond   A bond that has no coupon payments, just a single maturity payment. It will be sold at a discount to face value.

INDEX

accrued interest 99, 109
actual volatility 206
American-style options 144, 160, 161, 255
  boundary conditions 263–9
  early exercise 282–3
  pricing 289, 298
    Black's approximation 285–6
    minimum value 161
anticipatory hedge 184–5
arbitrage
  bond futures (enhancing bond portfolio returns) 135–8
  cash-and-carry *see* cash-and-carry arbitrage
  covered interest 232–4, 331–8, 361
  forward interest rates and 52–5
  with options 243–70
    boundary conditions 263–9
    option price convexity 259–63
    put–call parity 253–9
    reversals, conversions and options boxes 246–9
    synthetic futures 244–6
    synthetic options 249–53
  processes 135–6
  pure 29, 243, 269
  quasi-arbitrage 243, 269
arbitragers 10
  number of 270
ARCH models 297–8

Asian options 160, 162, 163
ask (offer) price 326
asset classes 387
asset mismatch 62, 67
at-the-money options 146, 187–8, 227, 233–4
  time value 149, 153, 218–19, 274
average rate options 160, 162, 163

Bank of England 325, 328–30
banks
  intermediaries in swaps 302–4, 311–12
  parallel money markets 40
  profits from FRAs 59–60
  profits from swaps 308
  warehousing 308–11
Barings Bank 240–1
basis 18
  change
    currency futures 339, 342–4, 363–6
    long-term interest rate futures 109–12
    stock index futures 30–3
basis point 120
basis risk 18, 32–3, 63
  forward yield curve and 64–6
  long-term interest rate futures 111–12
  short-term interest rate futures 64–8

sources of 32–3, 66–8
basis trading 27–8
bear call spread 211, 215–16
bear futures fund 369
bear put spread 210, 211, 214–15
bear spread 210–11
beta 15, 68
   appropriate strike price for stock index options 202–4
   hedge ratio 15, 19
   leveraged shareholdings 159
bid–offer (bid–ask) spreads 25, 53, 56, 59, 138, 326, 327, 368
   significance 334–8
bid price 326
Black–Scholes option pricing models 222, 271–99
   ARCH/GARCH models 297–8
   basic model (formula) 278–82
   bond options 289–92
   determinants of option prices 271–7
   early exercise 282–3
   option prices as costs of replication 277–8
   puts and American-style options 289
   smile effect 295–7
   variations 283–8
   volatility 292–5
Black's approximation 285–6
bond futures
   arbitrage (enhancing bond portfolio returns) 135–6
   see also fixed interest risk
bond options
   Black–Scholes pricing model 289–92
bond portfolio immunisation 116, 131–2, 133, 135
bond portfolio returns 135–8
bond portfolios, synthetic 378–81
boundary conditions 244, 263–9, 270
Bretton Woods system 1
Brownian motion 289
bull call spread 208–9, 215–16
bull futures fund 369–70
bull put spread 209–10, 211, 212
bull spread 209, 385
butterfly spreads
   futures 64, 75, 85–6, 372–3
   options 206, 232–5, 237
      price convexity 259–63
calendar spreads 206, 219–22

call options 7, 144–9, 168
   boundary conditions 263–9
   early exercise 282–3
   as hedging instruments 172, 173–4, 200–1
      delta hedging 191–3
   intrinsic value 145, 146, 147, 149, 271
   pricing 149, 275–6, 370, 385
      Black–Scholes model 283–8
   profit/loss profiles 145–9
   stock leverage 159
   synthetic 250, 252–3
   writing 155, 200, 370, 372, 375, 392
call ratio backspread 236–7
call ratio spreads 236–7, 372
capital asset pricing model 203–4, 396
capital protected funds 387–8
caps 184
cash-and-carry arbitrage 116, 269, 380–1
   long-term interest rate futures 91, 99–104
   stock index futures 15, 22–7, 130–1
   see also arbitrage; covered interest arbitrage
cash flows
   cheapest-to-deliver bond price 111
   discounted 113–14, 123
   hedging 96–7
   replication of option positions 277–8
   swaps 308
cash market 44, 46
certificates of deposit 40, 41, 60, 61
cheapest-to-deliver (CTD) bond 99, 111, 113, 132–3, 379–80
   hedging 119–21
class of options 158
clean price 109
clearing house 11, 12, 158, 169, 360, 369
closing out 12, 143, 342, 363, 365
closing purchase 158
closing sale 158
collars 184
commercial paper 40, 41–2
comparative advantage 305–8, 312–13
compensation formula (FRAs) 58–60
compound options 160, 162, 163
compound rate of return 47–8
conditional options 160, 162, 163
condors 237

confidence limits 37–8
constant ratio funds, implications of implicit options in 391–6
continuous compounding 279
controlled-risk index fund 370–4
conventional government bonds 92–3
convergence
  currency futures 343–4
  long-term interest rate futures 109–12
  short-term interest rate futures 66
  stock index futures 30–3
conversion arbitrage 243, 246–9, 253, 269–70
conversion factor (price factor) 98, 101, 112, 132–5
conversion premium 164–5, 166–7
conversion price 166–7
conversion rate 164, 165, 166
convertible bonds 143, 164–8
convexity of option pricing 244, 259–63, 270
cornering 112
corporation treasurer (role) 348–60
costs of option funds 385–6
counterparty risk 11–12, 354, 358
coupons
  coupon-bearing bonds 92–3, 125–6
  floating rate notes 316–17
covered call writes 200
covered interest arbitrage 323–4, 331–8, 361
covered warrants 164
covered writing 171, 194–200, 375
credit derivatives (potential role in fund management) 388–91
cross hedging 40, 60–1
cumulative normal distribution function 279
currency accounts 355–6, 360, 361
currency exposure (measuring) 351–2
currency forwards and futures
  see forwards and futures in currency risk management
currency futures 339
currency holding (profit/loss profile) 174–5
currency markets 324–6
currency options 255, 287
currency risk (nature of) 348–50

currency risk management see forwards and futures in currency risk management
currency swaps 301–2, 311–15, 318–20
cylinders 171, 181, 182, 370

date mismatch 66–7
dated bonds 92–3
dedicated portfolios 131
default risk 11, 303, 320, 360
delivery 97–8
delta 159, 166, 218, 386
  butterfly spreads 234
  call options 149, 188, 375–6
  put options 154, 375–6
  straddles 227–8
  valuation trading 206, 223
delta hedging 171
  of options 191–3
  replicated options 277–8, 391–2
  with options 185–91
demand and supply 324–5
diffusion processes 289–90
direct exchange rate quotation 326, 333–4
discount rate 123–5
discounted cash flows 113–14, 123
diversification 351–2, 387–8
dividend discount model 284
dividend paying stocks 283–6
dividend yield 203, 254–6, 385
down-and-out options 160, 162, 163
downside protection 199–200, 370, 382
duration 120, 122–30
  calculation 125–30
  matching 132
dynamic hedging 191–3
  see also delta hedging

early exercise 282–3
economic exposure 350–1
efficiency frontier 388
equity swaps 301–2, 315
eurocurrency market 40
European-style options 144, 160, 255
  boundary conditions 263–9
  pricing 298
    Black–Scholes model 283–5, 286–8
ex-dividend date 276, 282, 283
exchange-traded options 144, 156, 168, 359–60

exchange rates
    determination by demand and
        supply 324–5
    'guaranteed' 342–4
    quotation 326
    risk 348–50
    systems 1–2
    see also forwards and futures
        currency risk management
exercise price see strike price
exotic options 143, 160–3
expectations
    market expectations of volatility
        206, 223
        see also volatility trading
    profit 272
    and stock index futures prices 29
expiry 145
    profit/loss profiles
        at expiry 145–7, 151–2
        prior to expiry 147–9, 152–4,
            370–1
    time to 275–6
exposure, market see market exposures
external hedging techniques 356–60

fair prices
    bonds 123–4
    stock index futures 23–7, 33
    time value and options trading
        223–4
    see also Black–Scholes option pricing
        models
fair value premium 23
fat tails 295–6
fiduciary call 381–2, 383, 384, 385,
    386–7
financial engineering 3, 243
    building blocks of 249–50
financially engineered investments
    367–96
    constructing portfolio of capital
        protected funds 387–8
    credit derivatives (potential role in
        fund management) 388–91
    futures funds 367–75
    implications of implicit options in
        constant ratio funds 391–6
    options funds 381–7
    switching between stocks without
        trading in stocks 375–8
    synthetic bond portfolios 378–81

fixed hedging 171, 200–1
fixed interest risk 91–114
    basis and convergence 109–12
    cheapest-to-deliver bond 99, 113
    delivery 97–8
    discounting cash flows 113–14,
        123
    duration 120, 122–30
    futures contracts 93–5, 119–22
    government bonds 91–3
    hedging see hedging
    implied repos 92, 104–9
    invoice amount 99
    price factor 98
    prices 93–4, 112, 113
        determination 99–104
    underlying instrument 92–3
fixed ratio 396
floating rate loans
    hedging with FRAs 56–7
    interest rate swaps 302–4
floating rate notes (FRNs) 123, 302,
    316–17
floors 184
forfaiting 355–6, 360
forward foreign exchange market
    326–30
forward interest rates 49–55
    and arbitrage 52–5
    formula for calculating 52–5
forward premium/discount 314–15,
    327, 363, 365
forward prices and futures
    (relationship) 347–8
forward rate agreements (FRAs) 40,
    51, 56–60
    compensation formula 58–60
    hedging with 56–8
forward yield curve 55–6, 390
    and basis risk 64–6
forwards 3
forwards and futures in currency risk
    management 323–66
    comparison of futures and forwards
        346–8
    currency futures 339
    currency markets 324–6
    forward foreign exchange market
        326–30
    forward premium/discount 314–15,
        327, 363, 365
    futures contracts 339, 363–6

hedging currency risk with futures 339–45, 363–6
  pricing 323, 330–8
    interest rate parity 333–4
    significance of bid-offer spreads 334–8
    quotation of exchange rates 326
    relationship between futures and forward prices 347–8
    role of corporation treasurer 348–60
fund management
  potential role of credit derivatives 388–91
  see also futures in fund management
future rate agreements see forward rate agreements (FRAs)
futures 3, 4–7
  currency see forwards and futures in currency risk management
  delta hedging of options 191–3
  and FRAs 60
  hedging with see hedging
  long-term interest rate see fixed interest risk
  short-term interest rate see interest rate risk with futures
  stock index see stock index futures
  stock market risk with see stock market risk with futures
  vs options for hedging 201, 205
futures butterfly 64, 75, 85–6
futures contracts 6–7, 380
  currency futures 339, 363–6
  long-term interest rate futures 93–5, 119–22
  number required for hedging 34–6, 119–22, 363–6
futures exchanges 6–7
futures in fund management 115–39
  bond futures arbitrage (enhancing bond portfolio returns) 135–6
  duration 122–30
  equations 137–8
  hedge design 115, 119–22
  hedge ratios 115, 116–19
  hedged bond portfolios (as synthetic Treasury bills) 116, 131–5
  hedged equity portfolios (as synthetic Treasury bills) 115–16, 130–1
  implicit options 138–9
futures funds 21, 367–70, 381, 387

futures hedge ratio 344–5
futures margin accounts 361
futures options 243, 248–9, 255
  European-style call options 288
futures prices
  convergence to spot prices see convergence
  currency futures 323, 330–8, 347–8
  long-term interest rate futures 93–4, 99–102, 112, 113
  relationship between forward prices and 347–8
  short-term interest rate futures 43–7, 48–55, 61
  stock index futures 22–30
futures straddles 63–4, 74–85

gamma 193–7, 206, 227–8
GARCH models 298
geared bull futures fund 369–70
gearing see leverage (gearing)
gilt futures contracts 98, 136
gilt futures funds 387
gilt futures options 248–9
government bonds 91–3
  synthetic portfolios 378–81
  valuation 122–5
  see also fixed interest risk
Greeks 193–4
  see also under individual names
'guaranteed' exchange rate 342–4
guaranteed minimum value 382–3, 385–6

hedge design 119–22
hedge ratios
  currency futures 116–19, 344–5
  generic 63, 66–8, 88, 344
  long-term interest rate futures 113, 119–22
  stock index futures 18–19
hedged bond portfolios (as synthetic Treasury bills) 115–16, 131–5
hedged equity portfolios (as synthetic Treasury bills) 115–16, 130–1
hedgers 3, 4, 9–10, 205
  role in stock index futures pricing 29
hedging
  comparison of futures and options 201–2
  currency risk with futures 339–45, 353, 363–6

external techniques (relative merits) 356–60
fixed 171, 186, 200–1
fixed interest risk 95–7, 119–22
  cash flow 96–7
  value of a portfolio 95–6
  with futures 4–6, 42–3
    number of futures contracts required 34–6, 119–22, 363–6
  interest rate swaps 302–5
  options 171–204
    anticipatory hedge 184–5
    appropriate strike price 202–4
    covered writing 171, 194–200
    delta hedging of options 191–3, 391–2
    delta hedging with options 185–91
    as hedging instruments 172–80
    option sensitivities 171, 193–4
    options funds 385–6
    zero-cost options 171, 181–4
  short-term interest rate futures 42–7, 62
    advanced strategies 63–88
    cross hedging 40, 60–1
    FRAs 56–8
    strips and rolls 68–72
  stock index futures 6, 16–19, 34–6
  warehousing 308–11
historical observation method 37
historical volatility 37–8, 293–5, 297
horizontal (calendar) spreads 206, 219–22

IBM 314
illiquid bonds 390
immediacy 362
implicit options 102–4, 138–9, 391–6
implied repos 92, 104–8
implied volatility 222–3, 294, 295–6, 297
in-the-money options 146, 149, 153–4, 161, 187, 206–7, 233–4, 274, 295, 386
income component, creating 380–1
index-linked bonds 93, 123
indirect exchange rate quotation 326, 333–4
informational efficiency 10
initial margin 11, 368–9
intended purchases, hedging 184–5
inter-bank markets 40–1

inter-contract spreads 86–8
interest costs 305–8
interest rate derivatives 216–17
interest rate exposures, creating 379–80
interest rate parity 323, 333–4
interest rate risk with futures 39–62
  basic priciples of hedging 42–7
  computations and quotations 47–8
  cross hedging 40, 60–1
  forward rate agreements 40, 56–60
  forward yield curve 55–6
  prices 61
    determination 48–55
    quotes 43–7
  underlying markets 40–2
interest rate risk management (advanced strategies) 63–89
  basis risk 64–8
  butterfly spreads 64, 75, 85–6
  forward yield curve 64–6
  futures straddles 63–4, 74–85, 88
  inter-contract spreads 86–8
  non-linear yield curves 82–5
  strips and rolls 63, 68–72, 88
  variation margin leverage and tailing 64, 72–4
interest rate swaps 301, 302–8
  hedging interest rate risk 302–5
  pricing 317, 319–20
  reducing interest costs 305–8
interest rates
  and bond prices 124–5
  calculation and quotation 47–8
  duration as measure of risk 127
  forward interest rates 49–55
  instability 2
  inter-bank 40–1
  and option premiums 276
  term structure 39
intrinsic value 160, 161, 162, 163, 206–7, 230–1
  call options 145, 146, 147, 149, 271
  early exercise 282, 283
  put options 150, 152, 187, 271
invoice amount 99
irredeemable bonds 123
isolating market eposure 21–2
isolating stock selection 19–21
iterative processes 294

junk bonds 124

kappa *see* vega
knock-in/knock-out options 160

Leeson, Nick 240–1
leptokurtosis 295–6
leverage (gearing)
    futures funds 367–8
    gearing effect of options 217–18, 241
    stock index futures 36
    stock leverage and stock options 158–9, 276
liquid bonds 389–90
liquid markets 10
local authorities 40, 42
long-term interest rate futures *see* fixed interest risk
long-term interest rates 2
long option positions 173–4
lookback options 160, 161, 163

Macaulay's duration 125
maintenance margin 11, 368–9,
margin accounts 361, 380
margin system 10–12, 368–9
margined futures options 288
market expectations of volatility *see* expectations
market exposures
    currency forwards and futures 350–2, 362
    exchange rate risk 348–60
    futures funds 368
    isolating 21–2
    stock index futures 19–22, 382, 384
market practices and terms 158
marking to market 11, 347, 361, 369
Markowitz diversification 387–8
matching (risk management) 355
maturity matching 131–2
maturity mismatch 67
mean reversion 297
medium-term bonds 92–3
minimum portfolio value 202–4
mispricing 11
    arbitrage with options 243, 248–9, 269
    systematic by Black–Scholes model 295–7
modified duration 125–30, 138
money markets, parallel 40–2

money supply targets 2
Monte Carlo simulations 37–8

Nikkei 225 240
90/10 approach 381–2, 384, 386–7
no-arbitrage bands 15, 23–7, 138
    bond prices 102
    fair futures prices and 23–7
nominal (par) value 92, 119–20, 124, 289–90
non-linear yield curves 82–5
normal distributions 271, 272, 279, 295–6

offer (ask) price 326
opening purchase 158
opening sale 158
option cylinder 171, 181, 182
option delta *see* delta
option elasticity 159
option prices/premiums 3, 144–5, 155, 158, 168, 269–70, 271–2, 385
    boundary conditions 263–9
    convexity 244, 259–63, 270
    costs of replication 277–8
    delta, gamma and 193–4
    delta hedging 186–91
    determinants of 149, 272–7
    hedging and 172–3
    implied volatility 222–3
    mispricing *see* mispricing
    see also Black–Scholes option pricing models; intrinsic value; time value
option sensitivities 171, 193–4
option structures 389
options 3, 7–8, 143–69
    arbitrage with *see* arbitrage
    call options *see* call options
    convertible bonds 164–8
    exotic 160–3
    hedging with *see* hedging
    implicit 102–4, 138–9, 391–6
    market practices and terms 158
    put options *see* put options
    stock leverage and stock options 158–9, 276
    trading with *see* trading with options
    vs futures for hedging 201, 205
    warrants 163–4
    writing 155–7
options boxes 243, 246–9

438 • INDEX

options contracts 9
options exchanges 9
options funds 381–8
options on options 160, 162, 163
Orange County, California 108–9
out-of-the-money options 146, 149, 153, 187, 207, 219, 233–4, 274, 295–6, 370, 375, 386
over-the-counter (OTC) products 346, 358, 359
    futures *see* forward rate agreements (FRAs)
    options 9, 144

par (nominal) value 92, 119–20, 124, 289–90
parallel markets 40–2
participating forwards 171, 181
payoff profile (controlled-risk index) 370–1
perpetuities 98
perturbation 120, 121
piled-up rolls 68–72
plain vanilla swaps 302–4
portfolio of capital protected funds 387–8
portfolio insurance 382
premiums, option *see* option prices/premiums
price factor 98, 101, 112, 132–5
price quotes 43–7
price value of a basis point (PVBP) 120–1, 129, 379–80
price volatility 379–80
pricing bond valuation 122–5
pricing currency forwards and futures 323, 330–8, 347–8
principal invoice amount 99
profit/loss profiles
    at expiry 145–7, 151–2
    butterflies 233–4, 235–6, 372–3
    calendar spreads 220–2
    call options 145–9
    currency holding 174–5
    prior to expiry 147–9, 152–4, 370–1
    put options 151–4, 175, 176
    straddles 224–5, 235–6
    strangles 230–2, 235–6
profits
    expected 272–3
    from FRAs 59–60
    riskless 248–9

from swaps 308
protective put 382, 384, 385
pull to par 290
put–call parity 244, 253–9, 385
put options 8, 150–4, 168, 276, 375
    early exercise 282–3
    hedging 172–3, 174
    intrinsic value 150, 152, 187, 271
    pricing 289, 370
    profit/loss profiles 151–4, 175, 176
    synthetic 250–1
    writing 155
put ratio backspreads 236–7
put ratio spreads 236, 237

random walk 289
range forwards (cylinders) 171, 181, 182, 370
rates of return 197–9
ratio spreads 206, 236–41
rebalancing 22, 191
redemption yield 120, 124
reference asset 388–9
replication 381, 391–2
    costs of 277–8
repos 108–9
    implied 92, 104–8
return if exercised 197–9
return if unchanged 197–9
reversals 243, 246–9, 253, 269–70
rho 193–6
risk 2
    basis *see* basis risk
    controlled-risk index fund 370–4
    counterparty 11–12, 305, 320, 354, 358
    exchange rate 348–60
    fixed interest 91–114
    gearing effect of options 217–18
    hedging *see* hedging
    role 29–30
    systematic 15
    value at risk 36–8, 352
    see also forwards and futures in currency risk management
risk-free assets 381–3, 384–5, 386
risk aversion 30, 173, 207
risk management decisions 352–3
risk management with options 171–204
    appropriate strike price 202–4
    covered writing 194–200

INDEX • 439

delta hedging of options 191–3, 391–2
delta hedging with options 185–91
hedging anticipatory purchases 184–5
option sensitivities 171, 193–4
options as hedging instruments 172–80
zero-cost-options 171, 181–4
risk management techniques 354–5
riskless profits 248–9
rolls 63, 68–72

security market line 203
security selection 387
series, option 158, 171, 205
settlement price 99
short-term bonds 92–3
short-term interest rate futures (advanced strategies) *see* interest rate risk management (advanced strategies)
short-term interest rate futures (basics) *see* interest rate risk with futures
short-term interest rates 2
short option positions 173–4
simple returns 47–8
smile effect 295–7
speculators 3, 9–10, 205
    role in stock index futures pricing 29
split-synthetic 181
spot prices 161, 162
    convergence to *see* convergence
    and currency futures pricing 323–4, 342–4
spreads
    bid–offer 326, 327, 334–8
    calendar/horizontal 206, 219–22
    vertical 205, 214–16, 385
stacks 68–72
standard deviation 37, 275, 293
standardisation 339, 346
standardised normal distribution 279
stochastic volatility 296
stock index futures 384, 387
    hedged portfolios as synthetic Treasury bills 115–16, 130–5
    hedging *see* hedging
    see also stock market risk with futures
stock index options 286–7, 386

appropriate strike price 9, 200, 202–4
stock leverage 158–9
stock market risk with futures 15–38
    basis change and convergence 30–3
    futures funds 21, 368, 369, 371
    hedging 4–6, 16–19, 34–6
    prices 22–30, 370–3
    removing/enhancing exposures 19–22
    value at risk 36–8
stock options 158–9, 276
stocks
    dividend paying 283–6
    hedging value of a stockholding 186–91
    isolating stock selection 19–21
    put–call parity 253–9
    switching between (without trading in stocks) 375–8
straddles
    futures 63–4, 74–85
        non-linear yield curves 82–5
        rolling forward 82
        subsequent adjustments 80–1
        using 76–80
    options 206, 224–8, 235–6
strangles 206, 229–32, 235–6
strike (exercise) price 144, 161–2, 273–4, 370, 371–3, 375–7, 382–3
    appropriate when using stock index options 9, 200, 202–4
strips 63, 68–72, 88
swaps 3, 301–21
    currency swaps 301–2, 311–15, 318–20
    equity swaps 301–2, 315
    interest rate swaps *see* interest rate swaps
    pricing 302, 317–20
    warehousing 308–11
swaptions 320
synthetic bond portfolios 378–81
synthetic futures 22, 373–4, 375–8
    arbitrage with options 243, 244–6
    currency forwards and futures 331–2, 334–5
synthetic options 243, 249–53
synthetic Treasury bills 115–16, 130–5

table tops 237
tailing 64, 72–4

term structure of interest rates 39
theta 193, 206, 219
third party warrants 164
three-month interest rate futures 4–5, 39, 43–6, 66–8
ticks 12, 44
time to expiry 275–6
time value 187–8
   call options 147–9
   components 277
   net 208
   and option pricing 271, 274–7
   and options trading 205–6, 218–24
      volatility trading 221–2, 225–7, 230–2
   put options 150, 152
   see also theta
traded options 144, 156, 158, 168
traders, types of 9–10
trading with options 205–42
   basic principles 206–8
   derivatives prices (reading) 214–17
   effects of gearing 217–18
   strategies 206–7, 235–6
   time value and *see* time value
   vertical spreads 208–13
   volatility trading *see* volatility trading
transactions costs 25, 28, 102
transactions exposure 348–9, 351
translation exposure 349–50
transparency 346
Treasury bills synthetic 115–16, 130–5

undated bonds 93
underlying instruments
   combining options with positions in 174–80
   prices and trading strategies 206–8
underlying markets 40–2

valuation of bonds 122–5
valuation trading 222–3
value at risk 36–8, 352

value of a portfolio, hedging 95–6
value of a stockholding, hedging 186–91
variance/covariance models 37
variation margin 11, 16, 64, 111, 135, 368, 369, 380
   leverage and tailing 64, 72–4
vega 193–4, 195–6, 206
vertical spreads 205, 214–16, 385
volatility 19, 290, 292–5, 386
   actual 206, 221
   estimating 293–5
   historical 37–8, 293–5, 297
   implied 222–3, 294, 295–6, 297
   market expectations of 206, 221, 222
   modified duration 125–30, 138
   perturbation 120, 121
   stochastic 296
   systematic variation 297
   and time value decay 275
volatility trading 206, 224–41
   butterflies 232–6
   comparison of strategies 235–6
   ratio spreads 206, 236–41
   straddles 206, 224–8, 235–6
   strangles 206, 229–32, 235–6

warehousing 308–11
warrants 143, 163–4
Wiener process 289
World Bank 123, 314
writers 143, 155–7, 168–9

yield curve 135
   forward 55–6, 390
      and basis risk 64–6
   hedging yield curve risk with futures straddles 74–85
   non-linear yield curves 82–5
yield to maturity 124

zero-cost options 171, 181–4